CORN Publication Series 6

D/2001/0095/124
ISBN 2-503-51281-X

Labour and labour markets
between town and countryside
(Middle Ages – 19th century)

Edited by Bruno Blondé, Eric Vanhaute
& Michèle Galand

BREPOLS

CONTENTS

LIST OF CONTRIBUTORS

BRUNO BLONDÉ	University of Antwerp (UFSIA), Belgium
WILLIAM R. DAY JR.	University of Cambridge, United Kingdom
HARALD DECEULAER	University of Brussels (VUB), Belgium
STEPHAN R. EPSTEIN	London School of Economics and Political Science, United Kingdom
MICHÈLE GALAND	University of Brussels (ULB), Belgium
CARL A. HOFFMANN	Universität Augsburg, Germany
FRANZ IRSIGLER	Universität Trier, Germany
DEREK KEENE	University of London, United Kingdom
SYLVIE LEFÈBVRE	University of Brussels (ULB), Belgium
MARC LIBERT	University of Brussels (ULB), Belgium
MICHAEL LIMBERGER	University of Antwerp (UFSIA), Belgium
VICTORIA LÓPEZ BARAHONA	Universidad Autónoma de Madrid, Spain
ERIC MIELANTS	Fernand Braudel Center – State University of New York at Binghamton
MARTINA DE MOOR	Ghent University, Belgium
JOSÉ A. NIETO SÁNCHEZ	Universidad Autónoma de Madrid, Spain
VALÉRIE PIETTE	University of Brussels (ULB), Belgium
JOSÉ ANTONIO MATEOS ROYO	Saragossa University, Spain
JEAN-PIERRE SOSSON	Université Catholique de Louvain, Louvain-la-Neuve, Belgium
PETER STABEL	Ghent University, Belgium
ERIC VANHAUTE	Ghent University, Belgium
ADRIAAN VERHULST	Ghent University, Belgium

LIST OF FIGURES

LIST OF TABLES

Editors preface

This volume includes the proceedings of a conference held on December 18 and 19, 1998. The editors would like, firstly, to thank the Fund for Scientific Research – Flanders (FWO–V) and two research groups (directed by Prof. Dr. Erik Thoen, Ghent University, and Prof. Dr. Hugo Soly, University of Brussels (VUB)) of this foundation in particular for the structural support given. Prof. Dr. Claire Billen, backed by the "History and Societies" and "Rural History" research units at the University of Brussels (ULB), was generous in co-organising and hosting this conference. Additional financial support was given by the IUAP-project *Urban Society in the Late Middle Ages*.

Several texts had to be translated. In addition, Dr. Donald J. Harreld of Brigham Young University went through the final version of all texts originally written by non-native speakers. The editors also acknowledge Karin Roelant. Officially she was charged with the lay-out of this volume, but her contribution in homogenising the contributions and processing of maps for this volume proved to be invaluable.

September 2001

Bruno Blondé, Antwerp
Michèle Galand, Brussels
Eric Vanhaute, Ghent

General introduction

Bruno BLONDÉ, University of Antwerp – UFSIA
Eric VANHAUTE, Ghent University
Michèle GALAND, University of Brussels – ULB

On December 18 and 19, 1998 an international symposium was held at the University of Brussels (ULB) on the initiative of the research groups of the Fund for Scientific Research of the Flemish Community (FWO): "Labour, labour relations and labour markets in Western Europe, 1500–2000" and "Corn – Comparative Rural History of the North Sea Area", in co-operation with the "History and Societies" and "Rural History" research units at the University of Brussels (ULB).

The general topic of this scientific encounter covered labour and labour markets between towns and rural areas from the Middle Ages to the early 20th century. The conference brought together specialists in economic and social history who were challenged to explore a series of key mechanisms related to the organisation and development of, and relationships between, urban and rural labour markets.

Urban historians are, for instance, increasingly putting emphasis on the symbiosis in urban and rural economic developments. Of course, urban and rural markets did not coexist independently. The constant need to fill in population gaps resulting from the *urban graveyard* effect, pulled large proportions of rural inhabitants into town. Increasing levels of urbanisation, moreover, often caused the balance of power to shift towards towns. Needless to say, opposite movements with rural industries mushrooming and regional de-industrialisation of the urban world also occurred. Hence, conference participants were invited to look at price and wage differentials, migration movements, and other key topics related to regional economic developments, dynamics of migration, and urbanisation.

The regulatory environment within the walls of the city was of equal importance. How did the urban labour market respond to (predominantly incoming) migration flows? Did guilds contribute in organising a differential access to urban employment opportunities? If so, when and why? Why, when, and what strategies did towns develop in order to exclude unwanted countrymen?

In addition, conflicting interests of urban and rural industries had to be dealt with. Often, it was in the interest of urban authorities to safeguard urban monopolies, especially in the surrounding countryside. On the other hand, urban entrepreneurs and merchants did strive to maximise profits while moving production at lower costs to the countryside. In so doing they were 'shamelessly' making use of the economies of agglomeration offered by the nearby town while bypassing the accompanying price for urban centrality. Under what conditions did these urban strategies to monopolise production, distribution, and consumption succeed or fail?

Urban and rural markets largely behaved in a complementary fashion. Hence, scholars were invited to present research results and raise problems about occupations and employment structures in town and countryside. What influences did urban growth and decline exert upon occupational structures in town and countryside, and vice verse? What was the changing role played by rural shops, urban peddlers, periodic fairs, and permanent commercial infrastructures in shaping occupational structures, dividing labour between town and countryside, and organising regional labour markets? Finally, what was the effect of the integration versus the survival of regional labour markets in the modern period?

The research agenda drawn up at the start was vast. This did not prevent participants stemming from different regions, diverse chronological specialities and scholarly traditions to meet the challenge. Inevitably, however, the conference yielded a broad and very diverse set of research approaches and results. This inspired the editors to divide the proceedings of this symposium along chronological lines into four sections. Together with short introductory comments, the contributions have the goal of sustaining discussion and opening up new perspectives for future research.

The emergence of medieval towns from the early Middle Ages raises the question of their identity and of their links with the rural world, founded on migratory and commercial flows as well as on the birth of specialised 'urban' services. To what extent are we able to observe these phenomena for the most distant periods? Questions, doubts, and comments were presented by A. Verhulst and J.-P. Sosson for the towns of the Southern Netherlands, by F. Irzigler for those of the Rhineland and Westphalia and by D. Keene for the English towns, thus bringing to the fore the wealth and the limits inherent in making use of diplomatic sources, and also of archaeology.

These are fundamental questions as labour relations between the towns and rural areas would frequently crystallise around impediments to the urban corporative system and the possibilities of escaping it by developing certain craft and even pre-industrial activities in the rural areas. In this process, the textile industry explored numerous solutions, undertaking a distribution and even a division of labour between urban centres and the rural world. Industry developed sophisticated commercial relations between these poles of production, but also between the towns themselves. It was not surprising, therefore, that the textile sector was of particular interest to the participants. They were challenged by the diversity of the cases observed but also by the possibilities of comparison offered by the study of certain forms of de-localisation or of deregulation of labour. These developments required the interference of enterprising merchants capable of heading such a complicated organisation of production. E. Mielants raises the question in a theoretical manner by wondering about the transition between feudalism and merchant capitalism, thus questioning the overly rigid caesura between the Middle Ages and the beginnings of modern times. P. Stabel draws the picture of textile production in Flanders for this same period. He shows how the corporative constraints were overcome but also made use of in this heavily urbanised region. He points out the diversity of the solutions adopted, depending on the types of production, while wondering about the appropriateness of establishing a dichotomic distinction between towns and rural areas. C.A. Hoffmann studies the distribution of the labour market between towns and rural areas in Germany in the modern period, in a less urbanised region where the towns do not occupy a central place. In this context, the proto-industry compels recognition in a very variable manner, depending on the regions. For the same period, J.A. Mateos Royo deals with the question of labour organisation by concentrating on the conflicts of interest between urban corporations and urban councils as regards the control over the labour markets in the towns of Aragon. He does this in light of the economic development of the sixteenth century and the subsequent recession in the seventeenth century.

Among the cases analysed, the major towns provide some highly specific examples because they function as powerful poles of attraction that absorb the rural labour force. This way they contribute to their own demographic and economic development, while they become increasingly dependent on their hinterland for part of their supplies in food, raw materials, and certain manufactured products. The precocious and remarkable expansion of Florence in the twelfth and the thirteenth centuries, studied by W.R. Day, forced merchants to establish relations with remote towns. These relations ensured the sale of the textile production of the town at war with the other towns of Tuscany during the struggle between Guelphs and Ghibellines. This paradoxical situation had repercussions on the organisation of labour in the Florentine hinterland, eager to invest in improvements in order to increase agricultural yields. A town of the size of Antwerp in the fifteenth and the sixteenth centuries allowed for a series of industrial activities likely to find buyers there and to develop, essentially along the line of communication provided by the River Scheldt, as pointed out by M. Limberger. The comparative analysis of the three major towns of the Netherlands, namely Antwerp, Ghent and Brussels, as offered by H. Deceulaer, throws light on the complexity of the interplay of cities with their surrounding countryside in the eighteenth century. The demographic situation of the rural areas near these towns needs – among others – to be taken into account, including their economic development. This while considering the weight of proto-industrialisation around Ghent, the poverty in the Campine, an area neighbouring Antwerp, or the development of agriculture directed specifically to the local market, as in the suburbs of Brussels, well served by lines of communication. The trade in second-hand clothes, by establishing production and consumption links between the towns and the rural areas, is suggested as being an indicator in attempting to assess these complicated relationships. It is the particular geographical situation that allowed for organising the relations between Brussels and the neighbouring rural areas in a manner illustrative to modern times. The major town developed close to a large forest that served as a source for construction timber and wood for fuel. It is the role played upstream by the forest workers who frequently came from nearby rural areas for the purpose of finding a supplement to their meagre income, that is the object of the study by S. Lefèbvre.

The end of the Ancien Regime with its political and social upheavals necessarily had an impact on the traditional organisation of urban labour. While studying the craft of the butchers in Brussels at the turn of the eighteenth and the nineteenth centuries, M. Libert analyses the impact of the suppression of their corporation under the French Regime, but also the weight of traditions during this period of change. This same period also witnessed the growth of the proto-industry phenomenon explored by J.A. Nieto and V. Lopez for the region of Madrid and of New Castile. They prove the capacity of the town to invest in the industrial development of the region. The process saw the beginning of the exploitation of cheap female and child labour from the rural areas in 'spinning schools'. It is also the sex-related dimension of labour, this time of an urban nature, that is being discussed by V. Piette, who takes a thorough look at the status of unmarried women from rural areas seeking jobs as servants in Brussels, during the nineteenth century. Here again, the major town that provides jobs offers a particular example that allows for measuring the stereotypes attached to the status of these female workers as distorted testimonials of the contacts between these two worlds (i.e. the towns and the rural areas, but also between the different social classes destined to live next to each other). Finally, the geographical mobility and the diversification of the activities of farmers as well as their relations with the industrial world in Flanders at the end of the nineteenth century and during the first half of the twenthieth century allows us to understand the shock felt by the rural world hit directly by the competition of more attractive wages, the search for social security connected therewith, and the development of mechanisation, as shown by T. De Moor. These elements affected the organisation of rural wage labour in decline, which entailed changes in the size of the farms and, in some case, the use of foreign labour.

Distribution, specialisation and division of tasks, urban concentrations and rural delocalisation, mobility of labour and commercial links, organisation of working time, methods of remuneration, gender specialisation of activities, all these are topics that are to be studied within the framework of rural/urban labour markets. The renewed interest of social scientists in these research questions is shown by the diversity of the cases analysed according to geographical, demographic, economic, and political conditions. It also presents interesting possibilities of comparison for understanding the significance of labour in the organisation of societies in the course of the centuries that preceded and led up to the 'industrial age' in Western Europe.

PART I

MIDDLE AGES

Introduction to part I

Adriaan Verhulst, Ghent University

Henri Pirenne's theory – developed nearly a century ago – that towns as centres of industry and trade in North-Western Europe originated between the 9th and the 12th centuries as something totally new and profoundly different from the surrounding countryside and without any connection with the latter, has definitely been abandoned. The absolute contrast with a purely agrarian countryside deprived of any significant industrial and commercial activity, made it difficult to explain more particularly the sudden rise of the town as an industrial centre.

In spite of the growing contribution of archeology, as demonstrated by Keene's chapter on the industrial organisation of English towns before 1150, and nothwithstanding the evidence of industrial activities, commerce and wage labour on rural estates embedded in a manorial economy, provided by Verhulst and Irsigler in their respective chapters, it is still difficult to describe and explain the changes which between the 9th and the 12th centuries led to the shift of industrial activities from countryside to towns. This is caused, as Sosson emphasizes in his very critical chapter, by the paucity of written sources, the uncertainties of their terminology and especially the danger to project back into time concepts of a later period, like 'labour division'. At a later moment these difficulties for the most part disappear, as is demonstrated by Day's long contribution (in part II of the book) on the development of the Florentine textile industry during the 13th century, i.e. at the moment that written sources, particularly in Italy, become more numerous.

1 Some thoughts on mediaeval towns and the division of labour during the so-called pre-corporative period

Jean-Pierre Sosson, Université Catholique de Louvain (Louvain-la-Neuve)

I. Introduction

Whoever seeks to detect and subsequently interpret the first telltale signs of a 'division of labour' in mediaeval towns during the so-called 'pre-corporative' period within the ambit of the former Southern Netherlands is immediately confronted with three major obstacles, viz. a chronological, a conceptual and a heuristic one; and these issues must be addressed before any attempt is made, even if it means drawing inferences which are more tentative than conclusive, voicing truisms which are despairingly obvious, and having to concede that the documentation is sadly deficient.

While the aim is not to call into question the basic phenomenon represented by the emigration of countryside craftsmen towards the urban areas, their progressive organisation in this environment[1], and their eventual integration in a decentralised production process organised by the metropolitan trade systems, it is nevertheless important to point out an important degree of asynchrony and the very late appearance of the 'pre-corporative period' phenomenon in certain sectors at least. If we limit ourselves to the examples of the Flanders, Tournai, Brabant and Namur areas, the said period lasts until 1302 in Flanders and 's Hertogenbosch, until 1303 in Namur, 1305 in Malines, 1360 in Louvain, 1423 in Tournai, and between 1421 and 1435 in Brussels and Antwerp.[2] Thus one runs the risk of crediting the industrial scene between 1200 and 1250 with features which can be attested – and even then, with some reserve – only in the Lower Middle Ages.

Unless one agrees to view it in a 'High Middle Age' perspective – resorting to, say, Chapter 45 of the *Capitulare de Villis*[3] or to *Conflictus ovis et linis* (1068–1070)[4], the

[1] Moreover, there is great variety, as is evidenced, notably, by the example of the Namur county in 1289 (Genicot, 1982: 306, tableau XXVIII).

[2] Wyffels, 1951: 23; Goetstouwers, 1908: 3; not to speak of Germany with, for instance, the fishmongers of Worms from 1106–1107 onwards (Planitz, 1975: 291). Cf. also Des Marez, 1921: 412–446. The observation artificially complicates the perusal of documents. So for example, Martens 1958, clearly belongs to the pre-corporative period and contains a wealth of information on craftsmen, but dates from the 14th century.

[3] '(…) fabros ferrarios, et aurifices, vel argentarios, sutores, tornatores, carpentarios, scutarios, piscatores, aucipites, id est ancellatores, saponarios, siceratores (…)' (Boretius, A. *Capitularia regum francorum*, I, 87 (*M.G.H.*, LL, II]). With regard to him, see Verhulst, 1965: 175–189.

[4] It may be a somewhat overstated 'organisational' inference based on the sole use of the term *panni* to affirm that there is incontrovertible evidence that industry at the time 'featured a characteristic division of labour in which different categories of craftsmen were grouped' (trad.) (Verlinden, 1972: 399).

concept 'division of labour', which supposes 'a breakdown of complex processes into a repetition of simple operations' appears, if not as inaccurate, at least as largely anachronical (Samuelson, 1977: 53). The division of labour is not presupposed in the multiplication of labour units without intensification of productivity whose products are distributed non-locally. It must be granted that the division of labour 'often constitutes the only means to reach a level of activity sufficiently large to realise all the savings inherent in large-scale production' and is likely to allow the producer to impose his product more easily on the market; but this does not evacuate the requirement that 'the number of units produced must be sufficiently large to warrant the development of a sophisticated production organisation' (Samuelson, 1977: 84). But how is production to be assessed without recourse to documents allowing even a summary statistical evaluation?[5] And which is more, the 'division of labour' can be conceived only at the expense of a high degree of interdependence which, if it is to be successful, in turn supposes the concentration of all means (men as well as machines) and all production stages in a single spot, a minimum level of productivity on the part of the workforce, and the existence of a 'conductor' (Samuelson, 1977: 52).[6] At any rate, the concept cannot be extended beyond the limits of the work group where it was practised, and these limits were in turn dependent upon the equipment that the master could provide and control.[7] The supply of domestic labour was so abundant that one may wonder whether the division of labour through specialisation or mechanisation was likely to offer any advantage.[8] Of course one could, in a pre-industrial framework, think of 'dispersed but interrelated workshops' or 'disseminated factories'.[9] While it seems logical to postulate their existence, the evidence is still lacking. With the exception of textile production[10] and, more plausibly, of metallurgy[11], it would be more advisable to speak of 'vocational division' (*Berufsteilung*)[12] or 'vocational specialisation' by virtue of there being a finished

5 Fossier (1982: 739) insightfully notes (admittedly about the exchanges) 'one is seriously tempted to draw on the plentiful sources of the 13th century', and notes that with regard to the wage-earning class, 'the deeds prior to 1200 are virtually mute on his vital issue' (trad.) (Ibid.: 793).

6 In this respect one is bound to think of the role of the 'merchant contractor'; but besides some mythical figures – epitomised by a case like Boinbroke's, examined in Derville (1972: 357), – how much do and can we know, considering the state of the documentation? One may also, however, cite the less-known case of Michel Wichmar for Brussels (Despy, 1981: 147–165).

7 The point is rightfully insisted upon by Thrupp (1978: 251).

8 One may have one's doubts even in modern times and within the context of crafts and trades, cf. Sewell, 1983: 40; and for our own regions: Morsa, 1994: 234 ff.

9 These are insisted upon by Braudel, 1979: 259–263.

10 Even in the case, prudence is called for: did the 'labour division' apparently revealed by the Ypres census in 1431 (Pirenne, 1951: 479–480) exist as early as the 12th century? Unfortunately, for this region and this period we do not dispose of tax lists as accurate as those which exist e.g. for Paris in the late 13th century (Favier, 1970: 3). And even these documents testify only to 'vocational specialisation'.

11 One might here think of the case of Nuremberg, the capital of metalcrafts, but only in the 15th century, cf. Ammann, 1970 and Werner, 1965: 69–149.

12 The term was used by K. Bücher with reference to Frankfurt (quoted by Geremek, 1982: 15). In the large towns, for instance, it is evidenced by the high number of different crafts. Outside our regions, the most spectacular example is undoubtedly Paris in the 13th century (Depping, 1837; de Lespinasse and Bonnardot, 1879).

product or possibly a constant quality.[13] Even so, it must be remembered that in small production units, several tasks could, and probably were, entrusted to one and the same craftsman and his family[14], a situation which supposes a much wider range of skills, adding up to 'the capacity to practise a craft in all its aspects'.[15] In this respect, it is useful to highlight the remark of B. Geremek relative to Paris in the 13th–15th centuries, i.e. in the full 'pre-corporative' period: 'during the period under study, the labour division at the threshold of the craft workshop is a mere temporary accomodation, which does not entail any lasting specialisation' (Geremek, 1982: 15). The statement, based notably on the *Livre des métiers* of Étienne Boileau, is far from insignificant. Nor should one allow oneself to be misled on the grounds of 'inventories' of merchandise awaiting exportation or available on more or less distant markets; the variety of goods does not necessarily imply the existence of a 'labour division'.[16] The same holds for the existence specialised selling points[17], which, in the first analysis, testifies only to the importance of a fairly elaborate production and sales organisation. In brief, while we are relatively well informed of the trade, the 'organisational' modalities of the corresponding production remain in the dark.

As regard the heuristics, it does not take exceptional insight to realise that the available documentary evidence[18] prior to the appearance of corporations, which has been located and criticised for a long time, and which is abundant for our regions, does not, by virtue of its typological specificity, allow any spectacular demonstrations concerning labour in the urban context, and notably so when one seeks to delineate its first organisational structures and logic of production. The truly revelatory clues do not abound, and little agreement exists as to their functional relevance. Consequently, it seems advisable to rely more heavily on archeological evidence, which in the case under study is often the only data available as well as the only somewhat more convincing evidence.[19]

---

[13] In this connection, cf. D. Morsa's thoughts on the number of crafts (1994: 235–236).

[14] Carus-Wilson (1987: 654) righly insists on this fact. Cf. the reflections of Braunstein (1998: 306).

[15] Cf. the example of coachwork manufacture in Marx, 1965: 876.

[16] Such is the case, allegedly, of the stallage rates like those raised, for example, by Baudouin the 9th, Earl of Flanders, on July 15, 1199, which specify about textile goods '(...) ex quolibet panno suo scarlato (...) ex viridi uel brunetto (...) ex panno walonum (...)' (ed. *Thesaurus diplomaticus*, W380 / D383). Even if one may find surprisingly precocious evidence for the existence of 'specialised' products, like the stallage rate of the *Littersuerua* harbour recently edited by Verhulst et al., 1998: 143–172, notably 170: 'de panno albo laneo integro [...] de panno colorato [...]'.

[17] For instance, the '(...) domus in qua venduntur panni in Lovanio (...) in prenominata domo pannorum (...)' (Henry 1st, duke of Brabant, 1197; Thesaurus diplomaticus, W3773 / D4077; concerning this deed, see Vander Linden, 1908: 113–121; or the Huy cloth market first mentioned in 1209 (Joris, 1959a: 220 footnote 2).

[18] For Flanders and Brabant, for instance, one only needs to consult Wyffels, 1951 to realise this. For the Meuse region, one may refer to the thesis of Joris, 1959b: 282.

[19] Cf. the considerations of Schofield and Vince, 1994: notably 123: 'It is, for example, impossible to use documentary evidence to study urban crafts and industries in the eleventh or early twelfth centuries, and it is much clearer from archaeology than from documents that the mid to late twelfth century was a period of change in the organisation of a number of industries, among them potting, tile-making, dyeing, and non-ferrous metal-working', as well as Verhaeghe's contribution (1995: 271–293).

Although it can only be carried out – if at all[20] – for the years between 1250 and 1300, the experiment may be worth trying; but the operation requires a careful definition of the data to be examined and of the features to be regarded as relevant indicators.

The data are provided by the recent *Thesaurus Diplomaticus* (Tombeur et al., 1997), which provides a massive corpus, viz. a data base[21] of 12,800 documents, and a text base[22] of 6,000 diplomatic documents relative to the Southern Netherlands before 1200.[23] The normative documents which may cast a light on the first signs of organisation in one of the major 'industrial' activities in our regions, i.e. textile, the significant corpus constituted by the *Recueil de documents relatifs à l'histoire de l'industrie drapière en Flandre* (Espinas and Pirenne, 1906–1924; De Sagher, Van Werveke and Wyffels, 1961–1966) seems a self-evident choice, and, accessorily, the local accounts (the list of the published ones prior to 1302 is a rather short one[24]); these may, indeed, reflect the first forms of vocational consolidation, e.g. via the duties raised on a given trade.[25]

And the supposedly revealing clues? That is where the shoe pinches, for most of the documents contained in the *Thesaurus diplomaticus* deal with economic reality only incidentally, e.g. via the issue of seigneurial rights or 'through the keyhole of a church'.[26] One may therefore expect merchants[27] (stallages[28]) to be overrepresented in proportion to craftsmen. Moreover, it is interesting – albeit not very original – that even the first privileges granted to our towns are of more interest to the historians of law and institutions than the historian of the economy, even though some of these privileges give their explicit

[20] One may wonder whether the list of the 'esgardeurs', urban comptrollers in different branches of industry and trade in Douai about 1250 is the reflection of a real labour division, and whether one may presume they existed in the 12th century (Espinas and Pirenne, I, 1906: 28–29; cf. also Wyffels, 1951: 72–73.

[21] It contains an analysis of the diplomatic documents.

[22] It gives the complete text of the documents analysed, inasmuch as they have been previously published.

[23] They cover the territories of the county of Flanders, including Artois and the dependent counties, the duchy of Brabant, the principality of Liège, the duchy of Limburg, the counties of Namur and Hainaut, and the duchy of Luxembourg.

[24] They are all relatively late at any rate. The oldest ones are: Ypres (1267–) (Des Marez and De Sagher, 1909–1913); Bruges (1280–) (Wyffels, 1965–1971); Mons (1279–) (Piérard, 1971–1973); Calais (1255–) (Bougard and Wyffels, 1966); Ghent (1280–) (Vuylsteke, 1900); Arras (1241–) (Wyffels, 1964: 230–240); Tournai (1240–) (Verriest, 1904: 143–267).

[25] Yet one should not expect too much from this source, as is illustrated by the example of Ypres. The record of duties received in 1290 mentions the following entries: *Garenscale, Corenmarc, Blanders, Les estaus el markiet, Li Wullescale, Des brasseurs, Les epichiers, Li Zuvelmarc, Les dras, Li smede, Li vieu markiés, Li wesdier, Li ledermarc, Li taintenier à caudière, Li bolenghier, Li feutrier, Li houtmarc, Li waghe, Li vin* (Des Marez and De Sagher, 1909–1913, I: 101–102).

[26] The phrase comes from A. Chedeville (1973) *Chartres et ses campagnes (XIe–XIIIe siècles)*, Paris, p. 7, quoted in Carpentier, 1986: 12.

[27] The *Thesaurus diplomaticus* contains 85 occurrences (*mercator, mercatore, mercatorem, mercatores, mercatori, mercatoribus, mercatoris, mercatorum*).

[28] Despy, 1970: 253–287. 250 of the deeds compiled in the *Thesaurus diplomaticus* mention grants and exemptions of stallage.

support to economic development: '(...) ut omnis mercator ueniens aut recedens ad forum Valencenense assecuratur omni tempore ipse cum omnibus suis merchimoniis (...)'[29], and 'fiscalise' its traffic movements.[30] The normative documents, which frustratingly rare before 1250, may inform us of established situations (*more consueto*), but fail to tell us since when they prevail.

Which other clues might one then turn to? One may think of some large categories: these would definitely include the production agents, i.e. all types of craftsmen.[31] Other promising categories might be the infrastructures like markets[32] and market halls, 'industrial' facilities like mills, tanneries, forges and butcheries, inasmuch as these belong to urban centres, and excluding the corporations, i.e. all 'institutions' which group, protect or control the workforce like brotherhoods, guilds, *caritas* or *fraternitas*.

As to documents regarding the exportation towards foreign markets of products manufactured in our towns – such as the *pannos lineos vel laneos* sold in Cologne in 1103 by merchants from Huy[33] – any inferences based on such data are bound to be tentative if they seek to establish the existence of 'division of labour' or 'vocational division'.

II. The craftsmen

The inventory of craftsmen will not take us long[34], and will proceed in two stages. Let us first turn to a few examples of urban centres whose 'industrial' and commercial

[29] Excerpt from the *paix de Valenciennes* (1114) edited by Godding and Pycke: 103 (art. 1). Another remarkable example is the franchise charter granted to Saint-Omer on April 14, 1127 by William, count of Flanders (Vercauteren, 1938: 293–299; Van Caeneghem, 1982: 253–262), or the confirmation of municipal right granted to the burghers of the same town on December 4, 1164: *Constituta est etiam pax omni negotiatori omni ad mercatorem venienti ut securus cum suis rebus veniat securus* (de Hemptinne and Verhulst, 1988: 365–370, n° 233.)

[30] As is the case of the 'justice des lois' granted by Philip of Alsace, count of Flanders, to the new city of Nieuport in December 1163 (de Hemptinne and Verhulst, 1988: II–1, p. 344–348, n° 322).

[31] The inclusion of merchants seems less relevant. Of course, their existence bears witness to the commerce in diverse products, but throws no light on the 'division of labour'. The same objection might be raised against evidence inferred from the stallage rates.

[32] It would be interesting, for example, to be better informed of the division and allotment of stalls for a period prior to 1200. It is documented for Ypres at the end of the 13th century: 'Sors de illis qui vendunt pannos tinctos, sors de illis qui faciunt saios, sors de pannis enforciatis, sors de dimidiis pannis in Halla subter versus atrium, sors de illis qui vendunt' (Des Marez and De Sagher, 1909–1913, I: 23–25.

[33] Joris, 1959a: 218, note 2 (Cf. also Joris, 1959b: 65). It may be useful to note here that the deed of Frederick I, dated December 4, 1103 and fixing the tax rates to be paid by merchants from Liège and Huy on goods taken to Cologne is regarded as a forgery by Niermeyer, 1935: 131 ff en Despy, 1988: 105 footn. 3, who respectively date the document 1171 and 1200. Thus, the frustrating lack of texts is compounded by difficulties in chronology.

[34] All the more since books about the bourgeoisie at the time and in the region under study are rare: Ver-beemen, 1953: 65–74, in contrast to, say, Cologne, where the books have been kept since the 12th century.

activities prior to 1200 are above question. Let us take the case of Huy[35], where copper-work and braziery was a leading activity (Rousseau,1930: 103 ff), and the importance of drapery an established fact.[36] But may one actually speak of *Berufsteilung* on the basis of a record of rents handed over in 1189 to Our Lady's collegiate church (*Notre Dame*) by Conon d'Ocquier, which mentions three weavers (*textor*)[37], two bakers (*panifex*)[38], one carpenter (*carpentarius*)[39], one butcher (*carnifex*)[40] and one cobbler (*sutor*)[41]? Another case is Brussels in 1225, leaving aside the custom of millers of its five windmills (ca. 1173).[42] The three census records of Notre-Dame chapel yield a particularly poor result[43], as they mention a mere four weavers (*textor*), three blacksmiths (*faber*), two carpenters (*carpentarius*), two cobblers (*sutor*), one stonemason (*cementarius*) and one furrier (*pellifex*). What more is there to be said about three isolated documents, except that, for our purposes, they constitute an altogether haphazard collection of data; and this in turn raises the more fundamental question of whether trades like these are not bound to exist as soon as an urban community, no matter how small, has grown or has been growing for a certain time? The answer is a matter of common sense: it is no more than natural that under the tenure of Nicholas as an abbot (1180–1193)[44], there should appear among the *quidam morantes in oppido* of Saint Trond a few bakers (*bolengarii*), brewers (*cervisarii*), and maltsters (*sutarii*)[45]? And by the same token, one may raise doubts about the evidence for a real 'division of labour' based on Guiman's mentioning butchers (*carnifices*), bucklesmiths (*lorimerii*), tanners (*mesquiciarii*), millers (*molnarii*), bakers (*bolingarii*), cloth-shearers (*tonsores pannorum*) and cobblers (*cordeuuanarii*) in 12th-century Arras.[46]

Next, we must consider systematic records based on a 'population' of more considerable size. The attempt covers the period prior to 1200 and is limited to the diplomatic documents in Latin relative to the area covering actual Belgium.

---

[35] Joris, 1959b; Jansen, 1982 notes that we know very little about the labour organisation of the towns in the Meuse valley.

[36] As has been established by the studies of Ammann, 1953: 377–399; 1954: 1–63; Haase, 1976: 55–136; Joris.

[37] Evrardus, Emelinus and Philippus (cf. Joris, 1959a: 234, 236).

[38] Bastianus and Aboldus (cf. Joris, 1959a: 235).

[39] Stephanus 'carpentarius de curtili et wenda' (cf. Joris, 1959a: 235).

[40] Evrardus (cf. Joris, 1959: 37).

[41] Henricus Vacoz (cf. Joris, 1959a: 237).

[42] Lefèvre et al., 1993: 15, n° 9: '(...) dux Godefridus quinque molendinorum discipulis et eorum successoribus consuetudinem quam hactenus tenuerunt et supscriptam inperpetuum donavit'.

[43] Edited in *Thesaurus diplomaticus*, W3690–3692 / D3990–3992. Regarding them, see Des Marez, 1936: 92–93 and Godding, 1957: 169–180.

[44] *Monasticon belge*, VI: *Province de Limbourg*, Liège, 1976: 45.

[45] Cited by Des Marez, 1921: 433, after Ch. Piot (1870) *Cartulaire de Saint-Trond*, I, Brussels, n° 100 38 (CRH, in4–°): 'qui vulgo bolengarii, cervisarii, sutarii vocantur'. It is a confirmation of the safeguards issued on February 7, 1112 (ns) by Abbot Raoul to the 'bolengarii ceruisarii sutarii et qui alias hujusmodi merces vendunt super nostrum in oppido nostro' (ed. in the *Thesaurus diplomaticus*, W4897 / D4964; Ch. Piot, 1870: n° 28).

[46] Van Drival, 1875: 335. On the importance of this document for the history of Arras, see Vercauteren, 1978: 365–377.

Table 1.1 ***Thesaurus diplomaticus*****. Craftsmen: number of mentions**

Trade	Number of occurrences	Trade	Number of occurrences
agrimessor	–	latomus/lathomus[9]	1
alutarius	–	lotarius/lotor	–
apoticarius	–	machenarius	–
argentarius	–	makelardus/makellarius	–
aurifaber[1]	2	medicus	3
barbator/barbitons	–	mensurator	–
bermannus	–	mercemanus/mercenarius	
bolengarius[2]	8	molendinarius	24
brassator	–	molitor	–
buticularius	5	nebulator	–
caligarius/caligator/calsiator	–	panetarius[10]	3
carnifex[3]	3	pannifex[11]	2
carpentarius/carpentator[4]	13	parmentarius	–
cementarius[5]	7	pellifex[12]	6
cervisarius[6]	5	physicus	–
cirurgicus	–	piscator[13]	7
corriator	–	pistor[14]	17
corrigiarius	–	plumbifusor	–
cuparius	–	portitor saccorum	–
cyrothecarius	–	rotarius	–
faber[7]	39	sartor	–
figularius	–	sarcinator	–
formator	–	sutor[15]	9
fossor	–	tannator, tannarius	–
fullo[8]	1	tector	–
fusor campane	–	textor[16]	14
hallarius	–	tinctor[17]	1
hospes	–	tonsor	–
joculator	6	usurarius	1
laborator	–	vinarius	1
lapidarius/lapiscida	–		

Notes:

[1] aurifaber, 1; aurifabri, 1
[2] bolengarius, 1; bolengarium, 1; bolengarios, 2; bolengaris, 2
[3] carnifex, 2; carnifices, 1
[4] carpentarius, 6; carpentarios, 2; carpentario, 2; carpentarii, 3
[5] cementarius, 3; cementariorum, 1; cementariis, 2; cementarii, 1
[6] cervisiarii, 2; cervisiariis, 1; cervisiario, 2; cervisiarum, 5
[7] faber, 18; fabri, 13; fabris, 1; fabro, 5; fabrum, 2
[8] fullonis, 1
[9] latomus, 1
[10] panetarii, 3
[11] pannifices, 1
[12] pellifex, 3; pellifices, 2; pellificiis, 1
[13] piscator, 6; piscatore, 1; piscatorem, 3; piscatores, 9; piscatoribus, 3
[14] pistor, 15; pistore, 1; pistorem, 1; pistorum, 4
[15] sutor, 6; sutores, 2; sutori, 1; sutoris, 2, sutorum, 1
[16] textor, 14
[17] tinctor, 1

Source: Tombeur et al., 1997.

It is grounded on a Latin glossary using urban documents dating from the late 13th and early 14th centuries, and hence likely to mention precise trades. They are the accounts of the towns of Calais and Bruges, dating respectively from 1255 to 1302[47] and from 1280 to 1302[48], and both written in Latin; and the ducal census for the Brussels district of 1321.[49] The glossary mentions sixty different trades.

The results, albeit predictable, are surprising, and call for four observations. First, as regards the craftsmen, if one confines oneself to the sole occurrence of substantives referring to them, the yield – a mere 176 occurrences – is strikingly low. Second, the most significantly represented sectors were those one might have expected, i.e. in decreasing order, the blacksmiths, bakers, millers, carpenters, weavers, cobblers, masons, and furriers. Third, for those trades likely to feature 'industrial' activity and openings towards foreign markets, i.e. in the metal and textile sectors, the vocabulary is remarkably small, especially if one supposes the existence of a division of labour or *Berufsteilung*; but this argument may be discarded as meaningless, considering that the Latin terminology may not lend itself to detailed description. Fourth, the relative importance of the craftwork and/or industrial sectors represented, as well as the absence of some of these, raises questions. One cannot but be surprised, for example, by the dearth of references to the textile sector in regions where its importance is beyond question.

There is little to be learnt from so few data. To give but one example regarding a major sector (see Table 1.2): we note 14 occurrences of *textor*, which refer to 13 different craftsmen in 8 towns, only three of which have a real 'industrial' significance: Brussels, Huy and Ypres, and it is impossible to tell which place each of these craftsmen holds in the various stages of textile production. The only significant element may be that none of the entries is prior to the 12th century. With regard to two essential trades, the fowlers and dyers, we are forced to drop to the level of the anecdotal: a fowler, Radulfus, is mentioned in Tournai in 1198,[50] and a dyer, Marsius, is referred to in Saint-Omer in 1200.[51] The cloth-shearers, important as their specialty may be, simply fail to be mentioned.

Another example is constituted by metallurgy. We find 39 occurrences referring to *faber*, and another two to *aurifaber*. The numerical superiority of the former is unsurprising, and the term undoubtedly covers more varied specialisations than appears at first sight. Two other points need to be made, although they are not directly relevant to our argument. A fair number of the metalworkers are census payers, so for example Rucelinus, Iohannes and Lambertus in Brussels in 1225.[52] Others, more numerous, are mentioned as witnesses at the drawing up of deeds. Also, we must be sure that 'signum X fabri' does actually refer to a blacksmith – a fact that might be significant of their relative social status. But that is a different issue.

---

[47] Based on the glossary Bougard and Wyffels, 1966: 294–306.

[48] Based on the glossary Wyffels, 1971: 199–223.

[49] Based on the Latin glossary of Martens, 1958: 370–374.

[50] W3217/D2435 (cf. Table 1.2, references).

[51] W411/D414.

[52] D3990/W3690, D3991/W3691, D3992/W3692.

Table 1.2 Mentions of *textor*

Name	Place	Date	References
Adelelmus textor	Ypres[1]	1110	W2309/D2574
Adelelmus textor	Ypres[1]	1123	W2313/D2578
Hergerus textor	Ename[2]	1175	W979/D1229
Reinelmus textor	Arleux-en-Gohelle[3]	1175	W984/D1234
Stephanus textor	Flobecq[4]	1175	W1020/D1270
Evrardus textor	Huy[5]	1189	A. Joris
Emelinus textor	Huy[5]	1189	A. Joris
Philippus textor	Huy[5]	1189	A. Joris
Heribertus textor	Malmédy[6]	1200	W3794/D4100
Sifridus textor	Forest[7]	1200	W4623/D4837
Amelricus textor	Bruxelles[8]	1225	W3690/D3990
Henricus textor	Bruxelles[8]	1225	W3691/D3991
Baldricus textor	Bruxelles[8]	1225	W3692/D3992
Albertus textor	Bruxelles[8]	1225	W3692/D3992

Notes:
[1] property of St. Martin's at Ypres
[2] donation of a female serf by the name of Richildis, redeemed by her husband, a textor
[3] donation to Ename abbey
[4] record of incomes of the Ename abbey at Flobecq
[5] rents handed over to Notre-Dame at Huy
[6] Central domain of the abbey
[7] donations to the abbey
[8] domain of the Holy Sepulcre at Cambrai.
Source: Tombeur et al., 1997.
References:
W = registration number in 'Nouveau Wauters'
D = registration number in *Dictionnaire du latin médiéval diplomatique*
A. Joris = Joris, 1959: 233–237, n° 1.

III. The infrastructures

In this domain, the yield is almost nil. Besides a 'vic[us] sutorum'[53] and the fact that cloth was made in the L'Estrée quarter in Arras[54] in June 1177, references to markets and market halls can be counted on the fingers of one hand: in 1170, a 'dom[us] rerum venalium' at Oudenburg[55]; in 1187, in Aire, with 'great precision', 'omnes stalla qui ponuntur in foro Arie super qua omnia venalia venduntur'[56]; in 1189, in Avesnes, a

[53] W4421/D4737.
[54] Tock, 1991: 194–196, n° 174; W 5396/D5187.
[55] W2368/D2633.
[56] D5268.

'halla mea qui est in foro de Avennis'[57]; in 1191 a 'for[um] piscium' in Ghent[58]; and in 1197, a 'dom[us] pannorum' in Louvain.[59] The dearth must reside in the documents, and actual reality must have been quite different, as may be inferred from the 29 *mercato* and the 72 *foro* that can be spotted in the *Thesaurus diplomaticus*.

IV. Associative structures

Here again, one cannot but deplore the dearth of data. We find seven references to guilds[60], all at Saint-Omer, and neither of these allows to pinpoint a particular vocational specificity. Moreover none of the references to *fraternitas* (168 occurrences) and *societas* (83 occurrences) bear any relationship to the socio-economic world.

V. Conclusion

The verdict, as I see it, is clear: before the appearance and development of the corporations, the available diplomatic sources do not, or hardly, throw any light on the birth of a 'division of labour'. This observation may be explained in terms of typology, but there is likely to be a deeper-seated reason, namely that the question of labour division misses the point because it was not, or not yet, or rarely, asked in a socio-economic environment which – until proof of the contrary – did not yet know manufacture.

Let me conclude this paper by quoting an excerpt which, I feel, provides an eloquent illustration: 'The Nuremberg pin-maker is the fundamental element in the English pin-making manufacture; but while the former performed as series of twenty or so successive operations, in the latter twenty workers each performed only one of these operations, which, subsequent to later experiments, were to be isolated and subdivided into even smaller tasks.' Who is the author of these lines? No one else than Karl Marx![61]

---

[57] D4444/W4131.

[58] D78/W78.

[59] D4077/W3773.

[60] After 1127: D159/W158, D4990/W4947, D5124/W5285, D4196/W3890, D159/W158.

[61] Marx, 1965: 877.

Bibliography

Ammann, H. (1953) 'Huy an der Maas in der mittelalterlichen Wirtschaft', in *Städtewesen und Bürgertum als geschichtliche Kräfte. Gedächtnisschrift für F. Rörig*, Lübeck, pp. 377–399.

Ammann, H. (1954) 'Deutschland und die Tuchindustrie Nordwest Europas im Mittelalter', *Hansische Geschichtsblätter*, 72, pp. 1–63; reprinted in C. Haase (ed.) (1976) *Die Stadt des Mittelalters*, III: *Wirtschaft und Gesellschaft*, Darmstadt, pp. 55–136. (Wege der Forschung; 245).

Ammann, H. (1970) *Nürnbergs wirtschaftliche Stellung im Spätmittelalter*, Nüremberg. (Nürnberger Forschungen).

Bougard, P. and Wyffels, C. (1966) *Les finances de Calais au XIIIe siècle*, Bruxelles. (Pro Civitate, Coll. Histoire, sér. in–8°, 8).

Braudel, F. (1979) *Civilisation matérielle, économie et capitalisme, XVe–XVIIIe siècle*, II: *Les jeux de l'échange*, Paris.

Braunstein, Ph. (1998) 'Savoir et savoir-faire: les transferts techniques', in P. Beck (ed.), *L'innovation technique au moyen âge*, Paris, pp. 303–309. (Actes du VIe Congrès international d'archéologie médiévale).

Caeneghem, R.C. Van (1982) 'De keure van Sint-Omaers van 1127', *Tijdschrift voor Rechtsgeschiedenis*, 50, pp. 253–262.

Carpentier, E. (1986) *Orvieto à la fin du XIIIe siècle. Ville et campagne dans le cadastre de 1292*, Paris.

Carus-Wilson, E. (1987) 'The Woollen Industry', in *The Cambridge Economic History Europe*, II: *Trade and Industry in the Middle Ages*, 2nd. ed., Cambridge.

de Hemptinne, Th. and Verhulst, A. (eds) (1988) *De oorkonden der graven van Vlaanderen (juli 1128–september 1191)*, II–1: *Regering van Diederik van Elzas (juli 1128–19 januari 1168)*, Brussels. (Commissie voor Geschiedenis. Verzameling van de Akten der Belgische Vorsten).

de Lespinasse, R. and Bonnardot, F. (eds) (1879) *Le livre des métiers*, Paris.

Depping, G.B. (ed.) (1837) *Règlements sur les arts et métiers de Paris rédigés au XIIIe siècle et connus sous le nom du Livre des métiers d'Etienne Boileau*, Paris.

Derville, A. (1972) 'Les draperies flamandes et artésiennes vers 1250–1350', *Revue du Nord*, 54, pp. 353–370.

Des Marez, G. (1921) 'La première étape de la formation corporative. L'entr'aide', *Bulletin de l'Académie royale de Belgique*, 5th ser., 7, pp. 412–446.

Des Marez, G. (1936) 'Le domaine du Saint-Sépulcre de Cambrai à Bruxelles au XIIe siècle', in *Études inédites publiées par ungroupe de ses anciens élèves*, Brussels, pp. 91–96.

Des Marez, G. and Sagher, E. De (eds) (1909–1913) *Comptes de la ville d'Ypres de 1267 à 1329*, 2 vols, Brussels. (Commission Royale d'Histoire, in–4°).

Despy, G. (1970) 'Pour un corpus des tarifs de tonlieux de l'Europe occidentale au moyen âge, Ve–XIIIe siècles', *Acta historica Bruxellensia*, 2, pp. 253–287.

Despy, G. (1981) 'Secteur secondaire et tertiaire dans les villes des anciens Pays-Bas au XIIIe siècle', *Acta Historica Bruxellensis*, 4, pp. 147–165.

Despy, G. (1988) 'Recherches sur les tarifs de tonlieux dans le duché de Brabant au XIIIe siècle', *Publications de la Société historique de l'Institut grand-ducal de Luxembourg*, 104, pp. 103–129.

Drival, E. van (ed.) (1875) Cartulaire de l'abbaye Saint-Vaast d'Arras ... par Guiman, Arras.

Espinas, G. and Pirenne, H. (eds) (1906) *Recueil des documents relatifs à l'histoire de l'industrie drapière en Flandre*, I: *Des origines à l'époque Bourguignonne*, vol. I: *Aire-sur-la-Lys-Courtrai*, Brussels. (Commission Royale d'Histoire, in–4°).

Favier, J. (1970) *Les contribuables parisiens à la fin de la guerre de Cent Ans. Les rôles d'impôt de 1421, 1423 et 1438*, Genève-Paris. (Centre de recherches d'histoire et de philologie de la IVe Section de l'École pratique des hautes Études, V. Hautes études médiévales et modernes; 11).

Fossier, R. (1982) *Enfance de l'Europe. Aspects économiques et sociaux. 2: structures et problèmes*, Paris. (Nouvelle Clio; 17bis).

Genicot, L. (1982) *L'économie rurale namuroise au bas Moyen Âge*, III: *Les hommes, le commun*, Louvain-la-Neuve–Brussels. (Université de Louvain. Recueil de travaux d'histoire et de philologie; 6e sér., 25).

Geremek, B. (1982) *Le salariat dans l'artisanat parisien aux XIIIe–XVe siècles. Étude sur le marché de la main d'oeuvre au moyen âge*, Paris (repr.). (EHESS, Industrie et artisanat; V).

Godding, Ph. (1957) 'Note sur le domaine de l'abbaye du Saint-Sépulcre de Cambrai à Bruxelles au XIIe siècle', *Cahiers bruxellois*, 2, pp. 169–180.

Godding, Ph. and Pycke, J. (1979–1981) 'La paix de Valenciennes de 1114', *Bulletin de la Commission royale pour la publication des anciennes Lois et Ordonnances de Belgique*, 29, pp. 1–142.

Goetstouwers, J.-B. (1908) *Les métiers de Namur sous l'Ancien Régime. Contribution à l'histoire sociale*, Louvain-Paris. (Université de Louvain. Recueil de travaux publiés par les membres des conférences d'histoire et de philologie; XX).

Jansen, H.P.H. (1982) 'Handel en nijverheid 1100–1300', in *Algemene geschiedenis der Nederlanden*, II, Haarlem, pp. 148–186.

Joris, A. (1959a) 'Documents relatifs à l'histoire économique et sociale de Huy au moyen âge', *Bulletin de la Commission royale d'Histoire*, 124, pp. 213–265.

Joris, A. (1959b) *La ville de Huy au moyen âge. Des origines à la fin du XIVe siècle*, Paris. (Bibliothèque de la Faculté de Philosophie et Lettres de l'Université de Liège, 102).

Lefèvre, Pl., Godding, Ph. and Godding-Ganshof, Fr. (1993) *Chartes du chapitre de Sainte-Gudule à Bruxelles, 1074–1300*, Louvain-la-Neuve/Brussels. (Université de Louvain. Recueil de travaux d'histoire et de philologie; 6e sér., 45).

Linden, H. Vander (1908) 'Trois documents relatifs à l'hôpital de Louvain', in *Mélanges G. Kurth. Recueil de mémoires relatifs à l'histoire, à la philologie et à l'archéologie*, I: *Mémoires historiques*, Liège, pp. 113–121. (Bibliothèque de la Faculté de Philosophie et Lettres de l'Université de Liège, sér. Gd–in8°, 1).

Martens, M. (1958) *Le censier ducal pour l'ammanie de Bruxelles de 1321*, Brussels. (Commission Royale d'Histoire, in–8°).

Marx, K. (1965) *Le Capital*, I–xiv–1, French translation by M. Rubel, in Idem, *Oeuvres. Économie*, I, Paris, pp. 537–1406. (Bibliothèque de la Pléiade; 164).

Morsa, D. (1994) 'Les métiers aux Temps modernes, reflets de situations médiévales?', in P. Lambrechts and J.P. Sosson (eds), *Les métiers au moyen âge. Aspects économiques et sociaux*, Louvain-la-Neuve, pp. 537–1406. (Université Catholique de Louvain. Publications de l'Institut d'Études médiévales. Textes, études, congrès, 15).

Niermeyer, J.-F. (1935) *Onderzoekingen over Luikse en Maastrichtse oorkonden en over de Vita Balderici episcopi Leodiensis. Een bijdrage tot de geschiedenis van burgerij en geestelijkheid in het Maasgebied tot het begin van de dertiende eeuw*, Groningen.

Piérard, C. (ed.) (1971–1973) *Les plus anciens comptes de la ville de Mons, 1279–1356*, 2 vols, Brussels. (Commission Royale d'Histoire, in–4°).

Pirenne, H. (1951) 'Les dénombrements de la population d'Ypres au XVe siècle, 1412–1506. Contribution à la statistique sociale du moyen âge', in *Histoire économique de l'Occident médiéval*, Bruges, pp. 458–488.

Planitz, H. (1975) *Die Deutsche Stadt im Mittelalter. Von der Römerzeit bis zu den Zunftkämpfen*, 4th ed., Vienna/Köln/Graz.

Rousseau, F. (1930) *La Meuse et le pays mosan en Belgique. Leur importance avant le XIIIe siècle*, Namur. (Annales de la Société archéologique de Namur; 39).

Sagher, H.E. De, Werveke, H. Van and Wyffels, C. (eds) (1961–1966) *Recueil de documents relatifs à l'histoire de l'industrie drapière en Flandre*, II: *Le sud-est de la Flandre depuis l'époque bourguignonne*, Brussels. (Commission Royale d'Histoire, in–4°).

Samuelson, P.A. (1977) *L'économique. Introduction à l'analyse économique*, Paris. (Collection U).

Schofield, J. and Vince, A. (1994) *Medieval Towns*, London.

Sewell, W.H. Jr. (1983) *Gens de métier et révolutions. Le langage du travail de l'Ancien Régime à 1848*, Paris.

Thrupp, S.L. (1978) 'Medieval Industry, 1000–1500', in C. Cipolla (ed.), *The Fontana Economic History of Europe*, I: *The Middle Ages*, Glasgow, pp. 221–273.

Tock, B.-M. (1991) 'Les chartes promulguées par le chapitre cathédral d'Arras au XIIe siècle', *Revue Mabillon*, new series, 2.

Tombeur, P., Prevenier, W., Demonty Ph. and Laviolette M.-P. (1997), *Thesaurus Diplomaticus*, Turnhout, 1997 (1 CD-ROM and *User's Guide* by Ph. Demonty).

Verbeemen, J. (1953) 'Poortersboeken in de Nederlanden', *De Schakel*, 8, pp. 65–74.

Vercauteren, F. (ed.). (1938) *Actes des comtes de Flandre (1071–1128)*, Brussels. (Commission royale d'histoire; Series I, in–4°).

Vercauteren, F. (1978) 'Un exemple de peuplement urbain au XIIe siècle. Le cas d'Arras', in F. Vercauteren, *Études d'histoire médiévale. Recueil d'articles du Prof. Vercauteren publiés par le Crédit Communal de Belgique*, Brussels, pp. 365–377. (Crédit Communal de Belgique, Coll. Histoire Pro Civitate; sér. In–8°, 53).

Verhaeghe, Fr. (1995) 'Industry in medieval towns: the archaeological problem. An essay', in J.-M. Duvosquel and E. Thoen (eds) *Peasants and Townsmen in Medieval Europe. Studia in Honorem A. Verhulst*, Ghent, pp. 271–293.

Verhulst, A. (1965) 'Karolingische Agrarpolitik. Das *Capitulare de Villis* und die Hungersnöte von 792/93 und 805/06', *Zeitschrift für Agrargeschichte und Agrarsoziologie*, 13, pp. 175–189.

Verhulst, A., de Hemptinne, Th. and Mey, L. De (1998) 'Un tarif de tonlieu inconnu, institué par le comte de Flandre Thierry d'Alsace (1128–1168) pour le port de *Littersuerua* précurseur du port de Damme', *Bulletin de la Commission royale d'Histoire*, 154, pp. 143–172.

Verlinden, Ch. (1972) 'Marchands ou tisserands? A propos des origines urbaines', *Annales. Économies, sociétés, civilisations*, 27–2, pp. 396–406.

Verriest, L. (1904) 'La 'Charité Saint-Christophe' et ses comptes du XIIIe siècle', *Bulletin de la Commission royale d'histoire*, 73, pp. 143–267.

Vuylsteke, J. (1900) *Gentsche stads- and baljuwsrekeningen, 1280–1336*, Ghent. (Oorkondenboek der stad Gent, Ie Afd.: Rekeningen).

Werner, Th.G. (1965) 'Nürnbergs Erzeugung und Ausfuhr wissenschaftlicher Geräte im Zeitalter der Entdeckungen', *Nürnberger Mitteilungen*, 53, pp. 69–149.

Wyffels, C. (1951) *De oorsprong der ambachten in Vlaanderen en Brabant*, Brussels. (Verhandelingen van de Koninklijke Vlaamse Academie voor wetenschappen, letteren en schone kunsten van België, Kl. der Letteren; XIII).

Wyffels, C. (1964) 'Le contrôle des finances urbaines au XIIIe siècle. Un abrégé de deux comptes de la ville d'Arras, 1241–1246', *Bulletin de la Commission départementale des monuments historiques du Pas-de-Calais*, 8–3, pp. 230–240

Wyffels, C. (1965–1971) *De rekeningen van de stad Brugge (1280–1319)*, I: *1280–1302*, 2 vols, Brussels. (Commission Royale d'Histoire, in–4°).

2 On the preconditions for the transition from rural to urban industrial activities (9th–11th centuries)

Adriaan VERHULST, Ghent University

I. Introduction

Relations between town and countryside in the early middle ages have in recent years attracted increasing attention, since the rural economy of the Carolingian period is no longer considered as a closed system and since a new, less rigid definition of the concept of 'town' has made us aware of urban phenomena in that period other than the cities of late Roman origin (Hodges, 1982: 20–25). Some historians (Despy, 1968; Morimoto, 1991) even go so far as to take the rural expansion of the Carolingian period, which nowadays is commonly accepted by most medievalists (Flaran 10, 1988; Nelson, 1992: 19–40), as the main factor in the rise of new towns or the revival of older ones from the ninth century onwards. The agrarian production of the countryside is believed to have generated from then on a surplus, sold on an ever increasing number of markets (Nelson, 1992:30). Many of these markets had an urban character even when situated in small settlements which in a later period would not be considered as towns (Morimoto, 1991: 527–531).

On the other hand, interest in the predominantly rural economy of the early middle ages has for a long time overshadowed industrial activities that were going on both in urban and rural settlements. Since the post-war flowering of medieval archaeology brought them to light in both places, their role in the relations between town and countryside and particularly in the origin of towns as centres of industry must be investigated. Industrial activities in the countryside were indeed often organized on a large scale, both in workshops and within households of peasants or craftsmen (Jankuhn et al., 1981–1983), transforming some villages into real industrial centres (Janssen, 1983). In towns, however, these activities in many cases have been demonstrated archaeologically to have been situated at the edge of the settlement, often in a semi-rural environment.[1] A distinction between the rural or urban character of their location is therefore often difficult to make. Furthermore, taking into account certain rural features in urban crafts such as the textile trades in an early phase (11th century) – as for example their domestic location, the role of women, the continuation of old techniques etc.[2] – we should no longer speak of the shift of industry from countryside to towns (Van Werveke, 1954: 239–240), but of a long and gradual process of transition between the tenth and the twelfth centuries.

[1] Examples from Huy and Maastricht, both on the river Meuse, in: *La genèse et les premiers siècles des villes médiévales dans les Pays-Bas méridionaux*, 1990: 401–402, 446.
[2] Keene, this volume.

For all these reasons, it is well worth studying the written evidence for industrial activity, trades, specialisation, wage labour etc. in the countryside between the ninth century and the last quarter of the eleventh, a period for which written evidence on the organisation of industry and labour in towns is nearly completely lacking. This rural evidence may indicate labour practices which were also followed in towns. Archaeological evidence is available for some towns, but for many regions of North-West Europe during that period archaeological evidence is scarce, in both town and countryside (Demolon, Galinié and Verhaeghe, 1994; De Boe and Verhaeghe, 1997a). Notable exceptions are England, some regions and towns of the German Rhineland and some urban settlements along the Meuse, the Scheldt and the southern shores of the North Sea. The written evidence about the countryside is mainly of ecclesiastical and royal origin and concerns mostly the landed property of abbeys, churches and the Frankish king or emperor.

II. Landless unskilled labour reserve

The concentration of an industrial labour force in the towns, characterized by wage labour, predominantly of males, specialisation and even labour division, presupposes the presence in the countryside since the late ninth century of both an unskilled labour reserve that did not have a full employment in the agricultural sector and of forms of industrial production by specialized craftsmen.There is evidence from the ninth century that in several old settled and fertile regions of North-West Europe, like the Paris Basin, northern France and southern Belgium, demographic growth from about 850 onwards doubled the population in the course of two generations, i.e. in about sixty years (Verhulst, 1995: 481–483; Devroey, 1997). It caused emigration, mainly of women, to neighbouring regions, but its main effect seems to have been the presence on the big rural estates of a mass of young, nearly landless men, called by different names, *accolae, solivagi, haistaldi*, living somewhat isolated and mostly unmarried at the outer fringes of the estate (Goetz, 1995: 462; Kuchenbuch, 1978: 255–260; Devroey, 1997). As members of the lord's *familia* they were not really free. The *haistaldi* more specifically paid a significant yearly sum of money (12 d.) as a sign of their subjection, although their services on the demesne, unlike those of the unfree *mancipia*, were very limited and occasional. According to Dopsch and, in a less affirmative way, also to Perrin and Ménager, they were in fact wage labourers (Dopsch, 1922: 86–91; Perrin, 1934: 256). Even Kuchenbuch, although stressing their unfree status, admits that they worked for wages, either in kind or money (Kuchenbuch, 1978: 257–258). They were unskilled, unlike many of the *provendarii* who were another numerous group among the *familia* of abbeys and churches (Kuchenbuch, 1978: 254–255; Lesne, 1943: 192–198). Paid by a *provenda* normally consisting of food,they worked, though not all permanently, as specialized craftsmen inside an abbey or in the bourg or *vicus* next to it, where some had their *officina* and many of them their house.

III. Dependent specialised craftsmen and -women

In connection with the problem of the emergence of an urban population of wage-earners, it is important not only that *provendarii* seem to have enjoyed a more free and a better economic status than the *haistaldi*, but also that they were sometimes extremely specialized. In the sixth volume of his famous *Histoire de la propriété ecclésiastique en France*, Lesne brought together in a systematic way the evidence for the presence of specialized craftsmen in or near big abbeys (Lesne, 1943: 256–264, 273–276).

Tailors made the habits for the monks with the fabric delivered to the monastery by unfree or dependent women living on the estates of the abbey. These women either worked at home or in specialized textile workshops for women (*gynecea*) established on some large, mostly royal estates, situated in the countryside or even in towns of Roman origin like Tournai. The weaving of linen cloth (*camsiles*), woollen cloth (*sarciles*) and other fabrics (*panni, drappi,* and *mappae* for towels), almost exclusively by women, was in any case done outside the monastery, be it generally on command as an obligatory manorial service (Lesne, 1943: 259–260; Kuchenbuch, 1991: 139–175). Some monasteries acquired them by purchase, perhaps from independent female weavers like the six *camsilariae* working in the city of Tournai in the second half of the ninth century who bought off their manorial obligation and paid henceforth money to the abbey of Saint-Amand (Hägermann, 1991: 364–365).

Leather-workers with various specializations (*sutores, sellarii, scutarii, coriarii*) had their workshops within the precinct of a monastery or in the *vicus* next to it (Lesne, 1943: 257–258, 263). In the tenth century *coriarii* are cited in Ghent, not in the town itself, nor in the then destroyed *vicus* near St Bavo's abbey, but in the settlement (called *Oudburg, Vetus Castellum*) which was part of the count's castle, on the edge of the town. Centuries later they were still at the same place, and since the late Middle Ages the names of a street and a canal have commemorated their presence in this specialised district (Verhulst and Declercq, 1989: 56; Van Werveke and Verhulst, 1960: 11–13). This grouping, which in the tenth century was still in a manorial context, recalls the streets of specialized craftsmen in some abbey towns in the ninth and tenth century (Lesne, 1943: 418–422), and prefigures the same phenomenon visible in many towns from the twelfth century onwards.

The personal juridical situation of these different categories of craftsmen is not clear. Economically they probably enjoyed a certain degree of freedom, as there are indications that in some cases they sold their products. More obscure is their relation to the towns which from the late ninth and tenth century onwards emerged not far from some abbeys, as at Arras and Ghent, or within or near former royal estates, as at Tournai and Valenciennes (Verhulst, 1999: 75–86, 102–103). In Ghent the question is particularly relevant since the ninth-century *portus* near St Bavo's abbey was destroyed by the Vikings and a new *portus* emerged a few years later some hundred metres upstream along the Scheldt, while on the other edge of the town, as we have seen, a settlement of leather workers associated with the count's castle, existed about the same time (Verhulst and Declercq, 1989: 49–56).

IV. The disintegration of manorial organisation

So far two particular groups have been considered who may have contributed to the formation of an urban population of wage-earners: first, the different categories of landless people on the rural estates of the countryside, whose number rose during the ninth century because of population growth; secondly, the specialized craftsmen of usually unclear juridical status, working either within the precinct of an abbey, in a town-like *vicus* next to it, or on the territory of a royal estate near or on the site of a later town. The jurisdiction of an abbey, bishop or church over both place and people probably encouraged migration from the countryside into town.

There are, however, other factors to be taken into consideration as an explanation for the existence of a labour force reserve, which could be used as wage earners by industry from the moment of its location in towns.

The decline and disintegration of the manorial organisation from the late ninth century onwards was one of them (Ganshof and Verhulst, 1966: 305–319). Early examples of the commutation for money of agricultural services on the demesne can be found on the estates of the Alsatian abbey of Wissembourg (Dette, 1987: 61, 82). The splitting of the agricultural family unit, the *mansus*, also made hands available, since services rested on the *mansus* and not on each member of the family individually. Family members may not all have been engaged in agricultural work on the smaller but more intensely worked farms formed from splitting the *mansus*. Other services too, especially transport services, were redeemable, for instance on some estates of the abbey of Montierender from the middle of the ninth century and on some manors of St Remi de Reims in the tenth century (Droste, 1988: 141; Devroey, 1984: 77, 82, 85, 86).[3] Commutation of manorial services reached a peak in the eleventh and twelfth centuries when in many urbanised regions the whole system of services collapsed (Ganshof and Verhulst, 1966: 306–319).

Finally, the destruction or even the temporary desertion of abbeys caused by the Vikings in the southern Low Countries and Northern France at the end of the ninth century were responsible for the dislocation and sometimes the disappearance of industrial activities within the abbey or in its *vicus*.

V. Direct evidence of wage labour

Nevertheless, all these arguments and facts provide only indirect evidence of the existence of free labour relations and wages in the ninth and tenth centuries, just before the rapid rise and expansion of towns. There are, however, some direct proofs, although not very numerous, of wage labour in the countryside, in the economy of abbeys and even in some of the then existing towns. Dopsch emphatically although not exhaustively, brought them together (Dopsch, 1922: 167–171). Some examples quoted by him belong to the agrarian sector and are quite famous. The so-called 'statutes' of Adalhard, abbot of Corbie, from the year 822, indicate the possibility of 'hired labour' (*ad conducendos*

[3] '(…) facit vehituram in leugas XXX aut se redimit denariis (…).'

homines) as an extra help for work in the abbey gardens in autumn and even for industrial activities like brewing (Verhulst and Semmler, 1962: 250). The renting of carts (*carra conduci debent*) is also presented by Adalhard as a normal procedure (Verhulst and Semmler, 1962: 250 and note 233) as was the renting of ships elsewhere as early as the eighth century (Verhulst, 1970: 21). The money provided by Adalhard for the purchase of shoes (Dopsch, 1922: 171 note 2) implicates the existence of shoemakers selling the product of their work, although this is in fact an indirect proof, similar to the above mentioned practice of some abbeys to buy their cloth on the market.

Wage labour in the building trade seems to have been usual, notably in Lombard Italy, as early as the seventh century (Edictus Rothari), but also in Western Europe in the following centuries (Dopsch, 1922: 170; Lesne, 1943: 273–276).[4]

Finally, the famous Edict of Pîtres (864), in which Charles the Bald tackled a wide range of problems including the control of markets, prescribed the use of the same standards of weight and measure for the bakers and butchers selling their bread and meat by retail (*per deneratas vendunt*) and for those selling their wine (*per sextaria*), as for their colleagues who were bound to a bishop, abbot or count. A female baker similarly working for the market in Mainz is a redundant but nevertheless rare example supporting the hypothesis that the presence of free craftsmen/-women and merchants in towns in the Merovingian period continued through later centuries (Dopsch, 1922, 167–168).

VI. Industrial settlements in the countryside

As wage-labour was typical for urban industry, it may be interesting to know how in this respect the situation was in the industrial places of the countryside before the great expansion of towns. There were indeed places in the countryside where non-agricultural activities were predominant and had a real industrial character. This means that their production largely exceeded local demand and was suited to or even intended for export.

The textile industry, to begin with, is the most difficult case from this point of view, because of its decentralised organisation and its slight archaeological remains. On a few estates of the abbey of St Denis in the north of the Paris region several workshops of weavers have been archaeologically identified, each occupying a very small 'fonds de cabane' ('sunken hut'), dug out one metre into the soil and measuring one metre by one metre and a half. Their small number and location suggest that weaving was a side-activity of the peasant household, done mostly by women in a manorial context, as has been stated earlier on the basis of written evidence (Cuisenier and Gaudagnin, 1988: 275–288). Only the workplaces for women (*gynecea*) mentioned earlier in this paper, may have had, but certainly not always, an industrial character. Even there the work was done on a basis of dependence and not by wage-earners. A problem is raised by a charter of Charles the Bald (867) for the abbey of St Vaast at Arras. It stipulates that a large quantity of wool (400 *librae*) had to be brought to the abbey town (in the centre of the later medieval city) to be processed there instead of in the villages where it had been

[4] *Lexikon des Mittelalters*, 1991: 2084–2085, v° Lohnarbeit.

produced (Verhulst, 1999: 53–54).[5] Because of the reputation of Arras as a textile centre, both in late Antiquity and in the twelfth and thirteenth centuries, the question may be asked if this evidence for urban or proto-urban wool-processing in the ninth century may be explained by a continuing tradition of skill exercised by men and women who did not work in a totally manorial environment.

Iron-working was not exclusively the occupation of blacksmiths integrated in the manorial structures of a village or a group of farms. However, the only proof for the existence of industrial and centralised iron-working concerns possessions of the Carolingian king. In the neighbourhood of Bregenz in the Vorarlberg the income of a complete district consisted mainly of supplies of iron products paid to the representative of the king. The production of seven furnaces clearly exceeded local needs and perhaps also the needs of the king for weapons and military equipment, such as the famous metal shirt (*brunia*). The excess was probably marketed, notwithstanding the prohibition against export in several *capitularia* from 779 onwards. In the case of Bregenz as in those of several Carolingian abbeys to which deliveries of iron as rough ingots or as finished products were made by peasants as rent for their holdings, the production system however was fundamentally manorial. This was so even when an estate like that of the abbey of St Germain-des-Prés in the Perche (western France) was inhabited by a community of iron smelters (Verhulst, 1995: 501–502).

Documents concerning salt production on the estates of the abbey of Prüm in Lorraine, not far from Metz in Vic-sur-Seille, Moyenvic and Marsal, provide more information on a possible industrial organisation (Verhulst, 1995: 503–504; Kuchenbuch, 1978: 293–298). The abbey owned all the sources of salt, the collecting basins and the workplaces with pots. The manual workers (*operatores*) were Prüm's tenants and paid a tax on their person to the abbey as a sign of their dependent status. They worked in exchange for holdings where they could also grow crops. They had nevertheless to pay for the use of the infrastructure, but in return were allowed to keep part of their production for sale. Most of it, by means of transport services of tenants, went to the abbey, where the excess was sold on the local markets in the vicinity. Elsewhere in Europe there are only few references to salt extraction or processing; nearly all of them, except in Venice and at the estuary of the Po (in Comacchio), were in the hands of abbeys and organised in a manorial framework (Verhulst, 1995: 504).

The production of glass and ceramics is almost exclusively identified from archaeological evidence. The quantity and quality of the production, exported in the ninth century to Scandinavia, allow us to surmise that the production was on an industrial scale. The only two written references to glassworkers from the year 864 come from the abbey of St Amand in northern France, but are difficult to interpret with respect to their juridical and economic condition (Verhulst, 1995: 502).

Much more is known of Carolingian pottery, but exlusively from archaeological evidence, especially from one of the main centres of production, the village of Badorf between Cologne and Bonn (Verhulst, 1995: 503; Janssen, 1983: 348–373). The quality of the produc-

---

[5] Arras seems in this respect like London in the 8th century: see Keene, this volume.

tion and the sheer quantity apparent from the massive exports, clearly point to its industrial character. The later possessions of the archbishop of Cologne and the chapter of St Pantaleon of Cologne in the vicinity of Badorf are the only indication for considering these church institutions as the possible patrons of specialized craftsmen who are believed, rightly or wrongly, to have had no independent status at all (Janssen, 1983: 390–392). Although Ipswich in East Anglia was an important centre for pottery production on an industrial scale, where a pottery-making zone can be identified separate from the settlement, by contrast to other activities such as textile, leather and bone-working, nothing is recorded about its economic organisation and labour relations (Verhulst, 1995: 503).[6] The same is true for some *emporia* on the North Sea and Channel coast like Dorestad (Van Es, 1990: 173–175) and Hamwic (Southampton)[7], where production of textiles, iron and bone-working was spread over the whole settlement. In Haithabu there is evidence from the ninth century of iron- and bone-working around the central zone of the settlement (Steuer, 1990: 101).

In some places like the late Roman town of Maastricht or the late Roman *castrum* of Huy, concentrations of craftsmen can be observed at the edge of the town since the late Roman period and still in Merovingian times.[8] Although archaeological or written evidence is lacking in this respect for the Carolingian period, continuity through later centuries is not excluded.

VII. Conclusion: growing differenciation between towns and countryside

We should indeed not think of these urban or pre-urban centres as concentrated agglomerations such as they appear from the eleventh century onwards. Their structure was much more loose and some of their quarters had a rural character in those early centuries, with here and there some concentration of artisanal or industrial activity. At the edge of such agglomerations the difference between countryside and town may often have been hardly visible, except when there is evidence of a boundary ditch, like at Southampton or a defensive ditch like the one enclosing the London *vicus* in the ninth century. The really significant differences, however, between the early (8th–10th century) and the later towns (from the 11th century onwards) lay in their internal spatial organisation rather than on their margins.The later towns had more marked internal clustering of occupations, reflecting the growth of specialised markets and chains of production.[9] Finally, the contrast between rural and urban industry in the eighth and ninth centuries with respect to their economic and social and perhaps even technical aspects, was not so sharp as from the eleventh century onwards.One should be cautious therefore not to exagerate when speaking of the 'shift of industry from countryside to town'. The transition must have been gradual and may have lasted from the tenth to the twelfth century.

---

[6] Keene, this volume. Some inferences, however, can be made from the spatial distribution of the artefacts.

[7] Keene, this volume.

[8] See note 1, above.

[9] Some ideas of this conclusion were suggested to me by Dr. Derek Keene, Director of the Centre for Metropolitan History at London University, to whom I am also much indebted for other remarks, suggestions and corrections, and above all for his revision of my original English text.

Bibliography

Boe, G. de and Verhaeghe, F. (eds) (1997a) *Urbanism in Medieval Europe. Papers of the 'Medieval Europe Brugge 1997' Conference*, vol. 1, Zellik.

Boe, G. de and Verhaeghe, F. (eds) (1997b) *Rural Settlements in Medieval Europe. Papers of the 'Medieval Europe Brugge 1997' Conference*, vol. 6, Zellik.

La croissance agricole du Haut Moyen Age.Chronologie, modalités, géographie (1990) Auch (Flaran 10–1988).

Cuisenier, J. and Guadagnin, R. (eds) (1988) *Un village au temps de Charlemagne. Moines et paysans de l'abbaye de Saint-Denis du VIIe siècle à l'an Mil*, Paris.

Demolon, P., Galinié, H. and Verhaeghe, F. (eds) (1991) *Archéologie des villes dans le Nord-Ouest de l'Europe (VIIe–XIIIe siècle). Actes du IVe Congrès International d'Archéologie Médiévale (Douai 1991)*, Douai.

Despy, G. (1968) 'Villes et Campagnes aux IXe et Xe siècles: l'exemple du pays mosan', *Revue du Nord*, 50, pp. 145–168.

Dette, C. (ed.) (1987) *Liber Possessionum Wizenburgensis*, Mainz.

Devroey, J.-P. (1984) *Le polyptyque et les listes de cens de l'abbaye de Saint-Remi de Reims (IXe–XIe siècles)*, Reims.

Devroey, J.-P (1997) 'La démographie du polyptyque de Saint-Remi de Reims', in P. Demouy and Ch. Vuillez, *Compter les Champenois*, Reims, pp. 81–94.

Dopsch, A. (1922) *Die Wirtschaftsentwicklung der Karolingerzeit*, II, Weimar.

Droste, C.-D. (ed.) (1988) *Das Polyptichon von Montierender*, Trier.

Es, W.A. van (1990) 'Dorestad centred', in J.C. Besteman, J.M. Bos and H.A. Heidinga (eds), *Medieval Archaeology in the Netherlands. Studies presented to H.H.van Regteren Altena*, Assen/Maastricht, pp. 152–181.

Ganshof, F.L. and Verhulst, A. (1966) 'Medieval Agrarian Society in its Prime. France, The Low Countries and Western Germany', in M. Postan (ed.), *The Cambridge Economic History of Europe*, vol. 1, *The Agrarian Life of the Middle Ages*, Cambridge, 2nd. ed., pp. 291–339.

La genèse et les premiers siècles des villes médiévales dans les Pays-Bas méridionaux (1990) Brussels.

Goetz, H.-W. (1995) 'Social and military institutions', in R. McKitterick (ed.), *The New Cambridge Medieval History*, II, *c.700–c.900*, Cambridge.

Hägermann, D. (1991) 'Grundherrschaft und städtischer Besitz in urbarialen Quellen des 9. Jahrhunderts', in J.-M. Duvosquel and A. Dierkens (eds), *Villes et campagnes. Mélanges Despy*, Liège, pp. 355–365.

Hodges, R. (1982) *Dark Age Economics. The origins of towns and trade AD 600–1000*, London.

Jankuhn, H., Janssen, W., Schmidt-Wiegand, R. and Tiefenbach, H. (eds) (1981–1983) *Das Handwerk in vor- und frühgeschichtlicher Zeit*, 2 vols, Göttingen. (Abhandlungen der Akademie der Wissenschaften in Göttingen, Philologisch-Historische Klasse, 3d Series, nos 122 and 123).

Janssen, W. (1983) 'Gewerbliche Produktion des Mittelalters als Wirtschaftsfaktor im ländlichen Raum', in H. Jankuhn, W. Janssen, R. Schmidt-Wiegand and H. Tiefenbach (eds), *Das Handwerk in vor- und frühgeschichtlicher Zeit*, II, Göttingen, pp. 317–394.

Kuchenbuch, L. (1978) *Bäuerliche Gesellschaft und Klosterherrschaft im 9. Jahrhundert. Studien zur Sozialstruktur der Familia der Abtei Prüm*, Wiesbaden.

Kuchenbuch, L. (1991) '*Opus feminile*. Das Geschlechtsverhältnis im Spiegel von Frauenarbeiten im früheren Mittelalter', in H.-W. Goetz (ed.), *Weibliche Lebensgestaltung im frühen Mittelalter*, Köln, pp. 139–175.

Lesne, E. (1943) *Histoire de la propriété ecclésiastique en France*, vol. 6, *Les églises et les monastères, centres d'accueil, d'exploitation et de peuplement*, Lille.

Lexikon des Mittelalters (1991) vol. 5, München.

Ménager, L-R. (1965) 'Considérations sociologiques sur la démographie des grands domaines ecclésiastiques carolingiens' in *Etudes d'histoire du droit canonique dédiées à Gabriel Le Bras*, Paris, pp. 1317–1335.

Morimoto, Y. (1991) 'Considérations nouvelles sur les 'villes et campagnes' dans le domaine de Prüm au haut Moyen Age', in J.-M. Duvosquel and A. Dierkens (eds), *Villes et campagnes au moyen âge. Mélanges Georges Despy*, Liège, pp. 515–531.

Nelson, J.L. (1992) *Charles the Bald*, London-New York.

Perrin, Ch.-E. (1934) 'Une étape de la seigneurie. L'exploitation de la réserve à Prüm au IXe siècle', *Annales d'Histoire économique et sociale*, 6, pp. 450–466.

Steuer H. (1990) 'Die Handelsstätten des frühen Mittelalters im Nord- und Ostsee-Raum, in '*La genèse et les premiers siècles des villes médiévales dans les Pays-Bas méridionaux*, Brussels, pp. 75–116.

Verhulst, A. (1970) 'Der Handel im Merowingerreich: Gesamtdarstellung nach schriftlichen Quellen', *Antikvarist Arkiv* 39–*Early Medieval Studies* 2, Stockholm, pp. 2–54.

Verhulst, A. (1995) 'Economic Organisation', in R. McKitterick (ed.), *The New Cambridge Medieval History*, II, *c.700–c.900*, Cambridge, pp. 481–509.

Verhulst, A. (1999) *The Rise of Cities in North-West Europe*, Cambridge.

Verhulst, A. and Declercq, G. (1989) 'Early medieval Ghent between two abbeys and the Count's Castle', in J. Decavele (ed.), *Ghent. In Defence of a Rebellious City*, Antwerp, pp. 37–59.

Verhulst, A. and Semmler, J. (1962) 'Les Statuts d'Adalhard de Corbie de l'an 822', *Le Moyen Age*, 68, pp. 91–123 and 233–269.

Werveke, H. van (1954) 'Industrial Growth in the Middle Ages.The Cloth Industry in Flanders', *Economic History Review*, 6, pp. 237–245; reprinted in H. Van Werveke (1968) *Miscellanea Mediaevalia*, Ghent, pp. 381–391.

Werveke, H. van and Verhulst, A. (1960) 'Castrum en Oudburg te Gent. Bijdrage tot de oudste geschiedenis van de Vlaamse steden', *Handelingen der Maatschappij voor Geschiedenis en Oudheidkunde te Gent*, new series, 14, pp. 3–62.

3 From captive manorial trade to free urban trade. On the development of the division of labour in the Rhine-Westphalia region (9th–15th centuries)[1]

Franz IRSIGLER, Universität Trier

I. Introduction

The latest edition of the *Brockhaus*-Encyclopaedia defines 'division of labour' as 'the segmentation of working processes into partial specialisation and the distribution to different economic units (e.g. workforce, factories, enterprises, regions, states). Although division of labour is an essential feature even of the simplest cultures, it is particularly characteristic of fully developed economies'. As long ago as 1893, Karl Bücher postulated a series of economic steps extending from the middle ages to the modern period: 1. the formation of occupations, 2. the breakdown of occupations, i.e. 'the division of multilayered occupations into specialised occupations… and the combination of specialised activities to form a new profession', 3. the segmentation of the work process, i.e. the 'separation of production processes into several partial processes performed by one or more persons and/or technical facilities', and 4. the spatial division of labour, i.e. 'specialisation on the basis of most favourable location'.

The formation and segmentation of occupations is also called occupational division of labour, and this has to be distinguished from the economic division of labour, i.e. the distribution of labour and choice of the most appropriate location. The segmentation and diversification of the working process is regarded as a characteristic of the industrial era because it is related to mechanisation, automation and a sharp rise in productivity per worked man-hour. This historical demarcation is questionable in that segmentation of labour can be observed in the pre-industrial production of major centres of trade. Nonetheless I consider this model with its four successive stages to be useful, particularly when analysing the course of development in the Middle Ages.

This chapter focuses on those areas of Westphalia and the Rhineland with which I am very familiar. Broadly speaking, the period under consideration (the 9th to the 14th/15th centuries) can be divided into three phases. The formation of occupations can be viewed as a key element of the period of the developed manorial system or seigneurial lordship, i.e. the *Villikationsverfassung* (or bipartite system). During the urbanisation of the High Middle Ages we see certain occupations being divided, with an associated multiplication of guilds and specialist sub-guilds. Finally, in the Late Middle Ages there is clear evidence of some segmentation of the work process as well as a spatial division of labour regarding the extraction of raw materials and energy use.

[1] Translated by John Kidd and Herbert Eiden.

It is of course necessary to bear in mind that the process by which occupations were formed stretches back to a time prior to the development of the manorial system. Furthermore signs of a certain spatial division of labour can be traced as far back as the start of seigneurial lordship. It is even possible to argue that such a spatial division is a characteristic feature of the manorial system. During the 14th and 15th centuries the division of labour between towns, their environs and hinterland took on new forms. The decisive factors in this development and of the actual process of the segmentation of labour in the towns were the capital made available by merchants and the *Verlag* system (whereby work was subcontracted to homeworkers). Even so the process of the formation of occupations had not run its course by the end of the Middle Ages. Inventions and innovations meant that new technological and artistic skills were continually emerging, including those of the papermaker, the printer, founder, copper or steel engraver, cartographer, gunsmith, cannon founder, and so on.

II. The manorial system and the formation of occupations

As can be seen from the proceedings of conferences such as those at *Kleve* (Flink and Janssen, 1989), *Göttingen* (Rösener, 1989), *Trient* (Dilcher and Violante, 1999) and *Trier* (Haverkamp and Hirschmann, 1997), to name but a few, recent research on the agrarian economy now seems broadly agreed that the manorial system of the Early and High Middle Ages was not just the most important factor governing agrarian production in the broadest sense, but also a very significant and hitherto underrated nucleus of trade and market life, i.e. for a pre-urban and, ultimately, urban way of life. The separation of manorial and urban life was long considered useful for the purposes of historical analysis but now this view is being replaced by a more realistic model in which both spheres of life are inextricably entwined. This interconnection between town and countryside is a distinct feature of the urbanisation process in the High Middle Ages and its impact still lingered on in the later middle ages. Primarily urban elements such as a money-based economy, sophisticated markets, the intensification of commerce and international trade stimulated by a demand for high quality products and luxury goods can be regarded as already being an integral feature of the manorial system. This implies a certain limitation on the primary sector, no matter how important it was for human survival, and a greater emphasis on achievements in the secondary and tertiary sectors. Both sectors are fundamental to explaining the rise and decline of the urban economy.

The manorial system might therefore be defined as a system comprising all forms of production, subject to the seigneurial order, although not totally oriented towards the demands of the landlord. It was a system that was remarkably open to the outside world, offering considerable scope for economic activities in the domestic market (Irsigler, 1999).

I will begin with the secondary sector, i.e. production for trade, bearing in mind that the clear distinction of the sectors of production into primary production, production for trade and services, used by economists, was never so strictly distinguished in the day-to-day routine of the manorial economy. Very often *servitium* and *census,* the exaction of labour services and payments in kind or cash, were mingled. Demands on at least two sectors of production were the rule not the exception. For example, rents in kind paid in grain, cattle, wine, wood, textiles, metal goods or pottery were generally combined with the delivery of these products to the market or the manor house as the centre of consumption. Moreover, it is possible to find primary production and production for trade linked to the performance of certain services in the economic/administrative, political/military and cultural sectors, for the maintenance of law and order or communications. From the point of view of the centres of the great manorial estates with their widely dispersed properties, the organisation of manorial production was characterized by an almost extreme spatial division of labour. I do not intend to discuss this detail here and will confine myself to the remark that for most of the major ecclesiastical manors the possession of vineyards or holdings in saltmines and iron mines was essential for their economic survival. Remarkably efficient transportation systems were developed (Kuchenbuch, 1978; Devroey, 1984), which did not become obsolete until the 12th–13th centuries when wine, salt and iron tools could be bought much more cheaply at urban markets. In any case, the service sector in the manorial system had an enormous influence on professional specialisation and qualification, leading to a variety of new occupations, for instance in trade, which sometimes opened the way for a smooth transition to an urban lifestyle.

As for the evidence for a concentration of commercial production in the manorial system, research owes much to the interdisciplinary cooperation of archaeologists, mediaevalists, geographers and historians of technology. The increase in and the concentration of commercial production has always been accompanied by specialisation. In fact its segmentation has always been inherent in the formation of particular occupations. Here we might refer to the famous *St. Gallen* map, which has attracted so much scholarly attention (Horn and Born, 1979). The *officinae* are described not only as places of work but also as those of a great number of specialised crafts and occupations such as that of chamberlain, tailor, shoemaker, saddler, cutler and knife grinder, shieldmaker, turner, tanner, goldsmith, blacksmith, weaver, cook, brewer, baker, miller, cooper and other labourers and servants.

One should forget the idea that every peasant, even if he worked for the lord's home farm or tilled his own plot of land, had the time or ability to build the wheels for his plough or cart, forge an effective ploughshare or tan the leather canopy of a covered wagon by himself. Such work had to be done by specialists. Such specialists must have been numerous in wine-growing regions, where there was a great demand for coopers and builders of wine-presses; after all, beam and screw presses were highly complicated machines (Gilles, 1995). Moreover, every manor needed skilled craftsmen for the construction of water mills and other specialised buildings such as breweries, bakeries, kilns and smelting furnaces. Shipbuilding was also most certainly a job for the specialist, once the craft (under construction) became more complex than building the simple dugout canoe (Claude, 1981).

Facilities subject to the profitable *Bannrecht* (special rights within a protected area) and which were operated continuously, such as mills, wine-presses, bakeries, breweries or beer gruel houses *(Gruthaus)* needed qualified and specialised workers. For example, the knowledge of the beer gruel *(grut)* recipes needed for the brewing process were handed down from generation to generation. Here as in many other cases it seems to have been the rule that crafts and occupations were passed down the generations.

A striking example of the increase in commercial production and growing specialisation are the so called *Gynaecaea*. These were a kind of manorial cloth manufactory in which up to 40 female workers produced woollen cloth and linen cloth of a better and marketable quality. The existence of *Gynaecaea* can be traced in the sources back to as early as the 7th century (Irsigler, 1970). By the 12th century this institution, which was based on compulsory labour service, ceased to exist because of a general improvement in the position of villeins and serfs. Rural cloth production became a part-time job or a task performed at home to meet the needs of the family. However, we may discern in the heyday of the *Gynaecaea* the first signs of a division of the production process and the segmentation of work. For example in the *Gynaeceum* of the manor of Staffelsee (in the diocese of Augsburg), we find specialisations such as weaving, shirt-making and belt-making. Furthermore an entry in the *Capitulare de villis* suggests that spinning, weaving, dyeing and fulling was carried out by different specialists (Franz, 1974). The transition from rural and manorial cloth production to an urban textile industry seems to be associated with the introduction of the loom. From then on weaving ceased being a feminine activity and became a male occupation.

Many more crafts and occupations were linked to the manorial economy. Archaeological research has shown that centres for leather production, ivory and antler carving, iron working, lead smelting and potteries are to be found close to *Pfalzen* (palaces) and manors. Although the records are of a relatively late date – even though they are undoubtedly older than the *Liber annalium jurium* of the Archbishop of Trier, which was written in about 1200 AD (Rudolph and Kentenich, 1915) – there were concentrations of parchment-making and glass production in the countryside around Trier. The *Polyptychon Irminonis* for the estates of St. Germain-des-Prés enabled Konrad Elmshäuser and Andreas Hedwig (1993) to show a remarkable concentration of iron mining and trading activity around Boissy-Maugis in the region of the Drouais and in the Perche. And according to the *Urbar* (manorial extent) of 893, Wintrange, the only village of the abbey of Prüm which specialised in the forging of ploughs, was located in the Luxembourg *minette* area (Schwab, 1983).

A striking development took place in the building industry. As Frank Hirschmann (1998) has recently shown, all the cathedral cities in the wider area of the Rhine-Meuse region were major building sites from the 10th into the 12th centuries. Paderborn was one of these during the reign of the energetic Bishop Meinwerk (†1036). In order to carry out his ambitious building plans – the cathedral, the episcopal palace, the *Abdinghof* monastery, the St. Bartholomew chapel and the wall around the *civitas* (the episcopal castle and palace) – Meinwerk moved skilled building workers from all over his estates and settled them in Paderborn. He allocated them plots of land on both sides of the river Pader and instructed them to work on his building sites – without a doubt for a money wage rather than a mere payment in kind (Irsigler, 1970). Other episcopal landlords seem to have followed his example.

In my opinion we can generalise as follows: the craftsmen who were settled in Paderborn were not only highly skilled but were also highly specialised. Meinwerk needed, among others, bricklayers, carpenters, stonemasons, brickmakers, nailsmiths, ropemakers, tilers, plumbers and tin founders. Apparently their crafts were clearly differentiated in the manorial economy, which must have afforded sufficient freedom for the practice and perfection of these crafts and technical skills. The activities of these craftsmen could become their primary occupation and the trade was handed down the generations; workshops and specialised tools must also have been passed on from father to son.

Such a smooth transition from the rural-manorial sphere to the more liberal urban sphere with its municipal self-government may also be assumed for other areas of crafts and occupations. Since Gustav Freytag's famous book *Bilder aus der deutschen Vergangenheit* German urban historians have repeated his insightful comment that craftsmen were the populators of the towns (*Städtefüller*). Where did they come from? The answer of course is that in most cases they came from the manorial estates. Ideally, the graded migration model works on the assumption that peasants or agricultural labourers first move into small country towns and then migrate as craftsmen or petty merchants to the bigger towns or cities. Such movements were, however, the exception rather than the rule. Many of those who left their farms and villages migrated straight to the bigger towns, especially during the dynamic urbanisation after the 11th century. The transition from the captive crafts and trades of the manor to an urban occupation was easiest when the seigneurial lord held sway over the town as well, i.e. in cathedral towns, in towns owned by other religious houses and in the craft and merchant districts quarters close to or below the count's castle. The coexistence of manorial craftsmen and free craftsmen can be observed in all these commercial centres over a long period of time, and this normally only ends with the formation of guilds (Irsigler, 1985).

This development was a loss to the countryside. Substantial elements of an economic system already reliant on the division of labour moved to the flourishing towns. The huge range of professional skills active in secondary industry drained away from the manor to the town. Consequently, the fundamental authority of the seigneurial lordship was eroded and forced the manor to concentrate on the primary sector. A characteristic feature of the High and Late Middle Ages is, therefore, a *new* division of labour between town and countryside in which the latter was doubtless confined to primary production (agriculture, stock farming, specialised crops, mining). Apart from the domestic textile industry and moderate opportunities for extracting raw materials (forest products, tanning, mining, etc.) the only crafts that remained in the countryside were those essential for the work in the fields, forests, vineyards and for the processing of the crops. These would have included smiths, wheelwrights and cartwrights, millers and perhaps bakers who were also capable of brewing beer. In many cases these occupations were ancillary. Not until the emergence of the domestic putting-out system (*Verlag*) at the close of the Middle Ages and the beginning of the early modern times did the countryside again become integrated into the production process. One of the reasons for this reintegration was the rigid control of the crafts in towns by the guilds, who held an absolute monopoly. This ultimately enabled the countryside to win back some of the wide variety of crafts and trades that had grown up in rural areas during the Early and High Middle Ages.

III. Formation of occupations, division of occupations and the segmentation of labour in the towns of the High and Later Middle Ages

The new division of labour in the secondary sector between town and countryside and the ensuing increase in service trades in urban communities, greatly strengthened the status of towns as economic centres. This is reflected in particular in trade, coinage, the monetary system, health care (hospitals etc.), schools and those areas of activity that nowadays would fall under the heading of public services. This development furthermore weakened the significance of the countryside. Castles and monasteries could not be maintained because the majority of ecclesiastical institutions either took up residence in towns or were bound to nearby municipal communities. One should bear in mind that many occupations in the tertiary sector had already been shaped by the manorial economy. However, lack of space prevents me from following up this development in detail here. Nor, unfortunately, can I provide a thorough analysis of the increase in and the diversification of these occupations in the towns.

The smooth transition from the countryside to the town can be illustrated by the development of the various merchant occupations. A very telling example is the career of a petty rural trader from the manorial estate of St. Severin in Cologne. In 1181 he sold his tenement with the consent of the bishop because he became a merchant: 'institoris officium, plus coluit quam agrum et, ut ipse testatus est, propter urbis negotia concepit ruris fastidia', where in this context *urbs* of course means Cologne (Irsigler, 1999). Just as remarkable is the social and psychological argument for the move from the rural-agrarian into the urban-commercial sphere. It is unlikely that we would be mistaken in assuming that the seasonal traders who were bound to the manorial economy – like the peasants of Prüm or from the Bitburg area who as travelling peddlers sold the abbey's surplus of salt and wine as far as away as the Meuse region (Kuchenbuch, 1978) – had many positive memories of life at the markets and in the towns. The potentially large profits to be had from trade must have been the main motive for the migration of country dwellers to the town.

It is evident that it was not the towns of the High and Late Middle Ages which started off the process by which occupations were formed. Their achievement was a differentiation and diversification of occupations, i.e. the splintering of the occupations within the meaning of the definition given above. This splintering can already be discerned in the oldest guild charters of the Rhineland. The best example is the famous 1149 charter of the bed linen weavers *(Bettziechenweber)* of Cologne (Diestelkamp, 1967). The separation of a group of weavers who specialised in a certain textile product from the existing organisation of the wool weavers created a new profession, that of the bed linen weaver. Here the deciding factor was not the founding of the guild itself, but the decision of a relatively large group of weavers to specialise in a product that was in great demand. Ultimately, the guild organisation secured the continued existence of the new profession, because the specialisation in bed linen resulted in a monopoly for this product and the system of compulsory guild membership prevented other weavers in Cologne from making bed linen without joining the guild.

In general, the establishment of guilds did not create new occupations. Rather they reveal a certain consolidation in the process of the formation of occupations in a commercial economy characterised by the division of labour. That process had already begun in the pre-urban and proto-urban times. With the formation of guilds strict rules were established for the training of apprentices, the rights to practise a certain profession, the guarantee of equal opportunities for buying raw materials and free access to the market (entry rights, prohibition on prior sale) as well as a general acceptance of quality standards within a quality control framework operated either by the guild itself or by the municipal authorities.

It would go beyond the scope of this chapter if I were to try to follow in detail, for example in the case of Cologne, the long process of the division of occupations, the differentiation of commerce and trade until the provisional formalisation of the guild structure at 36 administrative guilds, so-called *Gaffeln*, at the end of the 14th century. Cologne was an international trading centre par excellence. The large number of guilds gives a good impression of the degree of professional differentiation (Irsigler, 1979). An account of the kind of specialisation of the guilds would require an analysis of their internal structure, as some of the *Gaffeln* were overarching organisations sheltering up to 10 sub-guilds (for example, the smiths and other metal trades). A compilation of the contemporary names of the occupations concerned would result in an extremely illuminating list of several hundred crafts and trades (von Loesch, 1907). Some research furthermore has been conducted in this area by linguistic historians. The most vivid expression of the fabulous increase of occupations by continuous differentiation and segmentation is provided by 'occupation catalogues' which present pictures of crafts and trades accompanied by brief descriptions. This type of literature first appeared around 1300 with the chess book of Jakob de Cessolis, a Dominican from Piedmont, and even in his time he had to place at least three crafts and trades on each of the eight squares of the *populares*. By the 16th century the number had increased to over 200, as can be seen in Jost Ammann's book (Kramer, 1995).

I would like to focus attention on two strikingly different strategies that shaped production based on the division of labour in the most important export trades of medieval towns: metalworking and textiles. The production of woollen cloth can be rightly called the 'mother of all textile guilds'. Almost all the workshops in the leading metal-trading cities of the German empire – Nuremberg has to be ranked above Cologne, Aix-la-Chapelle and Braunschweig – were small businesses, in which the entire production process, including the selling of the finished product, remained in the same hands. The division of labour in the workshop and in the family was no more than usual. Although cooperation existed, for example between cutlers and hilt makers, opportunities for such cooperation beyond the workshop were limited. A high standard of production was the result of ongoing specialization. For example, the different parts of a knight's armour (helmet, breastplate, tasses, cuisses, greaves, vambraces and tilting gauntlets) had to be bought separately from four or five specialised armourers. Nonetheless, this was not disadvantageous, because it improved the likelihood of finding well-fitting parts.

The differentiation between coppersmiths, brasiers, locksmiths and mechanics was extreme. The boundaries between craft and art became vague. Some of the most impressive artifacts of Nuremberg's metal masters (e.g. Master Henlein and others) can be still seen today. The Rhineland also has fine examples of craftsmanship to offer. About 1440, shortly before Gutenberg invented the letterpress, Girald Ferrose, a clockmaker, cannon founder and locksmith (*horologerius, balistarius, serralherius*) from Coblenz gave lectures to a kind of *ars artificialter scribendi* in Avignon, for which he was paid handsomely. In the metalworking trades the division of labour corresponds largely to the product or range of products sold (von Stromer, 1982).

The only exceptions are to be found in certain branches of the finishing or refining crafts which I will return to below. I must first go back to the textile industry. As I pointed out in referring to the female linen weavers and cloth weavers at the *Gynaeceum* in Staffelsee, differentiation by raw material is a pre-urban phenomenon, even though fustian and silk weaving appeared for the first time in middle Europe in the urban environment. Evidence for a division of occupation by specific product is rarely encountered. In Cologne, no other guild in the cloth trade developed after the *Bettziechen* weavers. Even in silk weaving, where one might expect some peculiarities, no further specialisations beyond braid trimming, embroidery or tablet-weaving are known. The development of the division of labour took the form of a segmentation of the working process. The female silk-spinners in Cologne were subordinate to the guild of the female silk-weaver masters. A further women's guild was formed by the gold-spinners. Their craft was the making of brocade: gold and silver leaves (*Lahn*) provided by gold-beaters were wound spirally round a core thread made of silk and linen (*Seele*). And yet another form of specialization, silk dyeing, appeared later on (Wensky, 1980).

The horizontal division of the working processes of woollen cloth production is well known. Every single piece of cloth went through numerous hands, technical devices and workshops. Both rural and urban wool spinners were involved; while the former twisted the thicker weft on spinning wheels, the latter spun the smooth strong warp with the distaff and spindle. The yarn was then processed by weavers, fullers, wool clippers and dyers. The spatial division of labour was magnified by shifting the processes of spinning, fulling, tentering (stretching the cloth on long wooden fences with iron hooks at top and bottom) and dyeing to different sites and workshops. One of the reasons for the decentralisation was the use of water power in the towns and country. It was not uncommon that weaving, dyeing or dressing was carried out in places far away from each other. A large amount of English cloth arrived undyed on continental markets; the material was often finished in the international trading centre of Antwerp, sometimes in Cologne and – if the customer so requested – in Frankfurt (Irsigler, 1979).

As a final example for how labour might become segmented as a result of the spatial division of labour, I would like to present two maps which illustrate the close contacts of the metal trades of Cologne with the hinterland on the right of the Rhine. The maps are based on statistical information derived from the assize records of Cologne dating from the second half of the 15th century (Irsigler, 1979).

Figure 3.1 Places of origin of ironmongers and coppermongers supplying Cologne, c. 1500

Figure 3.2 Places of origin of steel and steelworks supplying Cologne, c. 1500

Noticeable among the goods that were imported to Cologne are the thousands of pans and pan discs as well as other semi-finished products. Before being offered on the market they were finished in Cologne and might sometimes be stamped with the three crown mark, Cologne's trademark. In the Late Middle Ages this rural/small town trade east of the Rhine developed enormously and for centuries transformed the area between the rivers Sieg, Rhine, Ruhr and Lenne into the 'forge of Central Europe'. A similar economic development would not have been possible in Cologne itself or its environs due to the absence of specific structural conditions, such as sufficient energy supplies (water and charcoal), profitable mines and technical facilities for the processing work (iron works and hammer mills). On the other hand, in order to maintain their leading position on the market the merchants and putters-out of Cologne were very interested in the segmentation of the production process (semi-finished products in the countryside, finishing in the city). As a result this part of the Rhine-Westphalia area found itself in 'pole position' when the industrial age opened the way to a further leap in productivity on the basis of the division of labour.

Bibliography

Brockhaus (1996) *Die Enzyklopädie in vierundzwanzig Bänden*, vol. 2: *Art. Arbeitsteilung*, 20th ed., Leipzig/Mannheim.

Bücher, K. (1893) *Die Entstehung der Volkswirtschaft*, 17th ed., Tübingen. [orig. 1926]

Claude, D. (1981) 'Die Handwerker der Merowingerzeit nach den erzählenden und urkundlichen Quellen', in H. Jankuhn, W. Janssen, R. Schmidt-Wiegand and H. Tiefenbach (eds), *Das Handwerk in vor- und frühgeschichtlicher Zeit*, I, Göttingen, pp. 204–266.

Devroey, J.-P. (1984) 'Un monastère dans l'économie d'échanges: les services de transport à l'abbaye de Saint-Germain-des-Prés au IXe siècle', *Annales. Economies-Sociétés-Civilisations*, 39, pp. 570–589.

Diestelkamp, B. (1967) 'Quellensammlung zur Frühgeschichte der deutschen Stadt (bis 1250)', in C. van de Kieft and J.F. Niermeijer (eds), *Elenchus fontium historiae urbanae*, vol. 1, Leiden, pp. 1–277.

Dilcher, G. and Violante, C. (eds) (1996) *Strutture e trasformazioni della signoria rurale nei secoli X–XIII*, Bologna.

Dilcher, G. and Violante, C. (eds) (2000) *Strukturen und Wandlungen der ländlichen Herrschaftsformen vom 10. Zum 13. Jahrhundert. Deutschland und Italien im* Vergleich, Berlin.

Elmshäuser, K. and Hedwig, A. (1993) *Studien zum Polyptychon von Saint-Germain-des-Prés*, Köln/Weimar/Wien.

Flink, K. and Janssen, W. (eds) (1989) *Grundherrschaft und Stadtentstehung am Niederrhein*, Kleve.

Franz, G. (1974) *Quellen zur Geschichte des deutschen Bauernstandes im Mittelalter*, 2nd ed., Darmstadt.

Freytag, G. (1859 ff), *Bilder aus der deutschen Vergangenheit*ed, by Pleticha, München.

Gilles, K.-J. (1995) 'Römerzeitliche Kelteranlagen an der Mosel', in K.-J. Gilles (ed.), *Neuere Forschungen zum römischen Weinbau an Mosel und Rhein*, Trier, pp. 5–59.

Haverkamp, A. and Hirschmann, F.G. (1997), *Grundherrschaft – Kirche – Stadt zwischen Maas und Rhein während des hohen Mittelalters*, Mainz.

Hirschmann, F.G. (1998) *Stadtplanung, Bauprojekte und Großbaustellen im 10. und 11. Jahrhundert. Vergleichende Studien zu den Kathedralstädten westlich des Rheins*, Stuttgart.

Horn, W. and Born, E. (1979) *The Plan of St. Gall. A Study of the Architecture and Economy and of Life in a Paradigmatic Carolingian Monastery*, vols 1–3, Berkeley/Los Angeles/London.

Irsigler, F. (1970) 'Divites und pauperes in der Vita Meinwerci. Untersuchungen zur wirtschaftlichen und sozialen Differenzierung der Bevölkerung Westfalens im Hochmittelalter', *Vierteljahrschrift für Sozial- und Wirtschaftsgeschichte*, 57, pp. 449–499.

Irsigler, F. (1979) *Die wirtschaftliche Stellung der Stadt Köln im 14. und 15. Jahrhundert. Strukturanalyse einer spätmittelalterlichen Exportgewerbe- und Fernhandelsstadt*, Wiesbaden.

Irsigler, F. (1985) 'Zur Problematik der Gilde- und Zunftterminologie', in B. Schwineköper (ed.), *Gilden und Zünfte. Kaufmännische und gewerbliche Genossenschaften im frühen und hohen Mittelalter*, Sigmaringen, pp. 53–70.

Irsigler, F. (2000) 'Zur wirtschaftlichen Bedeutung der frühen Grundherrschaft', G. Dilcher and C. Violante (eds), *Strukturen und Wandlungen der ländlichen Herrschaftsformen vom 10. Zum 13. Jahrhundert. Deutschland und Italien im* Vergleich, Berlin, pp. 165–187.

Kramer, K.-S. (1995) *Bauern, Handwerker und Bürger im Schachzabelbuch. Mittelalterliche Ständegliederung nach Jacobus de Cessolis*, München.

Kuchenbuch, L. (1978) *Bäuerliche Gesellschaft und Klosterherrschaft im 9. Jahrhundert. Studien zur Sozialstruktur der Familia der Abtei Prüm*, Wiesbaden.

Loesch, H. von (1907) *Die Kölner Zunfturkunden nebst anderen Kölner Gewerbeurkunden bis zum Jahr 1500*, vols 1–2, Bonn.

Rösener, W. (ed.) (1989) *Strukturen der Grundherrschaft im frühen Mittelalter*, Göttingen.

Rudolph, F. and Kentenich, G. (eds) (1915) *Quellen zur Rechts- und Wirtschaftsgeschichte der rheinischen Städte. Kurtrierische Städte*, vol. I, Trier/Bonn.

Schwab, I. (ed.) (1983) *Das Prümer Urbar*, Düsseldorf. (Rheinische Urbare; vol. 5).

Stromer, W. von (1982) 'Zur "ars artificialiter scribendi" und weiteren "künsten" der Waldfoghel aus Prag und Girard Ferroses aus Trier, Nürnberg 1433–34 und Avignon 1444–46' *Technikgeschichte*, 49, pp. 279–289.

Wensky, M. (1980) *Die Stellung der Frau in der stadtkölnischen Wirtschaft im Spätmittelalter*, Köln/Wien.

4 Industrial organisation in English towns, 650–1150

Derek KEENE, University of London

I. Introduction

It is perhaps rash to address the topic of urban industrial organisation and labour markets during this half millennium of English history. The sources are fragmentary and unevenly distributed. We can only guess at the models of social and economic organisation, drawn from other periods and other disciplines, which may be appropriate to comprehending the phenomena. Moreover, some attempts to apply such models have hindered rather than aided understanding, and even the models themselves incorporate misunderstandings of the later societies from which they were supposedly derived (Hodges, 1989; Law, 1989). Nevertheless, the enquiry is worthwhile, for the evidential base has been growing steadily in ways which offer new scope for argument and hypothesis, and which promise to throw new light on continuities and discontinuities in the evolution of English urban crafts from the post Roman period onwards. Central issues to be addressed concern technological capacity; the nature of the demand and investment which sustained the manufacturing sector; the division of labour and the identity of specialised crafts within towns; the spatial organisation of production and the existence, or not, of craft neighbourhoods; the role of the household unit of production; the nature of any wider market for products; specialisation within the household, by status, sex or age; the degree to which production was controlled by, or was perceived to be the responsibility of, male heads of household; and the origin and remuneration of the labour force.

The textual evidence is largely restricted to the last one hundred and fifty years of the period. It primarily concerns individuals and locations identified by some form of occupational designation, and the existence of guilds of craftsmen. Despite its patchy survival, it offers much explicit information on the extent and organisation of manufactures in towns. The vocabulary of craft names alone can help us understand the degree of specialisation within certain sectors, while the spatial distribution of names can be important for understanding how production was organised. This body of evidence has been available for some time and is unlikely to increase in quantity. Archaeological evidence, by contrast, comes forth in increasing quantities. It throws light on the processes of manufacture and on the buildings and neighbourhoods within which they took place, and is thus directly relevant to questions of social organisation. At the same time, however, the physical processes of deposition, redeposition, and decay have often destroyed the features and associations of artefacts and structures which would have revealed the existence and organisation of crafts. Even when those associations survive, the archaeological contexts for which it is possible to investigate them amount to very small samples of urban areas. On the other hand, scatters of dateable, but not closely contextualised, archaeological material make an important contribution. It takes much time and skill to identify, interpret and publish the material evidence in a form which will contribute to a wider discussion. Unfortunately, the form of publication, in which it has been common practice to separate accounts of structures and of different categories of artefacts, has tended to inhibit that discussion. Nevertheless, this evidence has revolutionised our understanding of early towns and crafts, and we can expect that revolution to continue.

In simple terms, the history of English towns in this period falls into two phases.[1] In the first, from the seventh to the ninth century, the distinctively urban places – using the term urban to denote relatively large, dense aggregations of people pursuing specialised and primarily non-agrarian occupations – were on or had ready access to the sea. Southampton, London, Ipswich and York are the best-known examples, and Canterbury and its neighbourhood provide another. These settlements were undefended (at least until their later years), but were associated with sites of political authority. It is becoming increasingly clear that they were dense, highly-organised, permanent settlements, although constructed of simple, predominantly organic materials such as timber, wattle-and-daub and thatch. To judge from the physical extent and density of the towns, their populations were, at their peak, to be numbered in thousands, and possibly as many as five to ten thousand in the case of London. These towns were important sites of overseas trade, conducted with counterparts on the other side of the North Sea and English Channel. The items of commerce are not easily identified, but the exports probably included slaves, lead, textiles and agrarian products, while among the imports were probably wine, spices and other luxury goods traded along Continental river systems and thence to elite groups in England. Archaeology shows that the inhabitants of the towns practised many manufacturing crafts. The precise chronology of the settlements remains uncertain, despite the many assertions and complex arguments put forward by archaeologists. They seem to have flourished from the mid seventh century onwards (perhaps initially as sites of trade), to have reached a peak in size and in diversity of activities during the eighth, and to have been undermined by the Viking invasions and political discord of the ninth. Their populations then severely declined and shifted to new sites.

In the second phase, from the later ninth century onwards, the urban system was different. Towns were now predominantly defended places, with markets, mints and walls. An hierarchical network of many more identifiably urban centres emerged, occupying inland as well as coastal sites. The chronology of development was not even across the country, but by 1000 overseas trade, apparently with the same geographical pattern as in the first phase, had revived and was contributing to urban fortunes in both northern and southern England. Town growth was especially rapid during the eleventh and twelfth centuries. By 1100 London may have had as many as 20,000 inhabitants, while cities in the second rank, such as Winchester, Norwich or York had perhaps just under half that total. Small market towns, with just a few hundred inhabitants, were beginning to proliferate, especially in response to flows of traffic by land and water and to the commercial needs and initiatives of wealthy lawmen and monasteries. By the mid twelfth century the fabric of the larger towns was beginning to acquire a new inorganic solidity, expressed in stone and in the use of tiles for roofing. Such changes required an extended infrastructure of extraction and processing to support them. Yet much urban material culture – buildings as well as artefacts – bore a strong resemblance to that of the towns in the first phase, and technological development since then had been relatively slight.

---

[1] An up-to-date introduction to the urban history of this period will be found in Palliser, 2000. For a good archaeological survey, see Vince, 1994.

II. c.650–900

II.1. Sites and crafts

Archaeological evidence seems to indicate that there were few, if any, crafts pursued in the towns during the first phase which were not also practised in much smaller settlements. In many cases the products of the latter attained standards as high as or higher than those of the towns. This raises the question of the function of these smaller settlements, of which those best known from archaeology seem to have contained no more than about thirty houses. Were these smaller settlements in any sense 'small towns', with a role as centres of resort for a distinctive territory and a place in wider networks of production and exchange? Or did their inhabitants manufacture products primarily in order to meet the needs of, and at the direction of, the powerful lords or religious institutions which were based there? The model for the latter type would be the Carolingian *villa* or estate centre (Latouche, 1967: 176–189). Netherton (Hants), has been interpreted as the residence of a high-ranking layman where a small group of dependent craftsmen made goods appropriate to his status (Fairbrother, 1990) Other sites, including Jarrow, Whitby, Hartlepool and Barking, were monasteries which supported a range of the specialised crafts necessary to produce items for ecclesiastical use, as well as everyday goods such as cloth (Webster and Backhouse, 1991: 81–101, 138–141). These sites certainly acquired commodities by means of long-distance trade, but so far as it is possible to tell their products were not widely distributed. Some of them, however, may have been centres where essential raw materials were produced under royal or magnate control. Ramsbury (Wilts), for example, was a royal centre where in the early ninth century there was a substantial iron smelting industry; it probably also included a major church, and in the early tenth century became the seat of a bishop (Haslam, 1984: 94–97). Ramsbury's iron was perhaps distributed to blacksmiths at other settlements, including towns. At Brandon (Suffolk) an the eighth- to ninth-century settlement of at least twenty-five houses grouped loosely around a church and two cemeteries, producing high status metal goods, and containing a zone apparently devoted to the processing of flax, has been interpreted as a religious community (Carr, Tester and Murphy, 1988). But it is far from clear whether the entire settlement, which included men, women and children, functioned in that way, and whether the inhabitants of some houses served the needs of those in others. The houses are of a standard type and their disposition would be appropriate for either a secular or a religious settlement. It is possible that Brandon was one of those 'pseudo-monasteries', of which Bede complained and which proliferated in the eighth century as a device for laymen to secure from the king land which they could then pass on to their descendants (Wood, 1987). Archaeology has revealed several such sites, otherwise unknown either as settlements or as religious communities (Loveluck, 1998).

Places such as these played a significant part in manufactures between the seventh and the ninth century, not least because they promoted skills and the extraction and distribution of raw materials. The focus of this paper, however, will be on those much larger settlements whose function was more distinctively urban in terms which we would recognise today.

So far as we can tell, the major towns in the period c.650–850 all contained much the same range of crafts (Holdsworth, 1980; Cowie, Whytehead and Blackmore, 1988; Whytehead, Cowie and Blackmore, 1993 for 1989; Morton, 1992; Rogers, 1993; Hinton, 1996; Kemp, 1996; Andrews, 1997). Iron working was widespread. Gold, silver, lead, tin and copper alloys were worked in a variety of ways: by casting, the manipulation of sheet, the making of wire (usually by folding sheet, but possibly in some instances by drawing), and gilding. Precious metals were refined. Silver coins were struck. It seems that the basic metallurgical processes were understood as well as at any time during the medieval period. Many of the items made of non-ferrous metals were for dress or personal adornment, and included toilet items such as tweezers (although tweezers could have been used in working with gold thread). Most of these pieces were probably made in the town where they were found, although the evidence is such that it is rarely, if ever, possible to match the residues of manufacturing processes to the finished items. Glass was melted for use as beads and in other forms of jewellery. Widespread textile production is evidenced by the tools and other equipment for weaving, made from bone, wood, iron, and earthenware, although rural settlements seem to show more evidence of weaving than is apparent in some urban sites (Rogers, 1997). Antler, horn, and bone were extensively worked to produce combs, knife handles, tools and other items. Woodworking and leather-working are indicated primarily by the iron tools used, since the products themselves have decayed. Metals were brought from distant sources, where for the most part the ores had been processed. Small quantities of brass may have been brought from the Meuse valley, and there is other evidence of trade with the district of Huy, which supplied the essential ingredient for the alloy (Cowie, Whytehead and Blackmore, 1988: 91). Stone hones, mortars and other items were brought from distant parts of Britain and Scandinavia, and quern stones from the Rhineland. Overall, the quantities of material, both products and residues, are impressive, but possibly less than might be expected from comparable urban samples of the tenth and eleventh centuries. Comparison of this type of material between sites and periods is risky, however, and in the present state of research can be no more than impressionistic. Metals were certainly in short supply and were reused as much as possible. Thus only small quantities of gold and silver survive, and somewhat larger quantities of lead. Many of the copper alloy and iron items found were probably scrap destined for reuse. Glass, usually if not always derived from vessels imported from overseas, was extensively reused (Andrews, 1997: 217–218).

II.2. Patterns of exchange

The artefacts point to the existence of complex systems of transfer and exchange, both bringing materials into the towns and circulating them internally. Even antler and bone, which make hardly any impression on the documentary records of urban crafts surviving from later medieval periods (Keene, 1985: 282), involved elaborate processes to make them available to urban industry. The antler had generally been shed naturally and so had been gathered in the countryside. Bone and horn only became available after a number of tasks had been performed in the town, at least some of them by specialists: slaughter, dismembering the carcass, and the removal and processing of entrails, hides, and horn. The processing of horn was especially elaborate and time-consuming, and appears to have been the only trade involving the use of animal skeletons which had a distinctive impact in towns of the twelfth and thirteenth centuries, where horners and their pits can be recognised in the names of persons and places (Hodgett, 1971: 168; Palliser, 1978). We are as yet largely ignorant of leather manufacture in the towns of the first phase (but cf. Andrews, 1997: 31) although it was a major specialised urban activity from the tenth century onwards. The livestock breeding and arable farming which supported the early towns were evidently carefully organised and responded to distinctive urban needs. The social aspects of these distribution systems, however, remain unknown and are possibly irrecoverable.

Most of the surviving items made in these towns (principally goods of metal, antler or bone) appear to have been produced for consumption by their inhabitants rather than for distribution inland or overseas. As we have seen, the identification of places of manufacture is problematic. A recent discussion of the metalwork from Southampton points out that the town's products are not stylistically distinctive enough to be recognised if found elsewhere, and that this makes it difficult to assess whether or not they were distributed to nearby settlements: it seems unlikely, however, that they went much further than the immediate vicinity (Hinton, 1996: 98–101). Similar items are found at the smaller elite or 'monastic' settlements, but often in the company of higher quality or higher status products, including window glass, which may also have been made there. It is too early in the analysis of this rich body of material to come to firm conclusions about modes of production and distribution, but the contrast between the towns and the smaller settlements suggests several possibilities. Both small settlements and large towns seem to have manufactured specialised goods for internal consumption. This presumably involved some form of exchange between households, which in the case of the large towns may have taken the form of a complex internal market. At small elite settlements (whatever their function) higher status goods were also produced, presumably by 'command' rather than in response to a wider market. This elite production seems not to have been a distinctive or prominent feature of the large towns, as the case of Southampton in particular shows (Hinton, 1996: 101–102; 1998). Nevertheless, some of those towns contained high status residences or churches, which may have promoted high status manufactures in their vicinity, although clear evidence for that has yet to be found. Different forms of production and distribution, serving elite and mass requirements and responding both to 'command' and to a wider market may thus have co-existed. It is worth remembering that such a co-existence of forms was certainly apparent in later medieval towns. The matter to be assessed, therefore, is less whether one form of production succeeded another than the balance between forms which prevailed at any particular stage.

Some manufactured goods provide exceptions to this picture of localised or internal distribution of urban products. Coins travelled considerable distances from their mints. Textiles were probably made both for local consumption and for trade, since English blankets or cloaks (*sagi*) were exported overseas (Haddan and Stubbs, 1881: 497). Some towns may have specialised more in textile production than others. Thus the evidence for weaving appears much more obvious and widespread in London than in Southampton, although even in London weaving appears to have been a domestic industry, not in the hands of specialist craftsmen. Pottery was another manufactured item which was widely distributed. Most pots used in the towns were the hand-made products of local kilns. A few sophisticated, wheel-thrown pots came in on the back of Continental trade. Ipswich, however, had a distinctive pottery industry of its own, producing hand-made, but wheel-finished items which in the eighth and ninth centuries were widely distributed in East

Anglia, and further to York, London and eastern Kent (Wade, 1988; Cowie, Whytehead and Blackmore, 1988; Whytehead, Cowie and Blackmore, 1993 for 1989). Among the simple wares used in London in this period were ones imported from (or incorporating minerals from) the West Midlands (Bowsher and Malcolm, forthcoming), pointing to London's role as a town crucial to the interests of the Midland kingdom of Mercia.

II.3. Zoning and organisation

Within the towns there seems to be little indication of occupational zoning or clustering. The Ipswich pottery kilns, however, were situated on the edge of town, presumably to minimise the risk of fire. Indications that a specialised bone working site or neighbourhood existed in Southampton (Morton, 1992: 56–57, 150) seem in fact to be far from clear. This apparent occupational heterogeneity may reflect a household-based system of production directed essentially towards household needs and not strongly influenced by market- or command-driven specialisation. On the other hand, the apparent absence of spatial specialisation may reflect our reliance on the archaeological evidence alone. The substantial installations, such as dyehouses, tentergrounds and tanning pits, which enable us to recognise specialised craft districts in the archaeology of later medieval towns, have not been found, and perhaps may not have been present on account of the lack of capital to invest in them. London, however, has recently produced a group of substantial pits, apparently with an industrial function, which bears comparison with the tanning pits excavated in later Winchester and elsewhere, although it is as yet far from certain that the London pits were used for tanning (Biddle, 1990: 243–245; Bowsher and Malcolm, forthcoming). Such installations apart, it may be that the material evidence simply provides an insufficient basis, or has perhaps not yet been sufficiently analysed, to identify localised occupational characteristics. Much of the surviving material was redeposited as rubbish, thus destroying associations which might provide clues as to the organisation of production. Moreover, knowledge of the archaeology and documentary history of towns from the thirteenth century onwards, suggests that small finds often will not clearly reflect patterns of production and neighbourhood specialisation which were undoubtedly present and recognised by those who participated in them. Apart from the significance of rubbish disposal, this is because there was a fact a good deal of spatial intermixture between people in different crafts, so that patterns only become apparent when trades can be plotted across areas larger than those available for excavation, and perhaps only when there are textual sources to hand. Those patterns often took the form of combinations of interdependent trades in chains of production, rather than the domination of neighbourhoods by single trades. Moreover, the occupation of houses was very fluid, so that an artisan could easily by succeeded in a house by one in a different trade, without seriously affecting a local pattern of specialised production. In this way, flexible 'communities of skill' could persist in neighbourhoods over many centuries, despite the high mobility of the inhabitants and the intermixture of trades (Keene, 1985; Keene, 1996a). In the absence of substantial fixed plant, the archaeological expression of such communities, as surviving in the ground, can look undifferentiated and confusing.

Nevertheless, a group of about eight house sites in London occupied over a period of about one hundred and fifty years between the later seventh and the mid ninth century, and recently excavated in advance of the extension of the Royal Opera House, offers new insights into the organisation of production, especially when comparison is made with later periods (Bowsher and Malcolm, forthcoming).[2] The houses were set closely together and ranged along both sides of a street near the northern limit of the settlement. This arrangement, as well as the scale of the buildings, is paralleled in contemporary Southampton (Morton, 1992; Andrews, 1997) and closely resembles that of houses on densely built-up street frontages from the tenth century onwards, in London and other towns. In size and plan the structures resembled contemporary houses at Brandon and elsewhere, but their arrangement is in complete contrast and indicates distinctively urban conditions, in which the occupants' attention was drawn by the traffic, marketing or chains of production associated with the street, rather than focused on the household enclosure. Most or all of the structures seem to have been used both as domestic accommodation and for the routine practice of the crafts of weaving, as evidenced by the presence of weights from the warp-weighted loom and weaving tools, and the working of antler and bone, as evidenced by working waste. On two of the house sites metal-working was practised in addition to the other crafts. These were in fact the only two sites where weaving was *certainly* carried out, as indicated by the discovery of weights in rows as they had fallen from the loom, although the sheer number of loom weights from the other houses and their occurrence across the settlement as a whole, suggests that weaving was undertaken in most households. The occupants of one of the metal-working sites, on which there stood two houses in succession during the period, specia-lised in iron working. On the other site, where there were seven houses in succession (on account of their frequent destruction by fire) the occupants worked copper, silver and possibly gold. On this site it seems that weaving was not practised continuously throughout the period, for in one phase loom weights were present only in reused form as the surround for a hearth. A yard associated with this house contained the remains of high status foodstuffs such as venison and sturgeon, as well as items associated with fine metalworking, including a touchstone. At a third house site, ironsmithing was practised only in the latest phase of the settlement, in the mid ninth century.

These house sites present a complex picture which has some features in common with what we know of later periods. Close examination reveals that although the houses were similar in size and plan, the pattern of activity in the neighbourhood excavated was neither uniform nor homogenous. One house site, associated with fine metalworking, was clearly of higher status than the others. Moreover, it is possible to perceive household or family units of production, which seem also to be apparent in the less clear evidence for Southampton (Hinton, 1996), and perhaps also divisions of labour on gender and/or generational principles. Only a minority of households engaged in metalworking, which was perhaps practised or organised by male heads of household. The weaving and the bone- and antler-working which seem to have been present in all houses were perhaps the preserve of women, domestic servants and the younger members of the family. In one house, however, bone- and antler-working seems to have amounted to a specialism. Perhaps its occupants made finished products using blanks and other pieces roughed out by less skilled workers in neighbouring houses, although this hypothesis has yet to be tested against the distribution of finds. In those houses where metalworking was not

[2] The interpretation offered is provisional; analysis of the material is in progress.

practised, the specialist trade of the male head of household (if there was one) may have involved materials such as wood or leather which no longer survive, or may have been associated with the commercial activities of the river frontage, some 400 metres distant. In this neighbourhood, near the edge of the settlement, households seem to have been far from self-sufficient, and there is clear evidence of specialisation between them. We do not know, however, whether this pattern of specialised crafts simply repeated itself across the entire sixty hectares of the settlement, or whether there were distinct neighbourhood characteristics in the practice of crafts which are no longer apparent to us. Certainly the crafts evident at the Royal Opera House site were also practised in other parts of the settlement. Nor do we know how the products of the specialist households were distributed to consumers or to other crafts for further fashioning. The archaeological evidence alone does not indicate that those distribution systems were any different from those of later medieval periods.

The less well-preserved evidence from a group of houses near the limit of the built-up area of Southampton at about the same date enables us to add to this picture (Andrews, 1997). As in London, textile production and bone- and antler-working seem to have been undertaken at all or most houses in the group. Other crafts were more sparsely distributed. Blacksmiths were active at only two houses, both located at street junctions where they could catch passing traffic, in a setting very similar to that of blacksmiths in later medieval towns. The working of precious metals and copper alloys seems not to have been practised in this particular neighbourhood of Southampton, although the former was evident on site 50 metres away. There was a clear hierarchy of crafts which had a spatial expression, although it is unclear whether the market (if there was one) for the more specialised products was distributed throughout the settlement or was concentrated in particular spots.

III. c.900–1150

III.1. Crafts: specialisation and zoning

In the second phase of urban growth, from the late ninth century onwards, the archaeological evidence for crafts indicates a system of organisation which at first resembled that of the earlier period. The similarities between the houses of the Royal Opera House site and a smaller group of four house sites in tenth- and eleventh-century York are striking (Tweddle, 1990; Bayley, 1992; Ottaway, 1992; Hall, 1994; Rogers, 1997). The York houses were ranged along the frontage of the street known as Coppergate, not far from the business heart of the city. This street-name, first recorded about 1130, almost certainly denotes the turners who made wooden bowls (Palliser, 1978). The inhabitants of York presumably identified the street by its concentration of that activity, and a good deal of evidence for woodworking and turning has been recovered from the site. It is abundantly clear, however, that that other crafts were also practised there. The working of gold, silver and copper was associated with houses C and D. The occupants of house B, next to C, specialised in working iron. The iron coin dies found on the site have been taken to indicate that the occupants of C and D were engaged in the minting of coin, although the dies may rather have been present as scrap for use by the blacksmith in house B. In either case the dies perhaps indicate a business connection between neighbours following different technical specialisms. Textile production was also a feature of the neighbourhood. The distribution of spindle whorls, made of bone and other materials, suggests that in most houses people span yarn. There was a concentration of whorls in house C, but that may simply reflect the bone-working activities of its occupants, which are apparent from other finds. In other towns, too, spinning seems to have been almost ubiquitous in ordinary households for much of the medieval period and was presumably undertaken by women (Biddle, 1990: 201–203). Loom weights indicating weaving were found in all parts of the Coppergate site, but there was a concentration of them in an area to the rear of the houses. The physical and tenurial relationship of that area to the houses themselves is uncertain, so that it is impossible to say whether the weaving that appears to have taken place there was undertaken by the occupants of the houses or by an entirely different group. Certainly, neither here nor in the other urban sites is there any indication of weaving workshops in which weavers (presumably women) from different households or families may have worked together. It is possible that such workshops existed on rural sites, although the evidence for them has not been fully assessed (Rogers, 1997).

For the late ninth or early tenth century there is some striking evidence demonstrating a degree of integration between urban centres and a specialised technical response to the needs of urban production which had not been apparent earlier. In the earlier phase, before c.850, the ceramic crucibles used in fine metalworking in towns seem to have been locally made. In the ninth and tenth centuries the kilns at the town of Stamford became the site of a large-scale production of standardised pots which were widely distributed, in much the same way as Ipswich products earlier. The first Stamford wares to be traded to Lincoln and York were crucibles, which were used in preference to local wares and, being small, could readily be transported. Later, a much wider range of Stamford wares was used in these cities. The crucibles had presumably had been designed to perform to a high standard in response to the particular demands of goldsmiths (Mainman, 1990; Bayley, 1992; Mainman, 1993).

The Coppergate site may indicate a slightly greater degree of craft segregation in tenth-century York than was evident in London two hundred years earlier. This impression should not be given to much weight, however, for both groups of house sites were small and were subject to different conditions affecting the survival of finds. Moreover, our techniques for analysing the distribution of the material are far from perfectly developed. In addition, the London site was closer to the margin of the settlement than its York equivalent was. Changes in the evidence for the textile industry during the tenth and eleventh centuries, however, do suggest that in this substantial sector organisational changes were taking place, in response to an increasingly commercialised environment which favoured specialisation. Loom weights disappeared from Coppergate during the late tenth and early eleventh centuries, indicating either that weaving moved elsewhere or that it was undertaken using a different type of loom (Rogers, 1997). The warp-weighted loom, however, was being used at the York suburban site of Fishergate during the eleventh and twelfth centuries. In the eighth century, when that site was close to the then commercial hub of York, the crafts carried on there included fine metal-working as well as weaving with the warp-weighted loom, but when, about 1000, the site came to be reoccupied fine metal-working was not practised there (Rogers, 1993: 126–129). The warp-weighted loom seems generally to be have been associated with female weavers and the domestic mode of production (using the term 'domestic' to denote an activity which was probably not associated with the male head of household and which, though important, was probably secondary to the household's main source of income), although that need not preclude widespread marketing of the product. The York evidence may thus reveal a transition to a more specialised or professionalised system of production, in which weaving became the principle craft in certain houses. Domestic weaving, undertaken by women using the old-fashioned warp-weighted loom, became a feature only of marginal districts, and even there seems to have died out by the mid twelfth century.

The material evidence concerning Winchester between the tenth and twelfth centuries, when the city became a major centre of population, trade and manufactures, is similarly revealing (Biddle, 1990: 203–214). The warp-weighted loom was not used in the city, except possibly at the very beginning of the period, although it was employed in a hamlet close by. Thus by the tenth century (and perhaps at a later date in Yorkshire), there emerged a contrast between weaving practices in town and country. In the centre of Winchester at this period the artefacts suggest that weaving was carried out using a vertical two-beam loom, used to produce a cloth which later was widely marketed as a Winchester product. Cloth which could have been woven on this type of loom certainly became increasingly common in England from the tenth century onwards (Vince, 1991: 205). The horizontal loom, which facilitated more rapid production, but for which there is little if any archaeological evidence, presumably also came to be widely employed in Winchester and other towns during the eleventh century and later, thus contributing to the disappearance of the warp-weighted loom. Textile-finishing trades were practised in the heart of the city, especially in the street known as Tanner Street, where male dyers and fullers (but not weavers) are recorded as property holders in 1148. In or close to the houses associated with weaving and cloth finishing, copper working was also practised (Biddle, 1976: 113–116; Biddle, 1990: 97–98). It is possible that the weaving here was undertaken by women in a domestic context, although in later centuries there were male weavers in the vicinity, including weavers who probably used the vertical two-beam loom (Biddle, 1990: 207). The one male weaver in twelfth-century Winchester who can be connected with a particular site is to found in a suburb (Biddle, 1976: 430, 437–438).

In London the development seems to have been different again. As we have seen, weaving with the warp-weighted loom was a widespread in the large commercial settlement which between the seventh and ninth century lay just to the west of the city. The main settlement then shifted within the walls, where the warp-weighted loom continued to be used into the eleventh century, although not on the same scale as in the earlier settlement. Finds of weaving tools indicate that during the tenth and eleventh centuries the vertical two-beam loom was also used within the city walls (Vince, 1991: 167–168, 205).

Tanner Street in Winchester illustrates the specialised and dynamic character of urban industry from the tenth century onwards. The name, meaning 'the street of the tanners', is first recorded in 990, and archaeology has revealed at least one tannery operating there during the tenth and eleventh centuries. There were two male tanners among property holders in the street about 1110, but by 1148 the craft had moved to more marginal locations, in response to the rising land values and environmental constraints associated with the expansion of the city. In 1148 the street was characterised by its textile-finishing trades, a specialism which was to dominate the neighbourhood throughout the rest of the medieval period (Biddle, 1976: 60–61, 113–116, 235, 434–438; Keene, 1985: 295–318).

Almost all the persons associated with crafts recorded in the Winchester surveys and other documents concerning the city during the eleventh and twelfth centuries were men. This does not necessarily mean that women did not work in those crafts, but it does indicate the way in which specialised production was identified with those whom we presume to have been heads of households. In the earlier period, for which textual evidence specifically concerning towns is lacking, that may also have been the case with goldsmiths, blacksmiths, and a few other crafts, but it seems not to have been the case with weaving. Texts and graphic sources (most notably the ninth-century Utrecht Psalter and its derivatives) indicate a deeply-rooted cultural association between women, weaving (including use of the two-beam loom[3]) and other aspects of cloth production (James, 1935, fo. 263; Fell, 1984: 39–46; Van der Horst, Noel and Wüstefeld, 1996). The density of evidence for cloth production in London in the early period suggests that women there were producing for more than domestic consumption. In the eleventh and twelfth centuries, however, the rapid growth of commercial demands for ordinary cloth, and perhaps the adoption of new looms which required intensive working in order to repay the investment in them, meant that in towns weaving became a full-time occupation undertaken by men, while women continued in the textile industry only as spinners of yarn and as producers of certain elaborately-wrought, high-status textiles. The development of craft bynames as a means of identifying individuals, which in England seems to have taken place in the eleventh and twelfth centuries (Fransson, 1935; Tengvik, 1938; Biddle, 1976: 200–205), also suggests both increasing specialisation and a new focus on male heads of household as producers. In twelfth-century Winchester, at least one other important area of production, brewing, was distinctively associated with women, although a few men were described as brewers, anticipating the male take over of urban brewing in the late Middle Ages, as consumption of ale per head rose and beer emerged as a product with new commercial potential (Biddle, 1976: 60–61, 113–116, 235, 434–438; Keene, 1985: 265–269; Bennett, 1996).

Street-names provide an important indication of craft specialisation and groupings. They reflect networks of production and marketing, as well the environmental factors which determined the location of certain trades. The meaning of such names is not always certain, however, and, as we have seen, they should not be taken to denote exclusive concentrations of particular trades. Once more, Winchester's excellent records provide good evidence for the early period (Biddle, 1976: 231–239). Before the year 1000 the city had a street of butchers and one of shield-makers, as well as one of tanners, trades which were perhaps especially obvious for filth and smell. The shield-makers, recalling their namesakes at Saint-Riquier and in the *Capitulare de Villis* (Latouche,

[3] Many of the images in the Utrecht Psalter copy classical models. That certainly applies to the association between women and textile production, but apparently not to the depiction of the two-beam loom: Dufrenne, 1978: 87, Pl. 20.5, Fig. 11.

1967: 185, 244), suggest the way in which Winchester's role as a royal, aristocratic and military centre shaped its industrial structure. The particular concentration of elite demand in the city may also have contributed to the adoption there of the two-beam loom. By the early twelfth century there were in addition street-names indicating the presence of fullers, cloth-bleachers, and goldsmiths, the last known also from individual occurrences to be grouped near the royal palace and cathedral, where they had a prominent role in minting coin. By 1148 Winchester also contained street-names indicating shoemaking and perhaps tablet weaving (Brudene Street: cf. Page, 1985). Many of the Winchester street-names had probably come into existence long before 1100. At York before 1200 there were streets named after turners (Coppergate), cloth-bleachers, fishmongers, butchers, and shield-makers (Palliser, 1978), while at Chester by the same date there were features named after butchers and glovers (Dodgson, 1968), the latter perhaps already a key trade in the city. London was much larger, and probably more specialised in its crafts than these places, but its early records are less comprehensive. Nevertheless, they reveal that by 1200 it had streets or other locations whose names revealed specialised trading in fish, chickens, rabbits, bread, honey, corn, iron, lime, leather goods, candle wicks (possibly a distinctive innovation of the twelfth century) timber for building, firewood, charcoal, mineral coal, and distaffs for spinning yarn (Ekwall, 1954; Biddle, 1990: 991). This particular list reveals the great impulse towards specialised dealing and processing provided by the need to keep the bellies of urban populations full and their bodies warm.

The actual occupations recorded in the twelfth century, generally in the form of by-names, are also very indicative, though in a less systematic fashion. So far, only the Winchester evidence can be used to provide an overall picture, although it is one which probably accurately represents the state of affairs in the three or four cities which ranked immediately after London (Biddle, 1976: 200–205, 427–441). Fifteen distinct trades are recorded in a survey of the city about 1050, thirteen in one of about 1110, and forty-seven in the survey of 1148, which was the most comprehensive of the three. The increase in specialisation was probably not so great as suggested by these figures, for fourteen trades recorded in the two earlier surveys are not mentioned in the third, and we should also allow for the increasing incidence of bynames. Crafts in eleventh- and twelfth-century Winchester were highly specialised. The largest number of occupations (sixteen) was in the food-supply sector. Three terms were used to denote bakers, of which at least two seem to denote distinct types of product. There were three terms for leather-workers or shoemakers, which seemingly express a hierarchy of wealth and location within the city. Among manufacturing (as opposed to food-processing) trades, the leather sector seems to have contained the highest number of specialisms (nine), closely followed by metal-workers (seven), those concerned with cloth (five), and builders (four). Twenty-seven trades concerned manufacturing processes (excluding food and building). It is noteworthy that examples of food-processing trades and of crafts in all manufacturing sectors except for cloth, occur in all three periods covered by the surveys. Trades associated with cloth production occur only in 1148, possibly indicating that they were the last to emerge from a domestic environment into the public sphere.

In the twelfth century, towns smaller than Winchester contained fewer specialised trades. Among the rent-payers at the new market-town of Baldock (Hertfordshire) in 1185, only fourteen trades are recorded, all for males and only half of them in manufacturing (Lees, 1935: 66–69). At Winchester there were over twice as many trades concerned with cloth, over three times as many metal trades, and over four times as many leather trades. Highly specialised crafts such as sword-making, buckle-making, furbishing, copper-beating and parchment-making were present at Winchester, but not represented at Baldock. Nevertheless, Baldock contained at least seven makers or trimmers of clothes (*parmentarii*), six tanners, five smiths, and two ironmongers.

Around 1300 Winchester contained about seventy occupations, of which thirty-one concerned manufacturing processes, a total which seems in proportion to its size, by experienced marked growth and commercialisation between 1100 and 1300 (Britnell, 1993) but the increase in craft specialisation, as opposed to quantity of production, in Winchester seems less marked, especially bearing in mind the wider range of sources available for the later period and the growth of concern for occupation as a form of social and political identity. Commercialisation was perhaps expressed as much, if not more, in the spread of new towns and in the rapid growth of centres which had once been smaller than provincial centres like Winchester, as in an increasing division of labour and the specialisation of manufactures.

III.2. Organisation

How was urban production organised in the tenth, eleventh and twelfth centuries? Workshop sites, and sometimes their owners, can be identified. As in the earlier towns, houses and workshops were generally located on busy street frontages. But who ordered things to be made and owned the materials used? The Domesday survey in 1086 recorded the expansion (or as some now think the displacement) of the small town of Bury (Suffolk) which adjoined the great abbey dedicated to St Edmund. In the new houses there were seventy-five bakers, brewers, tailors, washerwomen, shoemakers, clothes-makers (*parmentarii*), cooks, porters and stewards, 'who all daily wait on the saint, the abbot and the brethren'. In addition, there were thirteen reeves in charge of the abbey lands who had their houses in the town, and thirty-four knights, both English and French (Beresford, 1967: 333–334). The impression given is of a community of craftsmen, officials and gentry who responded primarily to the requirements of the monks. St Edmund's was no pseudo-monastery, but in key respects the small town of Bury seems to have resembled the settlement at Brandon, and many other estate centres, three centuries earlier.

In large towns demands were more diverse than at Bury, and more market-oriented networks of production and distribution probably prevailed, on the lines of those that can be traced from the thirteenth century onwards. Nevertheless, the impact of religious institutions was important, and royal and aristocratic demands were a major stimulus to urban production. The surplus food rents of St Paul's cathedral, London, undoubtedly stimulated trade in the market streets nearby, while the demands of the cathedral canons and of the nearby royal palace presumably had a similar effect on luxury manufactures and the money market in the neighbourhood, as their equivalents did at Winchester (Brooke and Keir, 1975: 171–177; Biddle, 1976: 439). A mid twelfth-century London story is revealing (Barlow, 1992: 158). It concerns Maud, a 'noble matron of London', a phrase indicating that she belonged to one of the aldermanic or other ruling families of the city, who was skilled in the arts of dyeing with purple and decorating robes with jewels and gold embroidery. The Countess of Gloucester gave Maud an urgent commission, but on St Edward's day Maud was torn between carrying on work and honouring the saint. Her female servant, however, who seems to have been thoroughly imbued with an urban work ethic, continued to labour, mocking the 'rustic multitude' who worshipped the saint at his shrine in Westminster, just outside the city. For this God struck her down. This story reminds us of the continuing role of women, often of high social rank, as entrepreneurs in the luxury textile trades; it demonstrates the importance of aristocratic patronage and command in key areas of production; and it shows that such forms could co-exist with distinctively modern ideas concerning profit and the use of time.

By the late twelfth or early thirteenth century there several signs that entrepreneurs or middle men had an important role in production in the larger towns, putting out goods to be worked upon by others and then marketing the product. Direct evidence of the putting out system comes from London, where by the early thirteenth century it was the rule that goods found in dyehouses or in fullers' and dubbers' workshops could not be taken as distress for arrears for rent (Bateson, 1902: 494). This was presumably because those who paid the rent were often craftsmen who worked on cloth which had been put out to them by others. There are several indirect indications that such systems were common in the twelfth century. Mercantile groups probably had a key role in the organisation of production. In Winchester in the eleventh century was a guildhall where leading men drank together. By 1130 the property was known as Chapmen's Hall and served as a public market where linen cloths were sold. The chapmen (merchants) may have dealt in linen imported from overseas, but perhaps also gathered in linen woven in the city and its vicinity and organised production. Chapmen's Hall, from which the king received a substantial revenue, and which seems to have been one of a small number of institutions associated with the evolution of the city's communal government during the twelfth century, was close to the heart of business in High Street. Moneyers, who held a leading position in urban society as financiers, goldsmiths and traders in high-status goods, occupied properties near by. Later in the Middle Ages the site was a focus for the city's dyeing industry, suggesting that it had had a long association with mercantile involvement in the clothing industry (Biddle, 1976: 77, 421–422; Nightingale, 1982; Keene, 1985: 517–520). Today Marks and Spencer's stands on the spot. Another indication of mercantile or elite involvement in production concerns the situation of houses. The first mayor of London, Henry fitzAilwin, in the late twelfth century inhabited a site in the heart of the city, where he owned tenters for drying and stretching cloth and where his dwelling was surrounded by the smaller houses of dubbers, suggesting that his business affairs included entrepreneurial activity or investment in textile finishing (Keene, forthcoming). A fine stone house of the mid twelfth century in Tanner Street, Winchester, occupied a similar setting. The site had been of high status since at least as early as the mid eleventh century, and in the twelfth to thirteenth centuries included furnaces indicating specialised (but as yet not certainly identified) industrial activity. During the later Middle Ages, the residents of houses such as these were commonly active as entrepreneurs in the textile industry, employing or putting out work to craftsmen in neighbouring workshops. By the late twelfth century it was common for the dyeing of cloth, or rather the organisation of it, to be reserved to members of the merchant guilds, and dyers are among the first craftsmen known to have joined those guilds (Carus-Wilson, 1954: 222–227; Keene, 1985: 295, 303, 758).

Wage-labour is not explicitly recorded in English towns before the early thirteenth century, when anticipating a shortage of workers following a great fire in London the mayor set rates for several building trades, in a manner which indicates that working for a daily wage, with allowances for food and drink, had long been established practice (Bateson, 1902: 710–711). The use of money in England, and more particularly the monetization of urban property values apparent from the eighth century onwards (Keene, 1996b) indicate that wage-labour is likely to have been common well before 1100.

III.3. Guilds

In the thirteenth century the desire of mercantile groups to control craftsmen and to reduce them to economic dependency was a major source of conflict in towns. The making of this state of affairs is apparent in the twelfth century, especially in the textile trades. By 1130 guilds of weavers existed under royal licence at five towns, at one of which the guild was noted as a recent innovation. By the 1160s there were comparable weavers' guilds at two more towns. In 1130 Winchester also had a guild of fullers and Oxford also had one of shoemakers (*corvesarii*), while by 1156 London also had one of bakers. These guilds paid substantial sums to the king, by far the largest being due from the London weavers (Hunter, 1833: 2, 5, 48, 109, 144; Hunter, 1844: 4, 13, 29, 37, 39, 52; Unwin, 1938: 36, 44–46; Carus-Wilson, 1954: 225–226). In return the guilds presumably received royal protection. It is likely also that the king delegated to them powers to regulate standards in the trade, and perhaps also markets in labour and products, powers which formerly would have been exercised by royal officers. There is no direct reference to such responsibilities in twelfth-century sources concerning England, but the earlier evidence for the regulation of crafts by royal officers in Pavia (Bruhl and Violante, 1983) and the thirteenth-century references to the jurisdictions of the London fishmongers and bakers suggests that this is likely to have been the case. Bakers' guilds, in particular, met the need of royal officers to work through experts in regulating the basic element of urban food supply. Significantly, it is in a London document that we find the first record of the assize of bread, apparently operating before 1190 under the supervision of the king's bakers, who perhaps corresponded to the leaders of the bakers' guild (Riley, 1859: 374, Bateson, 1902: 710, 724). At some towns in the thirteenth century it was claimed that weavers' guilds had exercised a monopoly within the territory surrounding the town (Hill, 1948: 326–327), and London weavers certainly controlled their craft in settlements adjoining the city in the twelfth century (Consitt, 1933: 180–181). The widespread emergence of weavers' guilds probably arose from the rapid commercialisation of textile production, its shift out of the domestic sphere, and the desire of male craftsmen to defend their interests against merchants who were themselves forming guilds. Moreover, at the end of the twelfth century mercantile associations were assuming a controlling position in town governments (Reynolds, 1977: 82–84, 119–120), and were soon to constitute a particular threat to weavers.

The proliferation of guilds other than those approved by the crown indicates the increasing coherence of craft and other groups. Many such guilds had fraternal and religious functions which were intimately bound up with the economic interests of their members. Others appear to have had no trade connection. When such guilds had a craft connection it seems likely that the had emerged informally to protect the reputation of their products; to regulate technical processes, entry to the craft, relations between masters and employees, hours of work, and wages; and to provide a forum for apportioning work (Rosser, 1997). Such concerns, however, are not on record before the thirteenth century. Before 1200 Canterbury had a smiths' guild (Urry, 1967: 131–132). An inquiry in 1179–1180 into guilds which did not have royal licence revealed that in London there were guilds of pepperers, goldsmiths, butchers, and brokers or clothworkers (*pararii*), among others for which no trade connection is recorded. About 1190 there was a reference to the guildhall formerly used by the London tanners, who between then and the mid fourteenth century constituted a cohesive, but officially unrecognised, *societas* for the protection of their interests. By about 1200 the London saddlers regularly worshipped in a church close to the principal focus of their trade in the main market place of the city (Brooke and Keir, 1975: 279–282; Keene, 1994). There has been a tendency to downplay the significance of guilds associated with crafts in English towns before the 1260s (Reynolds, 1977: 61–62, 83–84; Veale, 1991), but the miscellaneous evidence for London, let alone the existence of guilds under royal licence both there and at other towns, suggests that they were already an important form of social organisation by 1180 and that their existence is good evidence for the growing specialisation and professionalisation of manufactures, especially in the textile sector, as well as for the overall increase in business and in the size of urban populations.

III.4. Labour supply

Members of the labour force engaged in urban industry presumably from the beginning of our period to town from the countryside, but we have no sense of the extent of urban migration fields before the twelfth century, when locative bynames begin to provide evidence. By that date the migration field of a city like Winchester was extensive, although the personal-names reflect political as well economic connections (Biddle, 1976: 197). Migration patterns were probably influenced by the flow of goods and raw materials needed in towns. For the late thirteenth century it is possible to detect the way in which specialised rural resources and skills interacted with urban crafts and dealing to create complex networks of family relationships and migration linking town and country. London's tanning and cutlery trades provide good examples (Keene, 1994; Keene, 1995), and there were doubtless others too. Such linkages almost certainly existed at a much earlier date. Another influence on the migration of labour was probably the connection between some urban properties and rural manors, generally situated within about 40 km of the town, which were in the same ownership (Biddle, 1976: 342, 382–385; Darby et al., 1952–1967). Such arrangements, recorded from the tenth century onwards but especially evident in Domesday Book, provided the rural landlord with a town residence, a rental income, and access to the urban market. The lord's agents and tenants probably travelled to and fro on a regular basis, movement which would encourage settlement in the town. It may be that at urban properties of this type, which were sometimes exempt from the routine jurisdiction of the town, manufactures were organised on a manorial basis, with part of the product being returned to the estate headquarters as rent. Such a system, for which the sources contain no direct evidence, would soon be eroded by commercial growth, causing the landlord's town headquarters to evolve into the combination of merchant house, workshops and lesser dwellings which, as we have seen, was common from the twelfth century onwards. Rents in kind may indicate the former existence of such systems. At Baldock in 1185, for example, a smith owed the making of two iron yokes as annual rent to the landlord of the town (Lees, 1935: 67). From certain larger towns the king took his dues in the form of distinctive local products: herrings (the product of industrial processing) at Dunwich and Lewes, and iron at Gloucester (Vinogradoff, 1908: 385–386; Tait, 1936: 37–38). Such dues suggest a way in which range of lords may have drawn profit from urban crafts, perhaps following a phase in which they had been more directly active in organising production.

The Gloucester iron (some of which went to make nails for the king's ships), the references to shield-makers and swordsmiths, and the great stock of body armour reputedly kept in London (Whitelock, 1979: 348), show that in the tenth and eleventh centuries the military needs of the state were a significant stimulus to urban industry. Likewise, the obligation of landholders in the territories around towns to contribute men to repair urban defences and bridges, or to provide money instead (Tait, 1916: 37–38), strengthened links between town and country and presumably influenced migration and the labour market. Other public or large-scale building projects, whether involving forced or hired labour, had a comparable impact. In 1097, when much labour was needed in the fields on account of the bad weather, men in many shires around London who owed labour and cartage services in the city were hard pressed on account of the wall being built around the Tower of London, the reconstruction of London Bridge following a flood, and the great hall then being erected for the king at Westminster. Labour for such works in London was due from as far away as Alfriston on the Sussex coast. At the same time, St Paul's cathedral in the city was being totally rebuilt after its destruction by fire, and the St Paul's estates were specially exempted from contributing to royal works in the city. (Stenton, 1970: 24; Whitelock, Douglas and Tucker, 1961: 163, 175) At Winchester, one outcome of the great investment in public building during the two generations after the Norman Conquest (at the castle, three great minsters, and the royal and episcopal palaces) was that masons were unusually prominent among the craftsmen of the city, in contrast to later centuries when carpenters were more numerous than masons (Biddle, 1976: 433). Such investment, by reducing transaction and transport costs, undoubtedly made stone more readily available for every-day building and promoted other skills in the construction and related sectors.

IV. Conclusion

Over the period as a whole there are few signs of development in the techniques of industrial production in English towns. The significant exception concerns the textile industry in the tenth and eleventh centuries, when the introduction of new types of looms, perhaps at first in southern England, or in centres of elite consumption such as Winchester, seems to have been associated with the rapid expansion of cloth production for a wide market and the marginalisation of domestic weaving. Otherwise, change seems to be expressed in the organisation and scale of production. Indeed, some changes which have been linked to technical innovation could in fact be organisational in character, involving the more common use of existing technologies in response to changes in the structure of the market. A case in point concerns the rapid decline in the use of hand querns in towns during the tenth and eleventh centuries. This may be less a response to changes in milling technology (as suggested in Biddle, 1990: 70) than an outcome of town growth which facilitated the emergence of the professional baker and a consequent decline in the preparation of grains at home. Bakers were substantial dealers in grain and operated urban mills; their substantial ovens were less of a fire risk than baking at home and, perhaps most important of all, were more economical with fuel. Specialised baking of bread may thus have emerged as towns reached a critical size. The appearance of bakers' guilds reflected this development, and it is no surprise that the first of them should be recorded in London. Archaeological evidence relevant to this change has yet to be systematically analysed.

Towns in our first phase, up to c.850, were distinctively urban environments. Their houses were set closely together and were aligned on street frontages, indicating that their inhabitants responded to traffic and to the exchange of goods and services in the public space of the street. The life of these towns was severely dislocated in the ninth century, but the urban environments which emerged thereafter seem in essential respects – including the materials, scale, density and arrangement of buildings and the distribution of specialised crafts such as metalworkers – to have resembled their predecessors. Material conditions did not significantly change until the eleventh and twelfth centuries, perhaps especially after 1100. In this second phase, however, the distinctively urban sites were more numerous and more widely distributed than before, and seem to have formed a more integrated system for the circulation of manufactured goods. Manufactures probably came to be more concentrated in towns, while 'non-urban' sites for the manufacture of high status goods appear to have become became less significant than they had been. There are also some archaeological indications – though far from conclusive and widespread – that specialised crafts came to be more concentrated within particular neighbourhoods of towns. This was perhaps especially the case with cloth finishing, although the emergence of the highly specialised dyeing industry, leaving substantial archaeological traces, was perhaps a feature of the twelfth to thirteenth century rather than earlier. At the same time some crafts ceased to be practised in a domestic environment. That was certainly the case with weaving and probably also with bone working, which in both London and Winchester, from the tenth and eleventh centuries onwards, became distinctly less widespread and perhaps more concentrated in specialist workshops (Biddle, 1990: 252–254; Vince, 1990: 175).

The texts which become available for consideration from the tenth century onwards reveal a high degree of specialisation in manufacturing processes and distinctive associations between neighbourhoods and particular crafts. By the twelfth century, in the larger towns, conditions in this respect were perhaps not very different from those in 1300, at the peak of urban population. The texts support the archaeology in revealing the rapid commercialisation of textile production. They also reveal aspects of entrepreneurial activity in several trades, and the social and political tensions which arose therefrom. Nevertheless, we should be cautious about concluding that the degree of specialisation and clustering of crafts revealed by the texts for the tenth and eleventh centuries was necessarily greater than in eighth-century towns. There are no relevant texts for the early period, and both texts and archaeology concerning towns in the central and later Middle Ages show that spatial heterogeneity of crafts with a town was not incompatible with highly specialised networks of production and with a recognition by contemporaries of the distinctive character of certain craft neighbourhoods. The picture that emerges, therefore, is of an essential similarity in the organisation of manufactures between the towns of the first period and those of the tenth and early eleventh centuries, despite the setbacks of the ninth century and the different character of the urban network established afterwards. Significant changes in organisation and infrastructure begin to be apparent in the eleventh and twelfth centuries.

It is unlikely that the contemporary texts can be forced to reveal much more on the topic of industrial organisation in English towns in the period up to 1150, except possibly through reassessment of the meaning of technical terms. On the other hand, the serious analysis of the abundant archaeological material has only just begun, and there has not yet been a truly comprehensive attempt at a unified interpretation of the artefactual evidence for different crafts with the evidence concerning the structures with which they were associated. To carry such a study forward into periods when the texts tell us much more about industrial organisation than they do for the twelfth century will enable us to put such continuities and changes as there were between 650 and 1150 into a better perspective.

Bibliography

Andrews, P. (1997) *Excavations at Hamwic. Volume 2: excavations at Six Dials. Council for British Archaeology Research Report 109*, York.

Barlow, F. (ed.) (1992) *The Life of St. Edward who Rests at Westminster*, Oxford.

Bateson, M. (1902) 'A London municipal collection of the reign of John', *English Historical Review*, 17, pp. 480–511, 707–730.

Bayley, J. (1992) *Anglo-Scandinavian Non-Ferrous Metalworking from 16–22 Coppergate*, London. (The Archaeology of York; 17/7).

Bennett, J.M. (1996) *Ale, beer and brewsters in England: women's work in a changing world, 1300–1600*, Oxford.

Beresford, M. (1967) *New Towns of the Middle Ages: Town plantation in England, Wales and Gascony*, London.

Biddle, M. (ed.) (1976) *Winchester in the Early Middle Ages: an Edition and Discussion of the Winton Domesday*, Oxford.

Biddle, M. (ed.) (1990) *Object and Economy in Medieval Winchester*, Oxford.

Bowsher, D. and Malcolm, G. (forthcoming) *Excavations at the Royal Opera House Site*, London.

Britnell, R.H. (1993) *The Commercialisation of English Society, 1000–1500*, Cambridge.

Brooke, C.N.L. and Keir, G. (1975) *London 800–1216: the Shaping of A City*, London.

Bruhl, C. and Violante, C. (1983) *Die 'Honorantiae civitatis Papie': Transkription, Edition, Kommentar*, Köln.

Carr, R., Tester, A. and Murphy, P. (1988) 'The Middle Saxon settlement at Staunch Meadow, Brandon', *Antiquity*, 42, pp. 371–377.

Carus-Wilson, E.M. (1954) *Medieval Merchant Venturers*, London.

Consitt, F. (1933) *The London Weaver's Company*, Oxford.

Corfield, P.J. and Keene, D. (eds) (1990) *Work in Towns 850–1900*, Leicester.

Cowie, R., Whytehead, R.L. and Blackmore, L. (1988) 'Two Middle Saxon occupation sites at Jubilee Hall and 21–22 Maiden Lane', *Transactions of the London & Middlesex Archaeological Society*, 39, pp. 47–163.

Darby, H.C. et al. (1952–1967) *The Domesday Geography*, 5 vols, London.

Dodgson, J.McN. (1968) 'Place-names and street-names at Chester', *Journal of the Chester Archaeological Society*, 55, pp. 29–61.

Dufrenne, S. (1978) *Les illustrations du Psautier d'Utrecht: sources et apport Carolingien*, Paris.

Ekwall, E. (1954) *Street-Names of the City of London*, Oxford.

Fairbrother, J.R. (1990) *Faccombe Netherton: excavations of a Saxon and Medieval Manorial Complex*, London.

Fell, C. (1984) *Women in Anglo-Saxon England*, London.

Fransson, G. (1935) *Middle English Surnames of Occupation 1100–1350*, Lund.

Haddan, A.W. and Stubbs, W. (eds) (1881) *Councils and Ecclesiastical Documents relating to Great Britain and Ireland, III*, Oxford.

Haslam, J. (ed.) (1984) *Anglo-Saxon Towns in Southern England*, Chichester.

Hall, R. (1994) *Viking Age York*, London.

Hill, J.W.F. (1948) *Medieval Lincoln*, Cambridge.

Hinton, D.A. (1996) *The Gold, Silver and Other Non-Ferrous Alloy Objects from Hamwic, and the Non-Ferrous Metalworking Evidence*, Southampton. (Southampton Archaeology Monograph; 6).

Hinton, D.A. (1998) 'Anglo-Saxon smiths and myths', *Bulletin of the John Rylands University Library of Manchester*, 80.1, pp. 3–22.

Hodges, R. (1989) *Dark Age Economics: the Origins of Towns and Trade, A.D. 600–1000.*

Hodgett, G.A.J. (ed.) (1971) *The Cartulary of Holy Trinity Aldgate*, London.

Holdsworth, P. (1980) *Excavations at Melbourne Street, Southampton, 1971–76. Council for British Archaeology Research Report 33*, London.

Horst, K. van der, Noel, W. and Wüstefeld W.C.M. (eds) (1996) *The Utrecht Psalter in Medieval Art: picturing the Psalms of David*, Westrenen.

Hunter, J. (1833) *Magnum Rotulum Scaccarii, vel rotulum pipae, anno tricesimo-primo regni Henrici primi*, London.

Hunter, J. (1844) *The Great Roll of the Pipe for the second, third and fourth years of the reign of King Henry the Second*, London.

James, M.R. (1935) *The Canterbury Psalter*, London.

Keene, D. (1985) *Survey of Medieval Winchester*, Oxford.

Keene, D. (1990) 'Continuity and development in urban trades: problems of concepts and the evidence', in P.J. Corfield and D. Keene (eds), *Work in Towns 850–1900*, Leicester, pp. 1–16.

Keene, D. (1994) 'Tanners' widows, 1300–1350', in C.M. Barron and A.M. Sutton (eds), *Medieval London Widows, 1300–1500*, London, pp. 1–28.

Keene, D. (1995) 'Small towns and the metropolis: the experience of medieval England' in J.-M. Duvosquel and E. Thoen (eds), *Peasants and Townsmen in Medieval Europe: Studia in Honorem Adriaan Verhulst*, Ghent, pp. 223–238.

Keene, D. (1996a) 'Metalworking in medieval London: an historical survey', *The Journal of the Historical Metallurgy Society*, 32, pp. 95–102

Keene, D. (1996b) 'Landlords, the property market and urban development in medieval England', in F.E. Eliassen and G. A. Ersland (eds), *Power, Profit and Urban Land*, Aldershot, pp. 93–119.

Keene, D. (forthcoming) 'Henry fitzAilwin', in *New Dictionary of National Biography*, Oxford.

Kemp, R.L. (1996) *Anglian Settlement at 46–54 Fishergate*, York.

Latouche, R. (1967*) The Birth of the Western Economy: Economic Aspects of the Dark Ages*, London.

Law, R. (1989) 'Slave-raiders and middlemen, monopolists and free-traders: the supply of slaves for the Atlantic trade in Dahomey, *c.* 1715–1850', *Journal of African History*, 30, pp. 45–68.

Lees, B.A. (ed.) (1935) *Records of the Templars in England in the Twelfth Century: the Inquest of 1185 with Illustrative Charters and Documents*, London.

Loveluck, C.P. (1998) 'A high-status Anglo-Saxon settlement at Flixborough, Lincolnshire', *Antiquity*, 72, pp. 146–161.

Ottoway, P. (1992) *Anglo-Scandinavian Ironwork from 16–22 Coppergate*, London. (The Archaeology of York; 17/6).

Mainman, A.J. (1990) *Anglo-Scandinavian Pottery from 16–22 Coppergate*, London. (The Archaeology of York; 16/5).

Mainman, A.J. (1993) *Pottery from 46–54 Fishergate*, London. (The Archaeology of York; 16/6).

Morton, A.D. (ed.) (1992) *Excavations at Hamwic. Volume 1: Excavations 1946–83, excluding Six Dials and Melbourne Street*, London.

Nightingale, P. (1982) 'Some London moneyers and reflections on the organisation of English mints in the eleventh and twelfth centuries', *Numismatic Chronicle*, 142, pp. 34–50.

Ottaway, P. (1992) *Anglo-Scandinavian Ironwork from Coppergate*, London. (The Archaeology of York; 17/6).

Page, R. (1985) 'Two problematic Old English words', *Leeds Studies in English*, new series, 16, pp. 198–207.

Palliser, D.M. (1978) 'The medieval street-names of York', *York Historian*, II, pp. 2–16.

Palliser, D.M. (ed.) (2000) *The Cambridge Urban History of Britain. Volume I: The Middle Ages*, Cambridge.

Rackham, J. (ed.) (1994) *Environment and Economy in Anglo-Saxon England. Council for British Archaeology Research Report 89*, York.

Reynolds, S. (1977) *An Introduction to the History of English Medieval Towns*, Oxford.

Riley, H.T. (ed.) (1859) *Munimenta Gildhallae Londoniensis, vol. I, Liber Albus, compiled A.D. 1419. Rolls Series*, London.

Rogers, N.S.H. (1993) *Anglian and Other Finds from Fishergate*, London. (The Archaeology of York; 17/9).

Rogers, P.W. (1997) *Textile Production at 16–22 Coppergate*, York. (The Archaeology of York; 17/11).

Rosser, G. (1997) 'Crafts, guilds and the negotiation of work in the medieval town', *Past and Present*, 154, pp. 3–31.

Stenton, F.M. (1970) 'Norman London', in D.M. Stenton ed., *Preparatory to Anglo-Saxon England*, Oxford.

Tait, J. (ed.) (1916) *The Domesday Survey of Cheshire*, Manchester.

Tait, J. (1936) *The Medieval English Borough: Studies on its Origins and Constitutional History*, Manchester.

Tengvik, G. (1935) *Old English Bynames*, Uppsala.

Tweddle, D. (1990) 'Craft and industry in Anglo-Scandinavian York', in P.J. Corfield and D. Keene (eds), *Work in Towns 850–1900*, Leicester, pp. 17–41.

Unwin, G. (1938) *The Gilds and Companies of London*, London.

Urry, W. (1967) *Canterbury under the Angevin Kings*, London.

Veale, E. (1991) 'The 'Great Twelve': Mistery and Fraternity in Thirteenth-Century London', *Historical Research*, 64, pp. 237–263.

Vince, A. (ed.) (1991) *Aspects of Saxo-Norman London, 2, Finds and Environmental Evidence*, London.

Vince, A. (1994) 'Saxon urban economies: an archaeological perspective', in J. Rackham (ed.), *Environment and Economy in Anglo-Saxon England. Council for British Archaeology Research Report 89*, York, pp. 108–119.

Vinogradoff, P. (1908) *English Society in the Eleventh Century*, Oxford.

Wade, K. (1988) 'Ipswich' in R. Hodges and B. Hobley (eds), *The Rebirth of Towns in the West*, London, pp. 93–100.

Webster, L. and Backhouse, J. (eds) (1991) *The Making of England: Anglo-Saxon Art and Culture, A.D. 600–900*, London.

Whitelock, D. (ed.) (1979) *English Historical Documents, c.500–1042*, London.

Whitelock, D., Douglas, D.C., Tucker, S.I. (eds) (1961) *The Anglo-Saxon Chronicle: a revised translation*, London.

Wood, I.N. (1987) 'Anglo-Saxon Otley: an archiepiscopal estate in a Northumbrian context', *Northern History*, 23, pp. 20–38.

Whytehead, R.L., Cowie, R. and Blackmore, L. (1989) 'Excavations at the Peabody site, Chandos Place, and the National Gallery', *Transactions of the London & Middlesex Archaeological Society*, 40, pp. 35–176.

PART II

MIDDLE AGES–16TH CENTURY

Introduction to part II

Stephan R. Epstein, London School of Economics and Political Science

The four papers that make up this session are distinguished by two broad themes. Stabel and Limberger focus on the division of labour between town and country and discuss the nature and outcome of the 'late medieval crisis'; Mielants and Day engage with the developmental role of medieval cities.

Stabel and Limberger address the development of the rural cloth industry during the fifteenth and sixteenth centuries. Although the process is well-known for much of western Europe after the Black Death and was described many years ago by Kellenbenz and later, among others, by van der Wee (Kellenbenz, 1963; Van der Wee, 1988), its full significance in the context of current debates on the sources of long run economic growth is still largely unexplored. For example, although it could be interpreted as a reversal of the traditional division of labour between town and country, and thus a move *backwards* in terms of functional specialisation, Stabel shows very clearly that it must be understood as part of a process of *increased* specialisation. Rural industry grew in response to market expansion (to which Stabel briefly refers, and which followed the increase in purchasing power by the lower to middle class consumers) and to declining industrial barriers to entry. Late medieval industrial expansion departed from the pre-existing, bipartite division of labour whereby an unskilled rural labour force produced inputs for urban industries that monopolised the final stages in the production process. In the period examined by Stabel and Limberger this traditional bipartite structure was replaced by a more complex tripartite one. Stabel describes how four major rural textile industries – in heavy woollens, light says, linen and tapestry weaving – developed in competition, or symbiosis, with urban manufacture in response to permutations between two factors, the nature of the labour force (specialised or unspecialised) and market size (regional or inter-regional and international).

The question inevitably arises, why some villages or regions were able to specialise to more skilled and higher value-added production while others remained wedded to low-skills, cheap manufacture. The contrast between the villages of Nieuwkerke and Hondschoote, whose success in the woollen industries propelled them to quasi-urban status, and the impoverished linen-producing countryside of inner Flanders is striking. Two crucial factors appear to have been at play. The first sine qua non of specialisation was that a rural community should be able to establish guild or quasi-guild-like structures that could enforce rigorous training standards and quality controls for export. This required being able to resist and circumvent the unremitting opposition by established urban industries towards rural competitors. As Limberger shows, rural specialisation required a degree of *political insulation* from urban institutional pressure.

Secondly, the industry had to be susceptible to significant product differentiation. High product differentiation in the woollen industry allowed rural producers to attain a significant level of skills before competing with more specialised urban industries. Product differentiation also made it possible for urban manufactures to exclude unspecialised producers – petty farmers and the like – from the higher industrial reaches (as Stabel notes, part-time by-employment was incompatible with higher quality cloth production). By contrast, the low levels of product differentiation within the linen industry and the resulting ease with which small-scale, unskilled peasants could engage in it part-time appears to explain why the rise of rural production did not challenge the traditional division of labour between town and country. Thus, by contrast with Stabel's suggestion that the distinction between urban and rural industry is 'futile', it seems to me that the difference between the two was still very much present in the period he describes. The distinction had, however, become more complex and functionally more differentiated, with, on the one hand, ostensibly still 'rural' communities growing into *industrial* 'new towns', and on the other hand, established towns retaining a monopoly throughout the period over commercial *distribution*.

Limberger's study of various types of rural by-employment, or proto-industry as he calls them, in the Rupel area of Brabant between the towns of Antwerp, Mechelen and Lier charts the complex range of activities that grew up from the late fourteenth century, including specialised cloth production, brick-making, ship-building, and the provision of fuel to the cities, in particular to Antwerp. Here also activities can be distinguished by the level of skill required and to some extent by the market they served. Low skill activities like brick and fuel-production, which remained a source of rural or 'proto-industrial' by-employment, depended strictly on the state of urban demand. This is quite the opposite of what the original theory of proto-industrialisation had stated, namely that proto-industry's stood in natural *opposition* to the urban economy. Moreover, the most successful rural industries – which, as in Flanders, specialised to wool cloth – were also those with the strongest 'urban' features. First and foremost, they were protected against urban encroachment by institutional 'liberties' (franchises) that enabled them to establish quality-enhancing guild structures.[1]

Limberger's use of proto-industrialisation as a descriptive tool is however not entirely felicitous. Having tested the theory of proto-industrialisation as an explanation for the social, institutional and demographic 'transition' to capitalism and industrialism, and having found it failing, historians in recent years have adopted one of two strategies. One reaction has been to use the term in a purely descriptive sense, as a synonym of rural by-employment or 'Z-goods' (Hyemr and Resnick, 1969); this is *grosso modo* Limberger's position. The second response has been to use it to describe any manufacturing activity not based upon urban crafts, thus for example including centralised manufacturies both in town and country (see Ogilvie and Cerman, 1996 for examples of both usages).

Both uses of the term are unsatisfactory. Both of them jettison some crucial distinctions of form and function between different kinds of rural production and by-employment that emerged from the debate over proto-industrialisation. It would seem more useful either to abandon the term entirely (since it is no longer associated with a theory of structural change), or alternatively, to work towards a new model of proto-industry that can account for newly discovered evidence about premodern rural manufacture. It should also retain the original distinction between production for external markets, which is

[1] Liberties were, of course, a necessary but not sufficient condition for industrial success, as the return into obscurity of the sixteenth-century industry of Walchem demonstrates.

historically distinctive and had significant structural effects, and rural by-employment in general, which is a near universal feature of agrarian economies and has few developmental consequences. Limberger mentions three particularly important factors that were missing from the original theory and which need to be integrated into a new one.

- ***Chronology.*** The original theory saw proto-industrialisation strictly as a seventeenth- and eighteenth-century phenomenon. We now know that it was preceded by a similar wave of rural 'industrialisation' between the late fourteenth and sixteenth centuries. Hohenberg and Lees explained the timing of these two waves in neo-Malthusian terms as a response to changing patterns of demand: 'proto-industry' expanded in periods of low or declining population pressure when demand for cheaper consumer goods increased, and contracted when population growth drove real wages down again (Hohenberg and Lees, 1985). Their model explicitly recognised the fact that proto-industry expanded when rural and lower-class urban living standards were *rising*. By contrast, it will be recalled that Mendels and Kriedte, Medick and Schlumbohm had argued from the supply-side that proto-industries had developed in response to *declining* living standards in the countryside, which forced impoverished peasants to abandon self-sufficiency for the 'risks' of the market. Thus, according to the original model, conditions during the late Middle Ages when the population collapsed across most of western Europe and average living standards rose, should have made it easier for peasants to retreat into self-sufficiency and to *avoid* market activities. The late Middle Ages should have been singularly unpropitious for rural industrial growth, rather than a period of rural manufacturing boom. In any case, as Limberger observes, rural living standards do not seem to be very accurate predictors for 'proto-industrial' activities, which flourished in both wealthy and impoverished parts of the Rupel countryside.

- ***Geographical distribution.*** Access to cheap raw materials and labour was not sufficient for a successful, e.g. institutionally independent and export led, proto-industry to arise. Institutional protection from urban interference in production was essential. Towns, or merchants based in towns, kept control of distribution, but that did not apparently inhibit rural production to the same extent.

- ***Developmental impact.*** The long-run structural consequences of 'proto-industry' appear strongly connected with its capacity to turn from an unspecialised and unskilled activity into a specialised one. This is because the former appears to be far more dependent on short-term market conditions than the latter. If proto-industries required a specialised, skilled labour force to achieve success, what some have described as the basic institutional *limitation* of European proto-industrialisation, namely its organisation through guild or corporate structures (a fact amply documented by both Stabel and Limberger), becomes less paradoxical. This is because the main purpose of guilds was precisely to provide their membership with a steady supply of skilled labour (Epstein, 1998).

As the reference to skilled labour suggests, Stabel and Limberger raise but do not specifically address important questions concerning the nature of late medieval and early modern labour markets. In a competitive labour market, individuals should specialise to their comparative advantage – farmers to agriculture, industrial workers to industry, others to services – and urban economies of scale and positive externalities should lead non-agricultural labour to reside in towns. Measured against this benchmark (typical of contemporary industrialised societies), rural by-employment and proto-industry is a highly inefficient use of resources. How can their persistence throughout the premodern era be explained? Two answers come to mind: either premodern markets were systematically inefficient – a hypothesis that conflicts with the widely held opinion that rural immigration kept urban economies in equilibrium with available resources – or premodern transport costs were too high to transfer large numbers of temporary wage labour from town to country at harvest time. In this view, transport and other transaction costs would have set a ceiling to the proportion of the rural population that could immigrate to towns on a permanent basis (Grantham, 1993). For indeed, neither in theory nor in practice were premodern labour markets limited to a one-way flow from country to town. Whereas skilled labour tended to fix in one place, unskilled labour was highly mobile and could easily – insofar as transaction costs allowed it – move back to the countryside from the town.

Mielants and Day's essays address one of the classic questions in economic history – the causes of medieval urban growth – from opposite ends, with the former emphasising the role of long distance trade, and the latter dwelling instead on the interaction between a great metropolitan city and its hinterland. In his wide ranging discussion of how various theories of the transition from feudalism to capitalism view the medieval economy and especially the late medieval crisis, Mielants argues that they all fail because they misconceive the role of medieval markets: Brenner ignores them, modernisation theory claims that they were monopolised by guilds, and Wallerstein misunderstands them. In fact, a large body of work shows that medieval markets were ubiquitous, and a satisfactory theory of the 'transition' must take account of this. Mielants' response is to identify capitalism with urban trade and to push back its origins into the dark ages. Mielant's solution is surprisingly traditional and side-steps the problem he attempts to address: when did the feudal economy come to an end? While one can agree with the main thrust of his criticism – virtually all theories of the 'transition' suffer from a nineteenth-century hangover with *Stufentheoretisch* ideal-types that reify trade as 'external' to feudalism – it is hardly original, as its most recent reincarnation in the burgeoning 'commercialisation' group of English medievalists attests (Bailey, 1998). Like the latter approach, Mielants' solution risks perpetuating the very error he denounces. By defining (medieval) trade as a form of commercial 'capitalism', he proposes afresh the old dichotomy between 'capitalism-as-markets' and 'non-capitalist' societies without trade. Mielants is aware of the danger of reifying markets. However, he does not provide a satisfactory answer to the obvious objection that a definition of trade as capitalism blurs historical distinctiveness, and easily leads to claims like those by Gunder Frank (who he explicitly criticises) that a 'world-system' organised around has been in existence for the past 5,000 years.

The source of the confusion that Mielants' denounces is arguably the tendency by many historians to equate *economic growth* – which is a consequence of trade and thus, institutionally, of markets – with *capitalism*.[2] This confusion is easily rectified however

[2] This is a particularly curious error for Marxist historians, for whom historical change should in principle be driven by technological progress, and for whom the postwar consensus that pre-

by drawing a clear distinction between growth – the consequence of a natural human proclivity to respond to scarcity by expanding productive powers (Cohen, 1978: 152) – and the capitalist mode of production, which is a historically contingent form of technological, social and market organisation associated with a certain *kind* (speed and trajectory) of growth. Having drawn this distinction, the next step is to distinguish between different *kinds of markets*, associated with different incentive structures and, thus, with different socio-economic equilibria. For example, markets would seem to have been a far more important focus of political rent-seeking in premodern than in capitalist societies. If so, why? Was the role of the state purely negative, as most public choice theory and new institutional economics assumes, or did the state also contrive to solve persistent market failures arising from co-ordination failures, prisoners dilemmas, and politically-based monopolies? Were towns the principal source of premodern growth, as Mielants seems to suggest and as has been recently restated by Grantham (Grantham, 1997), or were they also – in the guise of powerful political actors – rent-seekers that actively discouraged industrial and commercial competition, as Stabel's and Limberger's work reminds us? An approach to the 'transition debate' that is sensitive to the changing political economy of markets within different modes of production would seem to be more promising than old debates about the nature (capitalist or feudal?) of pre-modern trade.

In the context of Mielants' argument it is perhaps paradoxical that Day, who is concerned with the rise to metropolitan status of medieval Florence, never once mentions 'merchant capitalism' among the causes for Florentine success. For all that, Day's work reflects the recent shift from long distance trade to town-country interaction as the major source of premodern dynamic growth. We are presented with a classic 'Smithian' model of urban growth, similar to Grantham's previously cited work and much influenced by Wrigley's seminal work on early modern London (Wrigley, 1964; 1985). Florence emerges as a city whose extraordinary growth – from perhaps 25,000 to 125,000 inhabitants between the early thirteenth and early fourteenth centuries, according to Day – was fuelled largely by regional migration flows that in turn stimulated agricultural innovation and growth in the hinterland.

Like all claims to a virtuous cycle of growth feeding upon growth, however, the argument does raise some puzzles. The principal question – which applies equally to Grantham's important and wide-ranging claims – to be answered is, what drove urban growth in the first place? Why in particular was Tuscany so much more urbanised than other regions with apparently similar land and geographical endowments? Why did Florence emerge as hegemonic in Tuscany, and why did its neighbouring competitors – Pisa, Pistoia, Arezzo, Siena etc. – stop growing at roughly the time when Florence began to take off? To what extent did Florence divert regional resources for its own benefit already *before* it began to establish a fully fledged regional state after the Black Death? I suspect that the answer to all these questions may lie among those institutional variables that gave shape to premodern markets, and to which this interesting collection of essays has repeatedly pointed.

---

modern economies were technologically stagnant should have been anathema. The blind spot is most likely to be explained as a reaction against Stalinist *diamat*.

Bibliography

Bailey, M. (1998) 'Peasant welfare in England, 1290–1348', *Economic History Review*, 2nd ser., 51, pp. 223–251.

Cohen, G.A. (1979) *Karl Marx's theory of history. A defence*, Oxford.

Epstein, S.R. (1998) 'Craft guilds, apprenticeship and technological change in premodern Europe', *Journal of Economic History*, 53, pp. 684–713.

Grantham, G. (1993) 'Divisions of labour: agricultural productivity and occupational specialization in pre-industrial France', *Economic History Review*, 2nd ser., 46, pp. 478–502.

Grantham, G. (1997) 'Espaces privilégiés. Productivité agraire et zones d'approvisionnement des villes dans l'Europe préindustrielle', *Annales HSS*, 3, pp. 695–725.

Hohenberg, P.M. and Lees, L.H. (1985) *The making of urban Europe, 1000–1950*, Cambridge (Mass.).

Hymer, S. and Resnick, S. (1969) 'A model of an agricultural economy with non-agricultural activities', *American Economic Review*, 59, pp. 493–506.

Kellenbenz, H. (1963) 'Industries rurales en Occident de la fin du moyen âge au XVIII siecle', *Annales ESC*, 18, pp. 833–82.

Ogilvie, S.C. and M. Cerman, M. (eds) (1996) *European proto-industrialization*, Cambridge.

Wee, H. van der (1988) 'Industrial dynamics and the process of urbanisation and de-urbanisation in the Low Countries from the late middle ages to the eighteenth century. A synthesis', in H. van der Wee (ed.) *The rise and decline of urban industries in Italy and in the Low Countries (late middle ages – early modern times)*, Louvain, pp. 307–381.

Wrigley, E.A. (1967) 'A simple model of London's importance in changing English society and economy, 1650–1750', *Past and Present*, 37, pp. 44–70.

Wrigley, E.A. (1985) 'Urban growth and agricultural change: England and the Continent in the early modern period', *Journal of Interdisciplinary History*, 15, pp. 683–728.

5 Population growth and productivity: rural-urban migration and the expansion of the manufacturing sector in thirteenth century Florence[1]

William R. DAY JR., University of Cambridge

I. Introduction

In the later twelfth century, Florence was still a relatively minor town in Tuscany. The urban population of Florence was probably no more than about 15,000, and in terms economic if not demographic, the city was still overshadowed in Tuscany certainly by Pisa, probably by Lucca, and perhaps also by Siena. After about the middle of the twelfth century, however, the rate of growth in Florence had begun to accelerate dramatically. A new circuit of walls was constructed towards the end of the third quarter of the century in order to accommodate the sudden accretion, but continued growth soon rendered even these new walls obsolete, and construction on yet another much larger circuit of walls was initiated in 1284. By about the end of the first quarter of the fourteenth century, Florence had reached its apex. The urban population of Florence itself had assumed a figure perhaps as great as 120,000, while the population in the territory as a whole may have surpassed 400,000.[2] Moreover, the profound demographic expansion of Florence and its surrounding countryside was accompanied by sustained economic growth that was sufficiently robust to transform the city of Florence from a second-rate town in Tuscany into one of the larger and most economically dynamic urban centres in all of western Europe by the early fourteenth century.

---

[1] I would like to express my gratitude to Claire Billen, Bruno Blondé, Michèle Galand, and Eric Vanhaute for organising the conference from which this article stems and for extending to me an invitation to speak in Brussels. I would also like to thank Stephan R. Epstein and Chris Wickham for their guidance and suggestions. Special gratitude is owed to the Scholarships Office at the London School of Economics and Political Science; the Committee of Vice-Chancellors, administrators of the Overseas Students Research Award Scheme; and the University of London Central Research Fund for their generous financial support of my postgraduate studies. My research in the State Archives of Florence from September 1995 to January 1997 was funded by an Eileen Power and Michael Postan Award in Economic History, supplemented by a Studentship from the London School of Economics and Political Science and a grant from the Royal Historical Society.

[2] These estimates for the most part have been extrapolated from figures given by the fourteenth century chronicler Giovanni Villani. See Villani, 1823: bk. 11, chap. 94. Some of the estimates that have been put forward are summarised in the table found in Goldthwaite, 1980: 33. On the population of the city of Florence before the middle of the fourteenth century, see also Fiumi, 1950: 87, 106–118; 1957–1959: pt. 2, 465; 1977: 75–90, esp. 85–87. For figures from the early and later thirteenth century in the context of rank-size patterns, see Russell, 1972: 40–52. A brief discussion of the urban population of Florence before the advent of the Black Death in 1348 may be found in Herlihy and Klapisch-Zuber, 1985: 64–67. This work is an abridged translation, with substantial reorganisation, of Klapisch-Zuber, 1978; here, see 173–174. For the century from

The rapid growth of Florence from about the middle of the twelfth century through the first quarter of the fourteenth century has never been satisfactorily explained. In an age characterised by demographic growth and commercialisation, the Florentine example remains conspicuous. Florence continued to grow long after its Tuscan neighbours had ceased to expand, despite the fact that Florentine growth initially had been slower than that of other Tuscan towns. The peculiar political situation both within the territory of Florence and in Tuscany as a whole at first inhibited Florentine expansion. Before the beginning of the thirteenth century, Florence was unable to exercise control over large areas of its own countryside, much of which was dominated by a handful of exceptionally powerful comital lords. The Guelf political persuasions of the Florentine urban elite also conflicted with the Ghibelline sentiments that prevailed throughout most of Tuscany. The inability of Florence to control its own countryside meant that the city was unable to exert much influence on the production and distribution of foodstuffs within the territory, and antagonisms between Florence and its Ghibelline neighbours reduced opportunities for peaceful intra-regional trade. Florence was therefore compelled to look beyond the confines of its own territory and indeed beyond the confines of Tuscany in order to satisfy even some of its most basic requirements. The development of an export industry in woollen textiles and the cultivation of networks of inter-regional trade especially with such cities as Bologna, Faenza, Orvieto, and Perugia enabled Florence to overcome most of its food supply difficulties and to expand beyond the dimensions that agricultural production in its own territory would support.

Industrial development in the city of Florence provided strong incentives for the immigration of surplus labour from the countryside. Rural-urban migration in Florence precipitated a seven-fold increase in the urban population between about the beginning of the thirteenth century and the end of the first quarter of the fourteenth century. This was in spite of mortality rates that were probably four per cent or more even in normal years, and at any rate more than sufficient to offset any growth in the urban population through natality.[3] A steady flow of immigrants into Florence was therefore necessary

1280 to 1380, see De la Roncière, 1976, 2: 643–696. On the population of Florence from the fourteenth century through the early modern period, see Belloch, 1940: 127–149. On the rural population in the countryside of Florence, see again Fiumi, 1950: 87–105; 1977: 91–104, esp. 103. See also De la Roncière, 1976, 2: 659–678, esp. 677. For a discussion of the population in the Florentine countryside before the Black Death, see Herlihy and Klapisch-Zuber, 1978: 171–172; 1985: 65. For the Florentine countryside, Fiumi has given a figure of 245,000 for the year 1300 and 280,000 for 1338, but both De la Roncière and Herlihy and Klapisch-Zuber have regarded his estimates as being on the lower margin. De la Roncière has suggested that the total population in the territory of Florence was about 350,000 in the year 1300 and about 365,000 in 1338. Herlihy and Klapisch-Zuber have given even larger estimates, suggesting that the rural population alone stood somewhere between 280,000 and 320,000 around the year 1338, and that the population in the territory as a whole was greater than 400,000. My own estimates for the population of Florence and its surrounding countryside from the later twelfth century through the first half of the fourteenth century, reflected here and again towards the conclusion of this article, are put forward in Day, 2000: 119–147.

[3] The figure of 4% given as the probable rate of mortality in normal years pertains to Florence in the early fifteenth century and has been drawn from Herlihy and Klapisch-Zuber, 1978: 454–456; 1985: 269–270. A comparison of baptismal records and census data for Florence in the third

not only to fuel urban demographic growth but merely to compensate for natural losses, and recent immigrants probably constituted a substantial proportion of the population in the larger Tuscan cities (Herlihy, 1958: 39–42).[4] Of course, not all of the immigrants coming from the countryside of Florence and into the city entered the woollen textiles industry. New immigrants in Florence in the later thirteenth century included professionals such as notaries and judges, artisans and apprentices, and rural landowners (Nenci, 1981: 155–168). Immigrants from the Florentine countryside and beyond entered domestic service in Florence in large numbers, and they no doubt also swelled the ranks of the building trades and other professions.[5] The Florentine industry for woollen textiles nevertheless very clearly must have provided employment for a significant proportion of the new immigrants in the city in the thirteenth and early fourteenth centuries.

According to the fourteenth century Florentine chronicler Giovanni Villani, there were by about 1338 more than two hundred workshops in the city of Florence in which woollen textiles were fashioned and more than 30,000 Florentines, or perhaps as much as a quarter of the urban population, were earning a living through the woollen textiles industry. Thirty years earlier, before the Florentines had learned to produce fabrics from the finer grades of wool imported from England, there had been something on the order of about three hundred workshops in the city manufacturing woollen textiles. These workshops produced coarser and less expensive fabrics from local varieties of wool, but they produced from twenty-five to perhaps as much as forty-three per cent more

quarter of the eighteenth century suggests that the natality rate in Florence between 1751 and 1767 oscillated between 3.48 and 3.88% per year, which is roughly comparable to birth rates in other pre-industrial cities in Mediterranean Europe. The rate of natality hardly could have been higher in Florence during the early fifteenth century, not to mention the early fourteenth century. See again Herlihy and Klapisch-Zuber, 1978: 176; 1985: 68. See also Lastri, 1775: 94–95, 107–111. For examples of comparable birth rates for elsewhere in pre-industrial Italy, see Reinhard, Armengaud, and Dupaquier, 1968: 164–165.

[4] On the basis of the Florentine *Catasto* of 1427–1430, Herlihy and Klapisch-Zuber estimated that at least 10% of the urban population of Florence was composed of recent immigrants in the early fifteenth century, and at Pisa, nearly 20% of the urban inhabitants were recent immigrants. Elsewhere in Tuscany in the early fifteenth century, recent immigrants typically accounted for 5–6% of the urban population. See Herlihy and Klapisch-Zuber, 1978: 314; 1985: 112.

[5] In the early fifteenth century, as much as 60% of rural-urban migrants were entering domestic service in certain parts of the city. See Herlihy and Klapisch-Zuber, 1978: 320, and 321, tbl. 45. See also Guarducci and Ottanelli, 1982: 19–30; Nenci, 1981: 161. It should be noted, however, that at least some of the rural-urban migrants working as domestic servants in Florence probably provided low cost labour for the woollen textiles industry while working in the employment of masters of the wool guild. See again Guarducci and Ottanelli, 1982: 23. The most detailed study of the construction industry in Florence during the later middle ages and renaissance is that of Richard A. Goldthwaite. The author stressed labour mobility and the fluidity of employment in his work, but he did not discuss the immigrant component of the labour force. See Goldthwaite, 1980. The construction industry in Florence nevertheless must have been large enough to sustain a considerable amount of seasonal migrantion from the surrounding countryside between the seasons for reaping and sowing. In the later fourteenth and fifteenth centuries, according to Samuel Cohn, most of the common wage-labourers in Florence were probably day-labourers in the building industry, although he acknowledged that these labourers were only rarely identified by profession in the surviving notarial records. See Cohn, 1978: 69.

cloth by volume than thirty years later (Villani, 1823: bk. 11, chap. 94).[6] The nature of the surviving documentation for the Florentine woollen textiles industry renders it impossible either to corroborate or to discredit the testimony of Villani concerning its dimensions in the early fourteenth century, but the evidence from the second half of the thirteenth century clearly betrays an industry that had already achieved substantial proportions. The intention here is not to suggest that the depiction of the woollen textiles industry in Florence put forward by Villani should be regarded as a model of historical accuracy, but that it contains at least a kernel of truth, a notion which is borne out in the image of the industry that emerges from a consideration of the later thirteenth century sources.[7] The Florentine woollen textiles industry indeed must have been absorbing a appreciable proportion of the rural-urban migration in Florence particularly from the landless classes already before the middle of the thirteenth century.

II. The Plesner thesis

The Danish historian Johan Plesner has demonstrated that most of the documented immigrants in thirteenth century Florence were rural landowners from the surrounding hinterland who tended to maintain their landed possessions in the countryside after removing to the city. This clearly has important implications with respect to the assertion that the Florentine woollen textiles industry was absorbing considerable numbers of

[6] According to Villani, annual production in 1338 was between 70,000 and 80,000 pieces of cloth, generating revenues of more than 1,200,000 gold florins, which is to say an average between 15.00 and 17.14 gold florins for each piece of cloth. More than 10,000 pieces of cloth from northern Europe, worth an additional 300,000 gold florins, were also passing through Florence annually. Thirty years earlier, annual production had been more than 100,000 pieces of cloth, but this cloth was only half as valuable as the fabrics produced in 1338, which is to say that annual revenues in 1308, on the basis of 100,000 pieces, would have been between about 750,000 and 857,000 gold florins. Hidetoshi Hoshino, the Japanese historian of the medieval Florentine woollen textiles industry, has suggested that the figures for annual production given by Villani are vastly exaggerated. Although it may have been possible for the production of a single workshop to approach three hundred pieces of cloth yearly, Hoshino argued that the maximum average annual production per workshop was probably much closer to about one hundred pieces of cloth. See Hoshino, 1980: 196–203. On the credibility of the figures given by Villani more in general, see Fiumi, 1953; Frugoni, 1965; Green, 1972; Hunt, 1994: 268–271; Sapori, 1955, 1: 25–33. The figures given by Villani for the number of workshops in the Florence may be compared with the fact that 626 Florentines were actually matriculated in the wool guild in Florence in 1332, suggesting that the operations of each workshop were directed by two or three masters. See Hoshino, 1980: 226, tbl. 35, citing Archivio di Stato di Florence (ASF), *Arte della Lana*, nos. 18–20. In thirteenth and early fourteenth century Pisa, the workshops themselves were adopted for different phases in the productive cycle, and the various phases of the cycle required different numbers of labourers. The initial treatment of the wool usually could be accomplished by only a few workers, but succeeding phases required much higher labour inputs. See Castagneto, 1996: 166–178.

[7] The figures given by Villani for the size of the labour force in the woollen textiles industry in the early fourteenth century are also supported by later evidence. Nearly half of the ordinary wage-labourers in Florence that can be discerned in the notarial records from the second half of the fifteenth century were employed in the textiles industries, which by that time had expanded into the production of silk. See Cohn, 1978: 11, n. 19.

landless immigrants from the countryside. It also bears upon the increasing level of integration between the city of Florence and its surrounding countryside, a phenomenon distinguishable particularly in the thirteenth century. According to Plesner, the immigration of landowners from the countryside of Florence to the city enabled them to participate in the political life of the city and thereby advance their economic interests (Plesner, 1934).[8] This allowed the conjecture, subsequently articulated by Enrico Fiumi, that the growing interdependence between the rural and urban sectors in the territory of Florence in the thirteenth century was related to this wave of immigration and particularly to the consequent coalescence of the rural interests of the immigrating landowners with the interests of the city (Fiumi, 1957–1959: pt. 1, 429–434; pt. 2, 482–510).

The integration of an urban centre with its surrounding countryside typically is regarded as the essential condition for the demographic and economic growth of the urban centre in question in pre-industrial societies (Wrigley, 1991: 114–115).[9] Most scholars have

[8] Evidence dating from Pistoia in 1243 also lends support to the notion that the rural middle class contributed disproportionately to the wave of immigration from the countryside and into the city during the thirteenth century. In a tax assessment for 238 households in the rural commune of Piuvica, situated on the plain immediately south the city between the torrents of the Ombrone and the Stella, the average assessment for the thirteen residents identified as recent immigrants to the city was more than twice the average assessment for the commune as a whole, and two of these immigrants were among the wealthiest members of the commune. According to Herlihy, immigrants were identified in the assessment by phrases such as 'dicunt se esse cives' or 'habent libram cum civitate' following their names. The amendment was necessary because urban residence conferred upon the holder a different tax status. In the countryside, the system of taxation was based on a flat assessment levied against the community as a whole and then collected within the community on the basis of individual wealth. The system effectively required the wealthier inhabitants in the commune to assume the responsibility for the taxes of the poorest inhabitants, which resulted in a flight of wealth from the countryside to the city. See Herlihy, 1967a: 184–185.

[9] The term 'integration' is employed here to denote the economic and political integration of the city of Florence with the rural sectors within the territory as a whole, which is to say the dioceses of Florence and Fiesole. Economic integration is often defined in terms of price convergence or covariance, but the data for prices in thirteenth century Florence and its surrounding countryside are extremely exiguous. In the present case, economic integration refers simply to the degree to which the urban market dominated production and distribution strategies in the surrounding countryside. Political integration, on the other hand, refers to political hegemony, which was reflected most conspicuously upon the ability of the commune of Florence to administer justice and to impose taxes. The principal encumbrance to the economic and political integration of the city of Florence with its surrounding countryside lay in the fact that much of the Florentine countryside was dominated by three powerful comital lords: the Alberti, the Guidi, and the Ubaldini. The Alberti lords dominated in the valleys of the rivers Elsa and Pesa, in the lower valley of the river Arno, and in the western Mugello. The Guidi lords possessed enclaves throughout the territory but their power was concentrated in the upper valley of the Arno and in Romagna to the north and northeast. The Ubaldini lords controlled the valley of the river Sieve and the central Mugello. The Alberti lords submitted to Florentine authority in a series of agreements negotiated in the last years of the twelfth century and at the very beginning of the thirteenth century. The Guidi and Ubaldini maintained their autonomy, but Florence and the Ubaldini were reaching accommodations from at least as early as the year 1200. The expansion of the episcopal estate in the Mugello in the area around Borgo San Lorenzo in the later twelfth and early thirteenth centuries also favoured Florentine fortunes in Ubaldini territory.

agreed, however, that the rural and urban sectors in the territory of Florence, compared to those in the territories of other Tuscan towns, were neither politically nor economically very well integrated before the later twelfth century (Wickham, 1988: 131–133).[10] The relative lack of integration in Florence rendered the city slow to develop in relation to other Tuscan towns, but Florentine growth quickened dramatically as the city and its surrounding countryside became more thoroughly integrated in the thirteenth century.[11]

Earlier historians also had recognised the connection between urban demographic and economic expansion in Florence on the one hand and the integration of the rural and urban sectors in the territory as a whole on the other, but they regarded rural-urban integration as the consequence of the urban conquest of the countryside. For the German scholar Robert Davidsohn and his contemporaries, writing at the turn of the century, the integration of the city of Florence with its surrounding hinterland represented the subjugation of the feudal nobility in the countryside by the mercantile interests of the city (Davidsohn, 1977, 1: 926–928).[12] Like Davidsohn before them, both Plesner and Fiumi correctly perceived that urban growth in Florence was contingent upon the integration of the rural and urban sectors in the territory as a whole. The critical distinction between their respective lines of reasoning lay in the fact that whereas Davidsohn understood the processes of integration in terms of an urban conquest of the countryside, Plesner and especially Fiumi regarded the issue rather as an expression of the increasingly symbiotic relationship

---

[10] Some doubts about the low degree of integration in the territory of Florence before 1200 recently have been raised, but the evidence tends to bear out the notion that the level of integration between the rural and urban sectors in the territory of Florence around the middle of the twelfth century paled relative to that which was discernible in certain of the neighbouring Tuscan territories such as Lucca. For the recent dissenting opinion, see Dameron, 1996. It should be noted here that Dameron has focused specifically upon the relatively few urban landlords in Florence that undoubtedly possessed substantial proprietary holdings in the countryside, particularly the bishops of Florence and the cathedral chapter, though he has regarded these institutions and their proprietary interests not as exceptions but rather as a more or less accurate representations of the more generally pervading circumstances. On the bishops of Florence, see Dameron, 1991.

[11] Most estimates put the urban population of Pisa at the beginning of the thirteenth century between about 15,000 and 20,000 inhabitants. The Sienese urban population was probably between about 10,000 and 15,000, and the urban population of Lucca may have been around 10,000, although it must be acknowledged that meaningful figures from which to infer the populations of Siena and Lucca around the year 1200 are even more exiguous than those for Florence and Pisa. See Bairoch, Batou, and Chèvre, 1988: 40–49; Ginatempo and Sandri, 1990: 105–115; Russell, 1972: 39–52. Florence may have already surpassed Lucca and Siena in demographic terms by the beginning of the thirteenth century, but the economies of Lucca and Siena probably still enjoyed greater vitality owing at least partly to the position of these two cities on the via Francigena, the main pilgrimage route between Rome and the north. It was only in the early thirteenth century that the routes going through Florence, the via Cassia and the via Romea, became more heavily used.

[12] Davidsohn actually went so far as to speak of an urban 'reconquest' of the countryside, following what really amounted to a restriction of Florentine rights in the surrounding countryside by king Henry VI in 1187. The language of the 1187 act gives the impression of a royal concession, but the king conceded to Florence only jurisdiction of the immediately surrounding suburbs, and the nobility was to remain aloof Florentine authority even within this area. See De Rosa, 1995: 68. For evidence of the royal circumscription of Florentine rights in its surrounding countryside, see Ficker, 1868–1874: 4, no. 170, 1187 June 24, 213–214.

between the city and its hinterland. In this view, the integration of the rural and urban sectors in the territory of Florence was fostered by the immigration of rural landowners into the city who tended to maintain their proprietarial holdings in the countryside. Plesner and Fiumi had in fact utterly reversed the older paradigm, with the result that rural landowners were regarded not so much as the vanquished but more as the conquerors.

There can be little doubt that the immigration of rural landowners into the city facilitated in some measure the increasing interdependence between the rural and urban sectors in the territory as a whole during the thirteenth century, but rural-urban migration was not strictly speaking a causal agent. The immigration of rural landowners from the countryside of Florence and into the city itself should be seen collectively not as a catalyst of integration but rather as a phenomenon symptomatic of an already more or less advanced stage of integration. Rural landowners probably were more disinclined to remove to the city during the initial phases of integration than were landless peasants, in as much as they had more to lose in so doing. Urban communes in north-central Italy indeed often found it necessary to offer considerable incentives to rural landowners, professionals, and artisans in an effort to encourage immigration into the city from among the members of the middle and upper-middle classes.[13] Rural landowners removed to the city only when the projected benefits of participating more fully in the urban economy began to outweigh any perceived risks involved in becoming absentee landlords in the countryside. The immigration of rural landowners was thus for the most part subsequent to a transitional phase that entailed a much greater degree of risk and uncertainty. In modern developing economies, for example, it is worth noting that rural landowners have tended to be among the last to join the exodus to the cities, following upon a long train of landless immigrants (Grigg, 1982: 110–113).[14]

The predominance of landowners among those who can be seen to be immigrating from the countryside of Florence and into the city in the thirteenth century distorts the

[13] Preferred immigrants in Siena in the later thirteenth century were offered a variety of special privileges in the city, typically temporary exemptions ranging from five to ten years from taxes, personal service, or the obligation to construct a dwelling in the city. See Bowsky, 1967: 213. At Pisa, the preference for immigrants with notarial training is evident in the fact that two thirds of the notaries working in the commercial centre of the city in 1293 have been identified as recent immigrants. See Herlihy, 1958b: 41. The same preference can be observed at Florence in the second half of the thirteenth century. See Nenci, 1981: 165–168. In early fifteenth century Florence, close to 40% of one sample of urban notaries were recent immigrants from the countryside. See Herlihy and Klapisch-Zuber, 1978: 307–308; 1985: 114. Less desirable immigrants, on other hand, were sometimes faced with expulsion from the city or else were forbidden entry in the first place. For a perhaps hyperbolic reference to the expulsion of the poor at Siena in the early fourteenth century, see Pinto, 1978: 322, in which a Florentine grain merchant can be seen praising the ability of his native city to feed even its large indigent population, despite famine conditions, while the Siense expelled its poor. For measures taken to limit the indigent population at Pisa, see Bonaini, 1854–1870: 1, *Breve Pisani Communis*: bk. 3, rub. 51, 436–437, esp. 436.

[14] Land ownership can enhance opportunities for seasonal and other short-term migration when absence from the land is not likely to result in the loss of the land, but possession of immovable property discourages longer-term migration and especially permanent immigration. See Standing, 1981: 176.

reality. The notion that such immigration facilitated the increasing interdependence between the rural and urban sectors in the territory of Florence fails to consider the fact that the evidence in question almost entirely consists of notarial acts concerning the conveyance of landed property. The bourgeoisie and the more noble classes figure prominently in the extant documentation while those at the lower ends of the social spectrum are virtually absent. The overwhelming prevalence of the landowning classes among those who can be seen to be immigrating from the countryside of Florence and into the city in the thirteenth century therefore should not be regarded as necessarily indicative of the prevailing migration patterns. In view of the nature of the surviving evidence, it is very likely that poor and dependent cultivators are not adequately represented. In the early fifteenth century, a period illuminated by the far more comprehensive documentation of the Florentine *Catasto* of 1427–1430, only a small proportion of the recent immigrants in Florence were possessed of significant resources, and even these immigrants were typically recruited from the more important towns and villages in the countryside. Most of the immigrants in Florence came from among the rural poor and destitute (Herlihy and Klapisch-Zuber, 1978: 316–320; 1985: 113–114).

III. Undocumented immigration

A servile component in the thirteenth century immigrations from the countryside to the cities in Tuscany is nevertheless suggested in statutes and treaties that inhibited the ability of serfs to acquire citizenship. A statute promulgated at Lucca even before the end of the first quarter of the thirteenth century explicitly prohibited serfs from acquiring citizenship, and other potential citizens were required to hold property in the city (Vaccari, 1926: 83–86, esp. 85; De Stefani, 1894: 253–255, esp. 254). Pisan statutes of the early thirteenth century stipulated that the mobility of peasants living within the city walls and in the immediately surrounding suburbs was not to be restricted, except voluntarily, but the abandonment of the land by peasants in the deeper countryside was expressly forbidden (Vaccari, 1926: 86–91). In 1225, Florence negotiated a treaty with San Gimignano that prohibited either city from granting citizenship rights to serfs from the territory of the other city before the serf had spent ten years in continuous residence in the host city (Santini, 1895: *Miscellanea*, no. 23, 1225 November 19, 390–391).[15] The mere existence of statutes and treaties inhibiting the mobility of serfs indeed suggests that the flight of serfs from their stations on rural estates indeed may have constituted something of a problem for rural landowners. After the middle of the thirteenth century, it is even possible to observe large landowners in the Florentine countryside successfully pursuing fugitive serfs through the courts in the city (Santini, 1952, no. 192, 1255 January 21 and February 25, 399–400; no. 197, 1255 February 17 and 25, 403–404).

[15] It is likely that this clause was designed to discourage immigration from San Gimignano and its environs to Florence rather than the other way around. The text of the treaty strongly suggests that San Gimignano made the clause a condition for the repayment a large debt that it owed to Florence. Requirements from five to ten years of continuous residence in the city for newcomers before becoming eligible for citizenship were standard in north-central Italy in the thirteenth century for immigrants at the lower end of the social spectrum.

In the later thirteenth century, Florence actually liberated the serfs in its territory *en masse*, but the emancipation of the serfs is typically seen as an instrument employed by the commune to extend urban influence in the countryside rather than to encourage the immigration of labour into the city.[16] The degree to which the liberation of the serfs in the territory of Florence may have borne upon migration patterns remains a matter of conjecture, but it is worth noting that the liberation of serfs elsewhere was intended not to attract labour to the city but actually to discourage the abandonment of the land. The collective enfranchisement of the serfs in the territory of Bologna in 1257, for example, was motivated above all by fiscal exigencies, and particularly by the necessity to limit the flow of immigrants from the countryside and the loss of tax revenue that such population movements entailed (Vaccari, 1926: 100–110; Luzzatto, 1939: 197; Pini, 1978: 376–390, esp. 381–389). The establishment of new towns in the Florentine countryside beginning in the later thirteenth and early fourteenth centuries also may have been designed at least in part as a means by which to stem the tide of immigrants from the countryside and into the city (Pinto, 1984: 27).[17]

Undocumented immigrants from the lower strata of rural society nevertheless must have accounted for a considerable share of the growth in the urban population at Florence. They probably swelled not only the ranks of the labourers in the three hundred woollen textiles workshops in the city around the year 1308 (Villani, 1823: bk. 11, chap. 94), but they also may have accounted for a large proportion of the 17,000 indigent reported to have been in the city in 1330 by Villani (Villani, 1823: bk. 10, chap. 162). The documentation for Florence in the second half of the thirteenth certainly demonstrates that skilled

[16] The liberation of the serfs in the territory of Florence in 1289 was enacted only after communal officials in Florence were notified by ambassadors from several communities in the Mugello that the cathedral chapter in Florence had expressed its intention to alienate proprietarial holdings in the Mugello on which the tenants had owed annual services to the Ubaldini. The manoeuvres of the Florentine commune in this particular instance have been interpreted as an effort to limit the extension of the seigneurial power of the Ubaldini lords in the Mugello. See Vaccari, 1926: 112–122; Magna, 1982: 55–58; Luzzatto, 1939: 197. Evidence of the circumstances that gave rise to the emancipation can be found in Ildefonso di San Luigi, 1770–1789: 9, no. 17, [1289 July 30], 299–301, esp. 209; for the resulting provision that ostensibly liberated the serfs in the territory of Florence, see 300–301. The act is also published in Rumohr, 1830: pt. 2, no. 1, [1289 August 6], 100–103.

[17] On new towns in the Florentine countryside, see Higounet, 1962; Moretti, 1980. See also Friedman, 1974; 1988. Five new towns in the Florentine countryside were realised in the course of the first half of the fourteenth century. Castelfranco di Sopra, San Giovanni Valdarno, and Terranuova Bracciolini were founded in the upper valley of the river Arno between Figline and Montevarchi, and Firenzuola and Scarperia were founded north of the city, although it must be acknowledged that Scarperia existed as a market town already in the later twelfth century. Other foundations were planned in the valley of the river Ambra, just below the Passo della Consuma, on the Colla di Casaglia, and at Pian d'Albero from as early as 1285, but they never came to complete fruition. Firenzuola and Scarperia were established, or re-established, as a means by which to counter the seigneurial power of the Ubaldini lords in the Mugello and to provide greater security for travellers along the trunk routes between Florence and Bologna. The new foundations in the upper Arno valley were designed to facilitate the movement of staple foodstuffs to Florence.

and semi-skilled labourers were immigrating from the countryside and into the city, though the movement of unskilled labour towards the city has remained for the most part invisible.[18]

IV. Population movements in Tuscany

Rural-urban migration in pre-industrial Europe generally occurred over relatively short distances, with most immigrants rarely venturing beyond the nearest large town.[19] Immigration into Florence likewise came mostly from the immediately surrounding countryside, which is to say from the dioceses of Florence and Fiesole, but large cities such as Florence were able to attract immigrants from a much broader area. The languid growth of other major Tuscan towns from about the beginning of the second quarter of the thirteenth century in the face of continued rapid growth at Florence indeed suggests that Florence was absorbing much of the surplus labour immigration from the territories of other towns in Tuscany.

From the middle of the thirteenth century and until the Black Death, for example, the population density in the countryside of Pistoia was diminishing while the urban population remained virtually stagnant from 1219 through the thirteenth and early fourteenth centuries. This suggests that many immigrating peasants were not merely abandoning the countryside of Pistoia for the city but rather that they were abandoning the territory of Pistoia completely (Herlihy, 1967a: 56–77). Pisa appears to have attracted a greater

[18] The surviving evidence for Florence leaves much room for additional research, and the work thus far undertaken on migration into the city has merely scratched the surface. Maria Daniela Nenci was able to identify 1340 immigrants in Florence over the course of the second half of the thirteenth century. Artisans and apprentices were most numerous during the decade from 1291 to 1300, but much of the apparent increase in their numbers probably reflects the extant documentation, which swells towards the end the thirteenth century. The disparity favouring the last decade of the century is nevertheless more pronounced among artisans and apprentices than among the population of identifiable immigrants as a whole. The area of the city that received most of the identifiable immigration was the Oltrarno, but this again reflects the fact that the Oltrarno is the best documented area of the city in the second half of the thirteenth century. See Nenci, 1981. Research on labour migration in the region of Montpellier between 1293 and 1348, on the basis onomastic evidence, has identified sixty-seven out of a total of 208 contracts of apprenticeship or work that concern recent immigrants, which is to say 32.21%. About half of these immigrants had come from within a radius of fifty kilometres, and nearly 75% of them had come from within a one hundred kilometre radius. Immigrants from within a fifty kilometre radius were concentrated in the food trades, artisinal occupations, and menial labour. Artisans constituted an almost equal proportion of the immigrants from both within and beyond the fifty kilometre radius, but immigrants from farther afield were more likely to be engaged in either retail or wholesale merchandising. See Reyerson, 1979: 266–268. It should be noted, however, that even these immigrants were not common labourers, and the mere fact that their transfers to city are documented renders these cases somewhat exceptional.

[19] As already noted above, about half of the new immigrants in Montpellier between 1293 and 1348 came from within a fifty kilometre radius, and nearly 75% came from within one hundred kilometres, but more than 25% of the new immigrants came from beyond one hundred kilometres. See again Reyerson, 1979: 267.

number of immigrants from its surrounding countryside (Herlihy, 1958: 39–42, 124–125), but the most recent research on urban demography at Pisa suggests that the urban population may have registered little significant growth after about 1228 (Salvatori, 1994: 109–123). Immigration from the countryside of Pisa and into the city was either sufficient only to replenish natural losses or else was offset by emigration from the city of Pisa itself to other cities.[20]

The attraction of Florence was perhaps most sharply felt in nearby Prato, where the decline of the rural population was matched by demographic loss in the city. The population in the countryside of Prato was in continuous decline from about 1290 and until the Black Death, but it is abundantly clear that losses in the rural population were not fuelling urban demographic expansion at Prato. The urban population of Prato registered slight growth only in the last decade of the thirteenth century and during the first years of the fourteenth century, but the population in the city declined markedly from about 1305 (Herlihy and Klapisch-Zuber, 1978: 166–171; 1985: 61–64). The returns on papal tithes in the later thirteenth and early fourteenth centuries further suggest a considerable degree of depopulation throughout rural Tuscany (Osheim, 1976).[21]

---

[20] The period of maximum expansion at Pisa, on the basis of a variety of factors, was probably during the eleventh and twelfth centuries rather than the thirteenth century. The mid-twelfth century walls were never superseded by walls enclosing a larger space during the ensuing two centuries, and indeed the enclosed area of the city underwent little change even until the beginning of the twentieth century. Construction within the walls appears to have been most intense during the second half of the twelfth century, and despite some encroachment on the open spaces within the walls after 1200, the basic structure of Pisan urban topography was definitively rendered by the beginning of the thirteenth century. The political demography of the city may have been less ambitious than that of other north-central Italian cities in attracting certain classes of immigrants, especially those willing to undertake the heavy labour of the urban workshops. Moreover, justifiable doubts have been raised not only about the arguments on which population figures as great as 50,000 have been proposed for Pisa in the later thirteenth and early fourteenth centuries, but also about the methodology employed to arrive at such exorbitant figures. If the rate of population decline at Pisa had been similar to the admittedly steep rate of decline at Prato between the beginning of the fourteenth century and 1427–1430, then the maximum medieval population of Pisa at the end of the thirteenth century would have been about 31,440. If the demographic regression at Pisa was more along the lines of the milder rate of decline observable at Florence, however, then the Pisan population at the end of the thirteenth century would have been only about 24,000. By either measure, the urban population of Pisa around the year 1300 was not very much different from the figure between 24,000 and 27,000 inhabitants recently calculated by Enrica Salvatori for the year 1228. See Salvatori, 1994: 109–123, esp. 120. On the absence of any observable change in the urban topography of Pisa after the later twelfth century, see Redi, 1991: 140; Garzella, 1991: 210–248, esp. 242–243. On the eleventh and twelfth centuries as the period of maximum expansion at Pisa, see Cristiani, 1962: 162–231, esp. 164. On the political demography of Pisa, see again Cristiani, 1962: 180–187. On the rate of population decline at Pisa between the beginning of the fourteenth century and 1427–1430, see Herlihy and Klapisch-Zuber, 1978: 179; 1985: 71–72.

[21] Duane Osheim used the records for the collection of papal tithes in Tuscany during the periods from 1274 to 1280 and from 1296 to 1304 to argue that the traditional organisation of rural parish churches in Tuscany was being undermined by demographic regression in the countryside owing to rural-urban migration. The diminishing population of rural parishes throughout Tuscany

Within the territory of Florence itself, the city of Florence was not the only beneficiary of immigration from the more rural zones to more urbanised zones. Infrastructural development and improved drainage conditions on the plains and in the river valleys in the twelfth and thirteenth centuries helped to precipitate the blossoming of such lowland towns as Castelfiorentino, Certaldo, Empoli, Figline, Montevarchi, Borgo San Lorenzo, and San Piero a Sieve. Some of the communities that had been important seigneurial centres before the year 1200, on the other hand, either had ceased to expand or began to decline in the thirteenth century (Plesner, 1938: 5–11, 92–101; Fiumi, 1957–1959: pt. 2, 469–473, esp. 471).[22] The towns that benefited most from the realignment of the population in the territory became centres of artisan activity (Prunai, 1983; Masi, 1934: 213–217; ASF, *Diplomatico*, Passignano, 1233 February 24). The expansion of the lowland towns situated particularly on the periphery of Florentine territory no doubt came at the expense of population loss in the more marginal areas of the Florentine countryside that were poorly served by changes in the infrastructure, but their growth was also a product of depopulation in neighbouring regions.

Population movements within the territory of Florence and indeed within Tuscany as a whole were nevertheless most conspicuously oriented towards the city of Florence itself, and mechanisms of both incentive and coercion were operating to precipitate such movements. Perhaps the best evidence for incentives to encourage the immigration of artisans into a major city comes from Bologna in the early thirteenth century, thanks to the fortuitous survival of a particular set of records. The communal government in Bologna together with merchant entrepreneurs offered grants of citizenship, fiscal immunities, interest-free loans, rent-free workshops and residences, and machinery to textile artisans who agreed to live and work in the city for twenty years (Mazzaoui, 1967–1968: 276–284; Mazzaoui, 1984: 523–524; Pini, 1978: 378–379).[23] Closer to Florence, the commune of Prato likewise granted artisan immigrants from Verona fiscal exemptions, and they also offered them protection against creditors from their native city (Mazzaoui,

---

rendered it impossible for many parish churches to pay their ecclesiastical dues on a regular basis. The research conducted by Osheim assumes a positive correlation between the frequency of non-payment on papal tithes and the relative degree of demographic regression. On this basis, the evidence suggests that the depopulation of the countryside was most severe in the dioceses of Pisa, Fiesole, and Pistoia, respectively. The diocese of Florence was very clearly the least adversely affected by demographic regression, but the Florentine hinterland included the dioceses of both Florence and Fiesole. When the dioceses of Florence and Fiesole are considered in tandem, they still constitute the region least adversely affected, but much of the disparity between Florence and Siena, the next least adversely affected diocese, dissolves.

[22] A similar relationship between infrastructural development and the redistribution of the rural population between highland and lowland areas is also documented in the territory of Pistoia. According to Herlihy, only about 31% of the rural population in the territory of Pistoia dwelled on the plain and in the low hills in 1244, but the figure had increased to 40% by 1344 and to nearly 50% by 1427, despite demographic regression in the rural zones of the territory as a whole over the same period. See Herlihy, 1967a: 50–51. On demographic regression in the countryside of Pistoia, see again Herlihy, 1967a: 56–72. On the descent of settlement from hills to the plain in the territory of Perugia and infrastructural development in the Tiber valley, see Blashei, 1976: 39.

[23] Among those recruited into the woollen textiles industry at Bologna by such means were twelve Florentines. See Davidsohn, 1896–1908: 3, no. 988, 1231 February 13, 205

1984: 529). If any incentives of this particular variety were offered to encourage the immigration of artisans into Florence, no record of them has yet come to light, but there may be further scope for research on the topic in the registers of urban notaries from the later thirteenth and early fourteenth centuries.

V. The woollen textiles industry

The introduction of restrictive measures directed against independent textile producers in the countryside of Florence may have provided a coercive element of encouragement. The earliest surviving statutes of the wool guild in Florence, dating from 1317–1319, included numerous provisions that effectively inhibited the ability of independent artisans in the countryside to participate fully in the expanding market (Kotel'nikova, 1976). It was prohibited, for example, to sell textile products in Florence that were manufactured outside of the city of Florence or its territory, though exceptions were made for certain imported textiles (Enriques Agnoletti, 1940: bk. 2, rub. 37, 125–126). All salaried textile workers in the city or its suburbs, moreover, were required to be under the supervision of a master of the wool guild, who were based in the city (Enriques Agnoletti, 1940: bk. 3, rub. 2, 147–149). The fulling process was also concentrated in the city, and urban fulling mills were permitted to treat only the wool of masters of the wool guild or else wool that had been approved by the guild, though once again exceptions were made for northern European and Milanese wool (Enriques Agnoletti, 1940: bk. 2, rub. 25, 119–120). These proscriptions probably were instituted by the guild partly to maintain control over the quality of woollen textile production in Florence, but they also must have functioned to inhibit the rural manufacture of woollen textiles for the market.[24]

If these measures were indeed intended to attract manufacturing to the city, they very well may have been superfluous. Florence was particularly well-suited to become a centre of textile production. The river Arno provided Florence with a lengthy stretch of consistently fast-moving water, which was necessary for the fulling process.[25] Already by the middle of the thirteenth century, moreover, the emerging market for woollen textiles in the city was attracting business to Florence. In 1251, the bishop of Florence granted license to the members of the order of the *Humiliates* of San Michele di Alessan-

---

[24] Kotel'nikova has suggested that the intention of these proscriptions was to undermine rural competition against the Florentine woollen textiles industry. See Kotel'nikova, 1976. It is ultimately impossible, however, to determine the precise motivations underlying the proscriptions against the rural manufacture of woollen textiles for the market in the territory of Florence. It is nevertheless likely that the proscriptions encouraged the concentration of the woollen textiles industry in the city of Florence and its suburbs, and that they probably inhibited the rural production of woollen textiles for the market in all but the more remote areas of the territory of Florence.

[25] The various stages involved in the preparation of woollen textiles are described in Munro, 1988; Castegneto, 1996: 166–178. The considerable merits of the river Arno and another waterway, probably the torrent Mugnone, with respect to the service that they rendered for the woollen textiles industry were duly noted by an anonymous fourteenth century Florentine chronicler. See Frey, 1885: 119–123, esp. 120: 'Hoc quoque fluuium aquam suauem, ubi suauis exigitur, et riuus alius iuxta partem aliam civitatis aquam rigidam ad lauandas et extergendas lanas et alia necessaria non impetuose, sed abundanter producunt'.

dria to transfer their convent from the countryside of Florence to a location in the western suburbs of the city where they had already begun to manufacture woollen textiles more than ten years earlier. Most significantly, the record of the episcopal concession explicitly states that the purpose of the transfer was to enable the *Humiliates* to manufacture and to market their woollen textiles more easily, and to be less dependent on charity (Santini, 1952: *Miscellanea*, no. 31, 1251 September 11–13, 293–294).[26]

The arrival of the *Humiliates* in the Florentine suburbs in 1239 and the transfer of their convent to Borgo Ognissanti twelve years laters by no means constituted the introduction of the woollen textiles industry in Florence. On the contrary, the *Humiliates* very clearly had come to the Florentine suburbs to participate more fully in an already burgeoning industry. Partnership contracts dating from late in the first half of the thirteenth century indeed demonstrate that Florentines were investing considerable sums in the woollen textiles industry in Florence already before the *Humiliates* transferred their convent to the Florentine suburbs.[27] From even as early as the later twelfth century, moreover, guilds are attested in Florence that were organised around various aspects of the distribution and production of woollen textiles.[28] The mere existence of such bodies in early thirteenth century Florence by no means attests to a thoroughly developed industry for woollen textiles in the city by the middle of the century, and indeed wool guilds were a common feature in many north-central Italian cities with relatively modest woollen textiles industries, but it at least betrays a necessary level of organisation.

It must be stressed that Florence was no longer the same city in 1251 that it had been a half of a century earlier. By the middle of the thirteenth century, Florence had developed into a bustling medieval metropolis. At the beginning of the thirteenth century, only one bridge crossed the river Arno within the city, but three bridges were now spanning the

---

[26] The *Humiliates* transferred their convent to the western suburbs of Florence from its former location at San Donato a Torri, situated on the right bank of river Arno about ten kilometres east of Florence.

[27] See, for example, Santini, 1895: *Miscellanea*, no. 96, 1244 November 7, 481–482; ASF, *Diplomatico*, Strozziane Uguccione, same date. The contract records the establishment of a partnership by two Florentine investors for the purpose of manufacturing woollen textiles, with the total capital investment amounting to five hundred *libre*.

[28] The merchants of the Callemala, importers of northern textiles, are documented from 1192, and it is perhaps worth noting that the fabrics borne to Florence by these merchants may have provided the woollen textiles industry in Florence with the models that the Florentines sought to replicate. For the earliest reference to the merchants of the Callemala, see Santini, 1895: *Miscellanea*, no. 3, 1192 December 9, 365–367; ASF, *Diplomatico*, Strozziane Uguccione, same date. The wool guild in Florence is specifically attested from 1212, and the consuls of the merchants of the wool guild are documented from 1218. For the first specific reference to the wool guild, see Santini, 1895: *Miscellanea*, no. 12, 1212 June 1, 376; ASF, *Diplomatico*, Riformagioni, same date. For the earliest reference to the consuls of the merchants of the wool guild, see Santini, 1895: *Capitoli*, no. 66, 1218 March 21, 190–192. The wool guild was one of the seven major guilds in Florence in the early thirteenth century, and the rectors of these seven guilds, the *septem rectores qui sunt super capitibus artium*, are mentioned in a document of 1193, which suggests that the Florentine wool guild was in existence already in the later twelfth century. See Santini, 1895: *Capitoli*, no. 20, 1193 July 24, 31–33.

river within the space of about a kilometre already by the middle of the century and a fourth was about to be constructed.[29] Before the year 1240, the mint at Florence had already issued the silver *grossus*, the first known coinage of Florence, which was valued at one Pisan *solidus* and calibrated to issues of the same sort introduced by the mints at Pisa, Siena, and Lucca, perhaps to accommodate the exigencies of intra-regional trade.[30] The Florentine mint was also preparing to issue a new gold coinage, the *florenus*, in order to facilitate international trade. The gold *florenus* was first issued in 1252, and by that time, according to Villani, the urban population of Florence already may have been twice the size of the urban population of Pisa, or perhaps as great as 60,000 (Villani, 1823: bk. 6, chap. 53). The continued growth of Florence had even necessitated by 1258 the expansion of the urban enclosure to embrace the suburbs of San Niccolò, Santo Spirito, and San Frediano in the Oltrarno (Sznura, 1975: 94–97).

Within a few years of the immigration of the *Humiliates* to the western suburb of Borgo Ognissanti, the area was becoming a centre of industrial activity, and the *Humiliates* had invested in several mills on the right bank of the river there (Muendel, 1991: 370). Meanwhile, the abbey at Settimo had embarked upon its own ambitious programme of investment and construction on the river, and their purchases of mills on the river were accompanied by investment in the western quarter of the city in workshops and commercial establishments (Pirillo, 1995; Jones, 1956: 90–91).[31] By the early fourteenth century, investment on the river by the abbey at Settimo may have been so substantial that it precipitated frequent flooding on the right bank and constituted an obstacle for the transport of grain and other merchandise on the river (Pirillo, 1995: 84). Similar developments can be observed on the eastern periphery of the city even before

[29] The second bridge across the Arno after the Ponte Vecchio was the Ponte alla Carraia, constructed between 1218 and 1220. See Villani, 1923: bk. 5, chaps. 41–42. The construction of the third bridge across the Arno in 1237, the Ponte Rubaconte, was evidently accompanied by an ambitious programme of infrastructural development to pave the roads within the city. See Villani, 1823: bk. 6, chap. 24. In the year after the *Humiliates* had received license from the bishop of Florence to undertake the transfer to Borgo Ognissanti, the Ponte di Santa Trinità was constructed to provide the Frescobaldi merchant-bankers easy access to the city and the western suburbs from the Oltrarno where their possessions were concentrated. See Villani, 1923: bk. 6, chap. 50.

[30] There is a substantial bibliography on the *grossi* of the various Tuscan mints. It is generally thought that the five major Tuscan mints were striking *grossi* by the year 1240, that *grossi* were struck first in Pisa by 1231, and probably earlier, and that they were valued at twelve Pisan *denarii*, or one *solidus*. Within a relatively brief space of time, *grossi* were then introduced at Siena, Lucca, Florence, and Arezzo, repectively. See Lopez, 1967; Grierson, 1971–1972; Blomquist, 1986. See also Herlihy, 1954; 1967b. Michael Matzke has suggested that the Pisan *grossus* was first issued in the late twelfth century in connection with a revaluation of the Pisan *solidus*. Around the year 1190, Pisa introduced a new *solidus* of twelve *denarii*, were equivalent to fourteen old *denarii*, and Matzke understood the revaluation as associated with the first issue of the *grossus* in Tuscany. See Matzke, 1993.

[31] Investment by the abbey at Settimo on the left bank the river Arno at Porto di Mezzo, about a kilometre downstream from Ponte a Signa, can be dated from as early as 1217, but investment on the river at Ponte a Signa itself became intense only towards the middle of the century. For investment in the mill as Porto di Mezzo, see ASF, *Diplomatico*, Cestello, 1217 September 13. Investment in commercial property in the western quarter of the city is attested only from the early fourteenth century. See Jones, 1956: 90–91.

the middle of the thirteenth century, where the abbey of San Salvi combined prodigious investment on the river Arno with investment in commercial property between the old walls of the city and the late twelfth century walls (Vannucci, 1963–1964: pt. 2, 33). Farther upstream from Florence on the right bank of the Arno at Girone, the proprietors of a complex of grain mills transformed several of their mills into fulling mills, which they subsequently leased to members of a family that was already prominently involved in the Florentine woollen textiles industry (Hoshino, 1984). Developments of a similar sort were also taking place in the Oltrarno, both in the western portion where the Frescobaldi merchant-banking company was based and in the east around a place called the 'Fonte al Porto' where the monastery of San Niccolò as well as private interests possessed fulling mills (Sznura, 1975: 113). The proliferation of mills particularly on the Arno also may have given rise to significant technological improvements in mill construction that ultimately enhanced productivity in the Florentine woollen textiles industry.[32]

The numerous mills operating along the river Arno within the city of Florence and in its surrounding suburbs already before 1300 in particular attest to the vitality of the Florentine woollen textiles industry in the later thirteenth century. San Salvi was collecting grain rents on at least fourteen floating mills on the river at the port of Tempio, situated in the eastern suburbs of the city at the end of a street called the Corso dei

[32] In Tuscany, Florence appears to have been precocious in the introduction of a new type of mill, the so-called 'molendinum francescum' or French mill. This new type of mill was distinguished from older types above all by an overshot wheel, which is to say by an external vertical wheel propelled by water descending from a small aqueduct into buckets on the wheel itself. Before the advent of French mill technology, vertical mills typically had been propelled by a canal which turned the wheel from below. The French mill was ideally suited to the strong and steady current of water generally found on the Arno and on the lower reaches its larger tributaries. See Muendel, 1984: 225. The first absolutlely secure reference to the French mill in the territory of Florence occurs only in the first quarter of the fourteenth century, but the French mill appears to have come to the territory in tandem with the orbital mill, the *molendinum orbicum*, which can be dated to 1282. Moreover, a reference to a mill at Querceto in 1269 has been tentatively identified as an early example of the French mill. See Muendel, 1984: 217, 225–228. The first specific reference in the evidence for the territory of Florence to a fulling mill of the French type, a *gualchiera francesca*, comes from Razzuolo in the Mugello and occurs in 1333. See Muendel, 1984: 237, and 246, n. 30. On the retention of traditional milling technology in the countrysides of Arezzo, Pistoia, and Prato, see Muendel, 1984: 237–239. On the efficiency of French mills in the grinding of grains and the consequent increase in the value of mill rents, see Muendel, 1984: 229–230. The introduction of the French mill in Florence may have precipitated other technological developments. By 1337, for example, at least one notary in the city itself felt compelled to distinguish between looms of the 'French' type, the *telarium francescum*, and those of the 'Latin' type, the *telarium latinum*. See Muendel, 1984: 236–237, and 246, n. 29. Changes in the institutional organisation of the woollen textiles industry in the later thirteenth and early fourteenth centuries also may have generated economies of practice that rendered the production process more efficient. Certain tasks that had been performed by workers at home were removed to the workshop to facilitate closer supervision of the process, and other tasks were fragmented in order to allow workers to focus their attention on a smaller range of activities. The Florentine wool guild also began to collaborate more closely with the communal administration, and the guild itself became the preserve of wealthy investors. See Cohn, 1978: 9.

Tintori, by the end of the third quarter of the century (Pampaloni, 1973: no. 100, 1273 July 25, 177–179).[33] Another floating mill was anchored just across the river at the port of Camarzio in 1275 (Muendel, 1991: 368), and four suspension mills were leased by San Salvi at Camarzio in 1290 (ASF, *Diplomatico*, Badia di Ripoli, 1290 October 29). The Arno was indeed teeming with mills by the end of the first quarter of the fourteenth century, and it has been possible to identify securely no less than fifteen mills operating on the river within the third circuit of walls established between 1284 and 1326, largely on the basis of a series of court depositions. This is a very conservative figure, however, and there were no doubt others on the river within the urban enclosure, and many more just beyond the walls (Muendel, 1991: 370–371).

Of course, not all of the mills operating on the river Arno within the city of Florence or in its eastern and western suburbs were used for processing wool. Many mills were no doubt used exclusively for grinding the prodigious quantities of local and imported grain that were coming into the city to feed the swelling urban population, and indeed urban and suburban millers who leased their mills typically paid their rents in grain.[34] The evidence suggests, however, that the preparation of wool was concentrated increasingly in the city and its suburbs, and some urban and suburban mills may have combined fulling and grinding operations in varying degrees to service both the woollen textiles industry and the market for staple foodstuffs. Many of the mills introduced on the river especially after the middle of the thirteenth century, such as those in San Niccolò, were nevertheless dedicated exclusively to the fulling process (Sznura, 1975: 113). The documentation also suggests that the use of rural mills for the preparation of wool may have declined from the later twelfth century.[35] In addition to evidence for the concentration of

---

[33] See also Davidsohn, 1896–1908, 4: 444–445; ASF, *Diplomatico*, Badia di Ripoli, 1271 July 14. By the later thirteenth century, there were certainly three and probably four types of mill in use in the territory of Florence: the horizontal mill, the suspension mill, the floating mill, and probably also the orbital mill. See Muendel, 1981; 1984.

[34] For evidence of rent payment by suburban millers in grain, see again Pampaloni, 1973: no. 100, 1273 July 25, 177–179; on the payment of land-use taxes by urban millers, see Muendel, 1991: 371.

[35] Despite the increasing wealth of the documentation for the Florentine countryside in the thirteenth century, for example, fulling mills specifically designated as such are actually somewhat more richly documented in the twelfth century. My own investigations are far from exhaustive, but I have identified only four fulling mills in the Florentine countryside specifically identified as *gualchiere* in the thirteenth century. For evidence of one thirteenth century *gualchiera* near Legri in the valley of the torrent Marina, see ASF, *Diplomatico*, Cestello, 1201 January 13, 1202 February 21. Another thirteenth century *gualchiera* was situated at Bucine in valley of the torrent Ambra. See ASF, *Diplomatico*, Strozziane Uguccione, 1241 October 15. In the Chianti, there was a *gualchiera* on the torrent Dudda near Ponte a Stielle. See Pagliai, 1909: no. 543, 13th century, 245. The fourth *gualchiera* that I have been able to identify was on the river Greve near Impruneta. See Muzzi and Nenci, 1988: no. 109, 1279 August 1, 219, citing ASF, *Notarile antecosimiano* 1104, folio 14r. The evidence for fulling mills in the Florentine countryside in the twelfth century is by no means overwhelming, but my research has identified seven different *gualchiere* in the less abundant twelfth century documentation. Two of these, one situated on the torrent Cesto near Figline and another on the river Pesa near Sambuca, appear in the sources for the twelfth century as *gualchiere* but simply as a *molendina* when they reappear in the thirteenth century sources. For the twelfth century references to the *gualchiera* on the Cesto, see ASF, *Diplo-*

fulling mills in the city and its suburbs, the proliferation of commercial establishments in the urban records from the later thirteenth and early fourteenth centuries further supports the notion of a rapidly maturing manufacturing sector in Florence, driven largerly be developments in the woollen textiles industry.[36]

VI. Florentine trade

There can be little doubt that the Florentine woollen textiles industry was well developed already by 1275, and indeed probably by about 1250. The earlier development of the woollen textiles industry in Florence is much more obscure, but the evidence for Florentine commercial relations at least suggests an emerging export industry for woollen textiles in the city already in the early thirteenth century. Fabrics manufactured in Florence were being exported to Venice from as early as 1225, to Palermo from 1237, to Macerata

matico, Badia di Passignano, 1167 February 11, 1183 May 11 For thirteenth century references to the same mill as a *molendinum* rather than a *gualchiera*, see ASF, *Diplomatico*, Badia di Passignano, 1253 January 4. The 1183 reference makes it clear, moreover, that the *gualcheria* in question had ceased operation as a fulling mill by that time. For the *gualchiera* on the Pesa later identified simply as a *molendinum*, see ASF, *Diplomatico*, Badia di Passignano, 1179 March 24, 1214 September 8. Both of these mills are attested earlier in the twelfth century simply as *molendina*. The change between the later twelfth and the early thirteenth centuries may have been strictly terminological, and notaries may have referred to all mills increasingly as *molendina*. An early fifteenth century tax register of the mills in the Florentine countryside nevertheless goes some distance towards confirming the suspicion that the fulling process was increasingly centred in the city. Of the seven hundred and twenty-six mills that are documented in the Florentine countryside in the early fifteenth century, only sixty were engaged in the preparation of wool, and forty-five of these combined their fulling operations with the grinding of grain. Moreover, most of these fulling mills were located in remote parts of the Florentine countryside, which would have rendered access to urban and suburban fulling mills difficult. Competition between these remote fulling mills and their urban and suburban counterparts also would have been negligible. See Muendel, 1981: 91–102, esp. 98–99, 101–102.

36 Urban commercial establishments typically appear in documentary sources simply as *botteghe*, or in exceptional cases as *fundachi*. The *botteghe* were for the most part workshops, and the *fundachi* were probably warehouses appertaining to the larger merchant-banking companies. It is usually impossible to determine whether or not the *botteghe* and *fundachi* in Florence appertained in some manner to the woollen textiles industry, but is likely that many of the *botteghe* appearing in the documentary evidence were among the three hundred woollen textiles workshops to which Villani referred in his chronicle. The Del Bene merchant-banking family, which was involved in the woollen textiles industry in Florence both as an importer of northern European fabrics and as a producer of domestic cloth, already owned at least three *fundachi* in Piazza Santo Spirito in the Oltrarno by 1299. In the early fourteenth century, the Del Bene were leasing several *botteghe* in the square as well as other commercial and residential properties to labourers in various crafts, predominated somewhat by workers in the woollen textiles industry. See Sapori, 1955, 1: 305–352, esp. 305–309. The proliferation of *botteghe* in Florence in the later thirteenth and early fourteenth centuries is at least partly a reflection of greater documentary survival for the city itself and its suburbs especially after about 1275. Both the city of Florence and its immediately surrounding suburbs were very likely punctuated with numerous *botteghe* of various sorts already before 1250, but only a few of these urban and suburban *botteghe* are visible in the much more limited records for the early thirteenth century.

from 1245, and to Lucca from 1246. Products of Florentine manufacture have also been detected in the records of Genoa and Ragusa from just after the middle of the thirteenth century (Hoshino, 1980: 66; 1983: 184). Commercial treaties negotiated by Florence and Perugia in 1218 and again in 1235 further suggest an active trade in textiles between these two cities before 1250.[37] By about 1270, moreover, Florentine cloth merchants were the most prominent of all the groups of foreign merchants operating on the textile market in Bologna, where Florentine merchant-bankers had been conducting business from at least as early as the beginning of the thirteenth century.[38] Florence had also established trading relations with both Faenza and Imola in the early years of the thirteenth century.[39] Florentine trading relations with Orvieto date from at least as early as 1229, when the commune of Florence granted the citizens of Orvieto a ten year exemption from all taxes and tolls in the city of Florence and in the surrounding suburbs, suggesting an active commerce between the two cities by that time (Fumi, 1884: no. 189, 1229 March 9, 118).[40] In the early fourteenth century, raw wool from England, Sardinia, Tunisia, and

[37] The treaties establish customs duties to be paid on woollen textiles, among other things. For the treaty of 1218, see Santini, 1895: *Capitoli*, no. 66, 1218 March 21, 190–192; for the later treaty, see Bartoli Langeli, 1983–1991: 1, no. 148, 1235 March 14, 318–326. The earlier treaty suggests that Florence initially acquired access to external markets by accepting conditions that clearly favoured the other party. The conditions of the later treaty favour neither Florence nor Perugia, which suggests that the bargaining position of Florence had improved in the interim.

[38] Trading relations between Florence and Bologna are documented from 1203. A treaty dating from 1200 between Florence and the Ubaldini lords granting to the merchants of Florence safe passage 'in the usual manner' through Ubaldini territory between Florence and Bologna suggests that commercial relations between the two cities had been established even earlier. For evidence of trading relations between Florence and Bologna dating from 1203, see Muratori, 1738–1752: 4, 1203 September 13, cols. 453–454; Salvioli, 1784–1795: 2, pt. 2, no. 353, 1203 September 13, 248. For the agreement between Florence and the Ubaldini lords, see Santini, 1895: *Capitoli*, no. 32, 1200 October 15, 59–60. Commercial relations between Florence and Bologna are abundantly attested throughout the thirteenth century. On the prominence of Florentine cloth merchants on the Bolognese market in the third quarter of the thirteenth century, see Cuomo, 1977: 336–339, 350–352. Customs records for Bologna from 1264 mention only Milanese and northern European textiles, but Bolognese tariff data from 1279 and 1288 suggest a regular traffic in Florentine woollen textiles through Bologna during the last quarter of the thirteenth century. See Hoshino, 1980: 39, and tbl. 1, 50–51, esp. 51. By 1279, Florentine merchants established in Bologna had codified their own set of statutes, and the statutes suggest that the Florentines were selling a wide variety of fabrics in Bologna to both Bolognese clients and foreigners. See Gaudenzi, 1888.

[39] Florentine commercial relations with Faenza are attested from 1204, and the language of the document in question strongly suggests that woollen textiles were among the more conspicuous articles of trade. See Santini, 1895: *Capitoli*, no. 55, [1204], 144–147. The document is undated, but Florence was represented in the treaty by Ildebrandinus Cavalcantis, *consul Florentie*, who is known to have held an office as Florentine consul in 1204. See Santini, 1895: xlvii–xlviii. Relations between Florence and Imola are attested from 1238, and the treaty in question is published in Pini, 1975: no. 2, 1238 March 22, 95–96, citing Biblioteca centrale di Imola, Archivio storico, *Pergamene*, mazzo 1, no. 90. See also Davidsohn, 1896–1908: 3, no. 18, 6.

[40] Like the 1218 treaty between Florence and Perugia, the 1229 treaty between Florence and Orvieto suggests that Florence accepted terms weighted in the favour of Orvieto in order to achieve access to the Orvieto market. The strategy evidently paid dividends. By the end of the thirteenth century, Florentine woollen textiles constituted about 52.5% of all imported woollen

western North Africa was routinely transported to Florence on river boats that plyed the river Arno from Pisa, and they returned to Pisa bearing woollen textiles manufactured in Florence, Prato, Romagna, and northern Europe, which were probably destined for the southern Italian market.[41]

Bologna, Faenza, Orvieto, and Perugia clearly had become among the more important trading partners of Florence already by the middle of the thirteenth century, and they all shared several common charateristics. All four of these cities appear to have been net exporters of grain for most of the thirteenth century, which no doubt complemented the increasing dependence of Florence on grain imports to supplement domestic production, especially after about 1250.[42] In addition, all four of the cities were situated within the Papal States, and they all shared with Florence a Guelf political orientation. The common Guelf allegiances of these cities constitutes an exceedingly important factor in the development of Florentine trade especially beyond the frontiers of Tuscany, but also within the region. Florence had been the sole supporter of the papacy in Tuscany during the investiture controversy in the eleventh century, and it had remained a steadfast advocate of the papacy from that time. By the early thirteenth century, the consistency

---

textiles sold on the market at Orvieto, and from about 81.6 to 89.4% of all fabrics imported from within the Italian regions. See Hoshino, 1980: 68–69, and tbl. 6, 98–99, citing ASOrvieto, *Archivio notarile* 1, Registro del 1299.

[41] Genoese merchants were bringing substantial quantities of English wool to Florence by 1317, no doubt by way of the port of Pisa, and English wool destined for Florence was clearly going through the port of Pisa in 1327 and again in 1329. See Davidsohn, 1896–1908: 3, no. 691, 1317 October 29, 136; no. 887, 1327 March 30, 179; no. 944, 1329 February 13, 187. For imports and exports of raw wool and textile products at Florence during a period of almost a year in 1320 and 1321, see the table in Ciasca, 1927: 774–777, esp. 774–775, no. 20, 1320 November 16 – 1321 October 15.

[42] Precise figures are unobtainable, but it is reasonable to assume that net food imports in Florence during much of the thirteenth century amounted to 5–10% of total food consumption in the territory, tending more from the lower margin to the upper margin with passage of time. The first concrete figures from which to draw inferences about food imports come from a passage in the memoir of Domenico Lenzi, a Florentine grain merchant, written in May of 1329. According to Lenzi, grain production in the territory of Florence was sufficient to satisfy the food supply requirements of Florence for only five months per year. For Davidsohn, the passage indicated that grain production in the Florentine countryside was able to satisfy the total grain requirement of both the city and the countryside only five months per year. See Davidsohn, 1977, 5: 238; Davidsohn, 1896–1908, 4: 307–315, esp. 312–313. Giuliano Pinto has disagreed, however, suggesting that the author was referring only to the proportion of the urban grain requirement that was satisfied by production in the countryside, and he has taken this to mean that the needs of the countryside itself were for the most part met entirely. On the basis of an urban population of 120,000, a rural population of 300,000, and an average requirement of twelve Florentine *staria* per person per year, and assuming that the food supply requirements of the rural population were met entirely, the shortfall would have been about 16.67%. Scholars have generally agreed that Lenzi was referring to ordinary times, but 1329 was a famine year, and it is more likely that the entry reflects the conditions that were prevailing at the moment. Moreover, Florence was at or very near maximum expansion at the time that Lenzi was writing, and net food imports may have constituted a somewhat higher proportion of total food consumption in the territory than they did during the thirteenth century. See Pinto, 1978: 75–79, 317, n. 1.

of Florentine support for the papacy had earned Florentine merchant-bankers the privilege to serve as the principal bankers of the papal camera (Lunt, 1934, 1: 51–56).[43] Within Tuscany, moreover, Florence was clearly the primary benificiary of what Hoshino has called the 'guelfizzazione' of the Italian cities. Florentine merchant-bankers enjoyed privileged access to markets in Guelf cities, and the products of the Florentine woollen textiles industry were consumed throughout Guelf cities of north-central Italy (Hoshino, 1980: 67). The 'guelfizzazione' of Italy gained momentum in the second half of the thirteenth century after the Angevin conquest of southern Italy in 1266, which afforded Florentine merchant-bankers improved access to southern Italian markets.

Florence enjoyed especially close relations with Bologna, and the relationship between the two cities was in many respects complementary. Like Florence, Bologna produced woollen textiles for export, but rather than compete against exports from Florence, the Bolognese industry specialised in a higher grade of fabric than the coarse and less expensive fabrics that were produced for export in Florence before about 1319. It is also worth noting that Bologna was actually the only Guelf city to which Florentine merchants were able to travel without traversing the territory of a rival city-state in Tuscany. Moreover, the two cities lay on opposite escarpments of the Apennine chain. The mountains often functioned as a natural barrier to climatological disturbances affecting agricultural production, with the result that Tuscany and Romagna only rarely suffered from severe subsistence crises concurrently.

VII. Productivity

Industrial development in the city of Florence especially after about 1175 helped to attract surplus labour from the countryside and facilitated a progressive realignment of the labour force between the agrarian and non-agrarian sectors in the territory as a whole. The immigration of surplus labour from the Florentine countryside and into the city itself in turn led to a more efficient distribution of labour between the two sectors and generated substantial improvements in productivity. The development of the woollen textiles industry in Florence in particular provided the city with an export product that it was able to exchange for the staple foodstuffs necessary to fuel urban growth. Urban demographic expansion in pre-industrial Europe was contingent upon an adequate supply of vital resources, particularly staple foodstuffs such as grain. The development of an export industry in Florence afforded the city more or less regular access to imported foodstuffs, which in turn enabled the urban population of Florence to grow beyond the dimensions that agricultural production in the Florentine countryside was able to sustain efficiently. Urban growth in Florence from the later twelfth century through the second quarter of the fourteenth century is in fact a reflection of the steady improvement in overall productivity in the territory as whole over the same period.

[43] The involvement of Florentine merchant-bankers in the collection of papal revenues provided the merchant-bankers with periodic injections of large sums of capital, which they were often able to use temporarily in their own enterprises. The papal curia began to exercise stricter control over the amount of time that collections on behalf of the papacy could remain at the disposal of papal bankers only sometime after the beginning of the fourteenth century.

In poorly documented economies such as that Florence, evidence for demographic change provides usually the only means by which to measure productivity growth. In a closed economy, the urbanisation ratio in a given urban centre serves as a reflection of per capita agricultural production in the agrarian sector. Surplus agricultural production in the agrarian sector will provide the means by which to satisfy the food supply requirements of the non-agrarian sector, and the level of surplus production will determine the maximum size of the non-agrarian sector. An increase in the size of the non-agrarian sector thus implies a correlative improvement in per capita agricultural production in the agrarian sector while also providing a measure of the scale of change (Wrigley, 1985: 683–684).

Of course, it is never possible to isolate perfectly the non-agrarian sector from the agrarian sector in any developing medieval economy. A small segment of the rural population no doubt was engaged primarily if not exclusively in non-agrarian activities, just as some urban residents abandoned the city each morning to undertake agricultural work in the nearby fields, returning to the city again only at the conclusion of the labours. The proportion of the population resident in the primary urban centre of the particular region nevertheless provides an adequate approximation of the relationship between the two sectors (Wrigley, 1985: 683–684). Neither is it possible to sustain that the economy of Florence was closed even at the beginning of the thirteenth century. Food imports in Florence probably constituted between five and ten per cent of total food consumption in the territory of Florence under normal conditions. Adjusting for imports, however, such evidence as there is suggests that labour productivity in Tuscany as a whole, with Florence as its principal urban centre, grew at a rate between 0.15 and 0.35 per cent per year over the course of the thirteenth century (Persson, 1991: 124–143, esp. 133–139). Within the territory of Florence itself, it is very likely that the annual rate of productivity growth during the thirteenth century was even higher.

A means by which to conceptualise productivity growth in the countryside of Florence during the thirteenth century is through a purely theoretical model that takes into account the changing relationship between the total amount of land in the territory, the total population, and the distribution of the population between the city and the surrounding countryside. The actual extent of Florentine control over its subject territory at any given point in the thirteenth century is by no means certain, and indeed the precise dimensions of the territory are equally difficult to determine. Practically speaking, the territory theoretically subject to Florence in the thirteenth century was comprised of the dioceses of Florence and Fiesole. The medieval boundaries of the two dioceses correspond very roughly to the modern frontiers of the Florentine province, but Florentine control over the two dioceses was clearly incomplete at the beginning of the thirteenth century. Over the course of the century, Florence extended its control over the two dioceses and also began to encroach upon neighbouring territories. For present purposes, however, the figure of 390,000 hectares for the land area of the modern province may be employed to delineate the total land area in the territory of Florence throughout the thirteenth century. The figure actually needs neither to be accurate nor to account for qualitative differences in terrain, and indeed a completely hypothetical figure would suffice. With respect to the population in the territory of Florence and the distribution of the population between the city and the surrounding countryside, it has already be suggested that the urban population of Florence was probably about 15,000 around the year 1200. The rural population at the same time cannot have been less than 125,000, which gives an urbanisation ratio of 10.71%. By the end of the thirteenth century, the urban population was probably about 105,000, and the rural population been about 260,000, yielding an urbanisation ratio of 28.76%.[44]

On the basis of these figures, it may be surmised that the ratio between the total amount of land in the territory of Florence in hectares and the size of the total population at the beginning of the thirteenth century was about 2.78 hectares to each inhabitant. At the same time, about 125,000 rural inhabitants were producing enough foodstuffs to feed a total population in the territory of about 140,000, which is to say that each rural inhabitant was producing foodstuffs sufficient for about 1.12 inhabitants. By about the end of the thirteenth century, the ratio between the land and the total population was now only about 1.06 hectares to each inhibitant. Meanwhile, about 260,000 rural inhabitants were producing enough foodstuffs to feed a total population in the territory of about 365,000, which is to say that each rural inhabitant was now producing foodstuffs sufficient for about 1.40 inhabitants. Over the course of the thirteenth century, in other words, the ratio between the total area of land and the total population had actually decreased by a total of 61.87%, at a rate of 0.99% per annum. Nevertheless, per capita output among the agrarian population increased by about 25% over the course of the century, at an annual rate of 0.25%. Adjusting for estimated annual net food imports of 5% in 1200 and 10% in 1300, the decrease in the ratio between land area and population stood at 0.59% annually, while per capita output among the agrarian population increased at a yearly rate of 0.19%.

The results yielded by this exercise are by no means intended as precise representations of productivity growth in the territory of Florence in the thirteenth century, and they take little account of productivity change in the manufacturing sector, even if they reflect in some degree a realignment of the labour force from agriculture to manufacturing. The population estimates presented here for the city of Florence and especially for the Florentine countryside are highly conjectural before the later thirteenth century, and even later estimates must rely to a disturbing degree on a single chronicle source. The calculations nevertheless provide an illustration of what productivity improvements in the territory of Florence over the course of the thirteenth century might have meant in practical terms.

[44] The actual land area of the modern province of Florence is 387,964 hectares. See Barucci, 1964: 1. The methodology used to arrive at the population figures presented here is described in the third chapter of my PhD dissertation (Day, 2000).

VIII. Conclusion

Productivity growth in the territory of Florence in the thirteenth century was no doubt stimulated in a variety of ways. In addition to increased labour inputs as a consequence of demographic expansion and increased land inputs through the extension of arable, the expansion of credit markets generated greater possibilities for capital investment while insulating peasants to some extent from aggregate shock. Changes in property relations, agricultural and industrial specialisation, technological development and diffusion, the proliferation of market outlets for surplus production, and investment in infrastructure also contributed to productivity improvements. The common denominator of all of these stimulants was the emergence of Florence as a large urban centre and the vigorous development of the manufacturing sector mainly in the city itself over the course of the thirteenth century. The development of the Florentine woollen textiles industry in particular helped to attract surplus labour from the countryside and it stimulated a more efficient distribution of labour between the agrarian and non-agrarian sectors in the region as a whole. It also provided Florence with an export product and a means by which to obtain food imports to feed the growing non-agrarian component of its total population. The Florentine woollen textiles industry was not necessarily responsible for attracting to the city the overwhelming share of rural-urban migrants to Florence. The immigrants entering the industry were nevertheless vital to continued Florentine growth, because their labours ultimately enabled the city to expand beyond the dimensions that agricultural production in the countryside was able to sustain.

Bibliography

Manuscript sources

Archivio di Stato di Florence (ASF) (State Archives, Florence), *Diplomatico.*

Printed and secondary sources

Bairoch, P., Batou, J. and Chèvre, P. (1988) *La population des villes européennes de 800 à 1850*, Geneva.

Bartoli Langeli, A. (ed.) (1983–1991) *Codice diplomatico del comune di Perugia: periodo consolare e podestarile (1139–1254)*, 3 vols, Perugia.

Barucci, P. (1964) *Profilo economico della provincia di Firenze*, Florence.

Belloch, K.J. (1940) *Bevölkerungsgeschichte Italiens*, 2: *Die Bevölkerung des Kirchenstaates, Toskanas und der Herzogtümer am Po*, Berlin.

Blanshei, S.R. (1976) *Perugia, 1260–1340: conflict and change in a medieval Italian urban society*, Philadelphia. (Transactions of the American Philosophical Society, n.s., 66, 2).

Blomquist, T.W. (1986) 'Alle origini del "Grosso" toscano: dalla testimonianza delle fonti del XIII secolo', *Archivio storico italiano*, 144, pp. 243–260.

Bonaini, F. (ed.) (1854–1870) *Statuti inediti della città di Pisa dal XII al XIV secolo*, 3 vols, Florence.

Bowsky, W.M. (1967) 'Medieval citizenship: the individual and the state in the commune of Siena, 1287–1355', *Studies in medieval and renaissance history*, 4, pp. 195–243.

Castagneto, P. (1996) *L'arte della lana a Pisa nel duecento e nei primi del trecento: commercio, industria e instituzioni'*, Pisa.

Ciasca, R. (1927) *L'arte dei medici e speziali nella storia e nel commercio fiorentino dal secolo XII al XV*, Florence.

Cohn, S.K. jr. (1978) *The labouring classes in renaissance Florence*, New York.

Cristiani, E. (1962) *Nobilità e popolo nel comune di Pisa dalle origini del podestenato alla signoria dei Donoratico*, Naples.

Cuomo, L. (1977) 'Sul commercio dei panni a Bologna nel 1270', *Archivio storico italiano*, 135, pp. 333–372.

Dameron, G.W. (1991) *Episcopal power and Florentine society, 1000–1320*, Cambridge (Mass.).

Dameron, G.W. (1996) 'Patrimony and clientage in the Florentine countryside: the formation of the estate of the cathedral chapter, 950–1200', in S.K. Cohn jr. and S.A. Epstein (eds), *Portraits of medieval and renaissance living: essays in memory of David Herlihy*, Ann Arbor, pp. 259–281.

Davidsohn, R. (1977) *Storia di Firenze*, 8 vols, trans. Giovanni Battista Klein, rev. trans. Roberto Palmarocchi, indices eds. Lucia Belmonte and Lindi Clerici, Florence.

Davidsohn, R. (ed.) (1896–1908) *Forschungen zur Geschichte von Florenz*, 4 vols, Berlin.

Day, W.R. jr. (2000) *The early development of the Florentine economy,* c. *1100–1275*, London. Unpublished PhD dissertation, London School of Economics and Political Science.

De Rosa, D. (1995) *Alle origini della Repubblica fiorentina: dai consoli al "Primo Popolo" (1172–1260)*, Florence.

De Stefani, C. (ed.) (1894) 'Frammento inedito degli statuti di Lucca del 1224 e del 1232', *Archivio storico italiano*, ser. 15, 13, pp. 249–255.

Enriques Agnoletti, A.M. (ed.) (1940) *Statuto dell'arte della lana di Firenze (1317–1319)*, Florence.

Ficker, J. (ed.) (1868–1874) *Forschungen zur Reichs- und Reichsgeschichte Italiens*, 4 vols, Innsbruck.

Fiumi, E. (1950) 'La demografia fiorentina nelle pagine di Giovanni Villani', *Archivio storico italiano*, 108, pp. 78–158.

Fiumi, E. (1953) 'Economia e vita privata dei fiorentina nelle rilevazioni statistiche di Giovanni Villani', *Archivio storico italiano*, 111, pp. 207–241.

Fiumi, E. (1957–1959) 'Fioritura e decadenza dell'economia fiorentina', *Archivio storico italiano*, pt. 1, 115 (1957), pp. 385–439; pt. 2, 116 (1958), pp. 443–510; pt. 3, 117 (1959), pp. 427–502; reprinted in E. Fiumi (1977), *Fioritura e decadenza dell'economia fiorentina*, Florence.

Frey, C. (1885) *Die Loggia dei Lanzi zu Florenz*, Berlin.

Friedman, D. (1974) 'Le terre nuove fiorentine', *Archeologia medievale: cultura materiale–insedimenti–territorio*, 1, pp. 231–247.

Friedman, D. (1988) *Florentine new towns: urban design in the late middle ages*, New York/Cambridge (Mass.).

Frugoni, A. (1965) 'G. Villani, "Cronica", XI, 94', *Bullettino dell'Istituto storico italiano per il medioevo e archivio muratoriano*, 77, pp. 229–255.

Garzella, G. (1991) *Pisa com'era: topografia e insediamento dall'impianto tardo antico alla città murata del secolo XII*, Naples.

Gaudenzi, A. (ed.) (1888) 'Statuti dei mercanti fiorentini dimoranti in Bologna degli anni 1279–1289', *Archivio storico italiano*, ser. 5, 1, pp. 1–19.

Ginatempo, M. and Sandri, L. (1990) *L'Italia delle città: il popolamento urbano tra medioevo e rinascimento (secoli XIII–XVI)*, Florence.

Goldthwaite, R.A. (1980) *The building of renaissance Florence: an economic and social history*, Baltimore.

Green, L. (1972) *Chronicle into history: an essay on the interpretation of history in Florentine fourteenth-century chronicles*, Cambridge.

Grierson, P. (1971–1972) 'The origins of the grosso and of gold coinage in Italy', *Numismatiky Sbornik*, 12, pp. 33–44; reprinted in P. Grierson (1979) *Later medieval numismatics, 11th–16th centuries: selected studies*, London.

Grigg, D. (1982) *The dynamics of agricultural change: the historical experience*, London.

Guarducci, P. and Ottanelli, V. (1982) *I servitori domestici della casa borghese toscana nel basso medioevo*, Florence.

Herlihy, D. (1954) 'Pisan coinage and the monetary development of Tuscany, 1150–1250', *American Numismatic Society museum notes*, 6, pp. 143–168, plates xvi–xvii.

Herlihy, D. (1958) *Pisa in the early renaissance: a study of urban growth*, New Haven.

Herlihy, D. (1967a) *Medieval and renaissance Pistoia: the social history of an Italian town, 1200–1430*, New Haven.

Herlihy, D. (1967b) 'Pisan coinage and the monetary history of Tuscany, 1150–1250', in *Le zecche minori toscane fino al XIV secolo (Atti del 3º Convegno internazionale di studi del Centro italiano di studi di storia e d'arte, Pistoia)*, Bologna, pp. 169–192.

Herlihy, D. and Klapisch-Zuber, C. (1978) *Les Toscans et leurs familles: une étude du catast florentin de 1427*, Paris.

Herlihy, D. and Klapisch-Zuber, C. (1985) *Tuscans and their families: a study of the Florentine Catasto of 1427*, New Haven.

Higounet, C. (1962) 'Les "terre nuove" florentines du XIVe siècle', in *Studi in onore di Amintore Fanfani*, vol. 3, Milan, pp. 1–17.

Hoshino, H. (1980) *L'Arte della lana in Firenze nel basso medioevo: il commercio della lana e il mercato dei panni fiorentini nei secoli XIII–XV*, Florence.

Hoshino, H. (1984) 'Note sulle gualchiere degli Albizzi a Firenze nel basso medioevo', *Ricerche storiche*, 14, 2–3, pp. 267–289.

Hunt, E.S. (1994) *The medieval super-companies: a study of the Peruzzi company of Florence*, Cambridge.

Ildefonso di San Luigi, P. (1770–1789) *Delizie degli eruditi Toscani*, 24 vols, Florence.

Jones, P.J. (1956) 'Le finanze della badia cisercense di Settimo nel secolo XIV', in *Rivista di storia della Chiesa in Italia* 10, pp. 90–122; reprinted in P.J. Jones (1980) *Economia e società nell'Italia medievale*, Turin, pp. 317–344.

Kotel'nikova, L.A. (1976) 'La produzione dei panni di lana della campagna toscana nei secoli XIII–XIV e la politica delle città e delle arti della lana', in *Atti delle Settimane di studi dell'Istituto internazionale di storia economica "F. Datini", 2: Produzione, commercio e consumo dei panni di lana*, Prato, pp. 221–229.

Lastri, M. (1775) *Ricerche sull'antica e moderna popolazione della città di Firenze per mezzo dei registri del battistero di San Giovanni dal 1451 al 1774*, Florence.

Lopez, R.S. (1967) 'Prima del ritorno all'oro nell'occidente duecentesco: i primi denari grossi d'argento', in *Rivista storica italiana*, 79, pp. 174–181.

Lunt, W.E. (1934) *Papal revenues in the middle ages*, 2 vols, New York.

Luzzatto, G. (1939) 'L'inurbamento delle popolazione rurali in Italia nei secoli XII e XIII', in *Studi di storia e diritto in onore di Enrico Besta per il XL anno del suo insegnamento*, vol. 2, Milan, pp. 183–203; reprinted in G. Luzzatto (1966) *Dai servi della gleba agli albori del capitalismo: saggi di storia economica*, Bari, pp. 407–432.

Magna, L. (1982) 'Gli Ubaldini del Mugello: una signoria feudale nel contado fiorentino', in *I ceti dirigenti dell'età comunale nei secoli XII e XIII (Comitato di studi sulla storia dei ceti dirigenti in Toscana, Atti del 2º Convegno)*, Pisa, pp. 13–65.

Matzke, M. (1993) 'Vom Ottolinus zum Grossus: Münzprägung in der Toskana vom 10. bis zum 13. Jahrhundert', *Schweizerische Numimatische Rundschau / Revue suisse de numismatique*, 72, pp. 133–192, tbls. 1–4.

Mazzaoui, M.F. (1967–1968) 'The emigration of Veronese textile artisans to Bologna in the thirteenth century', *Atti e memorie dell'Accademia di agricoltura, scienze e lettere di Verona*, ser. 6, 19, pp. 1–47.

Mazzaoui, M.F. (1984) 'Artisan migration and technology in the Italian textile industry in the late middle ages (1100–1500)', in R. Comba, G. Piccinni and G. Pinto (eds), *Strutture familiari, epidemie, migrazioni nell'Italia medievale*, Naples, pp. 519–534.

Moretti, I. (1980) *Le "terre nuove" del contado fiorentino*, Florence.

Muendel, J. (1981) 'The distribution of mills in the Florentine countryside during the late middle ages', in J.A. Raftis (ed.), *Pathways to medieval peasants*, Toronto, pp. 83–115. (Papers in mediaeval studies; 2).

Muendel, J. (1984) 'The French mill in medieval Tuscany', in *Journal of medieval history*, 10, pp. 215–247.

Muendel, J. (1991) 'Medieval urban renewal: the communal mills of the city of Florence, 1351–1382', *Journal of urban history*, 17, pp. 363–389.

Munro, J.H. (1988) 'Textile technology in the middle ages', in Joseph R. Strayer et al. (eds), *Dictionary of the middle ages*, 11: *Scandinavian languages – Textiles, Islamic (693–711)*, New York, pp. 1–27; reprinted in J.H. Munro (1994) *Textiles, towns and trade: essays in the economic history of late-medieval England and the Low Countries*, Aldershot.

Muratori, L.A. (ed.) (1738–1752) *Antiquitates Italicae Medii Aevi*, 6 vols, Milan.

Nenci, M.D. (1981) 'Ricerche sull'immigrazione dal contado alla città di Firenze nella seconda metà del XIII secolo', *Studi e ricerche*, 1, pp. 139–177.

Osheim, D.J. (1976) 'Rural population and the Tuscan economy in the late middle ages', *Viator: medieval and renaissance studies*, 7, pp. 329–346.

Overton, M. and Campbell, B.M.S. (1991) 'Productivity change in European agricultural development', in B.M.S. Campbell and M. Overton (eds), *Land, labour and livestock: historical studies in European agricultural productivity*, Manchester, pp. 1–50.

Pampaloni, G. (ed.) (1973) *Firenze al tempo di Dante: documenti sull'urbanistica fiorentina*, Rome.

Persson, K.G. (1991) 'Labour productivity in medieval agriculture: Tuscany and the Low Countries', in B.M.S. Campbell and M. Overton (eds), *Land, labour and livestock: historical studies in European agricultural productivity*, Manchester, pp. 124–143.

Pini, A.I. (1978) 'Un aspetto dei rapporti tra città e territorio nel medioevo: la politica demografica "ad elastico" di Bologna fra il XII e il XIV secolo', in *Studi in memoria di Federigo Melis*, vol. 1, Naples, pp. 365–408.

Pinto, G. (1978) *Il libro del biadaiolo: carestie e annona a Firenze dell metà del '200 al 1348*, Florence.

Pinto, G. (1984) 'La politica demografica delle città', in R. Comba, G. Piccinni and G. Pinto (eds), *Strutture familiari, epidemie, migrazioni nell'Italia medievale*, Naples, pp. 19–43.

Pirillo, P. (1992) *Famiglia e mobilità sociale nella Toscana medievale: i Franzesi della Foresta da Figline Valdarno (secoli XII–XV)*, Figline.

Pirillo, P. (1995) 'Il fiume come investimento: i mulini e i porti sull'Arno della Badia a Settimo (secc. XIII–XIV)', in G. Viti (ed.), *Storia e arte della abbazia cistercense di San Salvatore a Settimo a Scandicci*, Certosa di Firenze, pp. 63–90.

Plesner, J. (1934) *L'émigration de la campagne à la ville libre de Florence au XIIIe siècle*, trans. F. Gleizal and the author, Copenhagen.

Plesner, J. (1938) 'Una rivoluzione stradale del dugento,' trans. Carmen Zimmer Storchi and the author, *Acta Jutlandica: Aasskrift for Aarhus Universitet*, 10, 1, pp. 1–104.

Prunai, G. (1983) 'Noterelle sul breve dei sarti di Figline del 1234', *Studi in onore di Leopoldo Sandri*, vol. 3, Rome, pp. 773–781.

Redi, F. (1991) *Pisa com'era: archeologia, urbanistica e strutture materiali (secoli V–XIV)*, Naples.

Reinhard, M., Armengaud, A. and Dupaquier, J. (1968) *Histoire générale de la population mondiale*, Paris.

Repetti, E. (1833–1845) *Dizionario geografico–fisico–storico della Toscana*, 5 vols and supplement, Florence.

Reyerson, K.L. (1979) 'Patterns of population attraction and mobility: the case of Montpellier, 1293–1348', *Viator: medieval and renaissance studies*, 10, pp. 257–281.

Rumohr, C.F. von (ed.) (1830) *Ursprung der Besitzlosigkeit des Kolonem im neuren Toscana aus den Urkunden*, Hamburg.

Russell, J.C. (1972) *Medieval regions and their cities*, Newton Abbot.

Salvioli, L.V. (ed.) (1784–1795) *Annali bolognesi*, 3 vols, Bassano.

Salvatori, E. (1994) *La popolazione pisana nel duecento: il patto di alleanza di Pisa con Siena, Pistoia e Poggibonsi del 1228*, Pisa.

Sapori, A. (1955) *Studi di storia economica (secoli XIII–XIV–XV)*, 3rd ed., 2 vols, Florence.

Santini, P. (ed.) (1895) *Documenti dell'antica costituzione del comune di Firenze*, Florence. (Documenti di storia italiana; 10)

Santini, P. (ed.) (1952) *Documenti dell'antica costituzione del comune di Firenze, Appendice*, Florence. (Documenti di storia italiana; 15)

Standing, G. (1980–1981) 'Migration and modes of exploitation: social origins of immobility and mobility', *Journal of peasant studies*, 8, pp. 173–211.

Sznura, F. (1975) *L'espansione urbana di Firenze nel dugento*, Florence.

Vannucci, V. (1963–1964) 'Vita economica di un monastero alle porte di Firenze dal sec. XI al XIII: la Badia di S. Salvi', *Miscellanea storica della Valdelsa*, pt. 1, 69 (1963), pp. 7–77; pt. 2, 70 (1964), pp. 22–61.

Villani, G. (1823) *Cronica di Giovanni Villani*, 4 vols, Florence.

Wickham, C.J. (1988) *The mountains and the city: the Tuscan Appennines in the early middle ages*, Oxford.

Wickham, C.J. (1996) 'Ecclesiastical dispute and lay community: Figline Valdarno in the twelfth century', *Mélanges de l'École française de Rome: moyen âge*, 108, pp. 7–93.

Wrigley, E.A. (1985) 'Urban growth and agricultural change: England and the Continent in the early modern period', *Journal of Interdisciplinary History*, 15, pp. 683–728.

Wrigley, E.A. (1991) 'City and country in the past: a sharp divide or a continuum?', *Historical Research*, 64, pp. 107–120.

6 The role of medieval cities and the origins of merchant capitalism

Eric MIELANTS, Fernand Braudel Center – State University of New York at Binghamton

I. Introduction

Each theoretical perspective copes with its own specific problems in dealing with the emergence of (merchant) capitalism. One of the main problems is that the role of medieval cities (and the relation to their rural hinterland) is consistently overlooked: Neo-Marxist Brennerianism ignores them, Modernization Theory dismisses them, and World System Analysis so far has been unable to effectively integrate them successfully into its framework, recent theoretical debates on 'world cities' notwithstanding. In this paper I emphasize the importance of the medieval inter-city state system in order to explain important historical continuities regarding the genesis of merchant capitalism in Europe. To be more precise, one should be careful not to miss the construction of an embryonic capitalist system in the period 1200–1400, hinged around European medieval cities and their hinterlands, precisely to understand the development of the world-economy in a much more intensified pattern, and on a larger scale in the subsequent period 1400–1600 (Wallerstein, 1993b: 11–12). Contrary to the most important theoretical perspectives which will be analyzed hereafter, I hope to demonstrate that cities, embedded in regional and 'international' long-distance markets, were not only an important aspect of the European Medieval economy,[1] but also a crucial variable in the occurrence of recurring growth in Western Europe in the long run.

II. Marxism: class struggle in the countryside

Essentially, Orthodox Marxism denies the importance of medieval cities in their relation to the emergence of capitalism because they fall outside the temporal framework of the Marxist conceptualization of Modernity. The Orthodox Marxist tradition of constructing an economic view of Modernity, reproduced by academics such as Christopher Hill, traditionally dates capitalism (and modern society) in the late 18th century with the Industrial Revolution at the forefront. It is only then that Orthodox Marxists see a real transition take place. Consequently, most of them could not care less about the

[1] The cities' dependence on the grain trade (for the consumption of the urban proletariat) as well as the textile market illustrate this quite clearly. Records indicate that in the 14th and 15th centuries French grain was transported via Ghent to Antwerp, where Dutch merchants had to pay toll to be able to transport it to Haarlem. At the same time, the import of grain from the Baltic area to the Low Countries (Aerts, Dupon and Van der Wee, 1985: 237) and from the Black Sea area to Genoa (Karpov, 1993) was an essential feature of the urban system. In return, the bulk of the western cities growing exports was directed to Eastern Europe (Van Uytven, 1983: 181).

Long 16th Century, let alone the Middle Ages.[2] At most, Marxists trace the early roots of capitalism to the 1640s in England (Cantor, 1973: 294). In the 1970s, however, a Neo-Marxian variant, the 'Brennerian approach', comes into the picture, and expands the Marxist temporal framework considerably. The Brennerian approach (unlike traditional Orthodox Marxism) is strongly preoccupied with the Middle Ages and the origins of capitalism. However, this perspective has specific problems since it tends to focus predominantly on class struggle and modes of production – hereby minimizing circulation of trade (Brenner, 1977) – overemphasizes agrarian production at the expense of urban centered production, and considers the nobility as nothing more than a 'surplus extracting by extra-economic compulsion' oriented class in order to indulge in so-called 'non-productive consumption' (Brenner, 1985: 232). Thus, Brenner remains encapsulated in a Marxist tradition that focuses predominantly on the mode of production and class warfare between peasants (the exploited) and the nobility (the exploiters) within a given territorial unit (the countryside of the nation-state being the unit of analysis).[3] Essentially, he explains the economic success of the English nobility, in comparison with the French nobility, as the difference between a class an sich (France) and a class für sich (England) (Byres, 1996: 67) which he labels 'extraordinary intra-class cohesiveness' (Brenner, 1985: 258). He also follows the Marxist path which juxtaposes 'absolutism in France' versus 'the development of classical capitalist relations on the land in England' (Brenner, 1985: 275; 284–299). He then constructs his narrative in such a way that it becomes either a prelude to Orthodox Marxist stagist historical evolution,[4] ending his story with the 'rise of a capitalist aristocracy presiding over an agricultural revolution' (Brenner, 1985: 299) which in turn created 'an upward spiral that extended into the industrial revolution' (Brenner, 1985: 327) *or* a particular variant of Modernization Theory (cf. infra), explaining why one territorial unit (England), unlike another one (France), managed to achieve an economic 'take-off'.[5] In both cases, capitalism becomes a characteristic of

---

[2] Although Marx (1977: 876) himself acknowledged that 'we come across the first sporadic traces of capitalist production as early as the 14th or 15th centuries in certain towns of the Mediterranean' he did not elaborate on this. His focus on the impact of industrial production and the modern factory system made him consider that the 'international division of labor, a division suited to the requirements of the chief center of modern industry' was as recent as the modern factory (Harvey, 1985: 47). The international division of labor is however older than the 19th century. It is quite clear that Marx was not really preoccupied with explaining the *origins* of capitalism since he was not interested in the Middle Ages or the early modern period. All his statements about them were no more but 'contextual observations dependent of his analysis of the capitalist production' (Guerreau, 1980: 57; Bois, 1985: 189).

[3] Brenner's thesis is essentially 'a base consisting of unfree peasants, the direct producers, and an aristocratic superstructure supported by rents which were extracted from the former. This critical process of extraction was possible because the lords owned the land' (Harvey, 1991: 16–17).

[4] Brenner (1985: 275) juxtaposes the general crisis 'on most of the continent' versus the 'critical breakthrough to self-sustaining growth in England'.

[5] 'It was the growth of *agricultural productivity*, rooted in the transformation of *agrarian* class or property relations, which allowed the English economy to embark upon a path of development already closed to its Continental neighbors' (Brenner, 1985: 323). Thus, English 'development' distinguished itself from the continent, suffering from sclerosis (Brenner, 1985: 275; 299). For Brenner, 'capitalism', 'development' and a 'breakthrough in economic growth' occur in England, while 'crisis, stagnation, absolute monarchy' are indicative of France. It is not only a very unilinear

one nation at a given moment in time. Another problem is to what extent peasants (in Brenner's view the rural 'productive base' of a society) were actually of servile status.[6] Also, in making class struggle and the mode of production that central, Brenner (1977; 1985; 1986) minimizes the market's importance. Certainly, one can claim that some peasants only sold products on the market to cover their monetary requirements, which were partially generated by coercive demands of their lords and/or state officials. Some agricultural producers were this way 'driven to the market' in order to obtain, via the sale of part of their production, the cash with which to meet their obligations, generated by 'extra-economic compulsion' (Aymard, 1993: 292–293). Yet, this does not mean one should minimize the importance of demographic change or the powerful dynamic impulses generated by the existence (and increasing significance) of the market itself: between the 11th and late 13th century, England's employment in market-dependent occupations grew more rapidly than the number of self-sufficient farmers. Not only within cities, but even in the rural economy, did specialization occur.[7] After investigating data available in the Domesday book, the economic historian Snooks estimates that 40% of the economy in 11th century England was involved in market activities (the market being the sector where 'all the major economic decisions in England were made') and 60% in subsistence.[8] These results challenge the conventional wisdom insisting only a very limited role for market forces at this time (Snooks 1995: 39). Hence, assertions such as Brenner's that individual feudal lords frivolously consumed surpluses either produced from rural estates, managed according to time-honored custom, or extracted from their tenants by various non-economic means, have to be seriously questioned (Snooks, 1995: 47). Of course, one cannot deny that a small minority (the nobility) in a given territorial unit imposed many substantial different financial extractions on the majority (peasants) without impressive re-investments occurring in the countryside (e.g. Thoen, 1988: 636–637). Nor does it mean that 'surplus extracting by non-economic compulsion' (Brenner, 1985: 232) did not take place. But it is important to acknowledge that strong cities, dominating their rural hinterland, exploited the countryside just as

way of thinking about historical evolution (Holton, 1985: 89; Torras, 1980: 262), but in focusing on rural class relations, Brenner's (1985; 1986) explanation of the transition from feudalism to capitalism fails to include the importance of cities in his 'narrative of socioeconomic change' (Howell and Boone, 1996: 323; Epstein, 1991: 258).

[6] According to Kominsky (in Harvey, 1991: 18), even in late 13th century 'feudal' England, 40% of the land occupied by peasants was free land, and about the same percentage of peasant households was free as well. Cf. Heers, 1992: 163–164.

[7] The intensification, specialization and commercialization of the countryside occurs in Flanders (e.g. Thoen, 1993) as well as in the Netherlands (Blockmans, 1993: 49–50). This 'commercialization changed the character of taxation. By 1300 the main tax on the laity was assessed on the value of personal movable property, [which] ensured that townspeople should be brought within its scope. Not only that, but towns-people usually paid tax at a higher rate than country people. In addition, customs duties fell directly on imports and exports. Edward I had enhanced their value in 1275 when he initiated the levying of a tax on wool exports. This levy on trade instantly became a principal support of royal finances, more regular than any other source of income. It was the foundation upon which the king established his credit when he wished to borrow money from Italian merchants' (Britnell, 1995: 14).

[8] Snooks (1995: 40) estimates that 32.3% of the English market sector in 1086 was rural and 7.8% was urban, hereby arriving at a total of 40.1%.

feudal lords did (Harvey, 1991: 19; Nicholas, 1971: 93; Epstein, 1992: 124–133). And, fundamentally, why would 'feudal structures' inhibit the emergence of markets? According to Bruce Campbell, peasant producers generally 'intensify production, specialize, and participate in the market exchange when they have to, and feudalism – through the extraction of their surpluses in various forms of feudal rent – obliged them to do precisely this' (1995: 133).

Peasants did produce abundant goods in regional market circuits (Derville, 1996: 123–136) as well as in truly international markets (Thoen, 1988: 277–279). Not denying or minimizing the significance of peasant resistance in the face of coerced extractions (Hanawalt, 1986; Imsen and Vogler, 1997), to consider the concept of 'power relations between lords and peasants as the primum movens of the Middle Ages would be absurd' (Guerreau, 1980: 108) since cities can not be excluded from the analysis of power relations in the Middle Ages (e.g. Cherubini, 1990: 129–130). Furthermore, one should not forget that 'primarily market structures determine the character and rate of economic development in a society. By contrast, since property relations are only one (albeit crucial) determinant of market structures, one may not deduce the course of economic development from a (reified) structure of property relations alone [...] one cannot infer a peasant smallholder's economic strategies from his ability to subsist on his own land (and his duty to pay rent to a feudal or other landlord); rather, his economic strategies will depend on how his access to markets is structured' (Epstein, 1992: 22).

That these markets are often located in an urban setting, and that many peasants were drawn to them, can not be denied (Fritze, 1985: 21–22). Yet by relegating the market's importance to a secondary position, Brenner and his fellow travelers (e.g. Wood, 1999) completely overlook the importance of medieval cities.

III. 'Modernization Theory': the non-existence of pre-industrial growth

Modernization theorists can ignore the socioeconomic importance of cities by referring to the importance of spiritual/religious/cultural values that form the basis of the emergence of capitalist accumulation (e.g. Weber, 1930; Tawney, 1926; Landes, 1998; Lal, 1998) or by considering a string of technological innovations as the crucial variable that would have led Europe on an unavoidable teleological path to dominance over 'the rest' of the world in subsequent centuries (e.g. Labal, 1962: 32–39; Gimpel, 1976; Ashtor, 1992: IV). Some Modernization theorists, however, do use a specific socioeconomic angle to explain the 'rise of the West', but usually do not consider a longue durée approach. As in Orthodox Marxism, the early modern period is often neglected and not associated with any form of recurring growth. Indeed, many scholars dismiss medieval corporations and guilds as synonyms of socioeconomic stagnation, decline and archaism (Munro, 1994: IX, 44; Boone, 1994: 3–5; Lis and Soly, 1997: 228). In Modernization Theory urban corporations and guilds have become the victims of an unduly unhistorical interpretation mainly because their presence is often related to what one defines as a feudal 'period of transition', whereas capitalism, identified as the 'real progress', takes over the pre-Renaissance 'decadent' medieval structures while 'installing modernity' (Boone, 1994: 4). The classic example of this traditional point of view in the Modernization/

Development School, is of course the most famous propagator of 'modern' economics, Adam Smith himself (1976: 69; 139). Thus, urban guilds became constantly depicted as medieval conservative remnants and 'socially inefficient cartels' (Hickson and Thompson, 1991: 127) that were obstructing the 'route to progress' (i.e. capitalism) with regulations and prohibitions (according to Modernization Theory detrimental to the increasing wealth of nations within a 'free' market).[9] In addition, guilds were, from the late 15th century on, the losing forces against ongoing centralization processes. Besides, the 19th/20th century liberal industrial nation-state was always significantly more interested and motivated in illustrating its own vibrant dynamism than in giving justice to its own predecessors, the medieval craftsmen and guilds (Braunstein, 1994: 23). Surely, capitalism could not have originated in the midst of this 'archaic pre-modern' world? For Modernization Theory, it seems nothing important or novel happened in the Long 16th Century: as in Marxism, the Industrial Revolution of the late 18th and early 19th century has to be looked upon as the real watershed in history, opening the gates of Modernity (Cantor, 1973: 298–301). As a result, the economic historian's principle interest in 'pre-industrial' economies lays in understanding the constraints that prevented their becoming modern. This 'stagnationist interpretation of medieval economic history' obviously had an impact on the course of historical debates and the assumptions many scholars shared about the state of the 'pre-modern' world in general. Only 'pre-modern' factors such as the availability of land and population growth became the key to understanding a 'pre-modern' world,[10] making commercialization, specialization and technical change peripheral topics for the history of a 'pre-modern' society (Britnell and Campbell, 1995: 8). Unfortunately, many still associate the Middle Ages with rural auto subsistence, ignorance, backwardness and general 'underdevelopment' (Pernoud, 1992: 16; Geremek, 1994: 15). However, regarding technological progress, dynamism and inventiveness, 'pre-modern' medieval labor formations can not, as Modernization Theory does, simply be dismissed as being 'pre-modern' as if a major gap would divide them from our 'modern' world. How can one imagine that these corporations, located at the heart of a medieval urban society, would have been nothing more but incarnations of conservative, stagnant and unproductive economic action without proper dynamism and innovation (Boone, 1994: 16)? Furthermore, pre-industrial (i.e. pre-19th century) markets were much more complex and varied than is usually envisaged (Epstein, 1993: 470). Yet, one should not only rethink the concept of the 'Industrial Revolution' as conceptualized by Modernization-Development Theory (Wallerstein, 1984: 179–180), but the term 'Agricultural Revolution' as well (Verhulst, 1989: 71–95; Verhulst, 1990: 17–28).[11] Unfortunately, Modernization

[9] Cf. Lis and Soly (1994: 366–369) but also Persson's (1988: 50–54) well-founded critique on Mickwitz (1936).

[10] E.g. Postan, 1966; 1973 and Postan and Hatcher, 1985. On the supposedly non-existence of technological progress in this perspective, which frames 'pre-industrial agrarian economies in a sort of Ricardo-Malthus trap' cf. Persson (1988: 3–4; 24–32). For a dismissal of pessimistic assessments regarding late medieval agricultural productivity and proficiency common to both Malthusianists and Neo-Marxists cf. Verhulst (1997: 91–92). For a revision of the ideal typical 'lymphatic peasants' à la Postan and the 'lackadaisical lords which sapped the agricultural sector of dynamism' à la Brenner cf. Campbell (1995c: 76–108).

[11] Some even situate the 'agricultural revolution' in the 13th–14th century (e.g. Dowd, 1961: 143–160 for Italy).

Theory dismisses not only the urban based guilds, but the entire 'pre modern' Medieval Era, as being rigid and suffering from sclerosis, only waiting to be swept away by the triumph of laissez-faire economics (Howell and Boone, 1996: 305). However, Marxism has the same obsession with 'modernity' in emphasizing the Agricultural Revolution and the Industrial Revolution in its 'stagist' perspective as Modernization Theory. Their dismissive attitude vis-a-vis the 'pre-modern' Long 16th Century or Medieval Era is quite similar. Therefore, Modernization Theory is incapable of assessing the importance of early modern urban networks and their creation of self-sustained growth. Last but not least, many Marxist and Modernization theorists tend to forget that 'the industrial revolution was *not* the source of modern economic growth' (North and Thomas, 1973: 157) but rather the *outcome* of different processes which have to be traced back in the period prior to the 'Industrial Revolution'.

IV. World-System Analysis (WSA): re-opening the transition debate

WSA attempts to explain the emergence of a Capitalist World-Economy in Europe parallel with the incorporation of regions through domination and colonization which brings about an international division of labor and an interstate system. In debunking 'Modernity' and 'Industrial Revolution' as concepts, WSA can not (unlike Modernization Theory and Orthodox Marxism) disregard Medieval Europe in its entirety since it has to 'reopen the question of how and when the capitalist world-economy was created in the first place; why the transition took place in feudal Europe and not elsewhere; why it took place when it did and not earlier or later; why earlier attempts of transition failed' (Wallerstein, 1979: 135).

Although WSA has not dealt effectively with the 'transition' problem, at least the Medieval Era comes back into the picture. Another positive element is that it illustrates how the 'Brenner Debate' between 'class history' versus the so-called 'objective economic forces, particularly those deriving from demographic fluctuations and the growth of trade and markets' (Torras, 1980: 253) can be overcome by stating that the 'exploitation of labor is not only determined by the wage bundle and the extraction of labor from labor power in the production process, but in substantial measure by the prices at which goods are exchanged between the economies that make up the world-system, or between the modes of production in a given economy' (Bowles, 1988: 434).

In this sense, WSA attempts to *integrate* the Marxist focus on production and the Smithian focus on the circulation of goods on the market in its relational model to explain the emergence of capitalism. Yet, as Thomas Hall (1996: 444–449) observes, many scientists agree that 'World-System Theory cannot be applied wholesale to pre-capitalist settings, before approximately 1500 AD'. This leads us to the question: is there no capitalist system before the Long 16th Century? The answer to this question depends whether one tends to agree with the spatial predisposition that there has been a period of transition from feudalism to capitalism wherein the existence of multiple systems converge in a single world-system (a world-economy centered around Europe) and a temporal predisposition, namely that this transition occurred between 1450–1650.

For Wallerstein (1974), capitalism evolved in Europe out of the crisis of feudalism in the Long 16th century and with the World-System one single new mode of production comes into existence. His magnum opus on the Long 16th century notwithstanding, his explanation about the transition remains unsatisfying. I tend to agree with the criticism of Cornelis Terlouw: 'During this long traditional phase, feudalism was slowly transformed into, and superseded by, capitalism. This can only mean that during at least two centuries feudalism and capitalism coexisted in one world-system. So what Wallerstein explicitly denies (the coexistence of two modes of production in one world-system) he implicitly assumes for the period 1450–1650. If one accepts that during a very long period, several modes of production coexisted in one single system, it is a small and completely logical step to admit that at any moment in the history of the world-system several modes of production could exist simultaneously' (1992: 57–58).

Like Marx himself, Wallerstein is more interested in the functioning of the Capitalist World Economy today. But this interest has some unfortunate theoretical implications: 'By focusing his attention on the emergence of the present world-system, Wallerstein inadequately theorizes about the temporal borders between world-systems. His fixation on the unity of the present world makes him blind to the intertwining of different social systems in the past' (Terlouw, 1992: 57).

Wallerstein (1980: 31) was of course aware of this problem. Calling the transition at a given moment in time completed (in the sense that capitalism has superseded other modes of production or that its logic appears to be predominant overall) is difficult, since 'it is always easy to find presumed instances of 'non-capitalist' behavior in a capitalist world – all over Europe in 1650 and 1750 and 1950. The mixture [of non-capitalist and capitalist behavior] is the essence of the capitalist system as a mode of production' (Wallerstein, 1980: 32). So who can really tell for sure when one system takes over (incorporates) the other one(s) at a specific moment? Unfortunately, the confusion does not end here. Wallerstein's reluctance to apply World System concepts such as core and periphery before the Long 16th century, is a result of the way he interprets the importance and impact of (long-distance) trade. However, the dichotomy which he creates between preciosities (luxuries) versus essentials or utilities (mass or bulk trade) can seriously be questioned, especially prior to 1500 (Schneider, 1991: 48). What goods can onc cxactly define as luxury or bulk trade: does one focus on the quantity of the goods exchanged or emphasize the nature of goods? Certain luxury items (as wine, sugar and salt) can become mass commodities,[12] being widely bought and sold, due to an increased market demand.

[12] 'Around 1300, England exported up to 15 million pounds of raw wool, and a year's export of about 25 millions gallons of wine from the Garonne valley was recorded. The wine trade found markets in Tunis and the Black Sea. Exotic commodities were more and more moved in bulk' (Mundy, 1991: 91). The production of wine for the market was enormous: 'La moyenne annuelle, pendant le premier tiers du XIVe siècle, se chiffre à 747000 hectolitres – 850000 environ en 1308–1309. Pour fixer les idées, en 1950 l'exportation totale de vin par la France est de 900000 hectolitres. Et cela ne concerne que les seules sorties par la Gironde: Bordeaux et Libourne' (Pernoud, Gimpel and Delatouche, 1986: 195). For the importance of 'regular, large-scale, well-developed trade between distinct but relatively integrated economies' of which the wine trade was illustrative, cf. Menard (1997: 236–248). For the Levantine sugar industry in the Late Middle Ages, 'a true capita-

But when do these 'critical' transitions from luxury goods to bulk goods actually occur?[13] In other words, when do 'luxuries' become 'necessities' (Wallerstein, 1993a: 294)? Furthermore, to what extent is it analytically useful prior to 1500 that such a dichotomy is drawn between the two? Schneider (1991: 52) and Adams (1974), for instance, are convinced that long distance trade in luxuries before 1500 was a 'formidable socioeconomic force in spite of its being confined largely to commodities of very high value in relation to commodities weight and bulk due to the high transport costs, and in spite of its directly involving only a small part of the population' (Adams, 1974: 247). And can the growing wealth of Europe not be measured by its increased demand for luxuries (Cheyney, 1962: 10)? Is it impossible to retain the importance and impact of luxury trade without reducing it conceptually to the same analytical level as bulk trade? Is it not conceivable that luxury trade (and certainly the serious profits involved) could have provided essential financial leverage for the same merchant entrepreneurs and families who were also engaged in 'bulk' trade, specifically prior to 1500?[14] And couldn't one argue that this leverage was necessary, if not essential, to further the increase of trade in mass commodities, stimulating the actual expansion of capitalism in the 'era of transition from feudalism to capitalism'?[15]

The transition from feudalism to capitalism invoked by Wallerstein c.1500 becomes even more problematic if one looks at other (non WSA) literature: for many scholars the Late Middle Ages stand for a period of 'acceleration' between 1270 and 1520 (Fossier, 1991: 337–441). This coincides with the 'Commercial Revolution' (Lopez, 1976; Jones, 1997: 152–332) between 1100 and 1350/1500 which in turn initiated the era of capitalism,

---

listic enterprise' cf. Ashtor, 1992: 237. For the salt trade, 'one of the unifying elements of the western economy' (Mollat, 1993: 65), cf. Bautier, 1992: V, VI; Mollat, 1968; Hocquet, 1979; 1985.

[13] One can pose the same question about other bulk commodities in the early 14th century, such as beer produced in Northern Germany and exported to the Low Countries (Aerts and Unger, 1990) or the lumber trade (North and Thomas, 1973: 50).

[14] A medieval 'super company' of the Peruzzi's or Bardi's c. 1300 in Italy invested and made huge profits in both textiles and large-scale grain trading (Hunt, 1994: 244). 'Since the latter part of the Middle Ages, the range of articles in long-distance commercial circulation was already a very diverse one, and encompassed consumer goods which were relatively commonplace, and which were not able to absorb very high transaction costs' (Torras, 1993: 202; cf. Cherubini, 1993: 282–283). Furthermore, 'the mass traffic of heavy products, such as salt and grain, and of cumbersome products such as wood, also corresponded to a certain division of tasks between the sea and land routes' (Mollat, 1993: 65). It is clear that 'de plus en plus, il faut se convaincre que l'essentiel des trafics méditerranéens était fait du sel, du blé, du vin, de l'huile, sans parler des cuirs, du bois, du fer, de l'alun, nécessaires à la vie de tous les jours, et que c'est sur ces produits pondéreux, sur celui des grains en particulier, que l'attention doit se porter, bien plus encore que sur les épices ou les soieries' (Bautier, 1992: VI, 224). It is thus a serious exaggeration to claim that industrial production in the Middle Ages was 'scattered, small-scale, and mostly geared to a luxury market' (Wallerstein, 1974: 123) or that 'there was no middle-distance division of labor [since] local zones did not generally depend on or count on such 'regional' (middle-distance) supply sources' (Wallerstein, 1993b: 5). For the importance of both bulk and luxury trade in the medieval economy cf. Mazzaoui (1981) and Bozorgnia (1998).

[15] Especially if one realizes that commercial expansion and industrial specialization both required unprecedented investment of capital (Schumann, 1986: 107).

disregarding whether various forms of technological innovations (White, 1962) or forms of agrarian development and surplus extraction as outcomes of specific class relations (Brenner, 1985: 11), were at the heart of the matter. According to Derville (1995: 243–250), the transition from feudalism to capitalism in the countryside takes place around 1150 AD. Several studies focusing both on urban production or trade and agrarian production for trade,[16] bulk/mass and luxuries alike, clearly indicate a historical continuity on all levels between the Late Middle Ages and the 16th century, which explains the political, economic and technological evolutions within the transition from feudalism to capitalism. Even a change in mentality,[17] the rational drive to ceaselessly accumulate capital, can be traced back to its roots in the Middle Ages (Le Mené, 1977: 160–190). Jacques Le Goff (1988: 9–10) considers the 13th century theological controversy regarding usury 'the labor pains of capitalism'.[18]

In addition, the mechanical clocks that were appearing on churches and town halls in the urban centers of Western Europe from the early 14th century onwards (Barnett, 1998: 80), brought about 'a historical revolution in the measuring of time, with far-reaching intellectual, commercial and industrial consequences' (Gimpel, 1976: 165; Pernoud, 1992: 140). Indeed, 'the rational outlook of the merchants and bankers was fundamental to the installation of mechanical clocks in the West. With their capitalistic mentality they had observed the value of time' (Gimpel, 1976: 170).[19] Besides, what is the essential difference regarding 'l'esprit d'entreprise' of a merchant like Jacques Coeur in the mid-15th century (Mollat, 1988), of a merchant like Jean Boinebroke in the late 13th century (Espinas, 1933; Koenigsberger, 1987: 223–224), or even of a merchant like Guillaume Cade in the mid 12th century (Derville, 1994: 52–54), all linked to the emergence of capitalism? This provokes the question: what is so *new* about the 16th century as far as features of capitalism are concerned (Bernard, 1976: 309–310)?

---

[16] Cf. essays on 14th century urban economies and putting-out production in Boone and Prevenier, 1993; Howell and Boone, 1996; for urban industries in the Low Countries and Italy cf. Van der Wee, 1988. For agrarian production for trade cf. Van der Wee and Van Cauwenberghe, 1978 and Thoen, 1992, 1993.

[17] 'Du Marx dans la pratique, six cents ans avant Le Capital! [...] La réussite ou l'échec d'une vie se mesurent à l'importance du capital accumulé' (Martin, 1996: 357–370).

[18] 'C'est avec le développement de l'économie monétaire, dès le XIIe siècle, que l'usure va devenir un sujet de la plus grande importance pour l'Eglise. C'est au XIIIe siècle que le problème s'est averé fondamental, alors que le capitalisme est en train de faire ses premiers pas, en usant précisément de pratiques condamnées par l'Eglise jusque-là' (Greilsammer, 1994: 810). Furthermore, '12th and 13th century urban authorities defended the practice of usury [...] synods that denounced canonical infractions such as usury hardly installed any fear in the 'monde des affaires' (Wyffels, 1991: 870–871) since 'money-lending was freely practiced in the Middle Ages among the poor as well as the rich. Usury was still forbidden by canon law, but there were all kinds of subtle devices for cloaking usurious transactions' (Du Boulay, 1970: 59 cf. Little, 1978: 180–183; Barnett, 1998: 60; Heers, 1992: 253–256).

[19] Barnett (1998: 61): 'God's time began to grant space to the new secularized idea of time required by a money economy'. For the implications of changes in the apprehension of time between 1300 and 1650, cf. Thompson (1993: 352–403). Time itself became a compartmentalized and rationalized commodity (Le Goff, 1991: 46–79; Martin, 1996: 168–174). Cf. also Epstein (1988), Crosby (1997: 75–93) and Dohrn-van Rossum (1996).

Let me at this point make it clear that it is not my contention to merely 'de-construct' theoretical perspectives and plead for a mere return to historical archival research in order to come closer to an 'objective Truth' (e.g. Grassby, 1999: 61–73). Historians' incessant warnings for 'pretentious and ill-founded grand hypotheses launched by some sociologists' (Dyer, 1991: 1) due to the latter construction of 'theories that seem to have been plucked out of the air' (ibid.) are however not an absolute virtue, for what is history without theory?

V. Medieval cities and the transition to a capitalist system

It should be clear that the concept *'age of transition'* implies that at least two coexisting modes of production were operating and, as time went by, one became more dominant over the other: if we want to analyze the rise of one mode of production and the demise of another, we have to acknowledge them working together. If not, should one not have to argue that feudalism simply disappeared in Europe during the Long 16th century? Instead, why not argue that the feudal system was very much alive in the 19th century, as well as some of its social structures? Could one not argue that from the 13th century onwards, features of capitalism became more apparent in Europe and that the mutual existence of feudalism and capitalism was entirely possible up to c. 1350, before a crisis made one logic become more dominant over the other as the medieval city 'brought about a fermentation process in the feudal mode of production [which] destroyed it in the long run' (Le Goff, 1998: 15). Therefore, the city has to be understood as a crucial variable in the long-term history of Western Europe.[20] Conceptually, most capitalist phenomena (wage labor, specialization of industries, class struggle, profits from trade, complex financial techniques and systematic incorporation of areas to further the ceaseless accumulation of capital) that one finds in the 16th century, are already apparent

[20] Referring to an inter-city state system, I do not wish to downplay the importance of the countryside in the Middle Ages since most Europeans did live there. Yet the 'modernization of the commercial infrastructure was only possible after the emergence of European cities who created ever more, new and optimal conditions for an increase of productivity and thus allowed successive series of increasing growth' (Van der Wee, 1981: 14). Cities are key to the 'international commerce [which] had become an extremely dynamic sector, of a vital importance to the growth of the European economy' (Van der Wee, 1981: 10) so they can be accurately labeled as the 'nodes of capitalism' (Rosenberg and Birdzell, 1986: 47) since in many regions of Western Europe 'a shift of economic emphasis from the countryside to the towns and cities [occurred]' (Tuma, 1979: 58). Much of the socioeconomic changes in the countryside were after all 'fueled by urban demand [which] stimulated an intensive and highly commercialized agriculture' (Yun, 1994: 116; Menant, 1993: 293). Without cities, it would not have been feasible let alone sensible for agricultural producers to specialize and commercialize (Wrigley, 1978: 301). Last but not least, it was primarily within cities that capital accumulation took place, since in the countryside 'the margin between incomes and outcomes was just too small to leave room for a significant accumulation of capital' (Toch, 1986: 180) while the upper class rural nobility spent most of its surplus obtained from extra-economic coercion on urban based goods or services, thus redirecting a lot of the cash flow back into the city (Spufford, 1981: 622; Lopez, Miskimin and Udovitch, 1970: 98).

in the Late Middle Ages, and more specifically in its urban centers.[21] It appears that c. 1200 AD, merchant capitalism was appearing in different places in Western Europe as re-allocations of capital took place from the medieval city to the countryside. The intercity-state system of the 13th–15th centuries featured more interregional trade characteristics than the dominantly local autarchic productions that characterized Europe prior to the 12th century or the more international space of flows that would shape the world economy from the 16th century onward, which is why I suggest to analyze the qualitative shifts that occurred in Europe in the 12th–14th centuries (i.e. the shaping of an intercity-state system within interregional trade patterns in the 13th century).

It is crucial to recognize the importance of early modern cities as 'power containers' of the bourgeoisie, just like nation-states later on (Giddens, 1981: 12; 148), as medieval cities were crucial to the development of capitalism. Wallerstein however, insists that the creation of the modern capitalist World-Economy took place not earlier than 1450. Of course, he is well aware of changes in Europe prior to that era, stating that 'the crisis of feudalism in Europe in the period of 1300–1450 [was] a crisis whose resolution was the historic emergence of a capitalist world-economy located in that particular geographic arena' (Wallerstein, 1984: 23).

Yet he does not really elaborate on this issue. No important historical continuity between 1300 and 1500 which could help explaining the transition, is acknowledged: what happened between 1150–1300 in Europe did not have an impact on the emergence of capitalism c. 1450 since Wallerstein (1979: 142) dismisses it as 'abortive'. But is there really such an extreme break with the past?[22] Is it not plausible that, precisely because several features of capitalism were already strongly apparent before 1500 in Europe – that is between 1100 and 1350[23] – and because of their overall continuing growing importance, the feudal system sunk into a crisis? Not that the feudal system was suddenly and completely replaced by a totally new system of accumulation. Instead, it fell in a slow period of decay as it became superseded by the dominant 'logic' of capitalism. As the economic historian Day points out, historical continuity is quite revealing: 'By the mid-14th century, merchant capitalism has already perfected the instruments of economic

[21] It is the *combination* of these features which constitutes a capitalist system. Profits derived from surplus value are *not* necessarily 'of greater historical significance' (Heilbroner, 1985: 66) than those derived from unequal exchange. Mollat du Jourdin (1977: I, 45) spells out the similarity between 16th and 14th century profits: 'L'intensité, la frequence en sont nouvelles [au 16e siècle], non la chose. Progrès quantitatifs certes; mais tonalité médievale'. (cf. also Mauro, 1988: 758).

[22] In a more recent article, Wallerstein (1999: 34) claims there is a fundamental difference between 'proto capitalist' systems with capitalist features (investments of capital, extensive commodity production, wage labor and weltanschauungen consonant with capitalism) on one hand and the 'genesis of a radically new system' after 1400 born out of the 'crisis of feudalism' on the other hand. Although Wallerstein's insistence on a fundamental rupture c. 1500 distorts the reality of historical continuity, I am convinced that looking for the existence of a world economic system which has been operating for thousands of years, as Frank and Gills (1991; 1992; 1993) want to demonstrate, is even more problematic.

[23] For the argument of continuity from medieval mercantile capitalism originating in Northern Italy and the Low Countries up to the emergence of industrial capitalism in Western Europe cf. Sée, 1928: 7–56.

power and business organization that were to serve it for the next four hundred years: foreign exchange, deposit banking, risk insurance, public finance, international trading companies, commercial bookkeeping' (Day, 1987: 199).[24]

Moreover, there was already a valid money market in the 14th century, where banking and trading companies had branches which dealt in paper currency (and, like every market, it was governed by the laws of supply and demand and was subject to various seasonal and cyclical fluctuations) (Bernard, 1976: 327). According to Braudel (1979; 1982) commercial, industrial, and banking capital[25] already existed in 13th century Florence (Brucker, 1998: 65–107) and has widened its grip over the economy ever since. Unlike Wallerstein, Braudel was *not* reluctant to apply the term capitalism in the Middle Ages, nor was he reluctant to apply WSA-concepts to that period (Braudel, 1979: 70). Indeed, why not use WSA terminology such as core, periphery, semi-periphery, incorporation etc., earlier than the 16th century, concerning the emergence of capitalism (De Wachter, 1996: 51–57)? And what about the *'incorporation'* of external arenas, by WSA defined as the 'historical process by which non-capitalist zones are absorbed into the capitalist world-system [where] inhabitants of territories that have been outside are brought into the system through colonization, conquest, or economic and political domination' (Dunaway, 1996: 455)? Cannot the conquest of Mediterranean islands by city-states in the 13th and 14th centuries or the Reconquista of the Iberian Peninsula be interpreted as an *identical* form of expansion, subjugation, domination and exploitation[26] or even Spain's conquest of the New World, albeit on a smaller scale?[27]

The exploitation of a rural periphery to the benefit of an urban core should not be overlooked either. The way cities such as Ypres and Ghent terrorized their countryside in the early 14th century to protect their monopoly in cloth production, resembles Wallersteins core-periphery model quite closely (Prevenier, 1997: 196). In general, the Italian city-states were the most successful in subjugating and dominating their rural hinterland, the contado (Nicholas, 1997: 87; Perrot, 1983: 93–97; Bowsky, 1970: 225–255) although

[24] The same is said by Bouvier and Germain-Martin, 1964: 21–22 and Lane, 1977. For the importance of credit instruments in 14th century overseas trade cf. Munro, 1994: X, 67–79. Using transfers of credit by exchange instruments 'inter-city exchange bankers' could avoid moving bullion over long distances (Blomquist, 1994: 345–346).

[25] Le Goff's conclusion of medieval banking: 'Par la masse d'argent qu'il manie, par l'étendue de ses horizons géographiques et économiques, par ses méthodes commerciales et financières, le marchand-banquier médieval est un capitaliste. Il l'est aussi par son esprit, son genre de vie, par sa place dans la société' (1962: 41).

[26] Cf. Bernard, 1976: 292–293 in general; cf. Le Mené, 1977: 207 (for the case of medieval Crete); Abulafia, 1993: I, 28–29 and Day, 1983: 198–200 (for medieval Sardinia); Ashtor, 1978: VI, 5–53 (for the Medieval Levant); the case of medieval Sicily is more doubtful (Epstein, 1989). But as Day (1985) points out, the colonialism which was practiced by the city-state of Venice in the Mediterranean, was not just political but financial as well. Thus, insisting on a fundamental difference between these forms of 'medieval' and 'modern colonialism' as Bartlett (1993: 306–313) does, is in my opinion not warranted.

[27] To what extent can one claim that 'à la fin du Moyen Age déjà, s'était établi un rapport pays développés – pays sous-développés entre l'Occident chrétien et les pays orientaux et maghrébins: l emprise économique a précédé la domination politique' (Ashtor 1992: IV, 385)?

the same can be said about early 14th century Toulouse (Mousnier, 1997: 347–379) or 14th century Bordeaux and the creation of its 'banlieu' (Bochaca, 1997). Since the urban hinterland was subordinated to the city-state in a hierarchical division of labor between town and countryside, and the city-state enforced a virtual monopoly position regarding the distribution of goods to the urban and rural population alike (Stabel, 1992: 352), some industries were more complementary than competitive with the urban ones.[28] It remains however unclear to what extent 'the international urban network' (Bartlett, 1993: 176) was a truly integrated one in the 14th century (Stabel, 1997: 72). Regional economies were certainly interconnected (Masschaele, 1997) while regional integration occurred and international trade was becoming more important. But it remains to be explored to what extent the economies of scale and economic differentiation in the Middle Ages have had a considerable impact on uneven regional development in the long run (cf. Ashtor, 1983: 375–433).

For Wallerstein (1993a: 294), the 'axial division of labor involving integrated production processes' is a conditio sine qua non when one wants to identify a system capitalistic in nature. Actually, from the late 11th century on, energetic merchant-entrepreneurs in Flanders started to produce standardized textile goods on a large scale, in particular woollen and linen cloth intended for export.[29] This urban based export industry drew its strength from a far-reaching division of labor, both employing semi-skilled and even unskilled workers in large numbers (Van der Wee, 1988: 320).[30] For Braudel (1982: 315) the boom of the 13th century arose out of the newly created division of labor as it proliferated. This increasing division of labor, especially apparent in the textile industry, but also in the mining industry (Braudel, 1982: 321–325; Pounds, 1994: 329; Molenda, 1989; Piccinni, 1994), had in turn a significant impact on social stratification and polari-

[28] At the same time one should consider to what extent the so-called 'buitenpoorterij' or 'bourgeoisie foraine', those who migrated from the city to the countryside – whilst retaining their citizenship – strengthened (juridically, socioeconomically and politically) the control of the city over its surrounding hinterland (Thoen, 1988: 400; 448–449; Boone, 1996: 715–725) and to what extent the 'landowning rural membership of an urban guild linked the town and the political life of its hinterland' (Carpenter, 1997: 63).

[29] For the importance of 12th century cloth from Champagne and Flanders to the Genoese market cf. Krueger, 1987. For the impact of market fluctuations on transformations in the urban textile industry cf. Munro, 1991. According to Chorley (1987), Northern cheap cloths exported to the Mediterranean in the 13th century exceeded those of luxury woolens, not only in volume but also in aggregate value.

[30] Thus in the Flemish textile industry, each of the tasks described was from the 12th century on performed by a specialist: breakers, beaters, washers, oilers, carders, combers, spinners, weavers, fullers, tenderers, teaselers, shearmen, dyers, pressers and so on (Munro, 1988: 1–27). 'Flanders and northern Italy had developed a genuinely capitalist mode of production in which the workers had effectively become wage earners, a proletariat, owing nothing but their labor, even though there was as yet no factories and the workers worked in their homes (...), the employment of these workers was subject to the fluctuations of the international market which they did not understand and over which they had no control. It is not surprising therefore, that both areas were beginning to experience industrial strife: strikes and urban revolts' (Koenigsberger, 1987: 225). In 1356–58 – after the great plague (!) – about 60% of the population in Ghent (then c. 65,000) was still involved in the cloth industry (Prevenier, 1975: 276–279). In Tournai, Maubeuge and Valenciennes, the situation was more or less similar (Bruwier, 1992: 261). In 14th century Florence 'between 40 and 60% of the population was engaged in the manufacturing of woolens' (Jacoby, 1994: 551).

zation in urbanized areas. Indeed, the mining industry – tin, lead, copper, bronze, silver, gold and iron – and finished products made from them, became quite significant in late medieval Europe (Braudel, 1982: 315) as metal-working gradually ceased to be a part-time occupation of the farming community and became the full-time pursuit of professional iron-workers (Braunstein, 1994: 23). Merchant capitalists who dealt in bar iron, first invested in ironworks, leased and operated them (Pounds, 1994: 327) [31].

In the inter-city state system, local oligarchic authorities also created deliberate policies of poverty-relief to increase the reserve of labor and depress wages. This poverty relief basically kept the urban poor who 'were not willing to jeopardize their miserable allowance' (Blockmans and Prevenier, 1978: 56) in perpetual dependence (Gonthier, 1978: 340). Although protests against living and working conditions did occur, they were generally unsuccessful in the long run since the 'magistrate worked hand in glove with the entrepreneurs' (Brand, 1992: 17). In most of Holland, the 'élites succeeded in preventing guilds from becoming powerful pressure groups' (Brand, 1992: 25). The very strict wage policies in the Low Countries set by the urban elite were actually not surprising: it was precisely the *fierce competition on the regional and international markets* which made the downward pressuring of wages combined with the increase of production the only effective way to make profit. This was done by exploiting fullers (and to a lesser extent weavers) who even in periods of economic upturn could hardly make ends meet (Brand and Stabel, 1995: 203–204; Boone and Brand, 1993).[32] Some 13th century merchants were capable of concentrating much power in the work place: they bought the raw materials to make cloth, controlled and supervised its fabrication, and preoccupied themselves also with the selling of the finished product on the market place (Derville, 1972: 360–361; Hodgett, 1972: 137–156).[33] It should be emphasized that capitalism not

[31] By 1430, the expansion of the metal industry in the rural areas of Namur and Liège lead to a take over of the industry by urban based merchant capitalists (Gillard, 1971). But paper-making, glass making and ship building were also important industries: 'the Venetian Arsenal, where standardized galleys were constructed along an assembly line, can probably claim to be one of Europe's first modern industrial factories' Modelski and Thompson (1996: 237). For the importance of capitalist relations in the medieval building industry cf. Hodgett (1972: 135–136).

[32] Since many 'drapeniers' in the Low Countries had no control over the price of primary resources (wool) because it had to be imported from England and Spain, 'textile guilds had very limited powers [...] their price-setting powers were limited, since they could not prevent competition in their major markets' (Munro, 1990: 44). 'The so-called weaver-guild was in reality an association dominated by master weavers who, as the chief industrial entrepreneurs, organized production by a domestic putting-out system. Most of their employees were unprotected, defenseless females whose piece-work wages the weaver-drapers controlled without difficulty' (Munro, 1994b: 383–384). A common feature of the 13th century was the 'steady multiplication and fragmentation of guilds – a tendency, it is suggested, deliberately fostered in places (Venice, Siena) by a calculated merchant policy to divide and rule [...] of which in turn further divisions emerged between capitalists, master craftsmen, and, marginalized by the whole guild system, the laboring population' (Jones, 1997: 250). According to Geremek (1994: 64–65) 'the cost of raw materials and the instability of the market, coupled with increasingly complicated technology demanding specialized skills and an extensive division of labor, often forced the craftsmen to submit and work for the merchants and entrepreneurs who organized production'.

[33] This also applied for 13th century England, where entrepreneurs 'bought wool and had it washed and dyed; they gave it out to carders and spinners; they employed weavers and fullers

only intensified in the cloth industry of the cities in the Low Countries, but also in the Italian cities that competed with them in the expanding European market,[34] which in turn was part of a larger world economic system (Abu-Lughod, 1989: 356–361). In addition, due to the restructuring of markets and because of a deliberate policy of entrepreneurs, constant 'reallocations' of capital from the urban centers to the countryside occurred (Heers, 1963: 121–124; Saey and Verhoeve, 1993: 107), since the latter 'offered more abundant and cheaper part-time agricultural labor, with a lower cost of living, virtually tax-free production, and an escape from specific guild and urban regulations' (Munro, 1994b: 378; cf. Holbach, 1993: 238–243; Stabel, 1997: 131). This aspect of capital reallocation which continued unabatedly up to the 16th century (Prevenier, Sosson and Boone, 1992: 164–166) also implied increased investments in technology there, such as windmills and water mills.[35] In general, this 'shift to lower wage zones and the possibility of further intra regional diversification' (Van der Wee, 1993: 205–208) was in direct competition with the urban proletariat (Brand and Stabel, 1995: 220), which caused the guilds of larger towns such as Brussels and Ypres to organize futile 'warlike expeditions to destroy looms in the rural areas around the towns' (Van der Wee, 1993: 209).[36] Only

---

throughout the town, under stringent supervision, at piece-rates fixed by themselves; and they sold the finished cloth at the great fairs of eastern England' (Miller and Hatcher, 1995: 112) Even small English towns as Stratford-upon-Avon were affected by the international textile trade: 'the monks of Winchcombe Abbey, who held 3 manors within easy carting distance from Stratford, contracted to sell the wool of their whole estate in the early 14th century to Italian merchants' (Dyer, 1997: 56–57). According to Lis and Soly (1994: 372–373), the 'overwhelming majority' of weavers in 14th century Cologne and Florence 'were working directly or indirectly as subcontractors for wealthy merchant-weavers who 'controlled all stages of the production process'. Although corporate regulations did exist, 'they did not hinder the concentration of production through networks of small workshops', thus making the latter centrally guided.

[34] 'As the workforce expanded, terms of employment hardened. Under the pressure (or pretext) of competition, working hours, including night hours, were stretched to the limits of endurance, wage rates lowered to what in many places by the 14th century was near starvation level, and wage earnings depressed by payment in debased coin or by truck in overvalued goods, and by loans and pay advances which tied workers to employers as much as peasants to landlords by rigid bonds of poverty and debt' (Jones, 1997: 251). In 14th century Paris artisans worked up to 16 or 17 hours per day in the summer and around 11 in the winter (Epstein, 1991: 189). In 14th century London, journeymen working in the cloth industry 'were used as piece workers (paid by the piece rather than by the day or week)' (Hilton, 1992: 84). Fullers in 14th century Ghent were mostly paid by the piece (Boone and Brand, 1993: 173); so were wool combers and carders in 13th century Genoa (Epstein, 1988b: 120).

[35] These technological innovations and techniques (mechanical fulling displacing labor power where water power was available) became widespread in the early 14th century (Carus-Wilson, 1952: 410–411) and their socioeconomic implications can not be underestimated: in 14th century England (pop. 6 million), for every 400–600 people there was a mill; in 14th century France (pop. 17.6 million) this was 440 persons per mill (Langdon, 1997: 284–285). According to Pacey (1978: 39), 'by 1250–1300, the foundations had already been laid for the later technological ascendancy of Europe'.

[36] In the Low Countries, only Ghent was very successful in controlling its immediate rural hinterland (Thoen, 1992: 56–57; Boone, 1990: 191–197). For an overview of military expeditions organized by urban militias against competing drapery production in the countryside cf. Nicholas (1971: 75–116; 203–221).

in a radius of a couple of miles were the guilds capable of eliminating competition from their immediate rural surroundings (Thoen and Verhulst, 1986: 54). The expansion of a putting-out (Verlag) system beyond the town walls was characteristic for preliminary highly labor intensive tasks like combing, carding and wool-spinning (Holbach, 1993: 235). Many urban centered industries eventually managed to adapt themselves to the changing socioeconomic situation (e.g. by specialization in higher quality products), but is likely that in several cities (especially those which had no staple rights for grain) wages of many unskilled unorganized workers were more exposed to market fluctuations and sudden economic downturns than their counterparts in the countryside. This made the urban based unskilled wage laborers prone to uproars since the fear of massive 'downsizing avant la lettre' and long term unemployment was a daily reality (Jones, 1997: 253). Not surprisingly, social explosions could be quite sudden and extremely violent during periods of economic recession. Obviously, social discontent was also (but far from exclusively) focused on questions of wages (Epstein, 1991: 116), not only on rates of pay because of high inflation, but also on such abuses as truck (Boone and Brand, 1993: 184; Holbach, 1993: 229). Clearly the cities' dependence on the market for textiles and grain supplies made them vulnerable for social unrest, especially given the nature of exploitative capitalism (Mackenney, 1987: 29). Essentially, the medieval 'proletariat' was a readily available pool of (often seasonal) extra labor, exploited when seen fit. This reserve labor pool was also increased by child labor (Epstein, 1991: 120). International competition, directly related to the social conditions of the lower social strata, was very real indeed since it induced the urban textile centers to shift their production of lower quality bulk goods towards more exclusive luxury goods for which demand was less elastic, while the countryside often took over the role of producing lower-quality products (Stabel, 1997: 144; Abraham-Thisse, 1993: 172–173).

VI. Conclusions

If all the above-mentioned parallels exist between late 13th century urban economies and socioeconomic processes in the early 16th century, what is actually so modern that one can see originating only around 1500 AD? [37] Can't we conclude that the term merchant capitalism is completely applicable to the medieval urban centers (Chaunu, 1969: 311)? Historical continuity seems to be undeniable. As a consequence, I suggest rethinking the temporal predisposition put forward by WSA. Let me end here by emphasizing that I do not challenge the fact that after 1500 the capitalist logic intensified because of the

[37] To quote Contamine et al. (1993: 403–409): 'Des formes d'investissement que l'on peut qualifier déjà de capitalistes étaient assez largement connues et pratiquées, en milieu rural comme en milieu urbain, sur terre comme sur mer [...] il importe de reconnaître que le capitalisme 'protestant' et 'nordique' des Temps modernes est largement issu des formes de capitalisme bien plus qu'embryonnaires apparues pendant les derniers siècles du Moyen Age'. However, I do not deny the qualitative shift which takes place in the 16th century when a global division of labor and the inter state system replace the inter city state system: city states were too small for the further ceaseless accumulation of capital on an ever wider scale: Genoa or Venwice could colonize and exploit their rural hinterland or their colonies (Crete, Cyprus, ...) in a core-periphery relationship but obviously not the Americas.

'the great maritime discoveries' (Sée, 1928: 41) and the subsequent increasing profits from trade and exploitation coming out of 'non-Europe' to Europe. Nor am I denying the emergence of an interstate-system after 1500 or the existence of different hegemonic cycles (Arrighi, 1994), processes which WSA has adequately theorized. How then can one accept general concepts of WSA and also explain the emergence of capitalism in the Late Middle Ages without falling into an extreme form of holism à la André Frank (1990a and 1990b)? If one accepts the fact that merchant capitalism was already maturing in Europe prior to the Long 16th Century, the development of a 'World'-System after 1492 is not empirically challenged. What needs to be rethought and explored is the emergence of merchant capitalism in Europe before it expanded in a 'World' capitalist economy: exploitation of wage labor, 'class' struggle, reallocation of capital and financial investments from a core (urban zone) to a periphery (countryside), substitution of labor power by technological inventions (wind mills and water mills) in order to minimize labor costs and further the endless accumulation of capital, the commodification of the material world and the rationalization of the spiritual world, in short, modern features of contemporary capitalism, found their roots in the Middle Ages. It was after all precisely within the urban nexus of medieval Western Europe that economic 'self-sustained growth' took place (Van Uytven, 1987: 127). As I attempted to point out, Modernization Theory, Marxist 'Brennerianism' and WSA all have certain problems with the emergence of capitalism in the medieval period because of their unwillingness to grasp the importance of medieval cities and their impact on recurring economic growth in the long run. The Late Middle Ages were after all far from being a rigid and stagnant artisan economy or a 'feudal system in crisis' only waiting to be swept away by Modernity under the cloak of capitalism. Instead, one should attempt to look at the Middle Ages without prejudices and see to what extent, why and how embryonic forms and features of capitalism came into being, matured and were capable of transforming themselves, while expanding and intensifying in the Long 16th Century. Then, medieval cities and their hinterland are likely to be central in our analysis of understanding why and how recurring growth occurred in Western Europe in the long run. Taking into account how city-states profited from their colonial territories is in this light a fundamentally important issue. To what extent was a medieval city's 'countryside' colonized and exploited in a similar way as its overseas colonies (such as Crete, etc.)? To what extent were notions of territoriality carved around medieval urban citizenship in opposition to its dominated countryside, carried over in the interstate-system of the 16th century? Practices of exploitation, colonialism and domination that were existent in early modern Europe are likely to have found their origins in medieval town and countryside relationships.[38] It is especially in the larger cities, whose exports were geared towards long-distance markets, that we

[38] Practices of territoriality which were pursued by mercantile states in the early modern period originated in the inter-city state system of the Late Middle Ages (cf. the phenomenon of the 'bourgeoisie fouraine' or buitenpoorterij). The city-state had extra-territorial powers beyond its proper walls in the sense that its citizens who were living far away in the countryside could only be tried by their urban magistrates. From the 12th century onwards, the well to do in the countryside purchased city-state citizenship even if they never lived there, precisely for all kinds of juridical and economic benefits. During the peak of the inter-city state system in Europe (1250–1400), many cities consistently implemented extra-territorial prerogatives as instruments of their imperialist strategies (Van Uytven, 1982: 250–252).

are most likely to find both the embryonic appearance of capitalist exploitation and class formations (Friedrichs, 1975: 45).

In addition, the nature of medieval cities is quite likely to explain why the emergence of capitalism occurred in Europe and not elsewhere.[39] Although some in WSA have advocated 'civilizational underpinnings', the existence of a European inter-city state system is most likely to be a crucial variable. As in the interstate system later on, constant competition due to the 'absence of a unicentric polity, that is, the existence of a multicentric political structure over most its space' (Mandalios, 1996: 283) is applicable to the Middle Ages as well. Furthermore, recognizing the importance of the political nature of the city-state system in direct symbiosis with the existing economic system of merchant capitalism, disarms the criticism that WSA is 'viewing political processes as epiphenomenal in relation to economic causation' (Zolberg, 1981: 255). Thus, bringing medieval cities back into the analysis of the above-mentioned perspectives, and especially in World System Analysis, is a most urgent and necessary endeavor.

Bibliography

Abraham-Thisse, S. (1993) 'Le commerce des draps de Flandre en Europe du Nord', in M. Boone and W. Prevenier (eds), *Drapery Production in the late medieval Low Countries: Markets and Strategies for Survival (14th–16th Centuries). Proceedings of the colloquium Ghent, April 28th 1992*, Louvain, pp. 167–206.

Abulafia, D. (1993) 'Southern Italy, Sicily and Sardinia in the Medieval Mediterranean Economy' in D. Abulafia, *Commerce and Conquest in the Mediterranean, 1100–1500,* Norfolk.

Abu-Lughod, J. (1989) *Before European Hegemony. The World System AD 1250–1350,* Oxford.

Adams, R. (1975) 'Anthropological Perspectives on Ancient Trade', *Current Anthropology*, 15, pp. 239–258

Aerts, E., Dupon, W. and Wee, H. van der (1985) *De Economische ontwikkeling van Europa: documenten,* Louvain.

Aerts, E. and Unger, R. (1990) 'Brewing in the Low Countries', in E. Aerts, L. Cullen and R. Wilson (eds) *Production, Marketing and Consumption of Alcoholic Beverages since the Late Middle Ages' in Proceedings 10th International Economic History Congress, Session B–14, Studies in Social and Economic History*, Louvain, pp. 92–101.

[39] For Hicks (1969: 38) 'the fact that European civilization has passed through a city-state phase is the principal key to the divergence between the history of Europe and the history of Asia'. In focusing on the European medieval inter-city state system, I do not wish to 'homogenize' the European town since it existed in different forms (Delumeau, 1998). But all over Europe, the cities at some point reached a very high degree of autonomy, sometimes independence, as they were ruled by their merchant-elite. This distinguishes them from, for example, Chinese cities (Deng, 1999: 108; 199), or Islamic cities (Udovitch, 1993: 792; Ashrafyan, 1998: 340) where merchants could not acquire significant political-military power.

Arenson, S. (1991) 'The Medieval Ship and Technological Decadence. The Case of the East', in C. Villain-Gandossi [et al.] (eds), *Medieval Ships and the Birth of Technological Societies*, Malta.

Arrighi, G. (1994) *The Long Twentieth Century*, New York.

Ashrafyan, K.Z. (1998) 'Central Asia under Timur from 1370 to the early 15th century', in M.S. Asimov and C.E. Bosworth (eds) *History of civilizations of Central Asia*, Paris, pp. 319–345.

Ashtor, E. (1978) *Studies on the Levantine Trade in the Middle Ages*, London.

Ashtor, E. (1983) 'Le Proche-Orient au Bas Moyen-Age. Une région sous-développée', in A. Guarducci (ed.) *Sviluppo e sottosviluppo in Europa e fuori d'Europa dal secolo XIII alla Revoluzione Industriale. Atti della Decima settimana di studio 7–12 aprile 1978*, Prato, pp. 375–433. (Instituto Internazionale di Storia Economica 'F. Datini'; Serie II, 10).

Ashtor, E. (1992) 'Levantine Sugar Industry in the Later Middle Ages' (III) and 'L'ascendant technologique de l'Occident Médieval (IV), in B.Z. Kedar (ed.), *Technology, Industry and Trade,* Norfolk, pp. 266–280 and pp. 385–413.

Aymard, M. (1993) 'Markets and Rural Economies in Mediterranean Europe (from the 14th to the 18th century)', in J. Torras [et al.], *Els Espais del Mercat,* Valencia, pp. 289–300.

Barnett, J.E. (1998) *Time's Pendulum,* New York.

Bartlett, R. (1993) *The Making of Europe. Conquest, Colonization and Cultural Change 950–1350,* Princeton.

Bautier, R.H. (1992) *Commerce méditerranéen et banquiers italiens au Moyen Age,* Norfolk.

Bernard, J. (1976) 'Trade and Finance in the Middle Ages, 900–1500', in C.M. Cipolla (ed.), *The Fontana Economic History of Europe. Volume I: The Middle Ages,* New York, pp. 274–338.

Blockmans, W. (1993) 'The Economic expansion of Holland and Zeeland in the 14–16th centuries', in E. Aers, B. Heneau, P. Janssens and R. van Uytven (eds), *Studia Historica Oeconomica. Liber amicorum Herman van der Wee,* Louvain, pp. 41–58.

Blockmans, W. and Prevenier, W. (1978) 'Poverty in Flanders and Brabant from the 14th to the mid-16th century', *Acta Historiae Neerlandicae*, 10, pp. 20–57.

Blomquist, T. (1994) 'Alien coins and foreign exchange banking in a medieval commune: 13th century Lucca', *Journal of Medieval History*, 20, December, pp. 337–346.

Bochaca, M. (1997) *La Banlieu de Bordeaux. Formation d'une juridiction municipale suburbaine (vers 1250–vers 1550)*, Paris.

Bois, G. (1985) 'Sur la crise du mode de production féodal', in B. Chavance (ed.), *Marx en perspective. Actes du colloque,* Paris, pp. 189–202.

Boone M. (1990) *Gent en de Bourgondische hertogen ca. 1384–1453. Een sociaal-politieke studie van een staatsvormingsproces,* Brussels. (Verhandelingen van de koninklijke academie voor Wetenschappen, Letteren en Schone kunsten van Belgie, Klasse der Letteren, jg. 52, nr. 133).

Boone M. (1994) 'Les métiers dans les villes flamandes au bas moyen Age (XIV–XVI siècles): images normatives, réalites socio-politiques et économiques', in P. Lambrechts and J.P. Sosson (eds), *Les métiers au Moyen Âge. Aspects économiques et sociaux,* Louvain-La-Neuve, pp. 1–22.

Boone, M. (1996) 'Droit de bourgeoisie et particularisme urbain dans la Flandre bourguignonne et habsbourgeoise (1384–1585)', *Revue belge de philologie et d'histoire*, 74, 3–4, pp. 707–725.

Boone, M. and Brand, H. (1993) 'Vollersoproeren en collectieve actie in Gent en Leiden in de 14e–15e eeuw', *Tijdschrift voor Sociale Geschiedenis*, 19, 2, May, pp. 168–192.

Boone, M. and Prevenier, W. (eds) (1993) *Drapery Production in the Late Medieval Low Countries: Markets and Strategies for Survival (14th–16th centuries)*, Louvain.

Bouvier, J. and Germain-Martin, H. (1964) *Finances et financiers de l'Ancien Régime*, Paris.

Bowles, S. (1988) 'Class versus World-Systems Analysis? Epitaph for a False Opposition', *Review*, XI, 4, pp. 433–451.

Bowsky, W. (1970) *The Finance of the Commune of Sienna 1287–1355*, Oxford.

Bozorgnia, S.M. (1998) *The Role of Precious Metals in European Economic Development*, Westport CT.

Brand, H. (1992) 'Urban policy or personal government: the involvement of the urban elite in the economy of Leiden at the end of the Middle Ages', in H. Diederiks, P. Hohenberg and M. Wagenaar (eds), *Economic Policy in Europe since the Late Middle Ages. The Visible Hand and the Fortune of Cities*, Leicester, pp. 17–34.

Brand, H. and Stabel, P. (1995) 'De ontwikkeling van vollerslonen in enkele laat-middeleeuwse textielcentra in de Nederlanden. Een poging tot reconstructie', in J.M. Duvosquel and E. Thoen (eds), *Peasants and Townsmen in Medieval Europe*, Ghent, pp. 203–222.

Braudel, F. (1979) *The Perspective of the World*, Berkeley.

Braudel, F. (1982) *The Wheels of Commerce*, Berkeley.

Braunstein, Ph. (1994) 'Les métiers du métal. Travail et entreprise à la fin du moyen âge' in P. Lambrechts and J.P. Sosson (eds), *Les métiers au Moyen Age. Aspects économiques et sociaux*, Louvain-La-Neuve, pp. 23–34.

Brenner, R. (1977) 'The Origins of Capitalist Development: A Critique of Neo-Smithian Marxism', *New Left Review*, 104, pp. 25–92.

Brenner, R. (1985) 'Agrarian Class Structure and Economic Development in Pre-Agrarian Europe' and 'The Agrarian Roots of European Capitalism', in T. Aston and C. Philpin, *The Brenner Debate*, Cambridge, pp. 10–63 and pp. 213–327.

Brenner, R. (1986) 'The social basis of economic development', in J. Roemer (ed.), *Analytical Marxism*, Cambridge, pp. 23–53.

Britnell, R.H. (1995) 'Commercialisation and economic development in England, 1000–1300', in R.H. Britnell and B.M.S. Campbell (eds), *A commercialising economy. England 1086 to circa 1300*, Manchester, pp. 7–26.

Britnell, R.H. and Campbell, B.M.S. (eds) (1995) *A Commercialising economy. England 1086 to circa 1300*, Manchester.

Brucker, G. (1998) *Florence. The Golden Age 1138–1737*, Berkeley.

Bruwier, M. (1992) 'Études sur le réseau urbain en Hainaut de 1350 à 1850' in *Actes du 15e Colloque International à Spa le 4–6 Sept. 1990 'Le Réseau urbain en Belgique dans une perspective historique (1350–1850)'*, Bruxelles, pp. 251–316. (Crédit Communal, Collection Histoire, série in–8; nr. 86).

Byres, T.J. (1996) *Capitalism from Above and Capitalism from Below. An Essay in Comparative Political Economy*, New York.

Campbell, B.M.S. (1995) 'Measuring the commercialisation of seigneurial agriculture circa 1300' in R.H. Britnell and B.M.S. Campell (eds), *A commercialising economy. England 1086 to circa 1300,* Manchester, pp. 132–193.

Campbell, B.M.S. (1995b) 'Progressiveness and Backwardness in 13th and early 14th century English Agriculture: The Verdict of Recent Research', in J.M. Duvosquel and E. Thoen (eds), *Peasants and Townsmen in Medieval Europe,* Ghent, pp. 541–560.

Campbell, B.M.S. (1995c) 'Ecology Versus Economics in Late 13th and Early 14th Century English Agriculture', in D. Sweeney (ed.) *Agriculture in the Middle Ages. Technology, Practice and Representation,* Philadelphia, pp. 76–108.

Cantor, N. (1973) *The Meaning of the Middle Ages. A Sociological and Cultural History,* Boston.

Carpenter, C. (1997) 'Town and Country: the Stratford Guild and Political Networks of 15th century Warwickshire', in R. Bearman (ed.), *The History of an English Borough: Stratford-upon-Avon 1196–1996,* Cornwall, pp. 62–79.

Carus-Wilson, E.M. (1952) 'The Woollen Industy', in M. Postan and E. Rich, *The Cambridge Economic History of Europe*, vol. II, Cambridge.

Chaunu P. (1969) *L'expansion européenne du XIIIe au XVe siècle,* Paris.

Cherubini, G. (1990) 'The Peasant and Agriculture', in J. Le Goff (ed.), *The Medieval World,* London, pp. 113–137.

Cherubini, G. (1993) 'The Market in Medieval Italy', in J. Torras [et al.], *Els Espais del Mercat,* Valencia, pp. 277–288.

Chorley, P. (1987) 'The cloth exports of Flanders and northern France during the 13th century: a luxury trade?', *Economic History Review*, 40, pp. 349–379.

Contamine, Ph. [et al.] (1993) *L'économie médievale,* Paris.

Crosby, A. (1997) *The Measure of Reality. Quantification and Western Society 1250–1600*, Cambridge.

Day, J. (1983) 'Terres, marchés et monnaies en Italie et en Sardaigne du XIème au XVIIIème siècle', *Histoire, Économie et Société*, 2e année, 2e trimestre, pp. 187–203.

Day, J. (1985) 'Colonialisme monétaire en Méditerranée au Moyen Age', in *Économies Méditerranéennes Équilibres et Intercommunications XIIIe–XIXe siècles. Actes du Ie Colloque International d'Histoire, Athènes, 18–25 septembre 1983*, Athènes, pp. 305–319. (Centre de Recherches Néohelléniques de la Fondation Nationale de la Recherche Scientifique).

Day, J. (1987) *The Medieval Market Economy,* Oxford.

Delumeau, J.P. (1998) 'Communes, consulats et la city-republic', in C. Laurent, B. Merdrignac and D. Pichot (eds), *Mondes de l'Ouest et villes du monde,* Rennes, pp. 491–509.

Deng, G. (1999) *The Premodern Chinese Economy. Structural Equilibrium and Capitalist Sterility,* London.

Derville, A. (1972) 'Les draperies flamandes et artésiennes vers 1250–1350: quelques considérations critiques et problématiques', *Revue du Nord*, 215, pp. 353–370.

Derville, A. (1987) 'L'héritage des draps médievales', *Revue du Nord*, 275, pp. 715–724.

Derville, A. (1994) 'Naissance du capitalisme', in F. Gasparri (ed.), *Le XIIe siècle. Mutations et renouveau en France dans la prémiere moitie du XIIe siècle*, Paris, pp. 33–60.

Derville, A. (1995) *L'économie française au Moyen Age*, Paris.

Derville, A. (1996) 'Douze études d'histoire rurale: Flandre, Artois, Cambrésis au Moyen Âge', *Revue Du Nord*, Hors Serie, 11, Lille III.

Dohrn-van Rossum, G. (1996) *History of the Hour*, Chicago.

Dowd, D. (1961) 'The economic expansion of Lombardy 1300–1500', *Journal of Economic History*, 21, pp. 143–160.

Du Boulay, F.R. (1970) *An age of Ambition. English society in the Late Middle Ages*, London.

Dunaway, W. (1996) 'Incorporation as an Interactive Process', *Sociological Inquiry*, 66, 4, November, pp. 455–470.

Dyer C. (1991) 'Were There Any Capitalists in 15th Century England?', in J. Kermode (ed.), *Enterprise and Individuals in 15th Century England*, Wolfeboro Falls, pp. 1–24.

Dyer, C. (1997) 'Medieval Stratford: a Successful Small Town', in R. Bearman (ed.), *The History of an English Borough: Stratford-upon-Avon 1196–1996*, Cornwall, pp. 43–61.

Epstein, S.A. (1988) 'Business Cycles and the Sense of Time in Medieval Genoa', *Business History Review*, 62, pp. 238–260.

Epstein, S.A. (1988b) 'Labour in 13th-Century Genoa', in I. Malkin and R. Hohlfelder (eds), *Mediterranean cities: historical perspectives*, London, pp. 114–140.

Epstein, S.A. (1991) *Wage labor and guilds in Medieval Europe*, Chapel Hill.

Epstein, S.R. (1989) 'The textile industry and the foreign cloth trade in late medieval Sicily, 1300–1500: a 'colonial relationship'?', *Journal of Medieval History*, 15, pp. 141–183.

Epstein, S.R. (1992) *An island for itself. Economic development and social change in late medieval Sicily*, Cambridge, 1992.

Epstein, S.R. (1993) 'Town and Country: Economy and Institutions in Late Medieval Italy', *Economic History Review*, 46–3, pp. 453–477.

Espinas, G. (1933) *Les Origines du Capitalisme. Sire Jean Boinebroke, patricien et drapier douaisien*, Lille.

Fossier, R. (1991) *La Société médiévale*, Paris.

Frank, A.G. (1990a) 'A theoretical introduction to five thousand years of world system history', *Review*, 13, 2, Spring, pp. 155–248.

Frank, A.G. (1990b) 'De quelles transitions et de quels modes de production s'agit-il dans le système mondial réel? Commentaire sur l'article de Wallerstein', *Sociologie et sociétés*, 22, 2, October, pp. 207–219.

Frank, A.G. and Gills, B. (1991) '5000 years of World System History: The Cumulation of Accumulation', in C. Chase-Dunn and Th. Hall (eds), *Core/Periphery Relations in Precapitalist Worlds*, Boulder, CO, pp. 67–111.

Frank, A.G. and Gills, B. (1992) 'The Five Thousand Year World System: An Inter-disciplinary Introduction', *Humboldt Journal of Social Relations*, 18, 1, Spring, pp. 1–79.

Frank, A.G. and Gills, B. (1993) 'World System Economic Cycles and Hegemonial Shift to Europe 100BC to 1500 AD', *The Journal of European Economic History*, 22, 1, Spring, pp. 155–183.

Friedrichs, Ch. (1975) 'Capitalism, Mobility and Class Formation in the Early Modern German City', *Past and Present*, 69, November, pp. 24–49.

Fritze K. (1985) 'Soziale Aspekte der Stadt-Land-Beziehungen im Bereich der Wendischen Hansestädte (13. bis 16. Jahrhundert)', in H. Sculze (ed.), *Städtisches Um- und Hinterland in Vorindustrieller Zeit*, Köln, pp. 21–32.

Génicot, L. (1968) *Le XIIIe siècle européen*, Paris.

Geremek, B. (1994) *Poverty. A History*, Oxford.

Giddens A. (1981) *A Contemporary Critique of Historical Materialism, vol. 1: Power, Property and the State*, London/Berkeley.

Gillard, A. (1971) *L'industrie du fer dans les localités du comté de Namur et de l'entre-Sambre-et-Meuse de 1345 à 1600*, Brussels.

Gimpel, J. (1976) *The Medieval Machine. The Industrial Revolution of the Middle Ages*, New York.

Gonthier, N. (1978) 'Dans le Lyon médiéval: vie et mort d'un pauvre', *Cahiers d'histoire*, 23, 3, pp. 335–347.

Grassby, R. (1999) *The Idea of Capitalism before the Industrial Revolution*, Oxford.

Greilsammer, M. (1994) 'Pour blanchir son argent et son âme', *Revue Belge de philologie et d'histoire*, 72, pp. 793–833.

Guérreau, A. (1980) *Le féodalisme. Un horizon théorique*, Paris.

Hall, T. (1996) 'The World System Perspective: A Small Sample from a Large Universe', *Sociological Inquiry*, 66, 4, Fall, pp. 440–454.

Hanawalt, B.A. (1986) 'Peasant Resistance to Royal and Seignorial Impositions', in F.X. Newman (ed.), *Social Unrest in the Late Middle Ages*, Binghamton, pp. 23–47.

Harvey D. (1985) *The Urbanization of Capital*, Baltimore.

Harvey, B.F. (1991) 'Introduction: the crisis of the early 14th century', in B.M.S. Campbell (ed.), *Before the Black Death. Studies in the 'crisis' of the early 14th century*, Manchester, pp. 1–24.

Heers, J. (1963) *L'Occident aux XIVe et XVe siècles. Aspects économiques et sociaux*, Paris.

Heers, J. (1992) *Le Moyen Age, une imposture*, Paris.

Heilbroner R. (1985) *The Nature and Logic of Capitalism*, New York/London.

Hicks, J. (1969) *A Theory of Economic History*, Oxford.

Hickson, C. and Thompson, E. (1991) 'A New Theory of Guilds and European Economic Development', *Explorations in Economic History*, 28, 2, pp. 127–168.

Hilton, R. (1992) *English and French towns in feudal society*, Cambridge.

Hocquet, J.C. (1979) *Le sel et la fortune de Venise*, 2 vols, Lille.

Hocquet, J.C. (1985) *Le Sel et le Pouvoir. De l'An mil à la Révolution française*, Paris.

Hodgett G. (1972) *A Social and Economic History of Medieval Europe*, New York.

Holbach, R. (1993) 'Some Remarks on the Role of 'Putting-Out' in Flemish and Northwest European Cloth Production', in M. Boone and W. Prevenier (eds), *Drapery Production in the Late Medieval Low Countries: Markets and Strategies fir Survival (14th–16th centuries)*, Louvain, pp. 207–249.

Holton, R. (1985) *The Transition from Feudalism to Capitalism*, London.

Howell, M. and Boone, M. (1996) 'Becoming Early Modern in the Late Medieval Low Countries: Ghent, Douai and the Late Medieval Crisis', *Urban History*, 23, 3, December, pp. 300–324.

Hunt, E.S. (1994) *The Medieval Super-Companies*, Cambridge.

Imsen S. and Vogler G. (1997) 'Communal Autonomy and Peasant Resistance in Northern and Central Europe', in P. Blickle (ed.), *Resistance, Representation, and Community*, Oxford, pp. 5–43.

Jacoby, D. (1994) 'The Migration of Merchants and Craftsmen: a Mediterranean Perspective (12th–15th Century)', in S. Cavaciocchi (ed.), *Le Migrazioni in Europa secc. XIII–XVIII. Atti della Settimane di studio 3–8 maggio 1993*, Prato, pp. 533–560. (Instituto Internazionale di Storia Economica 'F. Datini'; Serie II, 25).

Jones, E.L. (1981) *The European Miracle*, Cambridge.

Jones, Ph. (1997) *The Italian City-State. From Commune to Signoria*, Oxford.

Karpov, S.P. (1993) 'The Grain Trade in the Southern Black Sea Region: The 13th to 15th Century', *Mediterranean Historical Review*, 8, 1, June, pp. 55–71.

Koenigsberger, H. (1987) *Medieval Europe, 400–1500,* Hong Kong.

Krueger, H.C. (1987) 'The Genoese Exportation of Northern Cloths to Mediterranean Ports, 12th Century', *Revue belge de philologie et d'histoire*, 65, 4, pp. 722–750.

Labal, P. (1962) *Histoire. Le Moyen Age*, Paris.

Lal D. (1998*) Unintended Consequences. The Impact of Factor Endowments, Culture and Politics on Long-run Economic Performance*, Cambridge.

Lambrechts P. and Sosson J.P. (eds) (1994) *Les métiers au Moyen Age. Aspects économiques et sociaux,* Louvain-La-Neuve.

Landes D. (1998) *The Wealth and Poverty of Nations. Why Some are so Rich and Some so Poor,* New York.

Lane F. (1977) 'Double Entry Bookkeeping and Resident Merchants', *Journal of European Economic History*, 6, pp. 177–191

Langdon J. (1997) 'Was England a Technological Backwater in the Middle Ages?', in G. Astill and J. Langdon (eds) *Medieval Farming and Technology: the Impact of agricultural change in Northwest Europe*, New York, pp. 275–291.

Le Goff, J. (1962) *Marchands et banquiers du Moyen Age,* Paris.

Le Goff, J. (1988) *Your Money or Your Life: Economy and Religion in the Middle Ages*, New York.

Le Goff, J. (1991) *Pour un autre Moyen Age,* Paris.

Le Goff, J. (1998) 'Introduction', in J. Le Goff (ed.), *La ville en France au Moyen Age*, Paris, pp. 7–25.

Le Mené, M. (1977) *L'économie médiévale*, Vendôme.

Lestocquoy, J. (1952) *Aux origines de la bourgeoisie. Les villes de Flandre et d'Italie sous le gouvernement des patriciens (XIe–XVe siècles)*, Paris.

Lis, C. and Soly, H. (1994) 'Corporatisme, onderaanneming en loonarbeid', *Tijdschrift voor Sociale Geschiedenis*, 20, 4, November, pp. 365–390.

Lis, C. and Soly, H. (1997) 'Different Paths of Development. Capitalism in the Northern and Southern Netherlands during the Late Middle Ages and the Early Modern Period', *Review*, 20, 2, Spring, pp. 211–242.

Little, L. (1978) *Religious Poverty and the Profit Economy in Medieval Europe,* Ithaca.

Lloyd, T.H. (1977) *The English Wool Trade in the Middle Ages,* Cambridge.

Lopez, R. (1976) *The Commercial Revolution of the Middle Ages 950–1350,* Cambridge.

Lopez, R., Miskimin, H. and Udovitch, A. (1970) 'England to Egypt, 1350–1500: Long-term Trends and Long-distance Trade', in M. Cook, *Studies in the Economic History of the Middle East*, Oxford, pp. 93–128.

Mackenney, R. (1987) *Tradesmen and traders. The world of the guilds in Venice and Europe c. 1250–1650*, London.

Mandalios, J. (1996) 'Historical Sociology', in B. Turner (ed.), *The Blackwell Companion to Social Theory*, Oxford, pp. 278–302.

Martin, H. (1996) *Mentalités Médiévales (XIe–XVe siècle)*, Paris.

Marx, K. (1977) *Capital. Volume One*, New York.

Masschaele, J. (1997) *Peasants, merchants and markets. Inland trade in medieval England, 1150–1350*, Basingstoke.

Mauro, F. (1988) 'Les ports comme entreprise économique. La dynamique socio économique', in S. Cavaciocchi (ed.), *I Porti Come Impresa Economica. Atti della Diciannovesima Settimane di studi 2–6 maggio 1987*, Prato, pp. 751–777. (Instituto Internazionale di Storia Economica 'F. Datini'; Serie II, 19).

Mazzaoui, M. (1981) *The Italian Cotton Industry in the Late Middle Ages,* Cambridge.

Menant, F. (1993) *Campagnes Lombardes du Moyen Age*, Roma.

Menard, R. (1997) 'Transport costs and long-range trade, 1300–1800', in J. Tracy (ed.), *The Political Economy of Merchant Empires. State Power and World Trade 1350–1750,* Cambridge, pp. 228–275.

Mickwitz, G. (1936) *Die Kartellfunktionen der Zunfte und ihre Bedeutung bei der Entstehung der Zunftwesens. Eine Studie in spatantiker und mittelalterlicher Wirtschaftgeschichte*, Helsinki/Leipzig.

Miller, E. and Hatcher, J. (1995) *Medieval England: Towns, Commerce and Crafts 1086–1348*, London.

Modelski, G. and Thompson, W. (1996) *Leading Sectors and World Powers,* Columbia SC.

Molenda, D. (1989) 'Investissements industriels et investissements culturels dans les villes minières de l'Europe centrale aux XIIIe–XVIIe siècles', in A. Guarducci (ed.), *Investimenti e Civiltà Urbana secoli XIII–XVIII. Atti della Nona Settimana di Studi 22–28 Aprile 1977*, Prato, pp. 911–926. (Instituto Internazionale di Storia Economica 'F. Datini'; Serie II, 9).

Mollat, M. (ed.) (1968) *Le rôle du sel dans l'histoire,* Paris.

Mollat, M. (1977) *Études sur l'économie et la société de l'Occident médiéval XIIe–XVe siècles*, London.

Mollat, M. (1988) *Jacques Coeur ou l'ésprit d'entreprise au XV siècle*, Paris.

Mollat, M. (1993) *Europe and the Sea*, Oxford.

Mousnier, M. (1997) *La Gascogne toulousaine aux XIIe–XIIIe siècles. Une dynamique sociale et spatiale*, Toulouse.

Mundy, J.H. (1991) *Europe in the High Middle Ages 1150–1309*, London.

Munro, J.H. (1988) 'Textile Technology in the Middle Ages', in J. Strayer [et al.] (eds), *The Dictionary of the Middle Ages*, New York, pp. 693–711.

Munro, J.H. (1990) 'Urban regulation and Monopolistic competition in the textile industries of the late-Medieval Low Countries', in E. Aerts (ed.), *Proceedings 10th International Economic History Congress Leuven Session B–15*, Louvain, pp. 41–52.

Munro, J.H. (1991) 'Industrial transformations in the north-west European textile trades, c.1290–c.1340: economic progress or economic crisis?', in B.M.S. Campbell (ed.), *Before the Black Death: Studies in the 'crisis' of the early 14th century*, Manchester, pp. 110–148.

Munro, J.H. (1994a) *Textiles, Towns and Trade. Essays in the economic history of late-medieval England and the Low Countries*, Norfolk.

Munro, J.H. (1994b) 'Industrial Entrepreneurship in the Late-Medieval Low Countries: Urban Draperies, Fullers and the Art of Survival', in P. Klep and E. van Cauwenberghe (eds), *Entrepreneurship and the Transformation of the Economy. Essays in honor of Herman Van der Wee*, Louvain, pp. 377–388.

Nicholas, D. (1971) *Town and Countryside: Social, Economic and Political Tensions in 14th–Century Flanders,* Bruges.

Nicholas, D. (1997) *The Later Medieval City, 1300–1500*, London.

North, D. and Thomas, R. (1973) *The Rise of the Western World. A New Economic History*, Cambridge.

Pacey, A. (1978) *The Maze of Ingenuity. Ideas and Idealism in the Development of Technology*, Cambridge.

Pernoud, R., Gimpel, J. and Delatouche, R. (1986) *Le Moyen Age pour quoi faire?*, Paris.

Pernoud, R. (1992) *De Middeleeuwen. Een herwaardering*, Baarn.

Perrot, J.-C. (1983) 'Développement et sous-développement regionales', in A. Guarducci A. (ed.), *Sviluppo e sottosviluppo in Europa e fuori d'Europa dal secolo XIII alla Revoluzione Industriale. Atti della Decima settimana di studio 7–12 aprile 1978*, Prato, pp. 91–102. (Instituto Internazionale di Storia Economica 'F. Datini'; Serie II, 10).

Persson, K. (1988) *Pre-Industrial Economic Growth. Social Organization and Technological Progress in Europe*, Oxford.

Piccinni, G. (1994) 'Economy and Society in Southern Tuscany in the Late Middle Ages', in T. Blomquist and M. Mazzaoui (eds), *The Other Tuscany,* Kalamazoo, pp. 215–233.

Postan, M.M. (ed.) (1966) *Cambridge Economic History of Europe*, vol. 1, 2nd ed., Cambridge.

Postan, M.M. (1973) *Essays on Medieval Agriculture and General problems of the Medieval Economy*, Cambridge.

Postan, M.M. and Hatcher J. (1985) 'Population and Class Relations in Feudal Society', in T.H. Aston and C.H.E. Philpin (eds), *The Brenner Debate,* Cambridge, pp. 64–78.

Pounds, N.J.G. (1994) *An Economic History of Medieval Europe*, New York.

Prevenier, W. (1975) 'Bevolkingscijfers en professionele strukturen der Bevolking van Gent en Brugge in de 14de eeuw', in *Album Charles Verlinden*, Ghent, pp. 269–303.

Prevenier, W. (1997) 'Bij wijze van besluit: zoektocht naar het hart van de middeleeuwse stad', in M. Carlier, A. Greve, W. Prevenier and P. Stabel (eds), *Core and Periphery in late medieval urban society. Proceedings of the Colloquium at Ghent (22nd–23 August 1996)*, Louvain, pp. 193–199.

Prevenier, W., Sosson, J.-P. and Boone, M. (1992) 'Le réseau urbain en Flandre (XIIIe–XIXe siècle): composantes et dynamique' in *Actes du 15e Colloque International à Spa 4–6 Sept. 1990. Le Réseau urbain en Belgique dans une perspective historique (1350–1850)*, Brussels, pp. 157–200. (Crédit Communal, Collection Histoire, série in–8, nr. 86).

Rosenberg, N. and Birdzell L. (1986) *How the West Grew Rich. The Economic Transformation of the Industrial World*, New York.

Saey, P. and Verhoeve, A. (1993) 'The Southern Netherlands: Part of the Core or Reduced to a Semi-Peripheral Status?', in H.J. Nitz (ed.), *The Early Modern World-System in Geographical Perspective*, Stuttgart, pp. 93–114.

Schneider, J. (1991) 'Was There a Precapitalist World-System?', in C. Chase-Dunn and Th. Hall (eds), *Core/Periphery Relations in Precapitalist Worlds*, Boulder, pp. 45–66.

Schumann, R. (1986) *Italy in the last fifteen hundred years*, Lanham MD.

Sée, H. (1928) *Modern Capitalism. Its Origin and Evolution*, New York.

Smith, A. (1976) *An Inquiry into the Nature and Causes of the Wealth of Nations*, New York.

Snooks, G.D. (1995) 'The dynamic role of the market in the Anglo-Norman economy and beyond, 1086–1300', in R.H. Britnell and B.M.S. Campbell (eds), *A commercialising economy. England 1086 to circa 1300*, Manchester, pp. 27–54.

Spufford, P. (1981) 'Interventi', in V. Bagnoli (ed.), *La Moneta Nell'Economia Europa sec. XIII–XVIII. Atti della Settimane di studio 11–17 aprile 1975*, Prato, pp. 619–624. (Instituto Internazionale di Storia Economica 'F. Datini'; Serie II, 7).

Stabel, P. (1992) 'Markt en hinterland: de centrale functies van de kleinere steden in Vlaanderen tijdens de late middeleeuwen en het begin van de moderne tijd' in *Actes du 15e Colloque International à Spa le 4–6 Sept. 1990. Le Réseau urbain en Belgique dans une perspective historique (1350–1850),* Bruxelles, pp. 341–363 (Crédit Communal, Collection Histoire, série in–8, nr. 86).

Stabel, P. (1995) *De kleine stad in Vlaanderen*, Brussels.

Stabel, P. (1997) *Dwarfs among Giants. The Flemish Urban Network in the Late Middle Ages*, Louvain.

Tawney, R.H. (1926) *Religion and the Rise of Capitalism*, Harcourt.

Terlouw, C.P. (1992) *The regional geography of the World-System,* State University of Utrecht.

Thoen, E. (1988) *Landbouweconomie en bevolking in Vlaanderen gedurende de late Middeleeuwen en het begin van de Moderne Tijden*, Ghent.

Thoen, E. (1992) 'Technique agricole, cultures nouvelles et économie rurale en Flandre au Bas Moyen Age' in *Actes de Colloque Flaran 12 (1990)*, Ghent, pp. 51–67.

Thoen, E. (1993) 'The Count, the Countryside and the Economic Development of Towns in Flanders from the 11th to the 13th Century. Some Provisional Remarks and Hypotheses', in E. Aerts and R. van Uytven (eds), *Liber Amicorum Herman Van der Wee. Studia Historica Oeconomica*, Louvain, pp. 259–278.

Thoen, E. (1997) 'The Birth of 'the Flemish Husbandry': Agricultural Technology in Medieval Flanders', in G. Astill and J. Langdon (eds), *Medieval Farming and Technology: the Impact of Agricultural Change in Nortwest Europe*, New York, pp. 69–88.

Thoen, E. and Verhulst, A. (1986) 'Le réseau urbain et les campagnes dans l'ancien comté de Flandre (ca. 1350–1800)', *Storia della Citta*, 36, pp. 53–60.

Thompson, E.P. (1993) *Customs in Common. Studies in Traditional Popular Culture*, New York.

Toch, M. (1986) 'Lords and Peasants: A Reappraisal of Medieval Economic Relationships', *The Journal of European Economic History*, 15, 1, pp. 163–182.

Torras, J. (1980) 'Class Struggle in Catalonia. A Note on Brenner', *Review*, 4, 2, Fall, 253–265.

Torras, J. (1993) 'The Building of a Market', in J. Torras [et. al], *Els Espais del Mercat*, Valencia, pp. 197–212.

Tuma, E. (1979) *European Economic History*, Palo Alto.

Udovitch, A. (1993) 'Market and Society in the Medieval Islamic World', in *Mercati e mercanti nell'alto medioevo l'area Euroasiatica e l'area Mediterranea: Settimane di Studio del centro Italiano di studi sull'alto medioeve XL*, Spoleto, pp. 767–798.

Uytven, R. van (1982) 'Stadsgeschiedenis in the Noorden en het Zuiden', in D. Blok [et al.], *Algemene Geschiedenis der Nederlanden*, vol. 2, Haarlem, pp. 188–253.

Uytven, R. van (1983) 'Cloth in Medieval Literature of Western Europe', in N. Harte and K. Ponting (eds), *Cloth and Clothing in Medieval Europe. Essays in Memory of Professor E.M. Carus-Wilson*, London, pp. 151–183.

Uytven, R. van (1987) 'Economische groei in het Hertogdom Brabant tijdens de twaalfde eeuw', in R. Bauer [et al.], *Brabant in de twaalfde eeuw: een renaissance?*, Brussels, pp. 113–129.

Verhulst, A. (1989) 'Agrarian Revolutions: Myth or Reality?', *Sartoniana*, 2, 1989, pp. 71–95.

Verhulst, A. (1990) 'The Agricultural Revolution of the Middle Ages Reconsidered', in S. Bachrach and D. Nicholas (eds), *Law, Custom and the Social Fabric in Medieval Europe: Essays in honor of Bryce Lyon*, Kalamazoo, pp. 17–28.

Verhulst, A. (1997) 'The State of Research. Medieval socioeconomic historiography in Western Europe: towards an integrated approach', *Journal of Medieval History*, 23, 1, pp. 89–101.

Wachter, A. de (1996) *De Kempen in het Wereld-Systeem: Een verkennend onderzoek*, Ghent. Unpublished licentiate thesis University of Ghent, Department of Geography.

Wallerstein, I. (1974) *The Modern World System*, New York.

Wallerstein, I. (1979) 'From Feudalism to Capitalism: Transition or Transitions?', in I. Wallerstein, *The Capitalist World-Economy*, Cambridge, pp. 138–151.

Wallerstein, I. (1980) *The Modern World-System II,* New York.

Wallerstein, I. (1984) *The Politics of the World-Economy*, Cambridge.

Wallerstein, I. (1993a) 'World Systems versus World-Systems. A Critique', in A.G. Frank and B. Gills (eds), *The World System. Five Hundred Years or Five Thousand?*, London, pp. 292–296.

Wallerstein, I. (1993b) 'The Construction of a European World-Economy, 1450–1750'. Unpublished paper.

Wallerstein I. (1999) 'The West, Capitalism and the modern world-system', in T. Brook and G. Blue (eds), *China and Historical Capitalism*, Cambridge, pp. 10–56.

Weber, M. (1930) *The Protestant Ethic and the Spirit of Capitalism*, New York.

Wee, H. van der (1981) 'Productivité, progrès technique et croissance économique du XIIe au XVIIIe siècle', in S. Mariotti (ed.), *Produttività e tecnologie nei secoli XII–XVII'. Atti della Terza Settimana di Studio 23–29 aprile 1971*, Prato, pp. 9–16. (Instituto Internazionale di Storia Economica 'F. Datini'; Serie II, 3).

Wee, H. van der (ed.) (1988) *The Rise and Decline of Urban Industries in Italy and the Low Countries*, Louvain.

Wee, H. van der (1993) *The Low Countries in the Early Modern World*, Cambridge.

Wee, H. van der and Cauwenberghe, E. van (eds) (1978) *Productivity of land and agricultural innovation in the Low Countries (1250–1800)*, Louvain.

White, L. (1962) *Medieval Technology and Social Change*, Oxford.

Wood, E. (1999) *The Origin of Capitalism*, New York.

Wrigley, E. (1978) 'The Town in a Pre-industrial Economy', in P. Abrams and E. Wrigley (eds), *Towns in Societies. Essays in Economic History and Historical Sociol*ogy, Cambridge, pp. 295–309.

Wyffels, C. (1991) 'L'usure en Flandre au XIIIe siècle', *Revue Belge de philologie et d'histoire*, 69, 1, pp. 853–871.

Yun, B. (1994) 'Economic Cycles and Structural Changes', in Th. Brady, H. Oberman and J. Tracy (eds), *Handbook of European History 1400–1600. Late Middle Ages, Renaissance and Reformation*, vol. 1, Leiden/New York, pp. 113–145.

Zolberg, A. (1981) 'Origins of the modern world system: a missing link', *World Politics*, 33 (2), pp. 253–281.

7 Urban markets, rural industries and the organisation of labour in late medieval Flanders: the constraints of guild regulations and the requirements of export oriented production

Peter Stabel,[1] Ghent University

I. Introduction

For far too long, a clear dichotomy between town and countryside has prevailed in historical debate. The urban and the rural world are often considered as completely separate economic, political, social and cultural entities. The town walls symbolised this physical separation between two completely different societies. In the social and economic sphere, there was a clear division between the world of agriculture and related occupations, and that of the regulated, corporative world of urban guilds, between agriculture and industry, between self-sufficiency and commerce, between conservatism and innovation. And still today, social and economic historians are often divided into urban and rural historians, as if they were studying two different and separate disciplines. If and when interaction between town and countryside is assessed, it is usually seen more as confrontation than as close collaboration and coexistence. The most striking image of the late medieval urban-rural relations in the Low Countries is that of the urban militias which marched out in the first half of the fourteenth century to destroy industrial activity in the countryside as they defended the urban monopoly on manufacture and trade.[2]

And yet a multitude of studies in recent decades have pointed to often very complex systems of symbiosis between these two seemingly antagonistic ways of life. Cities and towns depended on their hinterland for the supply of food, of raw materials, and, of course, of people, and therefore of their labour force. The rural world functioned in a world wider than just its immediate surroundings and for this it also needed industrial goods and an urban commercial infrastructure. Furthermore, this interaction was not an exchange between two separate worlds. In fact urban settlements overwhelmingly kept many of their rural characteristics, and the so-called 'urban' ways of organising society and economy often spread very easily into the countryside. This took place all the more easily when a certain equilibrium between the urban and the rural world was achieved. Flows of population, of capital, of skill, and of industrial capacity went there and back.

---

[1] IUAP 4/14 Urban Society in the Late Medieval Low Countries.

[2] For general remarks and a bibliographical survey on urban-rural relations in the late medieval southern Low Countries: Thoen and Verhulst (1986) and Stabel (1996). It is striking how the focus in historical literature has been laid by many agrarian historians on urban real property in the countryside, while. urban historians have mostly focused on the juridical and administrative dominance of cities in their region and on the widespread dispersion of urban out-burghership in the countryside.

The still very poorly known migration flows in pre-industrial society present the most striking example of this interaction. In the Low Countries, with the possible exception of medieval Bruges and sixteenth-century Antwerp, the occupational structure of migrants in general and in particular the movement of unskilled and semi-skilled labour are impossible to quantify. But, as the scarce indicators of population movement seem to indicate, the image of the countryside as a mere deliverer of urban immigrants, and the town as a taker does not always live up to reality. Population mobility was much more complex, certainly in the smaller towns, where seasonal labour played an important part in constituting total income, and in rural areas with important industrial activity (and as in the case of Flanders many countrymen having the status of out-burgher, which meant that they enjoyed urban juridical status in one of the many towns). Moreover, a very significant number of people also left the smaller and secondary urban centres to look for opportunities in other towns or in the big cities. The former seem to have functioned as catalysts for the movement of skilled and semi-skilled labour and as reservoirs for immigration into the big metropolises of the fifteenth and sixteenth-century Low Countries.[3] In this way many towns, as well as the countryside, had to face a continuing brain drain of mostly skilled workers. Structural *multi-stage migration* became more frequent and the small towns often took upon themselves the initial training of unskilled rural workers, before they or their descendants migrated further towards the big cities. The pressure of a densely populated countryside characterised by very small agricultural holdings on the one hand, and different chances for employment and demand for substantially different technical skills, and hence difference of general wage levels in town and countryside, on the other hand were the main impetus for this continuous movement of people to small towns and big cities.[4] The polarity between an immobile rural society and a very mobile urban world is undoubtedly a false construction. Population movement was omnipresent in all kinds of pre-industrial societies and as the Flemish urban network was a very dense one, it must have influenced rural society in the county and far beyond its borders.

Movement of population implies not only the physical change of population structure, it also stimulates interaction with the conditions of labour in both town and countryside. In order to be able to have a grasp on labour relations and to avoid making generalisations based only upon the well-known Bruges case, which is atypical for the Low Countries as it was the top of the urban hierarchy and the gateway-city to a European commercial network (the city attracted mainly skilled craftsmen in retail, commerce, and service industries; artisans employed in the main export industries of Flanders were only an important minority, and migration was dominated by inter-urban movement) this paper will look with more detail at one of the most spectacular meeting-points of rural and urban systems of organising labour, the new industries of the 15th and 16th centuries which were established upon an already existing medieval industrial landscape in both town and countryside.

3 On migration patterns in late medieval Flanders: Stabel (1995a: 27–53; 1997a: 127–133), Thoen (1994: 335–354).

4 The characteristics of property structures in the Flemish countryside are discussed in Verhulst (1990: 109–118) and Thoen (1988: 845 ff). On the different wage levels in the small and secondary Flemish towns: Stabel (1995a: 204–213). The wage levels of skilled artisans in the countryside follow more or less the same pattern as in the towns, but they are usually much lower, 70% of that of an urban craftsman (Thoen, 1988: 957).

The town-countryside relationship was not only structured by property relations, surplus extraction of agricultural produce, and commercial exchange, there were also strong industrial links between the rural and the urban element. Polyfunctionality seems to be a general characteristic of the rural way of life in urbanised regions such as the Low Countries. The countryside not only produced agricultural goods and commodities related to the exploitation of natural resources (food, industrial crops, fuel, building materials), villages normally also had an important industrial component. Most villages had their own specialised craftsmen. Building activity, limited retailing functions, and industrial manufacture were not an urban monopoly, although the impact of urban markets and skilled artisans must have been a dominant feature in this most urbanised region in Europe. Occupational matrices permit, at least for the end of the pre-industrial era to mark out these semi-rural, semi-industrial functions of the countryside (Van Uytven, 1992: 29–79 and 1972: 172–203).[5] Urban settlements, on the contrary, usually had the monopoly of services and industries which were higher on the list of central goods and for which commercial viability depended upon patterns set by supply and demand. Urban staple monopolies often interfered with these patterns.[6] Only occasionally, however, did these urban monopolies disturb the pattern of functional distribution. This pattern, however, is not only valid for service industries and regional commercial functions, it can also be applied to the labour market for export commodities in this period.

II. Industrial landscapes and the rural industries in 15th and 16th century Flanders

The late Middle Ages have the reputation for being a difficult period of economic conversion in Flanders. A general pattern of industrial dislocation, of changes in manufacture, and of changing commercial routes and markets seems to dominate economic trends. Although there is no doubt that this period of crisis and transition caused a substantial decline in urbanisation (urban ratios seem to decline from 35% to less than 25% in two centuries), the urban system did not collapse. Patterns of urbanisation changed from the overall dominance of three capital cities in the county, to a more evenly distributed urban network (while the centre of gravity of urbanisation in the Low Countries shifted to the Brabantine cities of Antwerp and Brussels and to the North). After the general crisis of the fourteenth century, the absolute numbers for the urban population show no tendency for decline until the end of the sixteenth century. Declining urban ratios were caused by stronger growth in the countryside.[7]

---

[5] For eighteenth-century Flanders, see Stabel (1995b: 100–108). More general remarks in Stevens and Jaspers (1985) and Gijssels and Van der Straeten (1986). Because of the lack of sources revealing occupational hierarchies, more general urban hierarchies have been developed for the fourteenth, fifteenth and sixteenth centuries in Stabel (1997a: 241–261).

[6] The best known example is, of course, the commercial staple on grain trade and transport in Ghent (Boone and Howell, 1996: 300–324). For staple monopolies relating to the urban cloth industry, see Stabel (1995a: 85–121).

[7] On long-term development of urban ratios in the southern Low Countries: Klep (1991: 485–508), and Morsa (1997: 303–330).

On the contrary, in the same period, urban entrepreneurs and merchants were able to link up the restructured urban textile production to the new commercial outlets and to integrate very successfully rural industries in the urban commercial network (Van der Wee, 1988). These rural industries, producing for an urban commercial infrastructure, for the domestic market of textiles and for international demand, are an ideal case for studying the relation between the labour market in cities and towns on the one hand and in the countryside on the other. It would be, however, a false construction to generalise about labour relations in rural industries. Clear distinctions must be made between the various types of rural industries in Flanders. Indeed, in contrast to what is often suggested in the debate about proto-industries, the world of rural industries is not a monolithic one. Its structures and organisation not only depended on the added value of some types of manufacture (linen, woollen cloth, light drapery, tapestries), but on the organisation of the industries as a whole (the organisation of labour, the development of putting-out systems, the impact of corporate control, the organisation of commerce towards the commercial gateway, the impact of mercantile capital).[8]

In general terms, and as mentioned above, there were four types of rural textile production in late fifteenth- and sixteenth-century Flanders. Linen was produced in central Flanders (in the river basin of the Rivers Scheldt, Leie and Dender and in the regions north of Ghent), tapestries were manufactured in the same part of the county, but in a much more limited region (in the hinterland of the towns of Oudenaarde and Geraardsbergen). The rural woollen industry was located in many parts of the county, but a clear concentration can be noticed in western Flanders (in the vicinity of Ypres, Poperinge and Bailleul), and, finally, the manufacture of light woollens (the so-called says) was concentrated in western coastal Flanders (Hondschoote and its surroundings) and in southeastern Flanders (the semi-rural town of Ronse). But, in reality, regional discrepancies and different market orientations had created a still much more regionally diverse and complex industrial landscape. Four regions, four different industries and, therefore, also four different ways of organising labour and commerce.

III. Rural and urban woollens

The rural woollen industry in the village of Nieuwkerke and its neighbours (which, in the sixteenth century, produced medium quality woollens made from Spanish and even English wool) was structured along much the same lines as the traditional urban draperies, despite a century long rivalry with the regional cloth city of Ypres, once an industrial giant.[9] Although formally organised craft guilds (weavers, fullers, dyers, shearers, etc.) were either not present or only existed in an embryonic form, the cloth-entrepreneurs themselves, the drapers, had their own control mechanisms and organisations, in the same way as their urban counterparts in towns such as Ypres, Poperinge or

---

[8] For general remarks on proto-industries at the end of the Early Modern Period, see Duplessis (1997: 206–219), which gives also a survey of the most important literature.

[9] A quantitative assessment of production figures of the Flemish urban and rural cloth industries can be found in Stabel (1997c).

Menen.[10] They also took care of their commercial outlets: they visited regional fairs and they rented, and later on even owned, their own cloth hall in the gateway city of Antwerp. In order to achieve a standard quality they appointed a bailiff of the cloth industry and controllers (*eswarts* or *waerderers*) (Stabel, 1999).[11] A strict division of labour was enforced, whereby weavers were not allowed to full the cloth and vice versa. An ordinance of 1455 forbade drapers to be active as dyers (*qui sont deulx mestiers separez*), and, four years later, systems of vertical concentration of industrial manufacture (weaving, fulling, dyeing, etc.) were limited (De Sagher et al., 1966: 100–107). Entrepreneurial activity, the monopoly of drapers (they organised textile production, the finishing of woollens in Nieuwkerke itself or in cities which specialised in finishing textiles, and finally the commerce of Nieuwkerke woollens in the gateway cities and at the fairs in the Low Countries), was formally distinguished from any kind of industrial manufacture in the cloth industry of Nieuwkerke, a procedure which seems even stricter than in many of the secondary cloth towns (De Sagher et al., 1966: 101). All this implies a very 'urban way' of structuring the labour market.

The economic results of these policies were astonishing. Nieuwkerke drapers became formidable competitors for the decaying urban cloth manufacturers. In the middle of the fifteenth century they still manufactured mainly cheap and coarse woollens, but steadily they focused on the export market, despite growing frustration of urban entrepreneurs and occasional vigorous but vain attempts (by, for example, the Ypres magistrates) to limit rural production capacity. In the course of the sixteenth century the urban drapers stopped these attempts and there are many indications that a lot of the artisans migrated to the rural industrial settlement (De Sagher, 1966).[12] Other cities tried to attract Nieuwkerke entrepreneurs and artisans in order to restore the decayed urban cloth industries (Bruges, Dendermonde, Diksmuide). From the 1480s the cloth output of Nieuwkerke rose rapidly from 3,000 woollens to about 20,000 by the middle of the sixteenth century. Demand for labour and consequently the shortage of skilled artisans, was such that the strict division of the stages of production had to be abandoned. This did not lead to more relaxed regulation of the quality of the cloth. On the contrary, the middle of the sixteenth century was a period of strict regulation and many new ordinances were being issued (De Sagher et al., 1966).

Nothing of the sort existed in other rural cloth producing centres, both in western Flanders and on a more limited scale in coastal (around Diksmuide) and in interior Flanders (the region south of Ghent: Sint-Lievens-Houtem) (Thoen, 1988: 1011–1014; Stabel, 1997c: 136–139). Most of these centres focused on the manufacture of coarser woollens (*doucken*) for a domestic market. In the hinterland of Bruges and Ghent, urban monopolies had clearly succeeded in stopping a similar growth of rural woollen manufacture, and

---

[10] The corporative organisation of the semi-rural manufacture of light woollens, the so-called says of Hondschoote, is discussed in Coornaert (1930a: 317–411). For the small provincial town of Bergues, see also Coornaert (1930b).

[11] Sources on the organisation of the cloth industry at Nieuwkerke have been published in De Sagher et al. (1966: 93 ff).

[12] On the marketing of light cloth from the rural production centres in the early sixteenth century, see Stabel (1999).

the secondary towns in the river basin had also been more successful in implementing their privileges (Boone, 1993: 42–44; Stabel, 1995a: 138–142). But the main reason for the lack of woollen industries is a different industrial orientation. The urban draperies had resisted much better than they had in western Flanders (with the exception of Poperinge) to changes of commercial orientation. They had been able to switch rapidly and very effectively to the use of Spanish wool, they were present throughout the fifteenth century on the Hanseatic market, and they were even able to regain again access to the Mediterranean markets (Stabel, 1997c: 130–136). Moreover, as we shall demonstrate, the rural weavers in the river basin did not specialise in woollens, but in other types of fabrics, linens and tapestries.

Although the scale of the woollen industry in the various regions of manufacture did not resemble the *urban-style* organisation of the drapers in Nieuwkerke, a survey of rural industries in western Flanders (after another vain attempt by Ypres to limit rural manufacture in the 1480s) shows clearly that not only an important part of the out-burghers of this city were actively involved in the manufacture of rural woollens, but that there also existed strong industrial and commercial polarisation among rural entrepreneurs (in the same way as among urban drapers), and a minority of rural weavers controlled the bulk of manufacture of rural woollens. This polarisation grew as some of the rural centres followed the example set by Nieuwkerke drapers and oriented a part of their output towards the gateway-cities in order to achieve similar successes on the export markets (Dranouter, Eécke) (De Sagher et al., 1951: 24 ff.; 1961: 252–272).

The same development can be noticed in the production of the so-called light draperies, or says (which were, as is suggested in some surveys, not a monopoly of rural artisans). Local entrepreneurs put strong control mechanisms in place and a guild-like system was founded in what had been a mere village in the fifteenth century, Hondschoote. Yet the spectacular growth of Hondschoote (from a small village to a town of nearly 10,000 inhabitants in only half a century) was also stimulated by a strong commitment from merchants in the regionally important cities and in the gateway-markets. More than in the case of rural high-quality woollens, urban merchants were able to control the mechanisms of manufacture and commercial outlet of says (Coornaert, 1930a: 268–306 and 1950: 59–96). Although a formally recognised system of craft guilds usually was not allowed, the various structures which controlled the stages of production and marketing (the drapers' guild) organised relations between masters, apprentices and journeymen, prescribed the consecutive stages of manufacture and regulated the distribution of labour and the entry to the profession. And once growth was well established, drapers tried to defend their position in the region with the same methods as their urban counterparts in the fourteenth and fifteenth centuries, as did the Hondschoote entrepreneurs in the 1550s and 1570s. Big entrepreneurs, sometimes in close co-operation with the merchants, were able, at least in Hondschoote and probably also in the rural manufacture of *draperie ointe*, to concentrate production and to monopolise part of the output in the gateway-cities. This could even happen with the support of the local magistrates in the towns that adopted new types of production. The same systems of subcontracting and control of the supply of raw material (wool, dyes, alum) that were working in the urban cloth industries, seem to be present in the so-called rural industries.[13]

[13] On subcontracting in the urban cloth industries of late medieval Flanders, see Stabel (1997b:

Despite the very thorough studies by E. Coornaert on rural woollens and says, the unpublished research of J. Vermaut, and exemplary source editions on the draperies in Western Flanders,[14] surprisingly little is known about the organisation of labour in the rural draperies of the fifteenth and sixteenth centuries and the relation between craftsmen and urban entrepreneurs and merchants (the say-industry of Hondschoote – although a very specific industry – is the only exception). The rapid rise of industrial centres such as Nieuwkerke and Hondschoote must have caused structural changes in the regional labour market. More so, because gradually both centres must have attracted a labour force, which could no longer be sustained by the local agricultural infrastructure. This spectacular growth must have destroyed, therefore, at least partially the essence of what a rural industry was all about: the combination of agricultural and industrial activity. A lot of weavers and other artisans must have worked full-time at the manufacture of woollens.

This situation was completely different from the conditions of labour in the small-scale manufacture of woollens in the rest of the county and in the rural linen and tapestry industries. Both centres also had to adopt urban ways of regulating and organising labour, while, at the same time, watching out very carefully so that the overall advantages of rural labour were not completely lost in the process. Solutions to this problem in Nieuwkerke and Hondschoote were very different (perhaps because of the higher added value of the heavier Nieuwkerke woollens and the links with an industrial network of finishing industries). In the former the structures of 'urban drapery' were adopted, in the latter merchants kept more control over marketing procedures. But in other centres of rural cloth industry, the demands of an export oriented manufacture caused the entrepreneurs to standardise production, to broaden the scope of regulation, and to organise the labour market. At the same time, in the cities and towns themselves (and not only in Walloon-Flanders and Artois as Coornaert has stated), industrial change had lessened the impact of the traditional guilds, and new types of fabrics were being manufactured outside or on the edge of guild regulation. Hence the clear distinction between urban and rural ways of organising labour and output is no longer acceptable. Structures seem to have been put in place along very pragmatic lines; the economic realities of rural industries were more characterised by a gradual transition from 'urban' to 'rural' ways of organising production and labour, than by a clear-cut difference between the two.

IV. The linen industries in the river basin

Interior Flanders was characterised in the late medieval period by very dense population, high urban ratios, a dense network of transportation towards commercial cities, a very important subdivision into small, and therefore poor, agricultural units, and hence the availability of an important cheap rural labour force and an agricultural production, which was profoundly determined by urban demand and by the dispersion of industrial crops (dyes, such as woad and madder, and most of all flax) (Thoen, 1990: 51–67). These

---

79–98). General remarks in Lis and Soly (1994: 365–390).

[14] See Coornaert (1930a; 1930b; 1950), Clauzel and Calonne (1990: 531–573), Vermaut, (1988: 187–206), Espinas and Pirenne (1904–1920), and De Sagher et al. (1951–1965).

conditions were ideal for the development of a rural linen industry. The organisation of the rural linen industry is relatively well known thanks to the works of E. Sabbe and C. Vandenbroeke and, for the late medieval period, especially by the more recent research of E. Thoen on the rural economy in central Flanders (Sabbe, 1975; Vandenbroeke, 1979: 117–174; Thoen, 1988: 980–1010). From the late fourteenth century onwards, linens rather than woollens dominated industrial expansion in the countryside. In this period, Flemish linens appeared very suddenly on the English market, and later also in France, Italy, and the Hanseatic territories. But the importance of a huge domestic Low Countries market must also be taken into account (Stabel, 1995a: 176–189).

The initial commercial success of both rural and urban linens from an early stage, has undoubtedly stimulated the rapid development of the industry in large areas of the river basin. In this, the expansion of the culture of flax in the county and a sharp crisis of the rural economy in the 1360s and 1370s had been a decisive variable. The growth of an important linen industry was the answer for a countryside in the full swing of crisis and it compensated, although very partially, for declining demand and rising transaction costs, and hence declining volumes of exports of the urban industries, and it stimulated rural labour productivity by reducing periods of structural unemployment in the countryside.

Throughout the fifteenth and sixteenth centuries, the regional and international success of Flemish linens was continuing, despite short periods of crisis in the 1460s and at the end of the fifteenth century (because of war). The rural manufacture of linens spread very rapidly in the basin of the Leie, Scheldt and Dender rivers. The urban network very quickly monopolised the linen trade. Moreover urban merchants very often were able to control the finishing industries (bleaching, both in Flanders itself and for the high-quality urban linens also in Holland and Brabant) and they tried to standardise production for export purposes. Staple rights were established and towns also tried to lessen the impact of rural linen buyers – (but they never succeeded in removing them completely) by stapling the goods on urban transit-markets. Locally grown flax very soon became insufficient to supply the rural and urban weavers (farms in interior Flanders did not produce a significant surplus of flax) and a regional flax trade became necessary. Again this trade of raw materials was quickly monopolised by urban merchants and markets.

Many small farmers combined their weaving activities with the cultivation of flax and their industry became fully integrated with their holding, making it much more than simply supplementary income during calm periods (as had been the case for rural labour employed in the preparation stage of urban cloth industries). There was, however, a clear distinction between weavers with middle-sized farms, and those on very small agricultural holdings. In the hinterland of Oudenaarde in the middle of the sixteenth century, flax occupied between 12% and 18% of the cultivated area of farms between 0.5 and 4 ha (1.25 to 10 acres). Flax was most prominent at small farms accounting for between 0.5 and 1 ha (1.25–2.5 acres) or 18%. These percentages were considerably lower on holdings of less than 0.5 ha (less than 5%) and in those larger than 4 ha (5% to 7% of the cultivated land). There was a strong tendency to cultivate about 0.3–0.4 ha of flax per holding at both the small and the larger holdings. This acreage could produce about the quantity of flax a weaver could handle for a period of 140 days. Both the small and the larger holdings clearly favored cereals over flax, the former to provide themselves the maximum quantity of food possible, the latter to sell on the urban markets, while having enough flax to remain active as a weaver. The majority of very small-scale farmers in interior Flanders did not grow enough flax and had to buy their raw material. This made them completely dependent upon the supply of flax from the larger agricultural holdings or from the urban staple markets (Thoen, 1988: 997–1010).

Not only the cultivation of flax, but also the ownership of looms points to the importance of small farms in the linen industry. In particular farmers on very small and small agricultural holdings (0.5–4 ha.) were active as rural weavers. In the hinterland of Oudenaarde at the end of the fifteenth century, about 10% of all out-burghers of that city (in this region the majority of the country folk had this status) owned a loom for the manufacture of linens, in the 1520s their number rose to almost 50%. In the middle of the sixteenth century 63% of all farmers (with 2–4 ha. of land) had their own loom. Percentages were lower for very small farmers (less than 0.5 ha or 41%) or for the larger agricultural holdings (41% +4ha, 33% +15ha).

Entrepreneurial risks were therefore located in the countryside (weavers mostly owned their own looms and worked with their own raw material), but urban merchants and the more important farmers monopolised trade, the former also controlled linen finishing, and were involved in at least a part of the supply of raw materials. Systems of putting-out, as they existed in the traditional urban cloth industry and in the manufacture of tapestries were not dominant. Only occasionally did rural linen weavers work for piece-wages (the very small farmers, who were also active as journeymen on the larger holdings).[15] The rural linen industry remained the business of small-scale farmers living on the edge of subsistence, but who were able to purchase their means of production. In this way they could complement the income from their holding with the benefit of manufacturing linens and selling them through the urban market system.

Although there is evidence that some rural weavers specialised in more refined linens,[16] the majority of the output of expensive linen and specialised fabrics was still urban. In particular the town of Kortrijk (situated in the middle of a linen-producing countryside) had been specialising since the fifteenth century in the manufacture of damasked linen, table and bed linen (the most expensive fabrics were bleached afterwards in Holland and in Brabant, the cheaper ones were bleached locally, sometimes 'in a Dutch manner'). The social position of urban linen weavers was very different from that of rural linen weavers. Very quickly they turned into a proletarianised labour force. The success of Kortrijk linen boosted immigration from the overcrowded nearby countryside. The population rose from 5,900 in the middle of the fifteenth century to more than 9,000 one century later. The switch from the very specialised manufacture of the most expensive

[15] E. Thoen mentions how flax-producing farmers paid other countrymen a piece wage for the weaving of linens. Moreover, these farmers sometimes were active as real linen entrepreneurs and they owned stocks for market purpose (*coeplakenen*). He does not exclude, however, that at least some weavers worked as mere wage earners and that they did not own their own looms (Thoen, 1988: 1005–1006).

[16] Examples in Thoen (1988: 1000–1001).

woollens to the mass output of much cheaper linens, caused, however, drastic changes in the urban social structure. Nonetheless the manufactured goods (especially the figured damasks) still required a very skilled labour force (in contrast with the individual looms for plain linens in the countryside, each loom for damasks demanded two or three craftsmen, and the investment in means of production were also much greater) (Backhouse, 1976: 415–454; Stabel, 1995a: 180–185).

The urban linen manufacturers were organised in a traditional guild structure (the guild of Saint-Catherine's), but only from the end of the fifteenth century, when industrial conversion was already in full swing.[17] The ever-increasing refinement of guild regulation, which took place throughout the sixteenth century, was designed to control the output of manufacture between town and the linen-producing countryside in the Leie-basin and to protect urban market functions. Staple monopolies (of raw materials such as flax and linen thread, and of finished goods) strengthened the hold of urban merchants (the big firms in Lille and Antwerp had their own agents in Kortrijk, some of the important textile merchants even had Kortrijk roots). They acquired control over the commercial infrastructure: two linen halls were built for rural and for urban linens, a weekly linen market on mondays was organized (both measures had to stimulate trade and speed up marketing procedures: 'ten fijne dat de lieden van buuten hier huer lijnwaet te coope bringhen, goede ghereedscepe ende corte expeditie hebben mueghen'), and tolls on the linen trade, which were owned by local nobility, were bought by the city in 1518 (Stabel, 1995a: 183–184).

Yet, competition between urban and rural weavers was not abolished by guild regulation. Regulation, in particular relating to the manufacture of luxury linens, was aimed at concentrating manufacture in the city (all linens had to be sealed on the loom and in the linen hall, specific 'urban' patterns and formats were prescribed for the damasks, corporative control was centralised in the hall, etc.). Standard quality was crucial for the export linens, as it had been for the export woollens in the centuries before. Urban merchants were, nonetheless, allowed to market rural linens, and regulation also allowed rural weavers to come looking for orders at the urban market. Moreover, there were attempts to compensate, at least partly, the structural imbalance between rural and urban weavers (because of the fact that industrial income for rural weavers was only part of the family income), on the one hand by the strict urban monopoly on the manufacture of some more expensive fabrics (which was enforced by the guild), and on the other hand by other measures which influenced the costs of labour and of marketing in favour of urban fabrics (rural linen weavers who came to the town looking for work, had to pay 4 gr. for each order they received, which is about one third of the daily wage of a skilled artisan). The arguments in the Kortrijk linen privileges seem like copies from the privileges of the drapers: the constant search for good quality linens was good for the merchants and it avoided the decay of the industry and the town ('waer uute de vremde cooplieden zouden moghen ghefraudeert wesen ende 't Cortrijcx goedt mettertijdt gheblameert ter totale bederfvenesse ende ruyne van de vorseide neringhe ende stede').

---

[17] On the craft guild of urban linen weavers in Kortrijk: Bauwens and De Jaeghere (1986: 183–192).

As the Kortrijk example shows, the distribution of linen manufacture between town and countryside was the result of both a functional development (availability of skilled labour and of market infrastructure, property relations, the quality demands of an export commodity), and of a formal 'urban' organisation (by the urban guild, by merchants). Hence, the many similarities between the manufacture of cheaper cloth and of linen in this period. However, the rural linen weavers were never able to attract the manufacture of more refined fabrics, as some of the rural cloth centres had been able to do. These were successfully monopolised by urban craftsmen, because of the availability of labour, the presence of a commercial and industrial infrastructure in a decaying cloth town such as Kortrijk, and export demands. The growth of the industry in the sixteenth century in both town and countryside prevented any real conflict of interest and confirmed the functional distribution achieved early in the century.

Moreover, the growth of urban population in this period required a close interaction between town and countryside. The majority of its new burghers and other immigrants were recruited in the immediate hinterland of the town. Inevitably, many rural weavers must have been amongst them and, surely, many must have kept good relations with their place of origin. The fact that so many of the probate inventories of towndwellers (in Kortrijk and in the other important market towns for rural linens, such as Oudenaarde) contain small plots of real estate in the countryside, proves that even urban craftsmen often continued to combine their industry with some kind of agricultural activity (Stabel, 1997a: 95–106). Again the transition between urban and rural patterns is very gradual.

V. Tapestries: the dominance of an urban industry in the countryside

The relations between the rural artisan and the urban merchant or entrepreneur were different for the manufacture of tapestries. In contrast to the manufacture of rural linens and coarse woollens, this industry demanded high investments (not so much for the looms, although they appear to have been much more elaborate machines than linen looms, but especially for the raw materials: dyed thread, designs, etc.). The industry expanded rapidly in the region between Oudenaarde and Geraardsbergen in the course of the fifteenth century. Tapestries became one of the leading export commodities of the Low Countries during the sixteenth century (Pirenne, 1906: 644–656). The expensive tapestries were not only manufactured in urban centres of production (Tournai, Brussels, and in Flanders Aalst, Geraardsbergen and, of course, especially Oudenaarde, famous for its *verdures*), but an important part of the total output of smaller and less refined pieces were produced by rural tapestry weavers (Robijns, 1978: 33–129; Roobaert, 1957–1958: 39–53). In contrast to the rural weavers in the linen industry, these were integrated in urban systems of manufacture. The already existing links between urban cloth manufacture and the rural economy contributed to this seemingly smooth industrialisation of the countryside. Commercial networks were put in place to tighten contacts between the countryside and the town of Oudenaarde, and entrepreneurs and merchants also established (very often family) links with the firms in the gateway cities of the Low Countries (Duverger, 1960 and 1965: 30–73). In a few decades, the population of the town doubled and its industrial suburbs attracted hundreds of immigrants from the immediate surroundings and increasingly also from the neighbouring principality of

Hainaut. A letter of Philippe de Lalaing mentions a total of 14,000 people in the town and its surroundings who were dependent on the industry, and half of the active urban population in 1541 worked in tapestries (Vanwelden, 1979: 13; Stabel, 1995a: 190–194).

The beginnings of tapestry weaving in Oudenaarde and in its hinterland in the first half of the fifteenth century were very hesitant. The guild of Saint Barbara's was founded in 1441, as was usual in the case of export industries, partly 'omme de bewaernesse van den coepman' (in order to protect the interests of the merchants by guaranteeing the quality of the finished goods).[18] Before, the tapestry weavers were probably a dependent branch of the cloth weavers' guild, because there are many indications that already before 1441, there was a lot of tapestry activity and by the middle of the fifteenth century Oudenaarde had a serious reputation as a centre of tapestry weaving (a tapestry weaver who migrated from Oudenaarde to Antwerp was not obliged to have supplementary training in 1453, because the man in question was known as a *notabel werckman*). The urban part of the industry was concentrated, as was much of the cloth industry in the industrial quarters of the town, on the right bank of the River Scheldt (Pamele) and gradually also in the suburbs near the town gates and in neighbouring villages such as Bevere. The artisans used mostly the so-called *basse-lisse*, in contrast to the majority of artisans working on the luxury tapestries in Brussels, Bruges and Tournai, which were produced on a *haute-lisse* loom. The *basse-lisse* was a loom more in the tradition of the looms for woollen cloth, and it allowed a higher productivity than the *haute-lisse*. So, however different weaving procedures were, the technical equipment of Oudenaarde tapestry weavers was much the same for the manufacture of woollens and of tapestries.

Little is known about the actual organisation of the manufacture of tapestries during the fifteenth and sixteenth centuries in both town and countryside. Most studies deal with the seventeenth and eighteenth centuries, when the scale of the industry can no longer be compared with its peak in the middle of the sixteenth century. Yet, it is clear that a few entrepreneurs were able to establish very important enterprises. In 1541 each master employed an average of 29 artisans, but among them were many small-scale tapestry entrepreneurs, so a minority must have controlled the output of hundreds of weavers and dyers (Stabel, 1995a: 191). Entrepreneurs often leased out looms and provided the artisans and journeymen with the raw materials. The latter depended, sometimes for the rest of his career, on a particular entrepreneur because of various debts and financial obligations. This proved to be, in particular at times of labour scarcity, a serious obstacle to a free labour market.[19]

---

[18] On the organisation of the guild of tapestry weavers in Oudenaarde in the sixteenth and seventeenth centuries: Vanwelden (1979). Earlier developments are discussed in Vermeiren-Vanwelden (1995: 69–87).

[19] In 1553 an ordinance complains about the financial dependence of journeymen on the entrepreneurs, because they were not allowed to be employed by other masters: 'midts deselve cnapen so thaerwaert gheobligiert, dat sij nerghens en moghen andere meesters zoucken'. If particular indebted journeymen wanted to switch their masters, the latter had to clear all their debts (Vanwelden, 1979: 48).

In the fifteenth century, the scale of the industry was still very modest; few indications of large-scale enterprises, and of noticeable movable capital of tapestries and raw materials have survived. Only some probate inventories from town and countryside mention the presence of tapestry looms. Because of the high costs of investment, it seems that, in the course of the fifteenth century, a lot of tapestries were made specifically at the order of merchants and consumers.[20] Commercial specialisation in trade towards the centres of consumption had not occurred yet: local tapestry merchants usually also traded linens and woollens. In the sixteenth century, as Oudenaarde tapestries were more and more manufactured for the export market at Antwerp, this situation would change dramatically. Probate inventories of tradesmen for the sixteenth century contained unsold stocks, movable capital, etc. Specialist firms with branches in the centre of production, in the transit market cities and in the gateway cities appeared and got hold of the main trade flows, and urban entrepreneurs integrated, on a much larger scale, rural labour into the chain of production.

Master weavers were in theory not allowed to work for other masters. Yet various systems of subcontracting were readily being used: new masters could still carry out work for others as long as all their obligations towards their former employer were not fulfilled. Moreover, the larger scale of tapestry enterprises avoided the general use of subcontractors, as it existed in many of the urban cloth industries. Solutions for the growth of enterprises were therefore not only sought within the traditional guild system, but they were created by capitalistic systems of controlling the labour market. In contrast to the other centres of tapestry in the southern Low Countries, mastership in the guild of Saint-Barbara's was never an expensive affair, nor did candidates have to possess the status of burgher, although the entry for burghers was always cheaper and almost every entrepreneur in the town was at the same time a burgher because of some commercial advantages.

The few data about the relationship between artisan and entrepreneur show a very refined and hierarchical system of *putting-out*. Most of the rural weavers and the so-called 'shopmasters' (*winckelmeesters*) who took care of the link between the urban merchants and entrepreneurs and the smaller rural weavers, lived in a limited area on the right bank of the River Scheldt. In contrast to the linen weavers in the same region, who were small peasants who owned the tools and the raw materials they worked with, the rural tapestry weavers were in fact mere wage earners, complementing their agricultural income with *ad hoc* weaving activity. The high cost of raw materials and the very labour intensive production process effectively prevented the concentration of the means of production in their hands. They often received only piece-wages (often paid at a weekly base),[21] which depended on skill and the quality and quantity of the work. As the analysis of early seventeenth-century wages shows, their activity did not provide

[20] Examples from the Pamele records are cited in Vermeiren-Vanwelden (1995: 73).

[21] Weavers usually came to town, to show their master the amount of work they had produced (they measured this with their own ells) and they were paid accordingly. They received their new materials, which were already prepared for weaving in town. Discussions about the amount of work had to be solved by the guild authorities (Vanwelden, 1979: 53).

rural weavers with a sufficient income. Just like the linen weavers, they had to combine their industrial and agricultural income. They mostly did not own their looms, which were leased out by urban entrepreneurs, who also supplied them with the raw materials. The ties linking them to the urban industry were kept very close. Rural weavers had to be members of the urban guild of tapestry weavers, without, however, enjoying the same advantages as the urban master weavers; they were not allowed to have apprentices (and thereby they were robbed of an obvious way of hiring cheap labour), and most of all there were strict limitations as to their capacity to be involved in trade. Rural weavers were subordinated to the jurisdiction of the urban guild (*ghestelt onder den eedt ende onderdanigheyt vanden zelven ambochte*). The dominance of the urban entrepreneur seems to be complete. Urban and rural weavers had to comply with the guild regulations concerning quality and labour conditions; working for two entrepreneurs at the same time was forbidden; they could only use the raw materials and designs provided by the entrepreneur; they were obliged to work every work day during their commission unless authorised otherwise by the entrepreneur; they could not work for their own account, etc. The master on the other hand had to guarantee enough work during the period of the contract between him and the journeymen. The number of artisans working on one piece was strictly limited (usually only one journeyman) and any kind of association was forbidden.

VI. Conclusions

A survey of labour relations and relations between merchants, entrepreneurs, and craftsmen in the late medieval rural industries in Flanders shows a strong regional and typological differentiation. The scale of the various industries, the surplus value of labour, the investment in both industrial production (at various stages of manufacture) and commercial infrastructure, and the regional impact of urbanisation and property relations in the countryside caused such strong discrepancies. Yet there are also striking similarities between systems of production and of trade. Merchants in the secondary centres, and more so in the big cities, had successfully dominated the commercial infrastructure. They developed a hierarchical market-system, following more or less the same patterns as the Christallerian distribution of central places, oriented towards the commercial gateways, or in the case of rural woollens towards the cities which were able to develop a regional network of finishing industries. Local people, whether they were large-scale entrepreneurs such as in Oudenaarde or associated merchants and agents such as in Kortrijk, took care of concentration of manufactured goods at transit markets and of transport towards the commercial cities. Only entrepreneurs of heavy woollen cloth (such as at Nieuwkerke, and to a lesser degree also some entrepreneurs of light woollens) worked in the same way as the medieval urban drapers did, by taking care of commercial outlets and contacts with the international merchants themselves. But again, most of the smaller rural woollen industries were well outside such international orientation, and focused on the domestic market of the Low Countries, and even the regional Flemish market, for which regional commercial networks had been established.

Dislocation of textile manufacture towards new centres of production (both urban and rural) did not cause the collapse of the urban network. Nor was the dependence of rural communities upon industrial activities a completely new phenomenon. In the medieval cloth industry, the contribution of rural labour had been crucial, in particular for the preparing stages of woolens. Moreover, urban entrepreneurs did not hesitate to stimulate competition with urban workers and to organise elaborate systems of putting-out in the countryside, in order to guarantee cheap labour in this traditional urban industry. Because of urban political dominance and commercial monopolies, they were able to maintain control and to allow some competition from rural weavers. There was even strong inter-urban competition on these matters, so that the supply of raw materials was assured.

As the economic structures defining the location of textile industries changed urban merchants and entrepreneurs changed tactics, and urban industries changed to the manufacture of high quality goods, leaving the mass production of standardised goods to smaller towns and the countryside. The merchants concentrated on monopolising commercial infrastructure and finishing industries and divided industrial output between specialised and more expensive urban goods and mass-produced standardised fabrics in the countryside. There were certainly exceptions. Some rural centres were able to develop urban types of manufacture, and, as the say-industry of Hondschoote demonstrates, to even be incorporated, at least partially, in the urban network. In other sectors the more traditional image of rural industries prevailed (that of small farmers combining agricultural and industrial activities). The relations with urban entrepreneurs and merchants (and as some cases in the linen industry demonstrate, with big farmers in the countryside as well) could differ depending on necessary investments, on the impact of guild regulation in the countryside, on the market infrastructure, etc. Rural weavers could be mere semi-urbanised employees of large-scale entrepreneurs (Oudenaarde tapestries) or small farmers selling their own production at the staple markets and complementing their agricultural income. There seems to have been great diversity.

Another point is the futility of distinguishing between urban and rural industries. The great divide between two opposite societies never existed because of extremely high mobility, seasonal labour (of both town and countryfolk), property relations, market-orientation, industrial and commercial networks, etc. In the densely urbanised county of Flanders, peasants were active as rural weavers, but, as the many probate inventories demonstrate, urban craftsmen, in particular in the smaller towns, very often owned small plots of land in the countryside and urban middle class gladly invested in rural property. Temporary mobility of unskilled and semi-skilled people, although very difficult to grasp, must have been very strong. So even from an urban point-of-view the divide was nothing but artificial.

Bibliography

Backhouse, M. (1976) 'Korte schets van de socio-ekonomische en religieuze situatie in Kortrijk tijdens de XVe eeuw', *De Leiegouw*, 18, pp. 415–454.

Boone, M. (1993) 'L'industrie textile à Gand au bas moyen âge ou les resurrections succesives d'une activité réputée moribonde', in M. Boone and W. Prevenier (eds), *La draperie ancienne des Pays-Bas: débouchés et stratégies de survie (14e–16e siècles)*, Louvain/Apeldoorn, pp. 15–61.

Boone, M. and Howell, M. (1996) 'Becoming early modern in the late medieval Low Countries. Ghent and Douai in the late middle-ages', *Urban History*, 23, pp. 300–324.

Clauzel, D. and Calonne, S. (1990) 'Artisanat rural et marché urbain: la draperie à Lille et dans ses campagnes à la fin du moyen âge et au XVIe siècle', *Revue du Nord*, 72, pp. 531–573.

Coornaert, E. (1930a) *Un centre industriel d'autrefois. La draperie-sayetterie d'Hondschoote. XIVe–XVIIIe siècle*, Paris.

Coornaert, E. (1930b) *Une industrie urbaine du XIVe au XVIe siècle. L'industrie de la laine à Bergues-Saint-Winoc*, Paris.

Coornaert, E. (1950) 'Draperies rurales, draperies urbaines. L'évolution de l'industries flamande au moyen âge et au XVIe siècle', *Belgisch Tijdschrift voor Filologie en Geschiedenis*, 28, pp. 59–96.

Duplessis, R.S. (1997) *Transitions to Capitalism in Early Modern Europe, New Approaches to European History*, Cambridge.

Duverger, E. (1960) *Jan, Jacques en Frans De Moor, tapijtwevers en -handelaars te Oudenaarde, Antwerpen en Gent 1560 tot ca. 1680*, Ghent.

Duverger, E. (1965) 'De Stuerbouts, een Oudenaards-Antwerps geslacht van tapissiers', *Artes Textiles*, 6, pp. 30–73.

Espinas, G. and Pirenne, H. (eds) (1904–1920) *Recueil des documents relatifs à l'histoire de l'industrie drapière*, 4 vols, Brussels.

Gijssels, C. and Straeten, L. van der (1986) *Arbeid en tewerkstelling in West-Vlaanderen (1796–1815)*, Ghent.

Klep, P. (1991) 'Population estimates of Belgium by province (1375–1831)', in *Historiens et populations. Liber amicorum E. Hélin*, Louvain-la-Neuve, pp. 485–508.

Lis, C. and Soly, H. (1994) 'Corporatisme, onderaanneming en loonarbeid. Flexibilisering en deregulering van de arbeidsmarkt in Westeuropesesteden (veertiende–achttiende eeuw)', *Tijdschrift voor Sociale Geschiedenis*, 20, pp. 365–390.

Morsa, D. (1997) 'L'urbanisation de la Belgique (1500–1800). Taille, hiérarchie et dynamique des villes', *Revue du Nord*, 79, pp. 303–330.

Pirenne, H. (1906) 'Note sur la fabrication des tapisseries en Flandre au XVIe siècle', *Vierteljahrsschrifte für Sozial- und wirtschaftsgeschichte*, 4, 644–656.

Robijns, L. (1978) Bijdrage tot de studie van de Aalsterse tapijtwevers, *Alostana. Historische Bijdragen van Aalst*, 2, pp. 33–129.

Roobaert, E. (1957–1958) 'Het legwerkersbedrijf in het Land van Aalst, vooral te Geraardsbergen van ca. 1554 tot ca. 1564', *Artes Textiles*, 4, pp. 39–53.

Sabbe, E. (1975) *De Belgische vlasnijverheid. Deel 1. De Zuidnederlandse vlasnijverheid tot het verdrah van Utrecht (1713)*, Kortrijk.

Sagher, H.-E. de, Sagher, J.H. de, Werveke, H. van and Wyffels, C. (eds), (1951–1966), *Recueil des documents relatifs à l'histoire de l'industrie drapière en Flandre. Deuxième partie. Le sud-Ouest de la Flandre depuis l'époque bourguignonne*, 3 vols (vol. 1: 1951; vol. 2: 1961; vol. 3: 1966), Brussels.

Stabel, P. (1995a) *De kleine stad in Vlaanderen. Bevolkingsdynamiek en economische functies van de kleine en secundaire stedelijke centra in het Gentse kwartier (14de–16de eeuw)*, Brussels.

Stabel, P. (1995b) 'De-urbanization and Urban Decline in Flanders (16th and 18th centuries): dinsintegration of an urban system?', in D. McCabe (ed.), *European Urbanisation, social structure and problems between the eighteenth and twentieth century*, Leicester, pp. 87–108.

Stabel, P. (1996) 'Town and Countryside in the Southern Low Countries in the late 15th-early 19th century: preliminary reflections on the changing relations in a pre-industrial economy', in R. Ní Néill (ed.), *Town and Countryside in Western Europe from 1500 to 1939*, Leicester, pp. 1–28.

Stabel, P. (1997a) *Dwarfs among Giants. The urban network in late medieval Flanders*, Louvain-Apeldoorn.

Stabel, P. (1997b) 'Ambachten en textielondernemers in kleine Vlaamse steden tijdens de overgang van Middeleeuwen naar Nieuwe Tijd', in C. Lis and H. Soly (eds), *Werelden van verschil. Ambachtsgilden in de Lage Landen*, Brussels, pp. 79–98.

Stabel, P. (1997c)'"*Dmeeste, oirboirlixste ende proffitelixste let ende neringhe*". Een kwantitatieve benadering van de lakenproductie in het laatmiddeleeuwse en vroegmoderne Vlaanderen', *Handelingen van de Maatschappij voor Geschiedenis en Oudheidkunde te Gent*, 51, pp. 113–153

Stabel, P. (1999) 'Marketing cloth in the Low Countries: foreign merchants, local businessmen and urban entrepreneurs: markets, transport and transaction costs (14th–16th century)', in P. Stabel, B. Blondé and A. Greve (eds), *International Trade in the Low Countries (14th–16th century). Merchants, Organisation and Infrastructure. Proceedings of the International Colloquium. Ghent–Antwerp 12th–13th December 1997*, Louvain/Apeldoorn, pp. 15–36.

Stevens, C. and Jaspers, L. (1985) *Arbeid en tewerkstelling in Oost-Vlaanderen op het einde van het Ancien Régime*, Ghent.

Thoen, E. (1988) *Landbouwekonomie en bevolking in Vlaanderen gedurende de late middeleeuwen en het begin van de moderne tijden. Testregio: de kasselrijen van Oudenaarde en Aalst (eind 13de–eerste helft 16de eeuw)*, Ghent.

Thoen, E. (1990) 'Technique agricole, cultures nouvelles et économie rurale en Flandre au bas moyen âge', in *Plantes et cultures nouvelles en Europe occidentale au moyen âge et à l'époque moderne. Flaran 12*, pp. 51–67.

Thoen, E. (1994) 'Immigration to Bruges during the late middle ages', in S. Cavaciocchi (ed.), *Le migrazioni in Europa secc. XIII–XVIII. Atti della Venticinquesima Settimana di Studi, 3–8 maggio 1993*, Prato–Firenze, pp. 335–354.

Thoen, E. and Verhulst, A. (1986) 'Le réseau urbain et les campagnes dans l'ancien comté de Flandre (ca. 1350–1800)', *Storia della città*, 36, pp. 53–60.

Uytven, R. van (1972) 'Peiling naar de beroepsstructuur op het Brabantse platteland omstreeks 1755', *Bijdragen tot de Geschiedenis*, 55, pp. 172–203.

Uytven, R. van (1992) 'Brabantse en Antwerpse centrale plaatsen (14de–19de eeuw)', in *Het stedelijk netwerk in België in historisch perspectief (1350–1850). Een statistische en dynamische benadering. Handelingen van het 15de internationaal colloquium. Spa 4–6 september 1990*, Brussels, pp. 29–79.

Vandenbroeke, C. (1979) 'Sociale en konjunkturele facetten van de linnennijverheid in Vlaanderen (late 14e–midden 19e eeuw)', *Handelingen van de Maatschappij voor Geschiedenis en Oudheidkunde te Gent*, 33, pp. 117–174.

Vanwelden, M. (1979) *Het tapijtweversambacht te Oudenaarde 1441–1772*, Oudenaarde.

Verhulst, A. (1990) *Précis d'histoire rurale de la Belgique*, Brussels.

Vermaut, J. (1988) 'Structural Transformation in a Textile Centre: Bruges from the sixteenth to the nineteenth century', in H. Van der Wee (ed.), *The Rise and Decline of Urban Industries in Italy and in the Low Countries (late middle ages – early modern times)*, Louvain, pp. 187–203.

Vermeiren-Vanwelden, M. (1995) 'Omtrent het begin van de Oudenaardse tapijtweverij (1368–1500)', *Handelingen van de Geschied- en Oudheidkundige Kring van Oudenaarde*, pp. 69–87

Wee, H. van der (1988) 'Industrial dynamics and the process of urbanization and de-urbanization in the Low Countries from the late middle ages to the eighteenth century. A synthesis', in H. van der Wee (ed.), *The rise and decline of urban industries in Italy and in the Low Countries (late middle ages – early modern times)*, Louvain, pp. 307–381.

8 Early forms of proto-industries in the backyard of Antwerp? The Rupel area in the fifteenth and sixteenth centuries[1]

Michael LIMBERGER, University of Antwerp – UFSIA

I. Introduction

It may sound anachronistic, at first, to use the concept of proto-industrialisation for a study of fifteenth and sixteenth-century non-agrarian labour in the countryside. The concept originally referred to a phenomenon of the eighteenth century and is directly linked with the process of industrialisation. According to the hypothesis of F. Mendels, cottage industries oriented towards exportation to the international market, which he called proto-industries, formed a crucial step in the development towards actual industrialisation (Mendels, 1972; Clarkson, 1985; Ogilvie and Cerman, 1996). We cannot speak of a direct development towards industrialisation in the context of the fifteenth and sixteenth centuries, of course. If the assumption of a causal link between proto-industrialisation and industrialisation has been criticised as being teleological, it would be much more so if we extend it to the late medieval and early modern period. Nevertheless, H. Van der Wee pointed out in a critical assessment of the theory that rural industries, as presented by F. Mendels, were not a new phenomenon in the eighteenth century, but already existed from the late middle ages on in the Southern Low Countries (Van der Wee, 1988: 317–318; 1975; Clarkson, 1985). The rise of a rural textile industry in Flanders, producing for the international market dates from the thirteenth century. In fact, among the centres of textile production of the Low Countries in the late Middle Ages there were also numerous villages. The place that is cited most frequently in this context is Hondschoote, near Ypres. But there were several areas where rural textile industry developed in that period: western Flanders, the Lys-valley, in the South of Flanders, the Brabantine Campine area, and the villages of Weert, Hoorn and Maaseik along the river Meuse (Ammann, 1954: 16; Soly and Thijs, 1981: 37–43). Also P.M. Hohenberg and L.H. Lees assumed that there was a first wave of proto-industrialisation in Flanders and Brabant, taking place between 1300 and 1500 (1985: 121–122).

J.L. van Zanden, in turn, states that there were various non-agrarian activities in sixteenth-century Holland, which met the requirements of proto-industrialisation. In contrast to the Southern Low Countries, these were, however, not so much textile industries, but activities like fishing, international carrying trade, shipping or peat cutting. Although these types of economic activities generally are not considered typical fields of proto-

[1] Many thanks to Bruno Blondé and Stephan Epstein for their comments on the first version of this paper. The following abbreviations are used for archive-references: ARA: Algemeen Rijksarchief/Archives Generaux du Royaume, Brussels, RK: fonds Rekenkamer/Chambre des Comptes, MW: family archives Merode de Westerlo; RAA: Rijksarchief Antwerpen, OGA: Oud Gemeentearchief; SAA: Stadsarchief Antwerpen, SR: Schepenregisters.

industrial development, they fulfilled the same functions: that is, providing an additional source of income to the rural population, by profiting from the opportunities of the interregional market (1993: 29–40; 2001). Although in Flanders and Brabant, textile industries were the most important proto-industrial sector of this first wave, other kinds of non-agrarian occupations, comparable to those referred to by Van Zanden, developed there too. One example is the exploitation of quarries in the region around Brussels, which was a major economic activity during the fifteenth century, far beyond local importance (Maesschalck and Viaene, 1985). But, can we extend the concept of a first wave of proto-industrialisation to these kinds of occupations, as Hohenberg and Lees, and Van der Wee suggested?

In this paper, we will deal with an area where non-agrarian labour was particularly wide-spread during the fifteenth and sixteenth centuries, i.e. the area along the rivers Scheldt, Rupel, and Nete between Antwerp, Mechelen, and Lier, in the duchy of Brabant (see Figure 8.1). A major characteristic of this area, called the *Rupel area* hereafter, was the varied character of its economy. Although the plains along the rivers were fertile and favourable to intensive agriculture, different non-agrarian activities had arisen by the thirteenth century. Cloth weaving had been established by the fourteenth century in several villages between Lier and Mechelen, which became centres of cloth export in the fifteenth and sixteenth centuries. A second important sector was brick burning along the banks of the rivers Scheldt and Rupel. Already around 1400, bricks and tiles from Boom, Rumst and Hemiksem were in demand throughout the Low Countries (Hollestelle, 1976: 124–130). Furthermore, some other, although less spectacular, sectors developed in the Rupel area. These were especially inland navigation and small-scale shipbuilding, in Rumst and Boom, and, to a lesser extent, lumber trade. All these non-agrarian activities provided a source of alternative income for the local population outside agriculture, and therefore are comparable to the 'proto-industrial' occupations referred to by Van Zanden. Moreover, they were not limited to the local economy, but oriented towards the regional and even interregional market. Cloth weaving and to some extent brick burning can even be considered export industries. To what extent, however, do these non-agrarian activities, some of which were of rather modest dimensions, fit to the model of (late-medieval) proto-industrialisation? Does the definition apply to all of them or only to some? And, is it justified to call the Rupel area as a whole an early proto-industrialised area? In the following lines, we will look at some of the major characteristics of the non-agrarian activities of the Rupel area, such as their economic scale, their geographical range, their occupational structure and their organization, in order to detect differences and parallels between the different sectors. Some paragraphs will also be dedicated to the demographic and social impact of non-agrarian labour in the Rupel area. Through analysing different non-agrarian sectors within a limited area, this case study should help to answer the question whether the concept of a first wave of proto-industrialisation in Flanders and Brabant was limited to the textile industry, or whether it can be extended to other sectors.

Figure 8.1 Centres of non-agrarian labour along the rivers Scheldt, Rupel and Nete during the 15th and 16th centuries

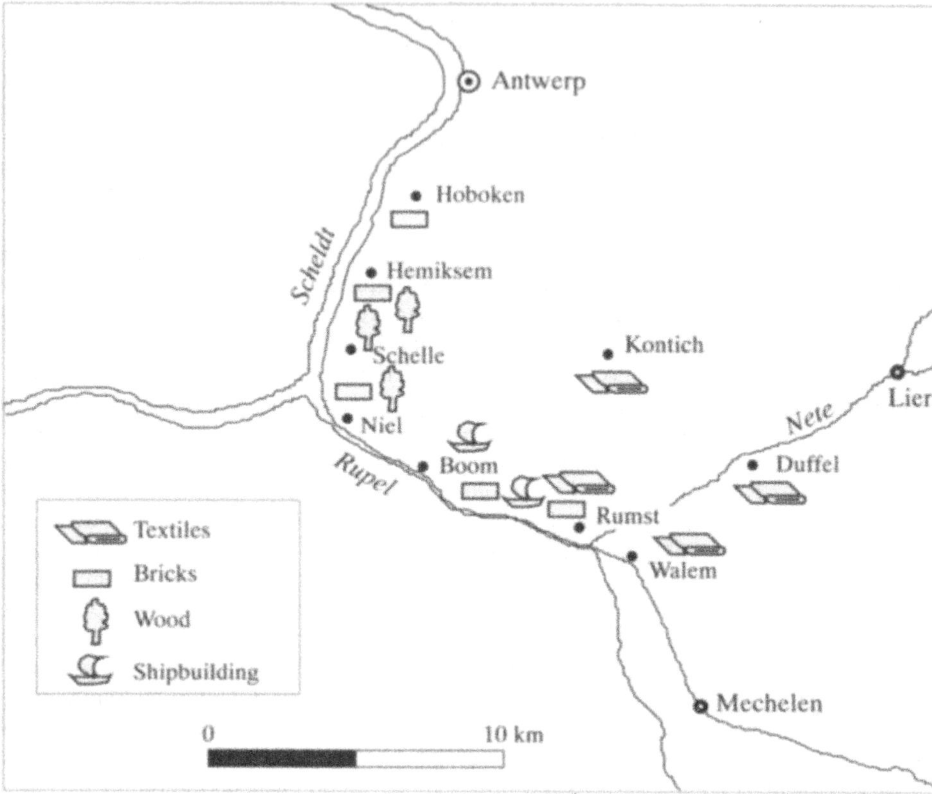

II. The draperies of Duffel, Walem, Kontich, and Rumst

The origins of wool-weaving in the countryside between Lier and Mechelen have to be seen as a result of the great number of sheep being raised in the area of Lier and in the adjacent Campine-area as early as the twelfth and thirteenth centuries (Van Uytven, 1976: 93). Weaving for local demand was a widespread occupation in pastoral regions during the Middle Ages and was not particular to the Rupel area. From a primitive form of cloth production, however, the villages of Duffel, Walem, Rumst, and Kontich, developed into centres of exportation, by the late fourteenth century. Among the economic factors that favoured the development of these rural draperies, the supply of raw materials, labour force, and easy access to a large sales market, seem the most important. On the supply side, raw materials were, without any doubt, abundant. Wool was available in great quantities in the Campine. The wool from the Campine was among the best of the Low Countries and was used in many Brabantine cloth centres. Although it was increasingly replaced by English wool, from the fourteenth century on, it remained important, especially for cheaper fabrics (Verhulst, 1974: 25). A second crucial factor was labour supply. The general hypothesis within the concept of proto-industrialisation is that cottage industries normally rose in areas with small holdings and a surplus of labour. Judging from population density, the latter condition was certainly met in the Southern Low Countries, which belonged to the most densely populated areas of Europe. For the Rupel-Nete area, the first quantitative evidence dates from the late fourteenth century. In 1374, Duffel counted 252 taxable persons, Rumst and Boom, taken together, 280, and Kontich 308. Although we do not know exactly by what criteria these 'taxable persons' were defined, the figures show that the population of the villages was substantial. The household count of 1437 confirms this impression: Duffel then counted 276 households, Rumst between 250 and 300, Kontich 189, and Walem 366, which suggests a population between ca. 1000 and 2000 inhabitants for each of these places. (Cuvelier, 1912: 10–11, 450, 466–468). The average population density in the Rupel-Nete area can be estimated, therefore, at more than sixty inhabitants per square kilometre, which is about as high as rural population density could get in the late Middle Ages. Landed property, accordingly, was split up into small holdings. More than half of the population held less than 2 ha of land.[2] Since raw materials and labour supply were available in large quantity, the third factor to look at, is the access to a sales market. It seems that the Rupel area was particularly well situated in this respect. The area was not only situated on the major Brabantine waterways, it was close to the two commercial centres of Mechelen and Antwerp, and an important international trade route, i.e. the road between the German Rhine area and Bruges, and the Brabant fairs of Antwerp and Bergen-op-Zoom (Van Uytven, 1976: 94). While the location along the route to Bruges may have led to contacts with German merchants, the Brabant fairs formed an ideal outlet for the rural cloth production, particularly from the fifteenth century on. In fact, cloth from Duffel and Walem was shipped regularly down the Scheldt towards these markets (Slootmans, 1985: 3, 150; Unger, 1939: 91, 611).

Besides these economic factors, institutional factors probably helped the cloth industry of Duffel, Walem, Rumst and Kontich too. Van Uytven stressed that many rural textile centres were communities with a privileged status, so called 'liberties', or were in the hands of powerful landlords (Van Uytven, 1975: 70). Both Walem and Rumst had the status of 'liberties,' and their landlords were members of the high Brabantine nobility (Wauters, 1975: VI C, 224–227, Galesloot, 1870: I, 135, 142).[3] The support of such a powerful lord at the ducal court could help to obtain privileges for the drapers against the opposition of a neighbouring town. Merchtem, near Brussels, lost its privilege to set up a drapers guild in 1411, only two years after it had been granted, due to the opposition

[2] In the manor of Helmont, in Kontich, for example, in 1431, the percentage of holdings of less than 2 bunders (2.46 ha.) was more than 66%. In Walem, ca. 50% of the holdings in copyhold in 1480 were smaller than 2 bunders (Van Passen, 1966; ARA, MW 327, Rent register Walem 1480).

[3] In the fifteenth century, Walem and Duffel-Perwijs was held by the family of Rotselaar, Duffel under the land of Arkel belonged to the family of Wezemaal. Both formed part of the high Brabantine nobilty. Rumst was held by Jeanne of Bethune, and later by her daughter Jeanne of Bar, wife of Louis of Luxemburg, count of St. Pol.

of the drapers of Brussels (Wauters, 1975: IV, 158). In the Rupel area, no such interventions by the neighbouring towns are known. Anyway, none of them was very likely to intervene. Mechelen did not have any juridical influence in the Rupel area, being a territory that did not belong to the duchy of Brabant. Antwerp on the other hand was more than fifteen kilometres away and was a commercial town, with an industry oriented toward cloth finishing, rather than an actual drapers town. Finally, the town of Lier, which was situated next to Duffel, did not oppose its rural competitor, either because of its smaller juridical influence, or because of the strong position of the landlords of Duffel and Walem.

Thus, by the fifteenth century, cloth production and export in the villages of Duffel, Walem, and Kontich had become prosperous. References to a dyeing workshop and a seal house, in fifteenth-century rent registers of Walem, indicate that the textile industry was already highly organized.[4] The fact that there was a 'weavers street' in the centre of the village, shows, furthermore, that weavers were specialized craftsmen, living in the village centre, rather than rural cottagers. The available data suggest that there was a certain division of labour within the village community: in the centre mainly houses with very small plots of land were to be found, whereas the larger agrarian holdings, including farms up to 20 ha, were situated outside the village.[5] For an explicit statement that the weavers of the area had actually given up agriculture, we have to wait, however, until the late sixteenth century: 'The inhabitants (of Duffel) who for a part are not active in agriculture, make a living of making cloth, *serges* and other woollens which are being sold to other countries and towns in great quantities' (Guicciardini, 1612: 121).[6]

Duffel, the place referred to in this text, developed quite exceptionally during the second half of the sixteenth century. From a late mediaeval cloth making village it developed into a centre of textile production, where cloth and other types of woollens, like 'sargiën', 'friezen' and 'baaien' were not only woven, but also finished and dyed. In the second half of the sixteenth century, woollens from Duffel were not only one of the leading export products of the Low Countries, but they were also to be found in many Antwerp households. Antwerp wholesalers were involved in the sale of the product. So we see Jan Andries, cloth merchant from Antwerp sign a contract with the aldermen of Duffel, which entitles him to sell woollens called 'Friezen' from Duffel for a period of nine years.[7] The drapery of Duffel was subject to numerous regulations in the sixteenth century. In 1553, Duffel had obtained the monopoly of making *serges*, a light cloth imitating a Spanish type of textile. Various regulations concerned the size and weight of each type of cloth, the quality of wool to be used, and even the wages of weavers and fullers per piece. Moreover, the drapers were obliged to make a cloth or baai after each six serges, probably in order to provide a larger variety of qualities, instead of limiting

---

[4] ARA, MW 327, Rent register Walem 1480: 'in de weverstrate': items nr. 2, 3, 6, 110, 134, 'het lombaerdenhuis': item nr. 81, 'het zegelhuis': item nr. 85.

[5] ARA, MW 327, Rent register Walem 1480.

[6] 'De inwoners (van Duffel) die eensdeels de landwinninge niet oefenen generen hen met laken, sargiën en andere wollenwerk welk in verscheidene landen en steden met grote menigte vercocht wordt.' This specification was added by Montanus after the first edtion in 1567.

[7] Contract from April 28th, 1586, cited in *Dufflaea*: 196–198.

themselves to the production of cheap serges. Six control officers who were appointed by the aldermen of the three local manorial courts guaranteed the quality of the textiles.[8] Although not being a town, in juridical terms, the cloth industry of Duffel had become urban in its form of organization, at least by the second half of the sixteenth century. This is illustrated also by its protectionist behaviour in a court case against the town of Lier in 1581, concerning the imitation of Duffel serges: the drapers from Duffel referred to their privilege of 1553, stipulating that the weaving of serges was an invention of Duffel, and that no other place in the Low Countries had the right to produce them (Dufflaea: 483–486). Hence, instead of the classical situation of urban protectionism against rural competition, we have a case of protectionism by a rural textile centre against an urban imitator.

The other villages of the Rupel and Nete area did not keep pace with the development of Duffel. Walem, which was still mentioned in the same breath with Duffel in the fifteenth century, as well as Rumst and Kontich, disappeared from the export registers during the sixteenth century. Duffel seems the only rural drapers' centre of the Rupel-Nete valley, which could fully profit from the export opportunities offered by the Antwerp market. The real breakthrough seems to have taken place in the second half of the sixteenth century. The basis for this success may have been the production of serges after 1553. The wars of the late sixteenth century, however, put an end to the Duffel cloth production. The weavers fled to the surrounding towns, and most of them stayed there. The serge-weavers from Duffel, residing in Mechelen were accepted into the local drapers' guild in 1632 (Dufflaea: 6). Duffel cloth continued to exist, however, as a trademark. According to several etymological dictionaries, the *Dufflecoat* owes its name to the old drapery in that village.

III. Brick burning

A second non-agrarian sector with an importance beyond the local level was brick burning. Like cloth weaving, its origins can be traced back far into the Middle Ages. According to most authors, brick burning was introduced in the Scheldt valley, south of Antwerp, in the second half of the thirteenth century, by the Cistercian monks of St. Bernard's of Hemiksem. Profiting from a thick layer of clay, which was very well suited for the production of bricks, it was probably them who built the first ovens on the banks of the Scheldt, in Hemiksem. Starting, hence, as a local production, probably on a very limited scale, brick production expanded steadily in the fourteenth century. Various documents from that period refer to brick ovens and lime kilns in Kallebeek (a part of Hemiksem), Rumst, Schelle, and Boom (De Schepper, 1953: 19–24).

The establishment of brick ovens in the area around towns was not unusual in the late Middle Ages. Every town tried to produce the bricks that it needed as close as possible. There were also brick ovens in the area of Nieuwpoort and Dunkerk and in Stekene, near Ghent, in Flanders, and in the area around Brussels and in the Campine, in Brabant (Hollestelle, 1976: 12; Meskens, 1987; Baetens, 1979: 137). Already in the late fourteenth

[8] RAA, OGA, Duffel Nr. 402: Order concerning the weaving of wool in Duffel, 18 Nov. 1574. Edited in *Dufflaea*: 467–482.

century, bricks from Scheldt and Rupel were not only sold in Antwerp, but also 'exported' to places outside Brabant. The growth of Antwerp, from the fifteenth century on, stimulated local brick production considerably. Hundreds of thousands of bricks and tiles were regularly shipped from brick ovens in Boom, Rumst, Niel and Hemiksem to the quays of Antwerp.

The owners of brick ovens were mostly members of what we might call the 'local upper class'. Brick burning was a rather capital intensive sector. The building of a 'steengeleg' required a plot of land at the riverside, where the oven was situated. For retrieving the necessary clay, it also included about a hectare of land, where the clay was dug. Furthermore, the owner of a brick oven had to supply the oven with large quantities of fuel to fire the oven throughout the whole production process, which took about three to four weeks for one charge (Hollestelle, 1976: 33). The local landlords and great landowners, such as the abbey of St. Bernard originally held the land on which the ovens stood. But much of the land, including the loam pits and brick ovens, was given out in copyhold against the payment of a yearly land rent, and so was in the hands of (relatively wealthy) tenants. By the early fifteenth century, we find Antwerp citizens among the owners of brick ovens (De Nave, 1978: 462–465). Their share in the brick production, however, was relatively limited, at that time. Only in the sixteenth century, would heavy investments by Antwerp citizens take place.

Besides land and capital, the production of bricks also required a labour force: The clay had to be dug, brought to the oven, and stamped. Then, the bricks or tiles were formed, and piled in the oven. In total, each oven required about six persons, of which the only skilled worker was the actual brick-maker, who formed the bricks. According to the estimate of Hollestelle, there were about fifty ovens in the villages of Hemiksem, Boom, Niel and Rumst taken together, by 1500. Thus, brick production provided work for about 300 persons, out of a total population of roughly 3500 inhabitants (Soly, 1977: 246).[9] Being predominantly unskilled work, brick making was a type of activity that could be easily combined with small-scale agriculture.

The almost explosive growth of Antwerp in the sixteenth century stimulated the expansion of the brick industry of the Scheldt and Rupel area. Between 1496 and 1568 about 5700 houses were built and many public buildings were erected in the commercial metropolis. The building fever reached its peak around 1550, when the entrepreneur Gilbert van Schoonbeke monopolized the public construction works of the town, including the building of the new fortifications. Together with his companion Jacob van Henxthoven, he established an organization, which H. Soly called 'a vertical building trust', which was unique in the history of the early modern Low Countries. To guarantee a cheap supply of bricks, they bought fifteen brick ovens in Hemiksem, which made them independent from other producers. In order to prevent the workers from leaving the ovens during the winter break, they had built sixty small houses near the ovens in order to

[9] The villages of Hoboken, Hemiksem, Rumst, Schelle and Niel, taken together, had 718 households, or ca. 3500 inhabitants. See: Cuvelier, 1912: 462–474. Soly estimates that there were only 20 ovens around 1500, but during the Antwerp building boom, around the middle of the century, their number increased, especially in Boom.

lodge them (Soly, 1977: 266). It is not impossible, therefore, that some of the workers immigrated to Hemiksem to work in brick production, during that period. However extraordinary the capitalist enterprise of Gilbert van Schoonbeke may have been, it was, nevertheless very short-lived. Already in 1554, the company with Van Henxthoven was liquidated, eleven of the fifteen brick ovens were sold to the brothers Jan and Peter van Boome, and the other four remained in the hands of Van Henxthoven. While for merchants like van Schoonbeke and Van Hencxthoven brick ovens were only a temporary investment, the van Boome's remained active in brick production until the seventeenth century (De Schepper, 1953: 26–27). The brick industry of the Rupel area flourished for some time, especially in Boom. During the Revolt, however, this activity diminished drastically. Only in the seventeenth century did a recovery take place. In 1650, production again reached the level of 1575. Further development of the Rupel brick industry can be described as one of slow industrialisation. The brick works of Boom and Hemiksem developed into an important industry and remained active until the twentieth century (Baetens, 1979).

IV. Other non-agrarian activities

Besides brick making and cloth weaving, some other non-agrarian activities existed in the Rupel area. Of course, there were craftsmen in the villages working for local demand, like carpenters, smiths, bakers, masons etc. But apart from these occupations that were common anywhere in the countryside, some others were typical for the villages of the Scheldt and Rupel valley. Woodcutting and wood trade, for example, were such activities concentrated along the Scheldt, especially near Schelle. There were larger woods in Brabant than those of Schelle and Niel, especially in the South of the duchy and in the Campine, but the position so close to Antwerp and the good transport facilities favoured their exploitation. Woods, which were owned by great landowners, were divided into plots that were cut in regular periods. These cuts, called 'hauwen', were bought by woodcutters, who acted as individuals or in small companies of two or three men. They cut the wood and sold it in Antwerp, and sometimes shipped it down the Scheldt (Slootmans, 1985: III, 1273). Considering the sparse character of Brabant woods, which hardly deserve to be called forests, the wood was sold as firewood, and hardly ever timber. Although woodcutting was not an industrial activity, it shared important characteristics with brick production. Both served essentially in the provisioning of Antwerp with raw materials. Both profited from the situation along the Scheldt, which was advantageous for the transport of relatively heavy products. Moreover, the woodmongers were part of the same social group, or even the same families, as the owners of brick ovens. Good examples for this link were the Antwerp building entrepreneurs Jacob van Henxthoven and Adriaan Spillemans. Spillemans was active in the wood trade himself (Soly, 1977: 266), and van Hencxthoven seems to have descended from a family of wood merchants.[10] Like the owners of brick ovens they acted as employers of workers for the actual

[10] ARA, RK 11907, Account Land van Mechelen oct. 1541–sept 1542. The van Hencxthovens had immigrated to Brabant in the 15th century from Germany. Jacobs father, Willem, lived in Duffel. Jacob, himself had properties in that place. SAA, SR, 207, f. 52 v. 19.7.1542.

woodcutting, which took generally place in autumn and winter, and thus provided seasonal wage labour for a number of unskilled workers.[11]

An advantage for both brick making and woodcutting were the transportation facilities offered by rivers Scheldt and Rupel. Along these rivers, a busy shipping activity developed. Although Antwerp, like most large towns, had its own corporation of boatmen, which had monopolies for the transport of merchandise, the rural boatmen were allowed to deliver local products to the town. The centre of the shipping activity along the Rupel was Rumst, a ducal toll-station and the major marketplace of the area. Here, and in the hamlet of Boom, several boatmen and shipbuilders were active. In the fifteenth century, they built barges for boatmen in Antwerp, Boom and Rupelmonde (Asaert, 1973: 382). We must, however, not overestimate the importance of the shipbuilding activity. The most important Brabantine shipbuilding centre, Mechelen, where fourteen master-shipbuilders were active in the fifteenth century, was situated only a few kilometres away. Even members of shipbuilding families like Pauwel Bertels and Henrik Pluym bought riverboats in Mechelen.[12] The families Pluym, and Bertels were the most active among the shipbuilders from Rumst. Like the owners of brick ovens and the woodmongers, they amassed considerable properties. Jacob Bertels, for example, owned, in 1461, a house with 1/2 bunder (ca. 0.66 ha) of land, at Boom, at the riverside, about 8 bunders (ca. 10.6 ha) of land which he held in fief from the lord of Rumst, situated next to the property of the Pluym children. Furthermore, Bertels was the owner of a brick oven, of 1.5 bunders, situated at the Scheldt.[13] This example shows how closely brickmaking, woodcutting, and shipping in the Rupel area were related to each other. The same families and even individuals were active in either of these activities, generally not so much as actual brick-makers or woodcutters, but rather as merchants or owners of an oven.

V. A proto-industrialised area?

This short survey shows that the area along the rivers Rupel and Nete witnessed the rise of a whole range of non-agrarian activities with more than local importance. To what extent, however, can these activities be regarded as part of a proto-industrial development? There are some reasons to make a distinction between the textile industry and the other sectors. First, the textile industry is the only one to fit to the strict definition of proto-industries given by Mendels, that is: home industries producing for exportation to the international market (Mendels, 1982: 77–79 cited in Ogilvie and Cerman, 1996: 6). The other sectors were essentially oriented towards Antwerp and the Brabantine economy, although bricks and wood were sent down the Scheldt to places outside Brabant. Hence, their development was not so much dependent on shifts within the international market, but rather of the growth of the regional economy, or that of the regional centre. In the case of Antwerp, however, the two were closely related. Antwerp was also crucial for

[11] Most of the contracts for buying a plot of wood for cutting date from the period between September and February.

[12] SAA, SR, 77, f. 234r. (25.10.1470), fo. 241 r. (7.11.1470) and SR 79, fo. 32 vo. (10.6.1471).

[13] SAA, SR 61 f. 182 r. (1461).

the rise of the rural textile industry, as an export market but also to a considerable extent through local consumption (Van der Wee, 1988: 334–335). A sector that shows this close interdependence of regional and international economy very clearly is inland navigation. Although regional in its range, it played an important role for the integration of the Flemish and Brabantine hinterland in the European commercial network. A second critical point is the fact that both brick production and the wood trade were heavily dependent on local resources and were therefore rural by definition. They were, therefore not subject to shifts from town to countryside, like for example textile industry. The term 'first wave' of proto-industrialisation, as opposed to a wave of urbanisation during the sixteenth and early seventeenth centuries does not really apply to these sectors.

If we have to distinguish, therefore, between the 'proto-industries' of the textile sector and the other sectors as two different, although closely related, phenomena, we can find, nevertheless, a major feature that they had in common: they all offered additional non-agrarian incomes to the rural population beyond the level of the local market. This is probably the most significant characteristic of proto-industries, and also the point that Van Zanden referred to. Of course the different non-agrarian sectors embodied distinct forms of labour, and different parts of the rural population were affected. In the textile industry, skilled or semi-skilled labour was predominant. In Duffel and Walem, weavers formed a considerable part of the village population from the fifteenth century on, in Kontich and Rumst their share was probably lower. In Rumst, there were, however, other kinds of skilled labour than weaving. A number of boatmen were active in Rumst and Boom, and several ship-builders had their workshops there, in which some assistants were employed.[14] These skilled or semi-skilled workers very likely dedicated a large part of their time to their non-agrarian occupation, although they may have cultivated some plots of land or tended some sheep or cattle. For brick burning and woodcutting, on the other hand, mainly unskilled workers were needed. The number of workers employed in woodcutting during the winter is unknown, but must have been considerable. In the case of brick production, the number of workers can be roughly estimated. During the Antwerp building boom, around 1550, some 400–500 persons may have worked in the brick ovens between Hemiksem and Rumst, most of which were unskilled workers (Soly, 1975: 343). Before and after this short peak period, the number was probably much lower. The great impact of the brick industry on the local economy shows in a testimony from 1570 which states that before the religious wars 'a great part of the inhabitants of Rumst had lived from the production of bricks and lime'(Cosemans, 1936: 349). Most of the workers employed in these sectors had a small plot of land and worked 'part-time' as woodcutters or in brickmaking. They were forced to, because both were seasonal occupations. A third group involved in the non-agrarian activities of the Rupel area can be categorized as small-scale entrepreneurs. These entrepreneurs were the owners of the brick ovens with surrounding plots of clay land, the woodmongers, and finally the cloth merchants organising the marketing of the woollens produced in the drapers' villages. They came largely from the villages of the Rupel area, where they formed part of the local upper class, holding large landed property and regularly serving as aldermen of the villages. Others lived in town, or eventually moved there, like

[14] ARA, RK 11909, account Land van Mechelen oct. 1556–sept.1557. 'Cornelis Wouters, shipbuilder, with two assistants'.

the two building entrepreneurs, Spillemans and Van Hencxthoven, who had their roots in the Scheldt area and in Duffel respectively. Although not directly involved in production, they had a considerable share in its organisation and even a greater share in the profits it generated.

As far as the social impact of the non-agrarian economy of the Rupel area is concerned, we can observe an extraordinarily high degree of demographic concentration in the villages along the Rupel and the Nete. Population density was higher in the villages along the rivers Scheldt, Rupel and Nete, than in other places of the area. In the second half of the fifteenth century, the population was concentrated in large village centres, which had obtained a nearly urban character. Duffel was called 'villa notabilis et populosa' in a document from 1488, on the occasion of a request to be allowed to rebuild the choir of the local church, 'novum magnum et sumptuosum' because the old one had become too small 'et tante communitate insufficiens'. A local historian of the seventeenth century, referred to the same place as 'renowned, rich and admired, adorned with many extraordinarily beautiful houses, because of the great trade with woollens, that is with serges, before the devastations of the war'(Dufflaea: 99, 185). In Walem, the houses around the church and the market square had proper names by about 1480 – (imaginative names such as, *the Eagle, the Red Shield, The Rose,* or *the Horse Shoe*) which suggests that that they were considerable in size and quality.[15] Rumst was a large market place with a yearly fair. In the late sixteenth century it had nine breweries which produced not only for local consumption but also for trade (Van Passen, 1988: 73; Cosemans, 1936: 315). The villages along the Scheldt did not reach the same dimensions. In contrast with the rural textile centres, none of the brick-makers' villages of the Rupel area developed into large agglomerations with a quasi-urban character, like Duffel, Walem or Rumst. This can partly be explained by the different economic structure of these places. The degree of organisation of brick makers was much lower than that of cloth weavers. The owners of the brick ovens made individual contracts with their clients, and were not so dependent on a strong organisation like the weavers of Duffel or Walem. Brick ovens were independent units, which required much space and direct access to the river, and less so the advantages that the concentration in villages may have brought about. So, they did not use common facilities, like a fulling pond, or a sealing chamber, as was the case for cloth production.

A negative impact that is attributed to proto-industrialisation, is proletarianisation and impoverishment. To what extent was this the case for the Rupel area? In the fifteenth century, the population was not only large but also relatively prosperous. The number of poor households, that is, the number of households which received poor-relief, and were therefore exempted from their fiscal contribution, was low in comparison with other parts of rural Brabant. In 1437, the rate of poor households of Duffel, Rumst, Kontich and Hemiksem ranged between 12 and 19% (Cuvelier, 1912: 450, 466–468).[16] The cited villages made up part of a whole area with a remarkably low average poverty rate of 9%, situated between Antwerp, Lier, and Mechelen. This was only half the rate of the district of Antwerp (20.7%), whereas in the districts of Brussels and Louvain the

[15] ARA, MW, 327, Rent register Walem, 1480.
[16] Duffel: 18.3%, Rumst 12.36%, Kontich 12.2% and Hemiksem 18.8%.

average poverty rate was between 30 and 40% (Blockmans and Prevenier, 1975: 517). In Walem, on the other hand more than half of the population was considered poor. In Hoboken, Niel, and Schelle, the other villages situated along the Scheldt, which were not so much hit by brick making as Hemiksem or Boom, the percentage of poor households was also higher (Cuvelier, 1912).[17] For the sixteenth century we have no comparable figures for the district of Antwerp. Only for Duffel and Walem, which were counted among the district of Brussels, are the poverty rates known for the year 1526: Duffel had 25.6% poor households, whereas Walem had only 17.5%. Although the rate of Duffel had increased strongly (which can maybe be explained by a plague that hit in 1515) these figures are still relatively low. The optimistic descriptions of Duffel and Rumst, from the second half of the sixteenth century, suggest that there was no visible tendency of impoverishment in these places before 1570. The available data are, however, insufficient to estimate the social impact of the expansion of the non-agrarian sector. Further investigation will be necessary to be able to compare the social situation of the population of the Rupel area with that of surrounding areas with a mainly agrarian economy.

VI. Conclusion

Although the Rupel area was limited to a number of villages strung along the rivers Scheldt, Rupel and Nete, it showed a remarkable economic potential. Within only few kilometres were concentrated a major rural cloth industry, the greatest centre of brick production of the Southern Low Countries, and the second greatest centre of shipbuilding within Brabant. Woodcutting and inland navigation formed additional non-agrarian occupations along the rivers. Each of these sectors, taken apart, fulfilled, to a certain extent, the function of creating extra-incomes for different classes of the rural population, which makes them comparable to the proto-industries of the eighteenth century. In terms of internal structure, two different 'proto-industrial' phenomena can, nevertheless, be distinguished: The cloth industry that was concentrated in some villages in the eastern part of the area in some respects formed a development apart. The rise of small centres of textile production for export is a development which took place in different parts of Flanders and Brabant during the fourteenth and fifteenth century, and forms part of the 'first proto-industrial wave' of the Southern low Countries' textile industry. The rural character of these cloth-making villages should not be overrated, however, especially in the case of Duffel and Walem. These drapers' villages were of considerable size and had many characteristics of small towns. Also the degree of organisation and regulation of cloth production in a place like Duffel reminds one strongly of the urban cloth industry of that period. Instead of a sharp antithesis between urban and rural industries, we should, therefore, speak of new centres of the cloth production, as opposed to the old established drapers' centres. Brick production, wood trade, inland navigation, and shipbuilding, between Antwerp and Rumst, on the other hand, formed a cluster of non-agrarian activities oriented mainly towards the supply of Antwerp. The location along a navigable river and the presence of raw materials such as clay and wood, in combination with the proximity of a big town, formed the major preconditions for the rise of these activities, which were closely interconnected. Rivers are known to have been the major focuses of

[17] Walem 50.5%, Hoboken 50.5%, Schelle 29.8% and Niel 34.2% (Cuvelier, 1912).

urban development of Flanders and Brabant in the Middle Ages (Van Uytven, 1992: 35–36; Prevenier, Sosson and Boone, 1992: 159–160; Stabel, 1997: 145). The clustering of non-agrarian activities in the countryside in the valleys of navigable rivers, and its socio-economic impact, however, is a phenomenon that has not yet been subject to systematic analysis. The fact that these two clusters of late medieval proto-industrial development were located within such a short distance of each other, and that their development also followed almost the same chronology, indicates that they had some major features in common. The most important was the impact of Antwerp. It stimulated the rise of the non-agrarian sectors (including the cloth industry) through an increasing local demand. For the textile industry, it served as a gateway towards the international market. The short, but exceptional, peak of both the production of woollens in Duffel, and the brick industry in Hemiksem and Boom around the middle of the sixteenth century also reflects the commercial and industrial boom of Antwerp during that period. To return to the question put forward in the introduction, if we can include the non-textile sectors of the Rupel area into the general concept of a first wave of Flemish and Brabantine proto-industrialisation, we suggest to answer the question with no. The rise of these non-agrarian activities is a regional phenomenon, related to the growth of an urban centre, and not part of the rise of the Flemish and Brabantine export industry. As this urban centre, Antwerp, became the major gateway for the Flemish and Brabantine cloth production, its impact on both types of rural activities was similar. In terms of the economic and social effects for the Rupel area, both types of non-agrarian activities can, nevertheless, be considered as proto-industrial. By offering sources of extra income, outside the local economy, it sustained a high population density and the growth of various large villages along the rivers Scheldt, Rupel, and Nete. The Rupel area was, therefore, an early case of a proto-industrialised area, or better, an area, where two different types of proto-industrial development coincided during the late Middle Ages and the sixteenth century.

Bibliography

Manuscript sources

Algemeen Rijksarchief/Archives Generaux du Royaume (ARA), Brussels, *Fonds Rekenkamer/Chambre des Comptes* (RK), 11907, 11909.

Algemeen Rijksarchief/Archives Generaux du Royaume (ARA), Brussels, family archives Merode de Westerlo (MW), 327, Rent register Walem 1480.

Rijksarchief Antwerpen (RAA), Antwerp, *Oud Gemeentearchief* (OGA), Duffel Nr. 402.

Stadsarchief Antwerpen (SAA), Antwerp, *Schepenregisters* (SR), 61, 77, 79, 207.

Printed and secondary sources

Ammann, H. (1954) 'Deutschland und die Tuchindustrie Nordwesteuropas im Mittelalter', *Hansische Geschichtsblätter*, 72, pp. 1–63.

Asaert, G. (1973) *De Antwerpse scheepvaart in de XVe eeuw (1394–1480). Bijdrage tot de ekonomische geschiedenis van de stad Antwerpen*, Brussels. (Verhandelingen van de koninglijke Academie voor Wetenschapen, Letteren en Schone Kunsten van België, Klasse der Letteren; nr. 72).

Baetens, R. (1979) 'Omvang en produktie van de baksteennijverheid in de Rupelstreek (16e–20e eeuw)', *Bijdragen tot de Geschiedenis*, 62, pp. 103–183.

Blockmans, W.P. and Prevenier, W. (1975) 'Armoede in de Nederlanden van de 14e tot het midden van de 16e eeuw: bronnen en problemen', in H.F.M. van den Eerenbeemt, P.C. Jansen and R. van Uytven (eds), *Armoede en armenzorg, Tijdschrift voor Geschiedenis*, 88, 4, pp. 501–535.

Clarkson, L.A. (1985) *Proto-Industrialisation: The First Phase of Industrialisation?*, Basingstoke/London. (Studies in economic and social history).

Cosemans, A. (1936) 'Het uitzicht van Brabant op het einde van de zestiende eeuw', *Bijdragen tot de Geschiedenis*, 27, pp. 285–351.

Cuvelier, J. (1912) *Les dénombrements de foyers en Brabant (XIVe–XVIe siècle)*, Brussels.

Dufflea. Bijdragen tot de geschiedenis van Duffel (1960–1962).

Galesloot, L. (1870) *Inventaire des archives de la cour féodale de Brabant*, 2 vols, Brussels.

Guicciardini, L. (1612) *Beschryvinghe van alle de Neder-landen; anderssins ghenoemt Neder-Duytslandt... vermeerdert... by den... autheur... Overgheset in de Nederduytsche spraecke, door Cornelium Kilianum. Nu wederom met verscheyden historien... vermeerdert... door Petrum Montanum Ghedruckt by Willem Jansz.*, Amsterdam.

Hohenberg, P.M. and Lees, L.H. (1985) *The Making of Urban Europe 1000–1950*, Cambridge (Mass.).

Hollestelle, J. (1976) *De steenbakkerij in de Nederlanden tot omstreeks 1560*, 2nd edition, Arnhem.

Maesschalck, A. and Viaene, J. (1985) 'Bouwmeester Jan van Ruisbroek herdacht (1486–1986)', *Tijdschrift voor Brusselse Geschiedenis*, 2, pp. 17–110.

Mendels, F.F. (1972) 'Proto-Industrialisation: the first Phase of the Industrialisation Process', *Journal of Economic History*, 32, pp. 241–261.

Meskens, F. (1987) 'Steenwinningen in Grimbergen', *Eigen Schoon en de Brabander*, 70, pp. 59–74.

Nave, F. de (1978) *Antwerpen, stad en land (1394–1402). De innerlijke vervlechting van stedelijk en landelijk milieu in de late middeleeuwen op basis van het privé bezit aan gronden en renten en andere soorten van goed*, Brussels. Unpublished Ph.D. thesis University of Brussels (VUB).

Ogilvie, S.C. and Cerman, M. (1996) 'The theories of proto-industrialisation' in *European proto-industrialisation*, Cambridge, pp. 1–11.

Passen, R. van (1966) 'Het cijnsboek van Helmont (Kontich) van 1431', *Bijdragen tot de geschiedenis*, 49, pp. 139–156.

Passen, R. van (1988) *Geschiedenis van Kontich*, 2nd edition, Kontich.

Prevenier, W., Sosson, J.-P. and Boone, M. (1992) 'Le réseau urbain en Flandre (XIIIe–XIXe siècle): composantes et dynamique', in *Het stedelijk netwerk in België in historisch perspectief (1350–1850). Een statistische en dynamische benadering/le reseau urbain en Belgique dans une perspective historique (1350–1850), une approche statistique et dynamique*, Brussels, pp. 157–200. (Handelingen 15de Internationaal Colloquium /Actes 15e Colloque International, Spa, 4–6 sept 1990).

Schepper, L. de (1953) *Hemiksem*, Antwerp.

Soly, H. (1975) 'Nijverheid en kapitalisme te Antwerpen in de 16de eeuw' in *Album aangeboden aan Charles Verlinden ter gelegenheid van zijn dertig jaar professoraat*, Ghent, pp. 331–352.

Soly, H. (1977) *Urbanisme en kapitalisme te Antwerpen in de 16e eeuw. De stedebouwkundige en industriele ondernemingen van Gilbert van Schoonbeke*, Brussels.

Soly, H. and Thijs, A.K.L. (1981) 'Nijverheid in de Zuidelijke Nederlanden', in *Algemene Geschiedenis der Nederlanden*, 6, Haarlem, pp. 27–57.

Slootmans, C.J.F. (1985) *Paas- en koudenmarkten te Bergen op Zoom*, Tilburg (Bijdragen tot de Geschiedenis van het Zuiden van Nederland; 64–66).

Stabel, P. (1997) *Dwarfs among giants. The Flemish Urban Network in the Late Middle Ages*, Louvain/Apeldoorn.

Unger, W.S. (1939) *De tol van Iersekeroord. Documenten en rekeningen 1321–1572*, The Hague (Rijksgeschiedkundige publicatiën; kleine serie 29).

Uytven, R. van (1975) 'Die ländliche Industrie während des Spätmittelalters in den südlichen Niederlanden', in H. Kellenbenz (ed.), *Agrarisches Nebengewerbe und Formen der Reagrarisierung im Spätmittelalter und19./20. Jahrhundert. Bericht über die 5. Arbeitstagung der Gesellschaft für Sozial- und Wirtschaftsgeschichte*, Stuttgart, pp. 57–78. (Forschungen zur Sozial- und Wirtschaftsgeschichte; 21).

Uytven, R. van (1976) 'La draperie Babançonne et Malinoise du XIIe au XVIIe siècle: grandeur éphémère et decadence', in M. Spallanzani (ed.), *Produzione, commercio e consumo dei panni di lana (nei secoli XII–XVIII), Atti della secconda Settimana di Studio*, Firenze, pp. 85–97.

Uytven, R. van (1992) 'Brabantse en Antwerpse centrale plaatsen (14de–19de eeuw)', in *Het stedelijk netwerk in België in historisch perspectief (1350–1850). Een statistische en dynamische benadering/le reseau urbain en Belgique dans une perspective historique (1350–1850), une approche statistique et dynamique*, Brussels, pp. 29–79. (Handelingen 15de Internationaal Colloquium /Actes 15e Colloque International, Spa, 4–6 sept. 1990).

Verhulst, A. (1974) 'La laine indigène dans les anciens Pays-Bas entre le XIIe et le XVIIe siècle. Mise en oeuvre industrielle, prouction et commerce', in M. Spallanzani (ed.), *La lana come materia prima: i fenomeni della sua produzione e circolazione nei secoli 13–17: Atti della prima Settimana di Studio*, Firenze, pp. 11–42.

Wauters, A. (1975) *Histoire des environs de Bruxelles ou description historique des localités qui formaient autrefois l'ammanie de cette ville*, Brussels. (Reprint of the 1855 edition).

Wee, H. van der (1975) 'Structural Changes and Specialization in the Industry of the South Netherlands, 1100–1600', *Economic History Review*, 2nd ser., 28, pp. 203–221.

Wee, H. van der (1988) 'Industrial Dynamics and the Process of Urbanisation and De-Urbanisation in the Low Countries from the Late Midle Ages to the Eighteenth Century.

A Synthesis', in H. Van der Wee (ed.), *The rise and decline of urban industries in Italy and in the Low Countries (late middle-ages – early modern times)*, Louvain, pp. 307–381.

Zanden, J.L. van (1993) *The rise and decline of Holland's economy*, Manchester.

Zanden, J.L. van (2001) 'A third road to capitalism? Proto-industriaization and the moderate nature of the late medieval crisis in Flanders and Holland, 1350–1550', in P. Hoppenbrouwers and J.L. van Zanden (eds), *Peasants into farmers? The transformation of rural economy and society in the Low Countries (Middle Ages–19th century) in light of the Brenner debate*, Turnhout, pp. 85–101. (CORN Publication Series; 4).

PART III

EARLY MODERN PERIOD

Introduction to part III

Bruno Blondé, University of Antwerp – UFSIA

Four different papers, using diverse methodological approaches, were grouped in this early modern section. Both Royo and Hoffmann offer interesting and encompassing studies, in which labour is not isolated from general economic and social developments, and special attention is devoted to the institutional framework and regulatory environment of labour markets. Hoffmann puts weight on rural labour markets and production, while Royo pays special attention to the city. In Royo's paper Aragon town councils and municipal guilds are dealt with as opposing forces, fighting for and compromising for control of urban labour markets. The balance of power, according to Royo, was dictated primarily by economic factors. In his article the countryside only comes to the forefront where migration and the willingness (and capacity) of the town to absorb rural inhabitants is dealt with. Carl Hoffmann's paper offers a nice overview of progress recently made in our knowledge of Southern German industrial developments. His approach is essentially a comparative one, in which four different regions (Bavaria, Baden, Württemberg and Swabia) are scrutinised. Hoffmann is studying a de-urbanising economy and in so doing is applying a flexible proto-industrial concept. Future research will be needed to explain why in some cases (Bavaria in the sixteenth century) population pressure stimulated restrictive guild policies, while in the Aragonese case (Royo) population pressure enabled municipal governments to limit the influence of guilds. Population pressure was probably not the strategic variable, but economic expansion (or contraction) perhaps was.

Like Hoffmannn, Harald Deceulaer has met the challenge to study the complexity of relationships between town and countryside in a comparative exercise. In his paper three cities with different "regional settings" and concomitant town-countryside relationships were studied. Ghent, located amidst a proto-industrial countryside, imposing and deriving urban centrality from a quasi-monopolistic situation in the middle of an 'urban void'. Antwerp, a former metropolis, rather weakly rooted in its agrarian context, and Brussels, a capital, but also a regional stronghold for a prosperous eighteenth-century countryside. A comparative analysis of the occupational structures in these cities inevitably points towards the rather exceptional position held by Ghent in cheap goods and affordable services destined for the rural customers of its proto-industrial hinterland. The case of the *oudkleerkopers*, second hand dealers often selling to low income groups in town and countryside, is illustrative in this respect. The structural strength of *oudkleerkopers* is, indeed, determined by a multitude of different factors. When it comes to explaining the occurrence of countryside shops and services, peddlers, or urban commercial circuits, no generally applicable models of town-countryside relationships existed. Hence, the effects of the eighteenth-century *urbanisation from below* are, according to Deceulaer, not equivocal. One aspect in particular, related to the demand side of the economy, may need to be investigated in more detail. While in some cities *oudkleerkopers* were forbidden to sell new goods, in other towns (such as Leuven) they were not. The possible impact of this different legal range of activities is, of course, enormous. Especially in cities were *oudkleerkopers* were prohibited to sell new consumer items, they may have fallen victim to the rapidly changing consumer and demand patterns of the eighteenth century.

In a more general sense, future research projects will have to devote more attention to demand factors, such as changing relative prices, fashion cycles, the propensity to by and sell on urban markets, etc. in order to interpret changes on the supply side, and in particular for labour markets . The example of the *oudkleerkopers* (Deceulaer) is illustrative in this respect. Moreover, what is puzzling in Royo's paper is the inability of the Aragonese economy to flexibly adapt to French fashion, a process in which *the opportunities for developing proto-industrial activity in the countryside were not exploited, due to the lack of native entrepreneurial activities.* To give another example, Hoffmann puts an emphasis on de-urbanisation and non-agricultural employment opportunities as part of a survival strategy. Can it be questioned, however, whether to some extent the *industrious revolution* concept (forwarded by Jan de Vries) also came into play?

One paper explicitly deals with the necessities dominating town-countryside relationships. In many respects fuelling pre-industrial cities posed even more difficulties than feeding them. In addition wood was also used as a primary material for building business, furniture and coach making and the like. Yet, prohibitive (land) transport costs were perhaps the strongest bottleneck to pre-industrial urbanisation processes. Hence the importance for the city of Brussels of the adjacent Forest of Soigne. Sylvie Lefèbvre offers us a vivid description of the variety of people officially and unofficially engaged in forest exploitation. By absorbing hidden unemployment during the winter season, the Forest of Soigne proved to be a source of extra income – sometimes even illegal – to country dwellers. On the urban market a lack of corporative structures didn't prevent wood merchants from powerfully lobbying in order to limit wood cutting and in so doing safeguard wood prices and personal incomes. The article doesn't teach us whether, and under what conditions, these actions proved successful or failed. Several other intriguing questions still remain open to debate. To what extent, for example, did secular population and price movements determine the conditions of the 'privileged' relationship between town and forest?

9 Municipal politics and corporate protectionism: town councils and guilds in the kingdom of Aragon during the sixteenth and seventeenth centuries

José Antonio Mateos Royo, Saragossa University

I. Introduction

This article analyses the relationship between town councils and guilds in the kingdom of Aragon during the sixteenth and seventeenth centuries. The study concentrates on the changes in council policies that affected craft activities and the influence of the guilds. Such changes were a response to the rapid demographic and economic growth of sixteenth century Aragon and the subsequent crisis of the following century.

The paper begins by outlining the demographic and economic developments in Aragon during the sixteenth and seventeenth centuries. There is then an analysis of how the guilds had developed in the kingdom during the late medieval period. The article then considers the changing relationship between town council and craft guilds by comparing the city of Saragossa, the capital of Aragon, and the smaller town of Daroca located near the Castilian border. The main issues considered are the economic goals and social influence of the guilds, the objectives of the municipal authorities and the changing character of migration between town and countryside.

II. The kingdom of Aragon during the sixteenth and seventeenth centuries

During the sixteenth century the kingdom of Aragon experienced rapid economic and demographic growth. The kingdom's population expanded greatly during this period, the peak being reached at the end of the century. A gradual decline then occurred during the early seventeenth century (Salas, 1991). A survey of the kingdom of Aragon in 1495 indicates that it then had 51,540 taxpaying households, which were referred to as *fuegos* (fireplaces). The next such survey, carried out in 1647, estimated that, despite the early seventeenth century decline, it still had 70,676 households. By 1711 it had 76,163 *fuegos*.

The demographic growth of Aragon during '*the beautiful sixteenth century*', as contemporaries called it, was accompanied by a number of economic developments. There was an expansion in the number of cultivated plots in rural areas. Civic institutions and a variety of social groups became involved in expanding the kingdom's network of irrigation channels (Colás, 1984; Mateos, 1998). These projects boosted agricultural production and, as a result, the internal consumption of goods in the countryside increased. The commercialisation of farming prompted the development of external trade, especially in frontier areas, and made demographic growth sustainable.

The economic development of Aragonese towns and cities during the sixteenth century was boosted by the growth of agricultural production. Wealthy merchants, nobles and

Figure 9.1 The kingdom of Aragon during the 16th and 17th centuries

clergymen benefited directly through their collection of tithes, first-fruits and other forms of land rent from peasants. A number of factors meant that a substantial portion of all these incomes was channelled into towns. First, many Aragonese nobles left the countryside during the sixteenth century and settled in Saragossa, the capital of the kingdom. Second, a large proportion of clergymen were based in urban cathedrals, parish churches, and convents. Third, urban economic activity and political power attracted lawyers and wealthy merchants to the towns. These groups monopolised the trade in agrarian produce and benefited most from the commercialisation of agriculture. Fourth, the expansion of grammar schools and the universities of Huesca and Saragossa attracted students from a wide area. This hinterland also supplied a constant flow of young migrants, who settled in towns as apprentices or servants.

Towns and cities were physically remodelled in Aragon by the construction of numerous buildings. The nobility built private palaces in Saragossa (Gómez Urdañez, 1987). Churches and collegiate churches were responsible for architectural and artistic development throughout the kingdom. Municipal authorities promoted public works outside and inside their towns. Councils assumed the responsibility for the construction of civic buildings, like the New Tower and the trade market, *La Lonja*, in Saragossa. In other cases, councils and religious institutions shared the cost of the improvement or remodelling of important religious buildings, like the collegiate churches in Barbastro or Daroca. The most striking symbols of this civic pride were the Town Halls, rebuilt in stone during the sixteenth century by numerous town councils in towns like Huesca, Bielsa, Jaca, Uncastillo, Alcañiz, la Fresneda, Valderrobres or Tarazona (Serrano, 1986). The water supply systems, to and within both towns and villages, were improved by constructing new aqueducts, cisterns, reservoirs, and fountains. The most impressive examples of such water engineering can still be seen in Teruel and Daroca (Mateos, 1998).

A great interest was taken in the improvement of communications during this century, so as to promote the commercial development of the kingdom through fairs and markets (Blázquez and Pallaruelo, 1999). Numerous wooden bridges were built or rebuilt. The construction or modification of stone bridges took place as well, such as those that were erected over the Jalón, Gallego and Cinca rivers. The condition of the roads was substantially improved, especially those linking northern Aragon to France, so as to improve communications along these vital commercial routes. Between 1560 and 1626 the Cortes (the Parliament of Aragon) provided significant financial support for these communication projects in northern Aragon. This was financed through incomes generated from the kingdom's customs.

The improvement of the roads north led to an increase in the quantity of French goods imported to Aragon via this route. From the middle of the sixteenth century, large numbers of French immigrants (Salas, 1985; Langé, 1993) also migrated south to work in the kingdom. This period of immigration reached its peak between 1580 and 1635. Most of these immigrants came from southwestern France – Bearn, Bigorre and Gascony –, but significant numbers also came from other areas, such as the Central Massif. The overpopulation of these parts of France, the increase of wages in Spain, and cultural affinities between both sides of the Pyrenees all promoted immigration. French immigrants usually settled in the urban centres of the northern part of the kingdom – Jaca,

Huesca, Barbastro – where they were employed as artisans and carriers. They were especially prominent in the capital. For instance, in 1642 990 out of 6,130 taxable householders were French immigrants who were engaged in a wide range of economic activities. Indeed, they almost monopolised some professions such as baking, milling, sawing, glazing, and woodcutting, and they provided many artisans for the woollen textile industry. French immigrants could be found also in the countryside working as shepherds and peasants.

In the favourable economic climate of the sixteenth century, craft and industrial activities expanded in urban areas (Desportes, 1999). Manufactured goods were produced to supply the needs of wealthier groups and more basic goods were produced to fulfil the demand by commoners who lived in both towns and the countryside. The textile industry was most important in Saragossa. However, traditional cloths had also been produced since the late medieval period in a number of middle-ranked and small towns – (Calatayud, Huesca, Teruel, Borja, Tarazona and Albarracín). Such cloths were good enough to supply the needs of most of the interior of the country. The sixteenth century also saw the development of new textiles which were produced in rural settlements near the Pyrenees Mountains – (Boltaña, Broto, Torla, Aínsa, Jaca) and in the southeastern border of the kingdom – (Rubielos, Alcalá de la Selva and Formiche).

The impressive growth of the sixteenth century was followed by a period of general crisis during the seventeenth century. In the past, historians used to associate the beginning of this decline with the expulsion of the *Moriscos*, ordered by King Philip III in 1610. *Moriscos* were the remnants of the formerly Muslim population that was forced in 1502 and 1526 to adopt Christianity in order to stay in Spain. The kingdoms of Aragon and Valencia contained the highest densities of these Communities, especially after the defeat of an important revolt in Granada (1568–71). It has been estimated that in 1609–10 *Moriscos* composed 18.85% of the population in Aragon and 26.77% in Valencia (Lapeyre, 1959). Previous historians have suggested that in Aragon they were entirely engaged in agricultural activities. However, their settlement in areas little suited to agricultural activity and a variety of civic sources indicate that many of them were also carriers or skilled artisans. *Moriscos* numbered around 14,000 families in 1610. They were mainly manorial vassals and lived in a small area that included the Ebro valley and its southern tributaries. After their expulsion, these territories were only partially resettled by Christians from nearby towns and villages. The newcomers were unable to reproduce the intensive systems of farming and artisanal production practised by the *Moriscos* (Salas, 1993).

Although the expulsion of the *Moriscos* had a negative impact on Aragon's economic and demographic development, recent research has demonstrated that the decline of Aragon preceded the exiling of the *Moriscos*. The kingdom's population reached its peak, both in the towns and the countryside, at the end of the sixteenth century (Salas, 1991). A number of factors interacted to halt demographic and economic growth. Accumulating debts during the sixteenth century led to a deterioration of the financial position of the most important nobles families (Abadía, 1993). Many town councils experienced economic difficulties by the end of the century (Salas, 1992). The bankruptcy of Aragonese merchants resulted in the Genoese and later French merchants seizing control of mercantile activities in the kingdom (Gómez Zorraquino, 1997a). From the end of the sixteenth century, the importation of foreign goods increased to such an extent that native production suffered greatly.

Difficulties grew during the seventeenth century. The long term scarcity of Aragonese currency became more serious because of commercial decline and the constant influx of debased Castilian and Valencian coins after 1620. Wars with France from 1635 heavily reduced external trade in the northern area and severed the kingdom's main commercial link. Subsidies that were demanded of all social groups by the Crown in the Aragonese Parliament increased dramatically after the *Cortes* of 1626 and during the Catalan war of secession between 1640 and 1652 (Colás and Salas, 1975, Solano, 1987, Sanz, 1997). Additional taxes were imposed on commoners by town councils, so that they could reduce their debts. The indirect way of taxing through foodstuffs also favoured town's wealthier inhabitants more than direct taxation. Despite these efforts, municipal finances fell into bankruptcy during the second half of the century. Furthermore, wars with France and Catalonia reduced the population and devastated the eastern part of Aragon. Between the years 1651 and 1654 bubonic plague spread throughout the kingdom and resulted in great mortality in towns and cities. For instance, municipal records suggest that between July 1651 and April 1652 Huesca lost around 1,400 people, about 29.31% of taxable inhabitants listed in 1646. A second outbreak of plague, which took place at Jaca between June and November 1654, resulted in the deaths of 1,092 people, about 42.50% of the population listed in the parish registers of 1653. Different sources estimate that between 2,500 and 6,000 deaths occurred in Saragossa during July and August 1651 (Maiso, 1982).

During this period, French merchants controlled internal and external trade in Aragon and carried out the most lucrative business, such as the tenancy of tithes, first-fruits and other land rights (Gómez Zorraquino, 1997a; 1997b). Production by rural and urban artisans could not rival French goods, because the French goods were cheaper and better made. The opportunities for developing proto-industrial activity in the countryside were not exploited, due to the lack of native entrepreneurial initiatives. So no significant textile industry was created in rural areas during the seventeenth century, even though it was favoured by a cheap supply of raw materials – (especially wool) and labour. Craft and commercial decline meant that economic activities became more and more focused on farming production and exportation of raw materials (Torras, 1982).

III. Crafts and guilds in Aragon: the medieval heritage

In the opinion of most social historians, craft guilds were a medieval development. Their evolution follows the urban renaissance and the growth of municipal organisation that took place in European towns and cities from the eleventh century onwards. In Spain, the development of the guilds was further influenced by the conquest of territories once held by Muslims by the Christians. This resulted in a redistribution of property and altered social relations. The oldest surviving records of craft associations come from British and German towns of the late eleventh or early twelfth centuries. These fraternities were devoted to religious and social purposes. Similar associations appear to have existed in France and the Iberian Peninsula by the twelfth century. In Aragon, master clothiers or *pelaires* were working by 1200 in Albarracín. The *Fuero* or charter for the town of Teruel, dated to the thirteenth century, alludes to leather artisans. In thirteenth century Saragossa, the Holy Spirit guild consisted of farmers, the Saint Francis guild of artisans and Saint Mary guild of merchants.

However, since the guilds were relatively weak at first many artisans still worked in Aragon during the thirteenth century independent of guild control. The earliest charters granted to craftsmen by the kings did not even specify the function of guilds and they allowed their members to write their own bylaws (Falcón, 1994). These guild regulations were originally orientated to religious and charitable purposes. Charters became more frequent and elaborate in Aragon in the course of the fourteenth century. After a relative decline in the second half of this century, their number rises during the fifteenth century. Development and diversification of craft activities prompted this increase: ancient and new guilds decided to define or reassert their professional identity by obtaining new charters from town councils and kings. Although ordinances dealing with craft activities were usually included in charters from the middle of the fourteenth century, regulations of apprenticeship and admissions to mastership only became common during the fifteenth century.

During the late medieval period, Aragonese artisans used the word *arte* or *oficio* to identify an ensemble of craftsmen who carried out the same profession. The term *cofradía* or *compañía* was used to describe the craft association of these artisans. These associations were usually under the protection of the Church and were orientated to a specific purpose. These fraternities exercised an effective influence over the *oficio*. On one hand, they carried out religious and charitable activities to support the member of the *oficio* and their families. On the other hand, they regulated artisan's professional life through ordinances that dealt with admission to apprenticeship and mastership. The normal practice for every craft guild was to form a religious fraternity.

Internal organisation of craft guilds always included a council (*capítulo, cabildo*) made up of all their members. This council met at least once every year and its main role was the modification of the guild's charters and ordinances. In Aragon these statutes had to be submitted to the municipality or the king for approval. The internal structure of guilds varied. Fraternities were typically run by the *mayordomos*, who represented the body, administered its finances and considered allegations of misconduct by its members. The *mayordomos* were often advised by the *consejeros*. *Veedores*, or searchers, were always present in crafts and often in guilds. After being elected by the *capitulo* or *mayordomos* and approved by the town council, the function of the searchers was to inspect artisanal goods in the market or workshops. The *cajero, clavario* or *limosnero* collected fees and fines from craftsmen and paid out alms and other expenses. However, in many *cofradías* the function of this official was assumed by the *mayordomos*. The secretary (*notario, escribano*) summoned the council and took the minutes of its sessions. The *sayón, andador, verguero* or *cercador* was an internal announcer and messenger. Finally, the *luminero* had the task of preserving the light before the altar of the guild's patron saint.

The Crown occasionally opposed the creation of craft guilds. From the late thirteenth century to the early sixteenth century, kings sometimes tried to ban them by issuing special proclamations (Asso, 1798). For instance, James I's charter for the city of Valencia forbade the formation of any guild there. He extended this policy to the rest of his territory due to the abuse of guild politics by the members. In 1311, James II passed an Act, called '*Ut monopolia*', that banned guilds in Aragon because of their monopolistic practices. Yet, such proclamations were ineffective for at the same time that they were being passed, both kings granted new guild charters to artisan groups.

In fact, it appears that Aragonese kings passed such suppressive legislation in response to petitions by town councils, which were afraid of the increasing political power of guilds during the thirteenth and early fourteenth centuries. In 1291–93, for example, the rival guilds of the Holy Spirit and Saint Francis combined to achieve political participation in the Saragossa city council. To prevent guilds from usurping their power, municipal authorities often supported the relaxation of restrictions on work in towns and cities so as to decrease the influence of guilds during the late medieval period. Guilds on the other hand demanded that artisans should be affiliated with their guild before they carried out their professions. However, during the fifteenth century the control of Aragonese town councils by wealthy citizens became firmly established. This was supported by the introduction by Queen Mary in 1442 of the *insaculación*, a new system to elect the main municipal magistrates (Falcón, 1988). Growing political stability also allowed councils to extend their influence over guilds and to regulate craft activities.

This political evolution was paralleled by economic changes within the feudal economy that favoured mercantile expansion. Throughout Western Europe the late medieval demographic crisis resulted in a decline of land rents and a rise in wages that transformed the manorial system. Landlords lost control over their serfs and traditional labour services were transmuted into money rents. Peasants and merchants acquired land. The commercialisation of agriculture and the higher incomes of the peasants resulted in the integration of the countryside into a market economy. In response, craftsmen had to modify their products to satisfy new market demands. Thus, the kingdom of Aragon witnessed an increase in the production, consumption and distribution of both rural and urban goods in the fifteenth century.

In respect to craft activities, it may be noted that some of the changes involved a simple expansion of production.[1] This started in the late fourteenth century and did not necessarily involve any technological innovation. Expansion without structural and technological innovation did not produce great benefits for the economy, but was important because of the number of artisans involved. By contrast, building and textile activities should be considered separately because they involved complex technological and economic structures, numerous skilled workers, and high levels of capital investment (Sesma, 1972).

[1] For instance, the number of pottery workshops increased in towns such as Calatayud, Huesca, Teruel and Villafeliche. High quality metalgoods, especially those of armours, were produced in the area surrounding the Moncayo Mountains. Saragossa skinners' work was noted throughout the kingdom. Shoemakers were particularly strong in Saragossa, Huesca and Calatayud. Clothmaking was carried out in urban settlements by predominantly Jewish craft fraternities. This clothmaking industry underwent significant structural changes in the fifteenth century as companies were created for the production and distribution of cloths (Sesma, 1972).

The building industry developed greatly in Aragon after the beginning of the fifteenth century as many private and public buildings were constructed (Falcón, 1986). Carpenters, masons, and coopers formed the Saint Stephen guild in Saragossa at the beginning of the century. It acquired a monopoly over production, controlled membership and regulated the admission to mastership. Guild statutes specified the correct use and proportions of plaster, bricks, tiles and wood. A separate fraternity for Muslim masons and carpenters operated in Saragossa between 1502 and 1526 (Gómez Urdañez, 1988). Notwithstanding this unusual example, Muslims and *Moriscos* carried out many construction activities in Aragon during the late medieval period and the sixteenth century without joining any guild or fraternity.

The textile industry became consolidated in Aragon by the last quarter of the fourteenth century (Sesma, 1972; 1992). Protective laws over native production were created by the Parliament in 1376 at a time when Catalan merchants and Jewish refugees were beginning to settle in Aragon and become involved in the textile industry. During the first half of the fifteenth century Aragonese cloths were sold abroad. By the middle of this century textiles were frequently provided with a certificate of origin and additional information about its type, quality, and colour.

Saragossa, as the capital, was the centre of this industrial activity. Other significant areas included western towns – (Tarazona and Calatayud), northern urban and rural settlements – (Huesca, Jaca, Aínsa, Broto and Sallent) and the southern border of the kingdom – (Albarracín, Teruel and Mora de Rubielos). This last area, favoured for the great amount of wool available and limited opportunities for cultivation, had a great textile tradition that was heavily orientated to the commercial market. While Albarracín and Teruel created traditional cloths, from the middle of the fifteenth century settlements surrounding Mora started making cloth in the style of the new European textiles. Apart from this, textile industry in Aragon during late medieval times concentrated on the production of a wide range of low and medium-quality cloth, orientated to local consumption rather than foreign trade. Foreign merchandise was also imported. A tax on these goods by the Parliament in 1376 included traditional cloths from the Low Countries (Ypres, Ghent, Louvain, Brussels, Malines) as well as new textiles from the Lys valley (Werwique, Courtrai) and England (London, Bristol, Colchester). French goods (Toulouse, Perpignan, Douai), were also imported and became increasingly important to the Aragonese market from the middle of the fifteenth century.

IV. The sixteenth century

During the sixteenth century, a wide range of economic factors contributed to manufacturing growth in Aragonese town and cities: the availability of raw materials, the growth of domestic demand, the fall in the cost of labour and low inflation. The expansion of markets and fairs – (Huesca, Barbastro, Daroca and Sariñena) facilitated the distribution of foreign and native goods throughout the kingdom. Towns simultaneously underwent a growth in mercantile, industrial, and craft activity. As a result of growing production and demand, councils tried to preserve the quality of the merchandise produced and sold in their towns. Town councils also promoted their own local industries.

So, guild control over foreign and native output and distribution was tolerated, but under strict supervision by municipal authorities.

As the economy expanded, the government attempted to limit the power of the guilds. In 1512 and 1515 the Saragossa city council instructed its delegates to petition the Parliament to ban the guilds. A municipal law, passed in 1527, opposed the guilds directly by granting Saragossa inhabitants free trade in goods and raw materials. The guilds' monopolistic practices were considered an obstacle to economic progress because guild searchers prevented free trade within the city. In 1522 several towns followed Saragossa's example and asked Charles V to suppress the guilds. Finally, at the express petition of town representatives, the Parliament banned all guilds in Aragon in 1528. Only their charitable and religious functions were to continue. This decision was confirmed by the Parliament of 1533 (Asso, 1798).

In some respects, the new law was not strictly applied. As the Saragossa city council soon accepted, banning guilds was inconvenient in practice. The quality of artisan goods declined in the capital because of the lack of control over work regulations. Since guilds were deprived of exam and entry fees, they lost their major source of income. As a result, several guilds had to ask the city council for financial support because they were unable to raise the investment capital necessary for their crafts. So, many guilds had their old powers restored (Seral, 1925, Mateos, 1997). Master clothiers or *pelaires* received new charters from the Saragossa city council in 1532, shearers, chemists and waxmakers in 1534, bookmakers, weavers and leather artisans in 1537, smiths in 1540, tanners and ropemakers in 1541, and tailors in 1550. Similarly, the municipal authorities passed new ordinances at Daroca to sanction guilds for shoemakers in 1544, for leather artisans in 1553, and for weavers in 1555. One after another, guilds had their rights and powers restored. The most powerful crafts got their rights back sooner. However, the less powerful experienced greater difficulties. For instance, the shoemakers' guild of Saragossa was only re-created in 1565, thirty-seven years after its initial suppression.

Although most guilds regained their traditional structure within a few decades, their influence over town councils remained weak for the rest of the century (Redondo, 1976). Wealthy citizens controlled town councils and they sought to ensure their monopoly of power. They did this by limiting access to the more important municipal positions to individuals of wealth and status. Artisans' political participation was restricted to the General Council. This was a kind of open assembly where decisions considered to be of general concern were submitted to the taxpaying citizens for approval. Although this development is most obvious in Saragossa, it also occurred in the rest of Aragon's towns as well. Even in smaller towns, such as Daroca, farmers and artisans only retained a few representatives on the town council as a relic from medieval times. The primary objective of these officials was the preservation of communal lands and the maintenance of the supply of basic foodstuffs to the town.

Once the political power of the guilds had declined, municipalities faced little opposition in controlling craft and industrial activities in towns and cities. Their public policy was directed to maintaining production standards. They also sought to supply the market efficiently by preventing any monopoly in either manufacture or distribution by artisans or merchants. To achieve these aims it was no longer necessary to ban the guilds. In 1575 the Saragossa council proclaimed the value of the guilds to the city not only because of their charitable activities, but because they served to organise their professions (Redondo, 1982). Magistrates regarded guilds as useful tools for the regulation of both the marketplace and the labour force. Since a large number of families were dependent on artisanal work, guilds were also useful as a mechanism for social control.

In order to preserve price stability the Saragossa city council could set the price of artisanal goods and raw materials such as leather, skin, hemp, wood or nails on some occasions during this century. This was done to avoid sudden price increases (San Vicente, 1988). Municipal policies were even introduced (1553–54, 1565, 1593, 1597) to fix the wages of farm-labourers and artisans. This was particularly common for those involved in building activities, such as carpenters or bricklayers. Following a well-established medieval tradition, the authorities also tried to avoid speculation or hoarding by merchants since this could make the cost of raw materials and, subsequently, the price of manufactured goods rise. Municipal officers and guild searchers supervised the quality of goods in markets and fairs and controlled production in local workshops. When more exceptional problems arose, councils set up public controls over particular aspects of production or trade. For instance, municipal searchers at Daroca were instructed to inspect imported leather in 1522 and home-made leather goods in 1553 (Mateos, 1997).

However, the Saragossa city council also adopted more draconian measures to control the quality of the goods guilds produced (Seral, 1925, San Vicente, 1988). If municipal authorities considered local production to be expensive or defective, they would invite foreign artisans to come and work in the city. For example, the council tried to attract foreign smiths in 1509 and foreign bricklayers and carpenters in 1565. On occasion Saragossa magistrates allowed artisans to carry out their professional activities against the wishes of guilds. Eventually, the municipality could temporarily suppress craft ordinances. This prevented guilds from controlling apprentices and journeymen and increased the opportunities for new immigrants into the city. For instance, the Saragossa council suppressed tailors' ordinances in 1567 and shoemakers' statutes in 1595 because of their poor workmanship. However, as soon as the guilds undertook to raise production standards, the old statutes were restored.

The control over the distribution of craft goods generated conflicts between a variety of public institutions (Desportes, 1999). For instance, several disputes developed between the Saragossa city council and *Diputación*, which was a sort of permanent government to preserve the kingdom's rights. The *Diputación* favoured free trade in native and imported goods in Aragon since this increased the incomes from the kingdom's customs. It therefore regarded intervention by guild searchers to be highly damaging. Since the Saragossa city council supported the controls exercised by the guilds, tensions arose. Such tensions reached their peak in 1535 when the Saragossa council demanded that the *Diputación* allow public searchers to be based in every significant settlement of the kingdom. After difficult discussions the *Diputación* blocked the demands of Saragossa. Public controls, such as those which took place in Daroca in 1522 and 1553, were, therefore, only occasionally adopted in towns as a result of council initiatives. Acting on its own initiative, the Saragossa council decided to apply stricter supervision over the production and marketing of textile goods in the city. To this end, in 1548, the council established the *Casa de la Bula* to act as a quality control centre for cloth goods. Public searchers who certified goods at the Casa and oversaw textile production throughout the city carried out its work. From 1602 the *Casa de la Bula* also employed searchers who were specifically responsible for supervising the city's dyers.

Finally, town councils engaged in the regulation of the labour force. The Saragossa council's involvement in the textile industry during the sixteenth century provides a good example of this (Desportes, 1999). As textile production became increasingly dispersed and the cloth market developed, it became clear that it was necessary to co-ordinate industrial activity, to maintain quality, and reduce the duration of the industrial process. Since the mercantile oligarchy, which had ruled the city since the late medieval period had failed to do this, *pelaires*, or cloth finishers, had started to fulfil this role by combining artisanal and entrepreneurial activities. *Pelaires* borrowed money, or sometimes wool, from merchants and ran textile production. These activities were carried out in workshops belonging to the *pelaires*, to other artisans, and to the guild. To increase their profits, *pelaires* even tried to ignore some guild regulations. Weavers and shearers were increasingly transformed into wage labourers working in shops rented by *pelaires*. The result was social polarisation: whilst *pelaires* and dyers prospered, weavers and shearers became proletarianised. This generated social instability, especially among the weavers, who before the council raised many complaints. After some hesitation, in 1576 and 1607 the Saragossa city council confirmed the *pelaires'* leading position in order to guarantee production standards. The council even temporarily suppressed weavers' ordinances in 1593 and 1613 to prevent them from interfering with the activities of the *pelaires*.

Municipal intervention was equally significant in conflicts between artisans. Saragossa civic records provide many examples of such disputes. City council considerations in such matters were orientated towards the preservation of the quality of the goods. This attitude was clearly demonstrated in the conflicts between woollen and linen weavers (1556, 1569, 1584) over new woollen cloths produced by techniques similar to those used for linen cloth. The city council allowed both craftsmen to carry out the production of these goods and delayed making a final decision over who could produce what. This was because, from the council's point of view, it did not matter too much who did the work so long as production standards were satisfactorily maintained. As a result, conflicts over this issue continued into the seventeenth century.

Developments in municipal politics and economic growth produced a favourable context for the reception of foreign artisans in Aragonese towns during the sixteenth century. Studies of parish registers have demonstrated that towns and cities received a constant influx of migrants, mainly from the surrounding countryside. Unfortunately, primary sources provide little information about the professional activities of immigrants. It is, however, clear that many worked as craftsmen. It has been estimated that about 50% of the apprentices working in Saragossa's textile industry came from the kingdom of Navarre (Desportes, 1999). In fact, some guild regulations seem orientated to retaining this labour force by reducing the high mobility of immigrants. For instance, the weavers and *pelaires* of Albarracín ordained in 1563 that foreign artisans could only become masters after their settlement and marriage in the town (Peiró, 2000). In Daroca, the parish registers of Saint Jacques listed at least 41 artisans out of 84 new parishioners accepted between 1541 and 1581 (Mateos, 1997).

The evaluation of guild ordinances and regulations has shown that it was rare for foreigners to be required to serve longer apprenticeships than local boys. However, over time guild regulations came to discriminate against foreigners because they had to pay higher fees to take the compulsory exam to become a master. From the middle of the century, ordinances began to specify that the sons of master artisans would only pay 50% of the fees payable to the guild (San Vicente, 1988; Mateos, 1997). Although there are some late fifteenth century precedents for this, during the 1550s this system was widely adopted in Aragonese towns and cities, such as Saragossa, Huesca and Daroca. This problem became more acute at the end of the century, especially in the capital, as the cost of exam fees rose steeply. Whilst the amount of money demanded from the aspirant by municipal officials, charitable institutions, and craft examiners remained small, fees payable directly to the guild increased sharply. Guilds justified these sudden rises to town councils by noting the financial support they provided for charitable and religious activities. Indeed, the requirement that guilds seek approval by the council for these increases helped to maintain the municipal control over guilds in this period.

The difficulties over the admission to mastership in late sixteenth-century Aragon are confirmed in the case of Saragossa by the existence of tensions in guilds (Desportes, 1999). Apprentices and journeymen complained that the higher exam fees were imposed so that masters could reserve professional advancement to their own sons. Masters also engaged fewer journeymen and paid them lower salaries as the century wore on. Since apprentices were cheaper, masters increasingly preferred to employ them, even though this resulted in a decline in the quality of their goods. As an expression of discontent, journeymen tried to create their own fraternities. The tailors' guild prevented such an attempt in 1556. In 1581 master weavers integrated 31 journeymen into their guild to prevent this happening. Finally, the *pelaires*' guild allowed 48 journeymen in 1606 to create a fraternity, but only on the condition that their own guild set its ordinances.

V. The seventeenth century

Economic decline in seventeenth-century Aragon created an unfavourable climate for artisans and immigrants. In particular, industrial activity faced a serious crisis after the middle of the century. The number of textile workshops at Saragossa fell by 51.10% between 1642 and 1721 and by 42.10% at Barbastro between 1619 and 1680 (Peiró, 2000). During a survey carried out by the *Diputación* in 1667 a similar situation was reported in several other Aragonese towns: Calcena, Caspe, Daroca, Alcañiz and Albarracín (Colás, 1974). In Calcena the council estimated that, of the 400 families engaged in the woollen textile industry in 1640, only 200 were still employed by 1667. Industrial stagnation in towns and cities prompted some expansion of craft activities in rural areas. However, in general rural artisans only produced low quality goods, which satisfied local demand but could not compete in wider markets.

In response to the economic decline, public institutions tried to protect native production by restricting the import of foreign goods (Redondo, 1982). So, although the *Diputación* had passed several statutes that supported free trade during the first quarter of the century – (1603, 1614, 1623), trade policy changed dramatically after the *Cortes* of 1626. This Parliament banned the importation of foreign cloths made from wool, silk, gold or silver. Foreign tapestries using these materials and some linen goods were tolerated, but charged with a 10% duty. Although this decision favoured guild interests, native production was also taxed to maintain royal revenues. A 5% levy was imposed for fifteen years on locally produced cloths of the types that were now subject to the import ban. Other native textiles attracted a 10% levy.

Unfortunately, these protective duties did not prevent the entry of French goods into the kingdom through smuggling and the black market. So in 1645–46 the *Cortes* recognised its failure and repealed the ban on cloth imports. Still, it increased customs by 3% during four years of the Catalan war of secession, which further stimulated the smugglers' trade. During the *Cortes* of 1677–78 Saragossa guilds and the city council intensified the pressure to adopt a more protective taxation system. In response, the Parliament doubled the kingdom's custom duties to a 20% levy on exports and imports and imposed an additional 10% duty on the import of foreign cloths of the type banned by the *Cortes* of 1626. Meanwhile, native textiles paid only a 5% duty. Finally, the *Cortes* of 1684–86 accepted the failure of its protectionist legislation. Customs rates were reduced to the previous 10% duty on imports and re-exports. Native goods were subject to a 5% export duty. The other new taxes were repealed and importation of foreign cloths made from golden and silver was permitted. The customs system was simplified and royal tolls were abandoned.

During this period, French traders and carriers increasingly became the target of native artisans and merchants, who considered them responsible for both commercial and industrial decline and the loss of silver from the kingdom (Redondo, 1985; Salas, 1985). Public institutions increasingly discriminated against French immigrants after the outbreak of war with France in 1635 and Catalonia's secession in 1640. The *Cortes* of 1645 banned immigrants from carrying out administrative services in the kingdom, attending the Parliament as political representatives or receiving honours and benefices. French communities were sometimes obliged to contribute to the military efforts with special 'donations'. In 1667, following an edict from King Charles II, their properties were seized. Some immigrants, and especially merchants, suffered violence from the common people of Saragossa in 1635, 1643, 1684 and 1694, when the city was disrupted by war or riots. These assaults were uncommon in the rest of Aragon, since councils were aware of the importance of the economic activities of immigrants. Their expulsion by municipal authorities from towns at the end of the century, such as Daroca in 1693 or Saragossa in 1695, was therefore only applied to non-naturalised merchants or vagrants. This was in accordance with the legislation approved by the Parliament in 1684–86 that prevented unmarried Frenchmen from carrying out commercial transactions in the kingdom.

During this period the relationship between town councils and guilds was extremely delicate. On the one hand, municipalities preferred to support local artisans by imposing heavy taxes on foreign merchandise. The Saragossa magistrates therefore supported guild demands in the *Cortes* of 1645–46 and 1677–78. They even banned the import into the city of foreign cloths in 1651 and 1675, a regulation which was almost immediately struck down by the *Diputación* (Redondo, 1982). On the other hand, such restrictions meant that the quality of local goods decreased while prices rose. Meanwhile, domestic inflation, the influx of debased Castilian and Valencian coins, and the high taxes imposed by both customs officials and municipal authorities encouraged the expansion of smuggling and the black market. The result was that, while nearly all trade had been conducted in the public markets during the sixteenth century, in the seventeenth century merchants increasingly conducted their business through private and illicit transactions, away from the gaze or control of the municipal authorities.

Difficulties were also growing for town provisioning. Increasing inflation and taxation resulted in the constant rise in the prices of artisanal goods, especially during the middle decades of the century. Guilds claimed that this inflation was due to the rising costs of raw materials (San Vicente, 1988; Mateos, 1997). So, the municipal authorities tried to fix the price of artisanal goods. When fixing prices, councils considered the costs of raw materials and sometimes the price of wheat as well, in order to ensure that artisans could earn a living. Town councils also regulated artisans wages. For example, in 1616 the Saragossa magistrates fixed weavers' wages for a fifteen year period and in 1629 they fixed the wages of shearers. In 1658 the city council set bricklayers' wages and the duration of their apprenticeship.

Town councils also faced problems in maintaining production standards. Many artisans used their control of local markets, which was particularly strong in small towns and villages, to prevent the sale of foreign merchandise (Mateos, 1997). On several occasions guilds at Daroca even stopped foreign artisans from carrying out casual work in the town. Poor quality raw materials were frequently used to produce low quality goods for the local markets. The failure of guild searchers to do their job properly resulted in the creation of municipal officers to preserve the quality of goods. Ironically the Daroca town council sometimes had to employ foreign artisans in order to ensure that such supervision was done properly. The municipal regulations passed in Saragossa during the century imply that the quality of goods was decreasing. In 1607 and 1658 the Saragossa magistrates even temporarily suppressed the ordinances of silk twisters and shoemakers because of their poor workmanship (San Vicente, 1988).

The survival of local industry thus became increasingly dependent on the maintenance of control over urban markets. Realising this, guilds tried to prevent the importation of merchandise into towns by either smugglers or regular shopkeepers. Supervision was especially tight during fairs because these events provided good opportunities for speculation and the illicit resale of such goods (Mateos, 1997). In 1644 the shoemakers' guild at Daroca forbade their own members from buying shoes for resale to artisans from Calatayud. Guilds did their best to prevent foreign artisans and merchants from extending their stay in the town beyond the duration of the fair. Guilds sometimes tried to convince town councils to ban foreigners from the fair on the grounds that their goods were defective. In 1647 shoemakers at Daroca even called for the burning of some shoes that had been brought by French merchants to the fair.

Despite the efforts of the guilds, they were unable to prevent the influx of French goods. The result was that native artisans faced impoverishment. To protect their own interests masters increasingly restricted the admission to mastership in guilds. They did this by raising the costs of the exams that all journeymen had to take before becoming masters. First, the entry fees payable to the fraternity for charitable purposes were substantially increased. Second, the amount of money requested as fees by examiners and guild officials who attended the exam rose. Third, if the aspirant passed the exam, he was expected to provide a meal for the members of the tribunal. However, from the beginning of the seventeenth century, several Saragossa guilds passed statutes that extended the differential between the fees and dues payable by the sons of masters and those paid by outsiders. The masters' sons now only had to pay half the exam attendance fees to examiners and guild officials demanded from the rest.

As a result of this situation, journeymen increasingly formed their own associations (Redondo, 1982; San Vicente, 1988). This process is especially clear in Saragossa because of its large number of guilds. Journeymen glovers, needlemakers and parchmentmakers founded their own fraternity at Saragossa in 1610 in response to the masters' strategy. Journeymen hatters followed their example in 1638 and journeymen woollen weavers in 1653. Although the master artisans and the city council only allowed these associations to carry out religious and charitable functions, they became an important focus for the journeymen. Such was their sense of group identity that in 1644 the journeymen *pelaires* of Saragossa asked the council to make it compulsory for all journeymen working as *pelaires* in the city to make a payment to their fraternity, even if they had not joined it.

Guild regulations and the growing indebtedness of artisans raised difficulties not only for journeymen, but for impoverished masters too (Salas, 1981; Mateos, 1997; Peiró, 2000). In 1630, the guild of Saint Calixto at Daroca tried to introduce a chapter in its statutes to prevent hemp master artisans who did not have their own workshop from selling goods. However, this was not possible for many could not afford to keep their own workshops. As a solution, the town council allowed them to use their own houses for business purposes and also houses or workshops that belonged to friends or were hired. In a similar effort to help artisans, the Teruel council permitted the weavers' guild to rent looms to impoverished masters in 1622. By 1666 *pelaires* had become absolutely dependent on the weavers at Albarracín for they had to borrow money from them to buy wool. By 1692 the *pelaires* at Teruel were so indebted that they had to sign an agreement with their creditors. *Pelaires* and weavers in Barbastro experienced similar difficulties, and the hosiers there were even free to give up their own guild in 1670. In 1691 and 1693 the hemp artisans and tailors' guilds at Daroca recognised the dependence of many craftsmen on merchants, who initially lent them money or raw materials and later assumed control of their output.

Guild regulations over admission to mastership increasingly effected the labour market and migrations within the kingdom. Thus, Teruel *pelaires* stated in their ordinances of 1622 that '*many journeymen came from distant lands and even from foreign kingdoms to the town*' and decided to give priority to Aragonese native artisans to carry out their profession (Peiró, 2000). In contrast the Saragossa magistrates, in 1672, accused guilds of being responsible for the migration of native journeymen to the countryside or smaller towns in the kingdom because of the excessive costs of mastership exams (Redondo, 1982). The suppression of these exams was brought before the *Cortes* of 1677–78, but was opposed by the urban representatives. Finally, the Parliament settled this matter by establishing two groups of artisan professions in the kingdom. It fixed the exam fees at 120 and 180 *sueldos* for most of the country and 150 and 300 *sueldos* in the capital.[2] In the *Cortes* of 1684 foreign immigrants who settled in Aragon were given a 50% discount of these exam fees. Once they had been accepted as masters within a guild, they had to pay one-sixth of the normal fee if they wished to qualify as masters of another activity governed by that guild.

From the above, it would seem that guild regulations played a key role in shaping the artisan labour market during this century. However, at the same time other factors were in operation, which reduced the real influence of the guilds. This was because readjustments in labour market enabled many craftsmen to circumvent guild controls and conduct their trades independently, both in their hometowns and in other settlements.

The expulsion of the *Moriscos* from Aragon in 1610 had a major impact on one hundred or so small towns and villages, mainly located in the Ebro valley, which had been dominated by these 'new' Christians. Since the *Moriscos* had carried out essential craft activities, town councils were forced to attract foreigners to replace them. A number of studies have demonstrated that these migrants came from the immediate hinterlands of the towns (Salas, 1993). Guilds had to tolerate this influx because of municipal support for these migrants. Moreover, guilds could do very little in some towns because many of these professions had been monopolised by *Moriscos*, who were never fully integrated into the guild system. Following the expulsion, new guilds were created in several towns to group the professions formerly controlled by *Moriscos*. In Daroca, the guild of Saint Paul and Saint Eloy was founded in 1627 to accommodate the metalworkers and the guild of the Transfiguration and Saint Joseph was created in 1636 for builders and carpenters (Mateos, 1997).

The outbreak of the war between France and Spain in 1635 created new possibilities for journeymen in Aragon (Redondo, 1982). In 1638 the Saragossa council tried to promote the recruitment of volunteer soldiers by permitting journeymen to carry out their profession without any mastership exam if they served in the company Saragossa contributed to the king's army. This tactic was also employed during the Catalan war of secession (1640–52) and other wars fought with France during the second half of the century.

It is difficult to assess the impact of this measure within the kingdom as a whole. However, various studies have examined its influence on particular towns and cities, including Saragossa, Calatayud, Barbastro and Daroca (Sanz, 1997; Mateos, 1997). On occasion councils tried to renege on their promises – (as several complaints from artisans in Barbastro

---

[2] 'Sueldo jaqués' was the official silver coin minted in the kingdom of Aragon during the medieval and early modern period (Beltrán, 1972; Sesma, 1986). The word 'sueldo' acquired the subsidiary meaning of a 'wage' because the coin was originally the standard daily wage for an agricultural labourer. Inflation meant that by the middle of the sixteenth century, the daily wage of a labourer varied between 1.5–2.5 sueldos. During the second half of the seventeenth century, it varied between 3–4 sueldos (Salas, 1981; Mateos, 1997).

indicate) but it seems clear that in general journeymen received their just rewards after finishing their service in the army. To control excessive demands, town councils could also use the grant of such concession by guilds, if provided in great number. The guilds protested vigorously to such impositions. For instance, in 1654 the hemp artisans' guild called for the suppression of exemptions before the Daroca council because it had resulted in a decrease in the income of their fraternity. However, its plea was ignored and the Saragossa magistrates made a similar response to protests raised in 1675 when 139 special licences were granted at this city. The significance of these exemptions was even greater in towns such as Daroca, because they were transferable and could, therefore, be given as a legacy to relatives. Attempts were even made to sell them for a profit.

Municipal politics continued to focus on trying to both moderate guild demands and preserve the quality of goods produced by them (Redondo, 1982, San Vicente, 1988, Mateos, 1997). If it is true that town councils often approved rises of exam fees, they also struck down guild regulations that interfered with the efficient running of the market. Some town councils, such as at Saragossa and Daroca, stopped several guilds from requiring candidates for mastership to provide a meal for examiners and other guild officials. Municipal authorities also reduced the exam fees of some journeymen in opposition to the wishes of guilds. When a particular guild was not strong enough, as frequently happened in medium or small towns, the council could even provide exemptions to some foreign artisans from the mastership exam. For instance, in Daroca the council exempted foreign weavers residing in the town from taking this exam until the final conformation of the guild in 1673. If guilds discriminated too much in the selection process for new masters, councils would designate their own examiners, as the Saragossa magistrates did in 1672. Moreover, in 1677 the Parliament sanctioned the right of every artisan to appeal to councils against guilds' decisions.

Town councils were able to pursue such policies because urban guilds often had an incomplete control over their crafts. In Huesca some guild complaints dated from 1595 and 1605 indicate that journeymen tailors were allowed to work at home on their own behalf if they were commissioned to do so. However, they were not allowed to offer their skills openly in the street, as some had tried to do (Arco, 1911). In 1643 a statute extended the right to all journeymen artisans working in Huesca (Arco, 1915). The Saragossa hemp and linen artisans' ordinances of 1633 accepted that shopkeepers who sold their artisan goods could join the guild without passing an exam (Redondo, 1982). Impoverishment of many families moved councils to moderate guild regulation, which tended to be particularly harsh during economic crises (Mateos, 1997). For instance, in 1655 the Daroca council supported women's right to weave cloths at home and sell them, just as the Parliament confirmed for the whole kingdom in 1677. In 1674 Daroca allowed master tailors to go to work in private houses for a fixed daily wage.

Economic decline therefore produced a readjustment of the labour market in Aragon. Migrations of artisans in the second half of the century were caused by general demographic stagnation and sharp population decreases in many towns occurred after epidemics of bubonic plague and the Catalan war of secession. Guilds tried to maintain the labour force by reducing the high mobility of journeymen. Daroca tailors' and linen weavers' guilds, for example, decided to introduce chapters in their ordinances to address this matter in 1679 and 1695. Municipalities faced a similar problem over farm labourers who temporarily emigrated to get better wages during harvest times (Salas, 1981, Mateos, 1997). Several town councils – (Barbastro, Daroca) banned them from taking this work until the end of the harvest and tried to fix strictly their wages and working hours.

Studies of parish registers have demonstrated the existence of migration and constant exchanges between town and the surrounding countryside during the seventeenth century. Thus, the collegiate church of Barbastro recorded that 41.5% of persons who got married in this town between 1641 and 1700 were foreigners (Salas, 1981). In seventeenth-century Huesca only 35% of the couples that got married had been born there (Salas, 1993). In Daroca, at least 51% of persons who married in Saint Mary collegiate church during this century were foreigners (Mateos, 1997). In the churches of Saint Jacques and Saint Michael, two of the other six parishes, these minimum estimates were 29.5% and 28.75%. It is impossible to provide accurate estimates about the professional activities of these migrants. However, it is clear that many artisans were involved. In Daroca, the parish registers of Saint Jacques listed at least 37 artisans out of 108 new parishioners accepted between 1662 and 1710. Saint Michael's registers included a minimum of 36 artisans out of 117 new parishioners admitted between 1657 and 1710.

VI. Conclusions

The study of the relationship between town councils and guilds in sixteenth and seventeenth-century Aragon produces a complex picture, for during this time both institutions competed for control of urban markets and their labour force. In this constant struggle, municipal authorities were forced to compromise with guilds. The exact terms of these agreements was dictated in accordance with the specific circumstances of the period.

Demographic and economic expansion during the sixteenth century made it easier for municipalities to limit the social influence of guilds. If town magistrates regarded guilds as useful tools for the regulation of the market and labour force, they were also aware of their important role in legitimising masters' control over apprentices and journeymen. This patronage allowed councils to modify guild regulations in order to maintain production standards. Expansion of industrial and craft activities resulted in foreign and native artisans being incorporated into guilds without real difficulties until the last decades of the century.

Economic decline during the seventeenth century reduced municipal and guild control of town markets, which were progressively invaded by French goods. In response, public authorities passed protectionist but ultimately ineffective laws to protect native artisanal production. Town councils also tolerated guild regulations introduced by masters to offer special treatment to their own sons. Interestingly, high mobility between town and countryside did not decline, but its character altered. As the economy worsened, migrant workers were increasingly 'pushed' from place to place in the search of work rather than being 'pulled' by the offer of better working possibilities elsewhere. A number of factors enabled journeymen to overcome guild control and carry out their professions independently. Municipal authorities assisted in this process to prevent guilds from abusing the monopoly position, to make sure the market operated efficiently and to retain as much of the existing labour force as possible in the towns.

Bibliography

Abadía, A. (1993) *Señorío y crédito en Aragón en el siglo XVI*, Zaragoza.

Arco, R. (1911) *Antiguos gremios de Huesca. Ordinaciones y documentos*, Zaragoza.

Arco, R. (1915) 'Estatutos dictados por el consejo general de la ciudad de Huesca', *Linajes de Aragón*, 6, pp. 128–139.

Asso, I. (1798) *Historia de la economía política de Aragón*, Zaragoza.

Beltrán, P. (1972) 'Los dineros jaqueses, su evolución y desaparición', in P. Beltrán, *Obras Completas*, Zaragoza, pp. 397–464.

Blázquez, C. and Pallaruelo, S. (1999) *Maestros del agua*, 2 vols, Zaragoza.

Colás, G. (1974) 'Las ciudades y la industria del reino de Aragón en los primeros años del reinado de Carlos II según diez cartas responsivas', *Estudios*, 74, pp. 121–129.

Colás, G. (1984) 'Las transformaciones de la superficie agraria aragonesa en el siglo XVI: los regadíos. Aproximación a su estudio', in *Congreso de Historia rural, siglos XV al XIX*, Madrid, pp. 523–534.

Colás, G. and Salas, J.A. (1975) 'Las cortes de 1626. El voto del servicio y su pago', *Estudios*, 75, pp. 87–140.

Desportes, P. (1999) *La industria textil en Zaragoza en el siglo XVI*, Zaragoza.

Falcón, M.I. (1986) 'La construcción en Zaragoza en el siglo XV', *Príncipe de Viana*, 2, pp. 117–143.

Falcón, M.I. (1988) 'Origen y desarrollo del municipio medieval en el reino de Aragón', *Estudis Balèarics*, 5, 31, pp. 73–91.

Falcón, M.I. (1991) 'Las cofradías artesanales de la Edad Media. Aspectos religiosos y sociales', in M. Barceló (ed.), *IX Jornades d' Estudis Històrics Locals. La manufactura urbana i els menestrals (segles XIII–XVI)*, Palma de Mallorca, pp. 193–222.

Falcón, M.I. (1993) 'La industria textil en Teruel a fines de la Edad Media', *Aragón en la Edad Media*, 10–11, pp. 229–249.

Falcón, M.I. (1994) 'Las cofradías de oficio en Aragón durante la Edad Media', *Medievalismo*, 4, pp. 59–79.

Gómez Urdañez, C. (1987 and 1988) *Arquitectura civil en Zaragoza en el siglo XVI*, 2 vols, Zaragoza.

Gómez Zorraquino, J.I. (1987a) *La burguesía mercantil en el Aragón de los siglos XVI y XVII (1516–1652)*, Zaragoza.

Gómez Zorraquino, J.I. (1987b) *Zaragoza y el capital comercial. La burguesía mercantil en el Aragón de la segunda mitad del siglo XVII*, Zaragoza.

Langé, C. (1993) *La inmigración francesa en Aragón durante el siglo XVI y la primera mitad del XVII*, Zaragoza.

Lapeyre, H. (1959) *Geographie de l' Espagne morisque*, Paris.

Maiso, J. (1982) *La peste aragonesa de 1648 a 1654*, Zaragoza.

Mateos, J.A. (1997) *Auge y decadencia de un municipio aragonés. El concejo de Daroca en los siglos XVI y XVII*, Zaragoza.

Mateos, J.A. (1998) 'The making of a new landscape: town councils and water in the kingdom of Aragon during the sixteenth century', *Rural History*, 9, 2, pp. 123–139.

Peiró, A. (2000) *Tiempo de industria. Las Tierras Altas turolenses, de la riqueza a la despoblación*, Zaragoza.

Redondo, G. (1976) 'Cargos municipales y participación artesana en el Concejo zaragozano (1584–1706)', *Estudios*, 76, pp. 159–190.

Redondo, G. (1982) *Las corporaciones de artesanos de Zaragoza en el siglo XVII*, Zaragoza.

Redondo, G. (1985) 'Las relaciones comerciales Aragón-Francia en la Edad Moderna: datos para su estudio en el siglo XVII', *Estudios*, 85–86, pp. 123–154.

Salas, J.A. (1981) *La población de Barbastro en los siglos XVI y XVII*, Zaragoza.

Salas, J.A. (1985) 'La inmigración francesa en Aragón en la Edad Moderna', *Estudios*, 85–86, pp. 51–77.

Salas, J.A. (1991) 'La evolución demográfica aragonesa en los siglos XVI y XVII', in J. Nadal (ed.), *La evolución demográfica bajo los Austrias*, Madrid, pp. 169–179.

Salas, J.A. (1992) 'Las haciendas concejiles aragonesas en los siglos XVI y XVII. De la euforia a la quiebra', in *Poder político e Instituciones en la España Moderna*, Alicante, pp. 9–66.

Salas, J.A. (1993) 'Migraciones internas y medium-distance en Aragón (1500–1900) in *I Conferencia Europea de la Comisión Internacional de Demografía Histórica*, Santiago, vol. I, pp. 189–215.

Sancho, L. (1925) 'El gremio zaragozano del siglo XVI', *Universidad*, 2, 3–4, pp. 613–648, 799–825.

San Vicente, A. (1988) *Documentos para una historia social y económica del trabajo en Zaragoza (siglos XV–XVIII)*, 2 vols, Zaragoza.

Sanz, P. (1997) *Política, hacienda y milicia en el Aragón de los últimos Austrias entre 1640 y 1680*, Zaragoza.

Serrano, C. (1986) 'Arquitectura civil pública del siglo XVI en Aragón', in *Actas del VI Coloquio de Arte Aragonés*, Zaragoza, pp. 115–131.

Sesma, J.A. (1972) *Transformación social y revolución comercial*, Madrid.

Sesma, J.A. (1986) 'La moneda jaquesa y la emisión de aragoneses de plata', in *Homenaje al doctor Antonio Beltrán Martínez, Zaragoza*, pp. 1029–1039.

Sesma, J.A. (1992) 'Rasgos precapitalistas en la producción industrial aragonesa (siglo XV)', *Medievalia*, 10, pp. 304–409.

Solano, E. (1987) *Poder monárquico y Estado pactista (1626–1652)*, Zaragoza.

Torras, J. (1982) 'La economía aragonesa en la transición al capitalismo. Un ensayo', in *Tres estudios de historia económica de Aragón*, Zaragoza, pp. 9–32.

10 Labour markets between the distribution of trades in the countryside and the loss of economic centrality in towns in the Holy Roman Empire. Examples of proto-industrial and non-proto-industrial areas in early modern South Germany (Baden, Bavaria, Swabia, Württemberg)

Carl A. HOFFMANN,[1] Universität Augsburg

I. Introduction

The research that has been done recently on proto-industry or craft production in the south German regions represents good progress in this field. Scholars have chosen either the state perspective or concentrated on companies, on towns, or on the countryside. In every case, increasing numbers of trades in the countryside played a characteristic role in the description of the economic system in the early modern period. This phenomenon can be recognised in politically fragmented Swabia as well as in absolutist and mercantilist territories, in areas exhibiting continuity from putting-out systems to industry in the nineteenth century and those that were primarily agrarian. The central question commonly was, how far does the described system fit into a theory of proto-industrialisation and how must this theory be altered. The following reflections are based on this recent research and concentrate on changes in the distribution of trade functions between town and countryside. Proto- and non-proto-industrial regions are included in order to differentiate developments that are connected with different special economic systems.

In this essay, I will first comment on some aspects of the state of research in the area under consideration concerning the question of labour markets with special attention to the proto-industrialisation process. Then, after a short survey of the different areas and their economic structures, a couple of parallel as well as contrary developments of the distribution of labour between towns and countryside are compared with regard to the question of whether or not there was really an overall decline of cities and towns after the Thirty Years' War and of how these results fit into the concept of proto-industrialisation.

II. State of research

Proto-industrialisation is a concept of economic and social history, which has been discussed in Germany since the early 1970s. In regard to our question, the original thesis states in short, that in the formative period of European capitalism, trade capital left the

[1] I have to thank Michele Zelinsky (University of Pennsylvania) for the correction of the English manuscript and Anke Sczesny (University of Augsburg) for the critical reading of the text.

old production centres and shifted in several regions to the countryside and the small towns, where no guilds existed. Production of goods then developed on a large scale. Much of the rural population, which concentrated on production at home and depended on urban merchants or manufactories, underwent a process of pauperisation. In addition, the population increased in relation to the spread of crafts in the countryside, because rural craftsmen were not subjected to corporate restrictions, for example as far as marriage allowances or admission to the crafts are concerned (Mendels, 1972; Kriedte, Medick and Schlumbohm, 1977). Peter Kriedte recognises in this phenomenon the reason for the economic crisis of the cities in the early modern period (Kriedte, 1982: 50). From a different perspective, Etienne François uses demographic figures to demonstrate the downfall of the old merchant cities after the Thirty Years' War and the rise of the resident cities of the princes (François, 1978). Proto-industrialisation has been regarded as a step between feudal agrarian economies and developed industrialisation.

After substantial criticism, this initial idea was developed in various directions during the following years. Current discussions show us a more flexible concept. Researchers now use the term 'proto-industrialization' to indicate a spectrum of economic relationships ranging from purely rural side line handicrafts working in a somewhat export-oriented putting-out system to highly concentrated economic monostructures in the countryside working for manufactories and export merchants in the large cities. The assumptions regarding an early capitalistic system generally free of corporate restrictions and connected with pauperisation of the rural workers, have been abandoned in favour of a plurality of developments, including the social consequences of this economic phenomenon (Kriedte, Medick and Schlumbohm 1992, 1998; Cerman and Ogilvie, 1994; Ebeling and Mager, 1997; Ogilvie, 1997a, 1997b). One can ask if this widening of the concept will erode proto-industrialisation to an empty term. In my opinion, the expression proto-industrialisation still usefully frames a special kind of economic and socio-historical circumstance which allows for the comparison of the very different developments from the late Middle Ages to the nineteenth century all over Europe.

Within South Germany highly export-oriented regions and those with hardly any export industry at all were situated closely together. An example of the latter is the duchy, and later Electorate, of Bavaria. As early as the 1960s research on this territory concentrated – as far as our question is concerned – on the phenomenon of people in the countryside who had no landed property (Fried, 1962; Schremmer, 1970, 1972). They could be identified in increasing numbers from at least the fifteenth century onward. In the early modern period they worked as day workers, side line handicraftsmen or even guild masters. But almost no proto-industrial structures (for example an organised putting-out system) were related with this development after the Thirty Years' War. So Bavaria is not seen as one of Germany's industrial regions ('Gewerbelandschaft') in the sense of Karl Heinrich Kaufhold's use of the term: above-average concentration and supra-regional importance of trades (Kaufhold, 1986: 114–116). A new work provides data for the whole Electorate concerning the number and types of crafts and their distribution between towns and countryside for the years 1771–81. The author shows, besides the broad distribution of basic handicrafts, concentrations of special trades with a regional importance in the towns and in the countryside (Denzel, 1998). Similar statistical data for a German territory exists only for Prussia. In this context, it would be interesting to see, if there were local initiatives by a greater number of 'craftsmen-merchants' who organised the sale of their colleagues products.[2] This would be a parallel to the phenomenon of the 'weaver-merchants' in Württemberg and Swabia which is discussed below. The demographic, economic and social consequences on the mostly small and middle-sized towns in seventeenth and eighteenth century Bavaria are discussed in a book on the Upper Bavarian towns with regard to state policy (Hoffmann 1997a, 1997b, 1998). What is missing, however, is research on the economic relations between towns and countryside and the working conditions and production levels of the rural craftsmen. Also missing is research on the question to what extent the decentralised rural craftsmen in Bavaria had business relations with the nearby Swabian Imperial cities. There are several indications of these relations. Answers to these questions would give us a better idea about the living conditions of the land-poor people and call into question assumptions about the process of their general pauperisation.

I have chosen the example of the small territory of the Margraviate of Baden only because of some interesting similarities with Bavaria. Most of our knowledge about the situation of rural handicrafts comes from articles by Eckard Schremmer whose main works are about the Bavarian economy. Unfortunately, nearly all of our information comes from purely statistical data about the distribution of rural and urban crafts and trades at the end of the eighteenth century (Schremmer, 1987a, 1987b).

A much better picture of proto-industrial structures and their socio-economic consequences from the seventeenth century onwards concerns the duchy of Württemberg. Within the last few years important research has been done on this subject. Hans Medick chose a micro-historical approach and analysed the developments of Laichingen between 1650–1900 (Medick, 1996). This village developed into a centre of linen production in close relation and also oppositon to the urban trade centre of Urach. Sheilagh Ogilvie concentrated on 'State corporatism and proto-industry' (Ogilvie, 1997a). She analysed the example of the worsted industry in the district of Wildberg, which belonged to the famous Calw textile region. Ogilvie stresses the correlation between economic development and 'state corporatism' which was widely determined by the fiscal necessities of the state. She systematically compares her results with modern international research on proto-industrialisation. Thus, she can demonstrate the progress made in different areas in this field of research. Nevertheless Medick is sceptical about her evaluation of the enforcement of state regulations and also about the general applicability of her example.[3] As Medick showed in his own study on Laichingen one can recognise some kind of free market for the weavers and 'weaver merchants' in the villages in opposition to privileged trading monopolies centred in the town of Urach during the eighteenth century. Finally, Reiner Flik presents a comparative study of the early industrialisation of the textile industries in Calw and Heidenheim from 1750 to 1870 in his dissertation. Primarily concentrating on the history of the different companies in the two towns, he also gives figures on the development of handicrafts in relation to the whole population

[2] See examples in Hoffmann, 1997a: 263–268.

[3] See his review on Ogilvie's work in *Historische Zeitschrift* 268 (1998): 201–202; see also Kriedte, Medick and Schlumbohm, 1998: 14 f.

in a synopsis between the two towns and their hinterland (Flik, 1990: 26–30). This modern research profits in many aspects from the data-rich work of Troeltsch on the 'Calwer Zeughandelskompanie' and its labour force from 1897 (Troeltsch, 1897).

The political structures and the basis for economic development in the Swabian area were totally different from the larger and middle-sized princely territories. The Imperial cities, with their wide-ranging export markets, had had close relations with their hinterlands through the putting-out system since the late Middle Ages. The textile industry of the Imperial cities, especially in Augsburg, has been described from various viewpoints, for example by Claus-Peter Clasen (Clasen, 1981, 1995). Lately research approaches have changed and interest has concentrated on the hinterland of the Imperial cities, the relationship between cities and countryside, and the production and living conditions of the rural weavers, spinners and trades people in Swabia. In this regard, our knowledge of the Swabian area is more advanced than that of Bavaria. This is mainly due to Rolf Kießling who is leading a research project on this subject at the University of Augsburg (Kießling, 1989, 1991, 1998a; see also Safley, 1993; Sreenivasan, 1995). Our knowledge about the development of the Imperial cities also has increased recently (Fassl, 1988; Huber-Sperl, 1991, 1995; Petz, 1998). As far as we can see at the moment, different modes of economic development in town and countryside were often at work simultaneously in the seventeenth and eighteenth centuries.

III. Labour markets and economic systems in different areas

III.1. Bavaria

The duchy of Bavaria became an electorate in 1623. In the early modern period, Bavaria was one of the more important middle-sized territories of the Holy Roman Empire. Historians have identified Bavaria as one of the fore runners of the administrative modernisation process in the first phase of early modern state building. At the same time, it must be described as a dominantly agrarian state. Handicraft production was decentralised and limited almost exclusively to the most basic crafts, which nevertheless were quite various (Schremmer, 1970; Störmer, 1981; Hoffmann, 1997a). Bavaria did not possess a source of income comparable to those of some other middle-sized territories, such as Saxony with its mining industry. Furthermore, Bavaria's towns were seriously disadvantaged with regard to trade connections. No important trade route crossed the territory, therefore it was impossible for Bavaria to establish a supra-regional fair. Researchers have shown that among the handicrafts the textiles were the only considerable export, and even this export diminished to a negligible quantity after the Thirty Years' War (Hoffmann, 1997a: 266ff. and passim). Denzel identified some trade centres with supra-regional importance using concentrations of numbers of craftsmen in towns or in the countryside at the end of the eighteenth century. Of all 123 towns in Bavaria around 1770 (Schmelzle, 1900: 23) only six had a greater concentration than fifteen percent in one trade compared to all other crafts. Besides the already well-known clock-makers in Friedberg, all the others were local textile centres. In the countryside there were only two centres which had a higher concentration than ten percent of all crafts: one for smiths (outside Traunstein) and one for potters (Kröning). The pottery of

Figure 10.1 Electorate of Bavaria (end of 18th century)

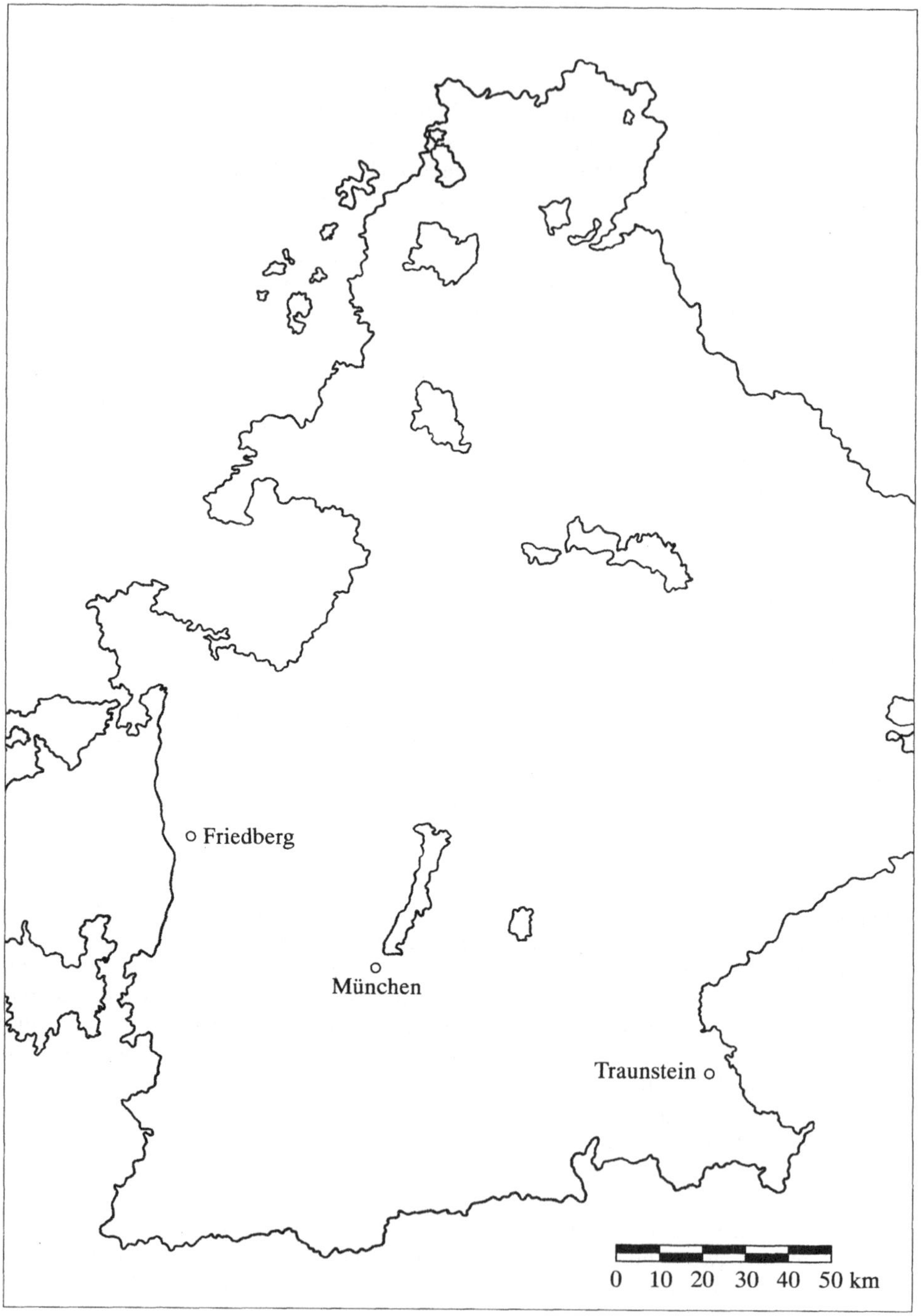

Kröning was exported into all neighbouring territories. Eight regional trade-centres which included towns and countryside existed in the Electorate with a concentration higher than twenty percent of all crafts, all connected with the production of textiles, mostly linen (Denzel, 1998: 426–436). These results seem to confirm the earlier estimation of the low significance of Bavarian exports. Nevertheless, the purely quantitative analysis of the distribution of crafts throughout the whole territory from 1771–81 requires more detailed research to differentiate our picture of a primarily agrarian society with a few regional trade centres at the end of the eighteenth century.

Population development is commonly used as a basic indicator for economic structure and development in the early modern period. In the sixteenth century the population of Bavaria had reached a level which caused a demographic crisis. The princely bureaucracy decreed prohibitions against marriage for non-citizens and non-peasants, immigration into the towns was restricted for non-citizens, and, finally, the number of masters in the towns was fixed at a maximum for more and more guilds. Sometimes this maximum was even lowered. This policy was enforced and steadily kept under surveillance by the central and local state bureaucracy (Hoffmann, 1997a: 77–91, 389 f.).

Population pressure caused an increase in the numbers of craftspeople and a spread in the variety of crafts into the countryside. A process of decentralisation began, which Eckart Schremmer called 'Territorialisierung des Gewerbes'. The spread of businesses was the result of the necessity for the non-peasant rural population to secure a livelihood for themselves. The generally poor economic conditions led to a levelling of the trade structure between the town and the countryside. 61 percent of all craftsmen (masters and journeymen) lived in the countryside in 1794, 25 percent in towns and 14 percent in market towns (Schremmer, 1972: 24). But the workshops were smaller in the countryside: 1.7–1.8 masters, journeymen and apprentices worked in an average shop in the towns and 1.2–1.4 in the countryside (Tyszka, 1907: 26 f.; Hoffmann, 1997a: 245 f.).

But even in organisational structures the countryside followed the towns. From the beginning of the seventeenth century we find guilds for rural craftsmen. The spectrum of trades was not as wide by far as it was in the towns. Of all 130 different types of crafts in Bavaria in 1771–81, twelve could be found in the villages and thirty-two in the market towns. The others were practised exclusively in the towns and cities (Schremmer, 1972: 26, 32 f.). The most widespread crafts in the countryside enjoyed the advantages of a common organisation. Unlike in Württemberg or Swabia this was not related to a significant putting-out system or any other proto-industrial structures. Demographic development forced people to work under new forms of business in the countryside. But we do not know of real centralising or organising efforts to establish a new export industry after the Thirty Years' War.

It has been recognized that in Bavaria in the eighteenth century a higher percentage of craftspeople lived in the districts of the nobles and monasteries ('Hofmarken') than in the countryside directly ruled by the princely bureaucracy (Schremmer, 1970: 362–365). Nevertheless, as far as we know, these small concentrations did not lead to the establishment of certain industries or production centres.

The towns underwent similar developments in their function as market places as they did in regard to the numbers of crafts. The annual fairs of most Bavarian towns served to provide a place for exchange only with the immediately surrounding area (hinterland). As already discussed for the crafts, the towns themselves also suffered an enormous loss of centrality in regard to the exchange of goods, which accelerated rapidly during the Thirty Years' War. More and more legal, as well as illegal, trade activities shifted to the countryside (Hoffmann, 1997a, pp. 278–301).

The residential town presents a different case. The well-known growth of the capital cities with its various demographic, commercial and cultural secondary effects can be seen in the example of Munich. But the results of this growth are relative. Around 1780, almost 40 percent of Munich's population was under princely rather than civic jurisdiction. As members of the princely household, administrative officers, court servants, craftsmen, soldiers etc. they belonged directly to the court. This portion of the residential city's population had grown continually from the sixteenth century. In contrast, the urban population under the city council's jurisdiction, namely the guild masters, reached its pre-Thirty Years' War level only around 1800 (Hoffmann, 1997a: 142–155, 224–233). This result qualifies the assumption of a general rise of the residential towns in the seventeenth and eighteenth centuries (François, 1978).

These developments had consequences for economic and property structures. Within the Bavarian towns one can perceive a structural decline of urban businesses. The de-urbanisation developments within the urban economy mentioned above found expression in net worth losses in taxable properties, which occurred in all the cities under investigation. Many of the craftsmen threatened by pauperisation sought an escape in socially degrading migrant work outside the towns. Agriculture as a side line occupation for craftsmen, already a normal way of subsidising one's income, increased in importance in the urban economy. We must proceed on the assumption that the restriction of immigration, of which the closing of guild membership is one example, probably hindered the further impoverishment of other civic groups. This assumption is supported by the positive effects on the capacity of the remaining guild masters to pay taxes, whenever a craft guild reduced the number of its members and restricted them to the level of demand. The shrinking of the guilds to a reasonable size, intended by territorial legislation, showed measurable success in these cases. The city of princely residence, Munich, was no exception. This shows that demographic increase alone is no indicator for economic growth (Hoffmann, 1997a: 243–275, 303–398). Nevertheless most craftspeople lived in poor or very poor conditions, in towns as well as in the countryside (Schremmer, 1972: 36; Hoffmann, 1997a, ut supra).

What is normally thought of as an essential for mercantilism – namely manufacturing – played at most a marginal role for exports. These manufactories very often were established to reduce the amount of imports and to improve the labour market. Rural and urban society was to be freed from the social problems that came from a growing part of the population with restricted income possibilities in danger of pauperisation. The textile manufactories especially were meant to enable the rural surplus population to earn money with spinning. Most manufactories in Bavaria were established by princely initiative, but they had little success in exports. There were some exceptions like the glass industry in northeastern Bavaria, but they had little importance for the economy of the territory as a whole. It has been estimated that at the end of the eighteenth century only about 10 percent of the territory's total handicraft production was exported, and the manufactories accounted for just 0.7 percent of the territories total exports (Slawinger, 1966; Schremmer, 1970: 480f).

Where possibilities for positive economic development in the cities existed, they were usually systematically destroyed by the state's need for revenue. Whenever the ever-empty treasury was involved, the last reserves of the territory and its cities were demanded. The discrepancy between demands for payment and ability to pay can be noticed clearly for the first time during the Thirty Years' War and it did not change through the end of the time period under consideration. The state's income usually had priority over territorial economic considerations. The inhabitants of the Imperial cities, especially the merchants, had no comparable problems. Their interests and the improvement of the economy played a crucial role in the policy of the magistrates. In contrast, Bavaria, which was under princely rule, lost capital-rich investors who might have improved the area's economy. Reasons for this were the state's steadily increasing claims for taxes or loans and the creation of state monopolies (salt, brewing of wheat beer) which nationalised important quantities of investment capital. So, the lack of initiative in putting-out ventures after the Thirty Years' War was extremely significant. Also, customs served (apart from solving treasury problems) primarily as a protective measure against imports and not as a way to stimulate an exchange of goods (Hoffmann, 1997a: 64–76, 93–98, 399–446).

III.2. Baden

Figure 10.2 Margraviate Baden-Durlach (end of 18th century)

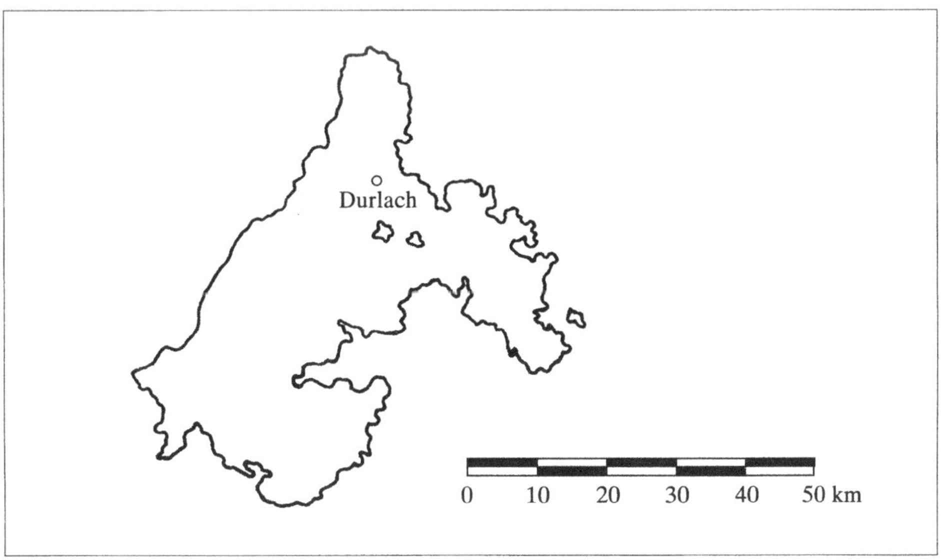

At the end of the eighteenth century in the margraviate of Baden-Durlach, a very small South German territory (98,418 inhabitants in 1767), the situation seems to have been similar to the electorate of Bavaria (Schremmer, 1987a, 1987b). Nearly three times as many craftspeople lived in the countryside than in towns in 1790. Of eighty-eight different types of crafts one could find fifty-five in the countryside. In many crafts, especially in the larger ones (except the weavers, which was the largest group), the number of craftspeople was considered to be too high. In the eighteenth century, the craftsmen sold their products only within a radius of five hours from home, i.e. the markets that they could reach within a day. Not even the weavers – by far the biggest group among the crafts – were able to produce a substantial quantity of exports. They worked, as far as we know, primarily for the internal market. As in Bavaria, the main reason for this development was the growth of the population in the countryside, where people could not earn their living by agriculture alone. On the other hand, income from handicrafts often was not sufficient to make a living, so most artisans in the towns had to subsidise their income with agriculture as a side line occupation.

According to an ordinance of 1577, the prerogative of the towns as the only places for craft production was not maintained in Baden. Finally, at the end of the eighteenth century, all objections to craft production in the countryside and competition with the towns were abandoned by the state bureaucracy as well. No one saw a way to avoid the 'Territorialisierung' of the trades. Also the 'Hofrat', the central council of the prince, valued the importance of the economy and state revenues as a whole, regardless of where craft production was situated. This attitude accompanied a more liberal economic policy. In addition, the new policy tried to encourage the establishment of export-oriented crafts and the education of future craftsmen. In both areas a great deficit was recognised. Nevertheless, the policy remained in the framework of mercantile (cameralist) thinking: as the prince ordered in 1794, one should primarily improve those professions that would bring foreign money into the margraviate.

This assessment was similar to the one made by state officials in Bavaria at the same time. In 1728 the Bavarian elector still tried to protect the guilds in Munich by prohibiting the erection of small houses for non-peasants around the capital. Normally, craftspeople without sufficient landed property in the countryside lived in such settlements. In 1799, when a new government with a more liberal policy was installed, all restrictions concerning the place of establishment for crafts production were abandoned (Hoffmann, 1997a: 109).

III.3. Württemberg

Smaller than Bavaria, Württemberg was also a middle-sized territory. The duchy's population development is similar to that of Bavaria to the East: expansion in the sixteenth century, which caused demographic pressure especially among the non-peasant rural people. During the Thirty Years' War Württemberg also lost half of its population. These losses were compensated by the end of the seventeenth century by high birth rates as well as by high immigration numbers. Again a demographic crisis in the eighteenth century forced parts of the surplus population to emigrate from the duchy. The number of emigrants was not higher than 20 percent of the yearly surplus of births (Boelcke,

Figure 10.3 Duchy of Württemberg (end of 18th century)

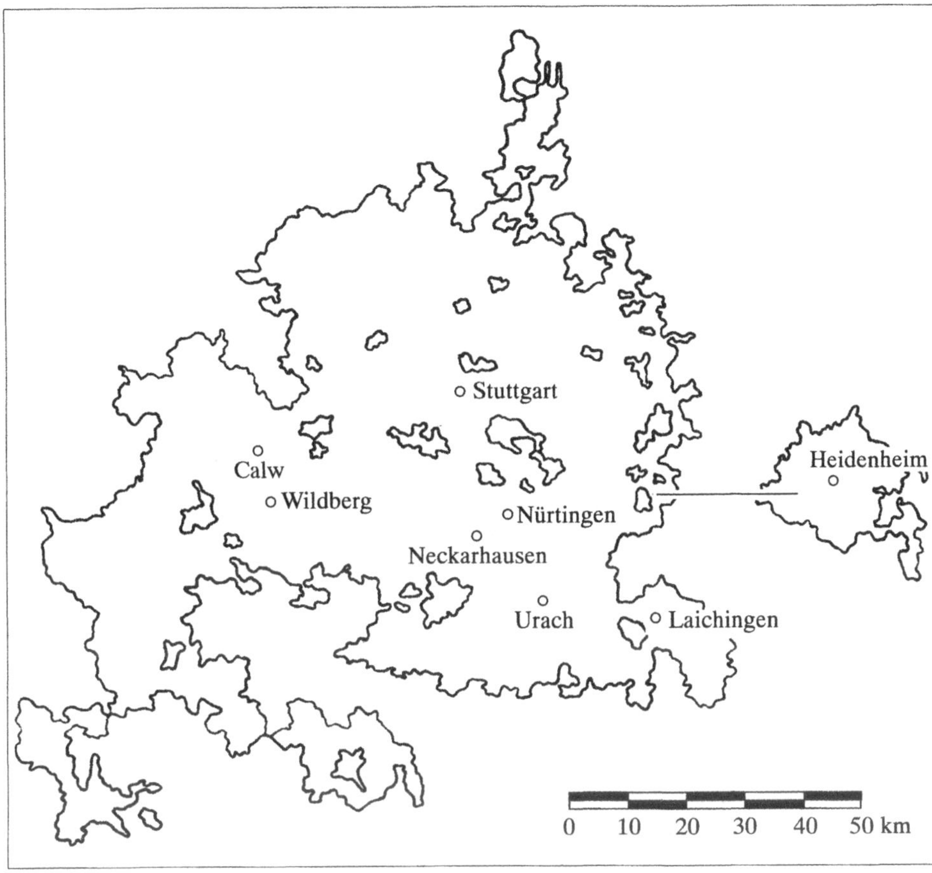

1987: 93–96). In 1707, 343,000 people lived in Württemberg, in 1794 there were 664,000 (Hoffmann, 1906: 31).

Demographic development found its expression also in the number of people practising a craft. In 1723, in Urach, a trade centre of linen production, there were 513 households with 454 practicing a trade. At the end of the century 1796 we can identify 597 households with 587 of them practising a trade. While the households increased 16 percent, the number of craft producers went up by 29 percent. These numbers do not indicate a boom in demand. Rather the urban crafts were overcrowded, and many handicrafts suffered from the lack of orders and impoverishment (Medick, 1996: 114). With the exception of the residential town of Stuttgart, all other Württemberg towns seem to have had a surplus of crafts too (Hoffmann, 1906: 31f.). The government as well as the guilds exercised little influence on demographic development. Population growth rates indicate this: from 1769 to 1802 Württemberg's towns grew between 1.01 and 2.21 percent a year

(Walter, 1990: 35). Unlike in Bavaria, access to the crafts and guilds, nevertheless, remained quite liberal. Together with the fragmentation of farms caused by the Württemberg law of inheritance, the result was a mixing of peasant and craft occupations in the eighteenth century (Flik, 1990: 34).

At the same time, the number of workshops in the countryside increased. We have evidence of conflicts between rural crafts and towns by the late fifteenth century (Scott, 1997: 104–108). In the mid-eighteenth century the total number of trades in the countryside surpassed that in towns. While, in 1663, 70 percent of Württemberg's master weavers lived in towns, it was only 35 percent in 1787 (Kaufhold, 1986: 146). But we know nothing about the total number of workers in Württemberg's enterprises in the eighteenth century (Flik, 1990: 30–36). In special cases urban handicrafts seem to have been economically more powerful than most of their rural colleagues. In Calw, one urban weaver of stockings provided work for ten to twenty rural masters as paid workers (Walter, 1990: 167). In this context another important finding of both Ogilvie and Medick is that there was no general pauperisation of the craftspeople working in the Württemberg textile industry in eighteenth century. One reason for this might be that they practised agriculture as a side line occupation. David Sabean is more sceptical about the situation in Württemberg's villages. In his example of Neckarhausen he shows a proletarianisation of the villagers in the first half of the eighteenth century onwards, primarily caused by an increase in population. People answered to this situation by specialising in trades (Sabean, 1990: 156–159). In Württemberg like in Bavaria, as far as we know, the manorial system had little influence on the development of crafts in the countryside (Ogilvie, 1997b: 112).

In the Black Forest, worsted weavers made up half of the families and employed three quarters of the female inhabitants of the villages as independent spinners. The weavers in villages supported themselves to a large extent with their own agricultural products (Ogilvie, 1997b: 109f.). These handicrafts had been export-oriented since the sixteenth century, and, for example, from 1582 onwards the worsted weavers in the region of Calw formed new guilds with privileges and jurisdiction over both urban and rural craftsmen. Previously, the weavers had sold their products to foreign markets directly. The worsted weavers in the districts of Calw and Wildberg exported their cloths to Horb, Strasbourg and Schafhausen, and bought wool from Strasbourg, Mühlberg, Nürtingen and Müncheningen. In 1650 the Calw Worsted Trading Company ('Calwer Zeughandelskompanie') was founded. For 147 years it was in the hands of Calw's dyers. This company acquired a monopoly over dyeing and exporting all worsteds produced in a fixed area, the so-called 'Calwer Moderation'. No one else was allowed to sell any product that was under the company's monopoly. The company was under a sort of surveillance by the state bureaucracy, especially regarding the selling of wool to the weavers, the prices of cloths, and the conditions of buying them from the weavers. The members of the Calw dyers were organised in a guild. This was fixed in the 1650 ordinance of the company, where the internal organisation was regulated, outsiders who had no proper guild training and mastership were excluded, and, finally, competition among members was forbidden in favour of internal harmony. This was the traditional idea of guilds, to give every member (nearly) equal income. The greatest portion of all Württemberg worsted weavers were always in the Calw region: in 1650, 500–550 of ca. 600; in 1728, 770 of ca. 970; in 1771, 989 of ca. 1,300 (Ogilvie, 1997a, 95–112, 129).

In the past, researchers concerned with Württemberg's textile industry attributed a leading role for the duchy's overall economy to the linen merchants' company in Urach ('Uracher Leinwandhandlungs-Compagnie' 1662–1794). This conclusion is challenged by Medick (1996: 59), though 35.5 percent of all Württemberg linen exports came from Urach alone (Walter, 1990: 177). Like the worsted company in Calw, the linen merchants in Urach had a monopoly over the buying and selling of all linen cloths produced within the district of Urach and the neighbouring districts (Medick, 1983: 270). The weavers in the town of Urach were organised in guilds similar to the weavers in the countryside. Medick shows that the weavers outside of Urach could produce less expensively. Therefore, the economic situation of the urban weavers worsened in the second half of the eighteenth century (Medick, 1996: 124). For fine linen products, the urban weavers remained the main producers, while mass production for export had primarily been located in the countryside since the 1760s (Medick, 1983: 278 f.). Finally, the weavers in the countryside broke through the monopoly of the company by the means of 'weaver-merchants'. In the second half of the eighteenth century they, together with their foreign wholesale dealers, dictated prices, and the rural weavers thus could overcome the prohibition to sell their products directly in another country. This was a victory for the rural weavers and the local guild organisation over the state monopoly of the Urach company (Medick, 1996: 137 f.).

Ogilvie demonstrates the decisive role of the state in the founding of the company in Calw. The dyers themselves were not able 'to set up a workable cartel or association between 1590 and 1650' without state assistance (Ogilvie, 1997a: 112). Also, guilds of the worsted and linen-weavers were privileged and supported by ducal officials. 'Guilds and companies could exercise greater internal regulation with state support, even while their external powers were being surpassed by those of the state' (Ogilvie, 1997a: 441 f.). Ogilvie shows, for example, that the fixation of official output quotas for the weavers was not related to a market with its free play of supply and demand. She believes both producers and merchants decided on the quantity of worsteds, 'based on the expected returns from producing and selling their products, in accordance with the predictions of standard economic theory'. These returns were determined through markets 'constrained by the institutional rules and privileges of powerful corporate groups supported by the state' (Ogilvie, 1997a: 224). Based on his results, Medick doubts the great importance of 'state corporatism', which Ogilvie stresses in her example of Calw.[4] The different views of Medick and Ogilvie are to some extent based in the different types of products in their samples. The old linen industry had a long tradition of rural-based weaving from the late Middle Ages onwards. The worsted industry was younger and more closely connected with state initiatives and state regulations.

In 1736, a subsidiary company of the Urach linen company was founded by princely initiative in Heidenheim with similar privileges. In 1767, the company went bankrupt, primarily because its owners had tremendous problems with their involvement in a silk factory in Stuttgart, a favourite project of the dukes. After that, different owners acquired the privileges and the monopoly. The number of weavers (masters) in the district ('Herrschaft') of Heidenheim changed drastically: in 1736, ca. 200; 1767, ca. 600; 1778,

---

[4] See note 3.

ca. 400; 1789, ca. 700. In Heidenheim the number of handicrafts increased above the average after the foundation of the company in 1736. In a couple of years the obligation of the weavers to sell their cloth to the company was suspended because of the bankruptcy. But even after the reestablishment of the 'Moderation' weavers opposed the restrictions. They preferred to sell the linen to foreign merchants, who were usually connected to wholesale dealers in Ulm, Günzburg or Switzerland. Nevertheless, even after protests against the monopoly in 1765/66 and 1788, they had no success, as far as legal restrictions were concerned (Flik, 1990: 29, 96–105). It is not yet known if 'weaver-merchants' were also active in Heidenheim, as in the Urach district.

Not enough research has been done to evaluate the success or influence of trading and customs policies in Württemberg. Flik prefers not to ascribe to this policy any impact on foreign trade. In his study for the second half of the eighteenth century, Rolf Walter primarily described theoretical reflections. His evidence for a prohibitive mercantilistic policy in the eighteenth century together with the criticism of contemporaries, regarding the pre-eminence of state income over the encouragement of exports (Walter, 1990, 39–55), suggests a practice very similar to the electorate of Bavaria. Likewise, Medick stresses the customs policy of the Württemberg dukes as a barrier to trade and export (Medick, 1996: 61f.).

III.4. Swabia

The situation in the textile-producing region of Swabia is much more complex, especially in eastern Swabia, where the most research has been done. The political framework of this area was not a single territory but a mixture of Imperial cities of different sizes and influence (for example Augsburg, Ulm and Memmingen) and small or even tiny territories (for example Burgau, Oettingen). Swabia is called, in contrast to the greater territories, a 'territorium non clausum', meaning that different kinds of rights and influences were at work, which could not always be separated by clear boundaries. As in Württemberg or Bavaria, state privileges and monopolies for trading companies could also play a role in these small territories of Swabia. At the beginning of the eighteenth century the Habsburg government of Burgau initiated a new economic policy to make the capital of Burgau, Günzburg, into a textile centre. This policy led to competition, above all, with the Imperial city of Ulm. Both Burgau and Ulm erected trade barriers against each other (Kießling, 1990: 38).

From the late Middle Ages, the area was one of Germany's most important textile regions. From the centres of Augburg, Ulm, Memmingen, Mindelheim, Ravensburg, Günzburg etc., a huge number of spinners and weavers in the hinterland were organised and affiliated with markets in the cities (Kießling, 1989; Safley, 1993: 121). Furthermore, a system of local markets in the smaller towns (sub-centres) around the metropols was established to provide a link between the spinners and weavers in the hinterland and the merchants in the big cities (Kießling, 1998b). Already in the fifteenth century quarrels between the urban and rural weavers were reported. From the beginning of the seventeenth century this system was affected by the textile crisis. After the Thirty Years' War, the number of weavers in the cities never reached its pre-war level. From then on production in the

Figure 10.4 Swabia (end of 18th century) (*Territorium non clausum*)

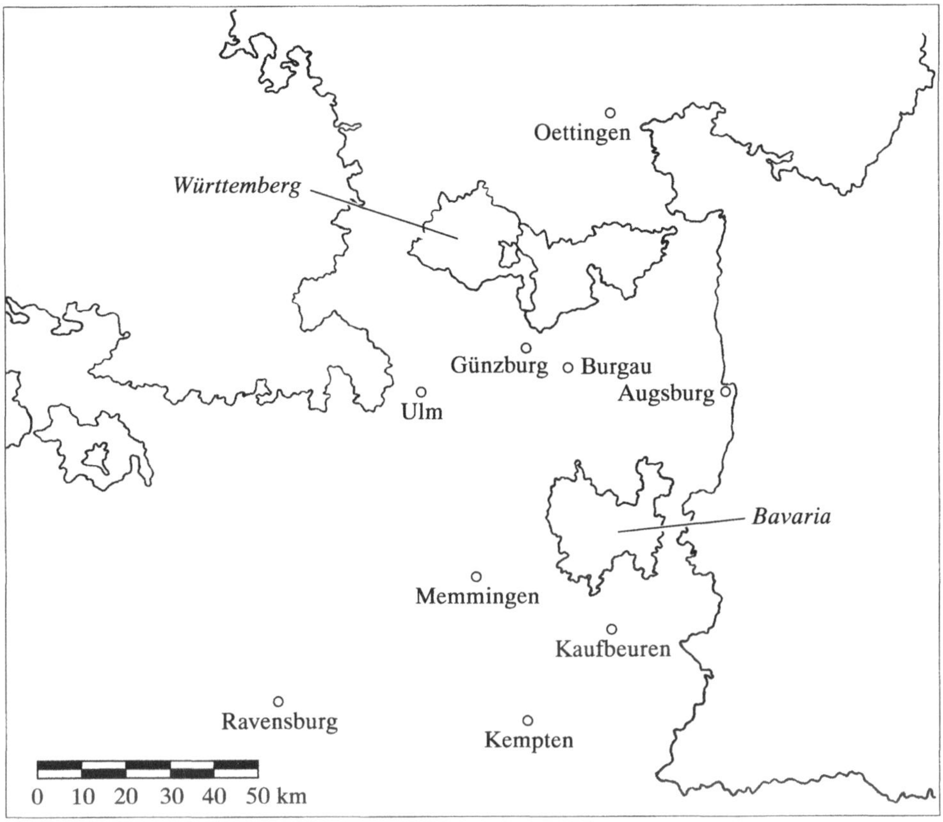

countryside surpassed that in the merchant cities (Kießling, 1998a: 50, 54). For Augsburg, however, the assumption of a general decline in the seventeenth and eighteenth centuries has been called into question (Kießling, 1991: 36f.). The manufactories in the city played a crucial role in the industrialisation of the nineteenth century. In the eighteenth century in Kaufbeuren as well as in Augsburg proto-industrial mechanisms were closely related to the cotton manufactories. Merchants from the cities also played a vital role in the traditional structures of the putting-out system especially in the traditional linen production. The old centre of Ulm regained a leading position in this field in the eighteenth century like it had had in the early sixteenth century (Kießling, 1998a: 16). The city obtained this position within the Württemberg territory as well as the Swabian. The centre of Urach always remained second to the Imperial city of Ulm. On the other hand, the Imperial city of Memmingen, which had supra-regional and international importance in the textile industries with an advanced putting-out system before the Thirty Years' War, declined to a middle-sized town with only a local market in the eighteenth and nineteenth centuries (Huber-Sperl, 1991, 1995). As a result, we cannot fully accept the thesis of an overall decline of Imperial or merchant cities in the late seventeenth and eighteenth centuries.

New economic structures developed after the Thirty Years' War, which cannot be found in the nearby territory of Bavaria.

In Augsburg and Kaufbeuren cotton finishing played a central role, while all other steps of production for the most part were put out into the hinterland. It is not yet completely clear if the losses suffered during the textile crisis of the seventeenth century were compensated for by the new techniques and labour organisation of the eighteenth century, which revived the old living and working relations between cities and the countryside of the sixteenth century (Kießling, 1998a: 75f.). Equally unclear for the Swabian region is whether or not a general proletarianisation of weavers was combined with this development. Given the situation in Württemberg, it is likewise improbable for Swabia. On the other hand, we find uprisings of urban weavers between 1580 and 1656 in the Allgäu (Upper Swabia), who feared deprivation from foreign competitors (Safley, 1993: 135–144). This was not a conflict between town and countryside, but an unsuccessful attempt to secure an exclusive market. Nevertheless, these weavers saw the danger of pauperisation in a free market in the sixteenth and seventeenth centuries.

Besides this orientation towards the big centres, textile production in the countryside increased and, at least periodically, was more important than in the cities in the eighteenth century. From the end of the seventeenth century onwards we find, for example, local merchants and the new organisation of rural guilds. All steps of linen production and marketing, from cultivation to export, were centred also in local markets. The new rural guilds played quite a significant role. They adopted the rules of the urban guilds only to the extent that they were useful for them. Guild rules were in the interest of the weavers (legal status) as well as of the merchants (guarantee of quality) (Kießling, 1998a: 64 f.). Also, 'weaver-merchants' had played a role since the early eighteenth century (Kießling, 1998a: 71). There are certain suggestions that local independent nobles acted like the princes of the larger territories, favouring the establishment of production and trade (sub-) centres on their estates ('Herrschaft') (Kießling, 1991: 32, 41–45, 48). As in Burgau, the local rulers in Swabia assisted in these developments by supporting the initiatives of local merchants in their territorial towns, especially in the eighteenth century. Consequently, these sub-centres increased in importance. Concomitant with the economic efforts of the local rulers to institute mercantilist policies, manufactories also were established in their territories and by their initiatives, partly in competition with the Imperial cities. Capital came in part from merchants in Imperial cities (Kießling, 1990: 39; Kießling, 1998a: 60 f.).

In summarising this development, Kießling describes these structures in the countryside as a mixed economy, which counterbalanced the power of the capital-rich merchants in the Imperial cities and their exploitation of rural productive resources. This must have been a barrier against a 'forced proto-industrialisation' (Kießling, 1998a: 76). During the seventeenth and eighteenth centuries, traditional economic and social structures were combined with new proto-industrial developments in the region (Sczesny, forthcoming).

IV. Conclusions

A comparison among the four areas under consideration is constrained by the varying amounts of research done on each one. Clearly, these results must be confirmed or modified by further analysis on the region under consideration. We urgently need comparative studies on the different regions, using the same methodological approach. Nevertheless, we can identify some similarities and differences at this point.

We can see similarities in the following developments and structures:

1. In comparison to the cities, the countryside gained more and more economic importance. Not only did the number of craftspeople increase, but the location of the exchange of products shifted to a large extent to the countryside. This can be demonstrated, for example, by the growth of the local markets, or by the increase in exporting directly from the local production centres. These developments were independent of a special economic structure (proto-industrial or not) but closely related to demographic growth. The more specialised crafts remained solely within the domain of the towns and cities.
2. Accompanying the economic ascension of the countryside, institutional structures also grew stronger. The organisation of the rural handicrafts in guilds gave them a better defence against exploitation as well as against exclusion by the urban guilds. These rural guilds institutionalised the stronger economic position of the countryside.
3. Princes and the bureaucracies of the territories no longer protected the separation between towns and countryside. No later than the sixteenth century had rural crafts won legal status in the ordinances of all areas under consideration. At the end of the eighteenth century liberal economic theories led to the end of the last restrictions for the practice of trades in the countryside.
4. In the territories, state bureaucracy gave the economic system (which consisted for example of guild ordinances, manufactories, and rules for admission to the crafts, production conditions etc.) a certain legal framework, which was under steady state surveillance. Within this system, the extent of state intervention varied (for example Württemberg seems to have been more liberal on the admission to the crafts than Bavaria). Enforcement of state policy also reached its limits when social reality and group interest came into opposition with the legal framework (for example, the demographic development in Bavaria, and Württemberg's monopolies).
5. The trade and customs policies of the princes were intended to protect the territories from imports. Even if monopolies were erected, the founding of manufactories was promoted etc., the primary aim of this policy was to improve the income of the treasury. This could be a crucial disadvantage for economic progress (Bavaria), but could also bring new economic possibilities (Burgau, and to some extent Württemberg).

We can see differences in the following developments and structures:

1. In contrast to Swabia or Württemberg, in the territory of Bavaria hardly any signs of proto-industrial structures have been identified, with the exception of some specialised manufactories. In western Bavaria, only a few crafts profited from nearby Augsburg. Most other crafts lacked money from capital-rich merchants who could have invested in the putting-out system.
2. While in the Württemberg area concentrations of export-oriented weavers had existed since the sixteenth century, in the territories of Bavaria and Baden (at least in

the late eighteenth century) handicrafts were – with some exceptions – decentralised and diverse outside the towns. They were also not oriented for export.

3. In the eighteenth century, manufactories in the territory of Bavaria were founded under the initiative of the prince in order to improve the labour market and to avoid imports as much as possible: a purely mercantilistic policy. In contrast, the Württemberg princes granted monopolies to merchants to secure a high rate of exports. In the Imperial cities this idea played no role at all. Foundations of manufactories were inspired primarily by capitalist goals.

4. Even as the countryside won enormous parts of craft production and trade, in comparison to the cities and towns all over south Germany, the corresponding effects on the urban economies varied. While in Württemberg the centres of Calw and Urach lost economic potential, their craftspeople increased in number and were in danger of pauperisation, Bavarian towns reduced their productivity and numbers of craftsmen, and tried to match the demand of their own inhabitants. On the other hand, the Imperial cities of Augsburg and Ulm were able to win new markets after the crisis of the seventeenth century. In Augsburg some of the eighteenth century manufactories were forerunners of modern factories. Ulm and Memmingen, which were also important centres for the early modern putting-out system in textile-production, had no such similar continuities. Memmingen declined dramatically in the seventeenth and eighteenth centuries.

5. While the nobles had little influence on demographic and economic developments in the bigger territories, in their own estates, free Imperial lords (reichsunmittelbare Herrschaften) could exert successful initiatives for the improvement of their crafts and trades.

In view of these results, proto-industrialisation cannot be described as a homogenous phenomenon on the way to the industrial age in south Germany. Nevertheless, everywhere population increases necessitated the excess rural population to find opportunities for income outside of agriculture. By the eighteenth century, all basic crafts were located in the villages. A new self-confidence consequently found its expression in the rural guilds. These guilds can be interpreted as an important step towards the integration of rural craft production into the early modern economic system. The cities and towns underwent different developments that depended on the interplay of political and economic factors. The towns under princely rule in Bavaria suffered tremendous losses and in Württemberg most were overcrowded with producers. Some Imperial cities regained a leading position in textile production over a certain hinterland after the crisis of the textile production in the seventeenth century, while others declined to an average town with only a local market. There was a steady exchange of the labour force between town and countryside, but the towns were not able to counterbalance the great demographic shifts. Regardless of whether immigration to towns was open or restricted, the results of the demographic 'explosion' of the eighteenth century were decided in the countryside. These very different developments and problems cannot be explained by a single teleological concept alone.

Bibliography

Boelcke, W.A. (1987) *Wirtschaftsgeschichte Baden-Württembergs von den Römern bis heute*, Stuttgart.

Cerman, M. and Ogilvie, S.C. (eds) (1994) *Proto-Industrialisierung in Europa. Industrielle Produktion vor dem Fabrikzeitalter*, Wien.

Clasen, C.P. (1981) *Die Augsburger Weber. Leistungen und Krisen des Textilgewerbes um 1600*, Augsburg.

Clasen, C.P. (1995) *Textilherstellung in Augsburg in der frühen Neuzeit*, 2 vols, Augsburg.

Denzel, M.A. (1998) *Professionen und Professionisten. Die Dachsbergsche Volksbeschreibung im Kurfürstentum Baiern (1771–1781)*, Stuttgart.

Ebeling, D. and Mager, W. (eds) (1997) *Protoindustrie in der Region. Europäische Gewerbelandschaften vom 16. bis zum 19. Jahrhundert*, Bielefeld.

Fassl, P. (1988) *Konfession, Wirtschaft und Politik. Von der Reichsstadt zur Industriestadt. Augsburg 1750–1850*, Sigmaringen.

Flik, R. (1990) *Die Textilindustrie in Calw und Heidenheim 1750–1870. Eine regional vergleichende Untersuchung zur Geschichte der Frühindustrialisierung und der Industriepolitik in Württemberg*, Stuttgart.

François, E. (1978) 'Des républiques marchandes aux capitales politiques: remarques sur la hiérarchie urbaine due saint-empire a l'époque moderne', *Revue d'Histoire Moderne et Contemporaine*, 25, pp. 578–603.

Fried, P. (1962) *Herrschaftsgeschichte der altbayerischen Landgerichte Dachau und Kranzberg*, München.

Hoffmann, C.A. (1997a) *Landesherrliche Städte und Märkte im 17. und 18. Jahrhundert. Studien zu ihrer ökonomischen, rechtlichen und sozialen Entwicklung in Oberbayern*, Kallmünz.

Hoffmann, C.A. (1997b) 'Integration in den frühneuzeitlichen Staat und ökonomischer Funktionsverlust – die altbayerischen Kleinstädte vom 16. bis zum 18. Jahrhundert', in H.T. Gräf (ed.), *Kleine Städte im neuzeitlichen Europa*, Berlin, pp. 83–110.

Hoffmann, C.A. (1998) 'Urbanisation et déurbanisation dans l'Électorat de Bavière aux XVIIe et XVIIIe siècles', *Cahiers d'histoire*, 43, pp. 439–453.

Hoffmann, L. (1906) *Das württembergische Zunftwesen und die Politik der herzoglichen Regierung gegenüber den Zünften im 18. Jahrhundert*, Krefeld.

Huber-Sperl, R. (1991) 'Handwerk, Verlag, Manufaktur – oder weshalb in Memmingen keine große Industrie zu Hause war', in J. Jahn and W. Hartung (eds), Sigmaringendorf, pp. 70–87.

Huber-Sperl, R. (1995) *Memmingen zwischen Zunfthandwerk und Unternehmertum. Ein Beitrag zur reichsstädtischen Gewerbegeschichte 1648–1802*, Memmingen.

Kaufhold, K.H. (1986) 'Gewerbelandschaften in der frühen Neuzeit (1650–1800)', in H. Pohl (ed.), *Gewerbe- und Industrielandschaften bis ins 20. Jahrhundert*, Stuttgart, pp. 112–202.

Kießling, R. (1989) *Die Stadt und ihr Land. Umlandpolitik, Bürgerbesitz und Wirtschaftsgefüge in Ostschwaben vom 14. bis ins 16. Jahrhundert*, Köln/Wien.

Kießling, R. (1990) *Günzburg und die Markgrafschaft Burgau. Die Entwicklung eines ländlichen Raumes im Spannungsfeld der Großstädte*, Günzburg.

Kießling, R. (1991) 'Entwicklungstendenzen im ostschwäbischen Textilrevier der Frühen Neuzeit', in J. Jahn and W. Hartung (eds), *Gewerbe und Handel vor der Industrialisierung. Regionale und überregionale Verflechtungen im 17. und 18. Jahrhundert*, Sigmaringendorf, pp. 27–48.

Kießling, R. (1998a) 'Ländliches Gewerbe im Sog der Proto-Industrialisierung? Ostschwaben als Textillandschaft zwischen Spätmittelalter und Moderne', *Jahrbuch für Wirtschaftsgeschichte*, pp. 49–78.

Kießling, R. (1998b) 'Kleinräumige Jahrmarktzyklen in Schwaben. Zur wirtschaftlichen Erschließung des Landes im Spätmittelalter und in der beginnenden Frühen Neuzeit', in H.P. Becht and J. Schadt (eds), *Wirtschaft–Gesellschaft–Städte. Festschrift für Bernhard Kirchgässner zum 75. Geburtstag*, Ubstadt-Weiher, pp. 139–156.

Kriedte, P. (1982) 'Die Stadt im Prozeß der europäischen Proto-Industrialisierung', *Die alte Stadt*, 9, pp. 19–51.

Kriedte, P., Medick, H. and Schlumbohm, J. (1977) *Industrialisierung vor der Industrialisierung. Gewerbliche Warenproduktion auf dem Land in der Formationsperiode des Kapitalismus*, Göttingen.

Kriedte, P., Medick, H. and Schlumbohm, J. (1992) 'Sozialgeschichte in der Erweiterung – Proto-Industrialisierung in der Verengung? Demographie, Sozialstruktur, moderne Hausindustrie: eine Zwischenbilanz der Proto-Industrialisierungs-Forschung', *Geschichte und Gesellschaft*, 18, pp. 70–87, 231–255.

Kriedte, P., Medick, H. and Schlumbohm, J. (1998) 'Eine Forschungslandschaft in Bewegung. Die Proto-Industrialisierung am Ende des 20. Jahrhunderts', *Jahrbuch für Wirtschaftsgeschichte*, pp. 9–20.

Medick, H. (1982) 'Freihandel für die Zunft. Ein Kapitel aus der Geschichte der Preiskämpfe im württembergischen Leinengewerbe des 18. Jahrhunderts', in *Mentalitäten und Lebensverhältnisse. Beispiele aus der Sozialgeschichte der Neuzeit. Rudolf Vierhaus zum 60. Geburtstag*, Göttingen, pp. 277–294.

Medick, H. (1983) 'Privilegiertes Handelskapital und 'kleine Industrie'. Produktion und Produktionsverhältnisse im Leinengewerbe des alt-württembergischen Oberamts Urach im 18. Jahrhundert', *Archiv für Sozialgeschichte*, 23, pp. 267–310.

Medick, H. (1996) *Weben und Überleben in Laichingen 1650–1900. Lokalgeschichte als Allgemeine Geschichte*, Göttingen.

Mendels, F.F. (1972) 'Proto-industrialization: The First Phase of the Industrialization Process', *The Journal of Economic History*, 32, pp. 241–261.

Ogilvie, S.O. (1997a) *State corporatism and proto-industry. The Württemberg Black Forest, 1580–1797*, Cambridge.

Ogilvie, S.O. (1997b) 'Soziale Institutionen, Korporatismus und Protoindustrie. Die Württembergische Zeugmacherei (1580 bis 1797)', in D. Ebeling and W. Mager (eds),

Protoindustrie in der Region. Europäische Gewerbelandschaften vom 16. bis zum 19. Jahrhundert, Bielefeld, pp. 105–138.

Petz, W. (1998) *Zweimal Kempten – Geschichte einer Doppelstadt (1694–1836)*, München.

Sabean, D.W. (1990) *Property, Production, and family in Neckarhausen, 1700–1870*, Cambridge.

Safley, T.M. (1993) 'Production, Transaction, and Proletarianization: The Textile Industry in Upper Swabia, 1580–1660', in T.M. Safley and L.N. Rosenband (eds), *The Workplace before the Factory. Artisans and Proletarians, 1500–1800*, Ithaca/London, pp. 118–145.

Schmelzle, H. (1990) *Der Staatshaushalt des Herzogtums Bayern im 18. Jahrhundert*, Stuttgart.

Schremmer, E. (1970) *Die Wirtschaft Bayerns. Vom hohen Mittelalter bis zum Beginn der Industrialisierung. Bergbau–Gewerbe–Handel*, München.

Schremmer, E. (1972) 'Standortausweitung der Warenproduktion im langfristigen Wirtschaftswachstum. Zur Stadt–Land–Arbeitsteilung im Gewerbe des 18. Jahrhunderts', *Vierteljahrschrift für Sozial- und Wirtschaftsgeschichte*, 59, pp. 1–40.

Schremmer, E. (1987a) 'Zünftige und nicht-zünftige Gewerbetreibende in der Markgrafschaft Baden-Durlach im Jahre 1767', in H. Henning, D. Lindenlaub and E. Wandel (eds), *Wirtschafts- und sozialgeschichtliche Forschungen und Probleme. Karl Erich Born zur Vollendung des 65. Lebensjahres*, St. Katharinen, pp. 48–84.

Schremmer, E. (1987b) 'Zu wenig städtisches und zu viel ländliches Gewerbe in Baden um 1790?', in H. Kellenbenz and H. Pohl (eds), *Historia Socialis et Oeconomica. Festschrift für Wolfgang Zorn zum 65. Geburtstag*, Stuttgart, pp. 316–329.

Scott, T. (1997) *Regional Identity and Economic Change. The Upper Rhine, 1450–1600*, Oxford.

Sczesny, A. (forthcoming) *Zwischen Kontinuität und Wandel. Ländliches Gewerbe und ländliche Gesellschaft im mittleren Ostschwaben des 17. und 18. Jahrhunderts*, Augsburg, Doctoral dissertation Universität Augsburg. [or. 2000].

Slawinger, G. (1966) *Die Manufaktur in Kurbayern. Die Anfänge der großgewerblichen Entwicklung in der Übergangsepoche vom Merkantilismus zum Liberalismus 1740–1833*, Stuttgart.

Sreenivasan, G.P. (1995) *Land, Money, and Power at Ottobeuren (1525–1710)*, Cambridge (Mass.).

Störmer, W. (1981) 'Wirtschaft und Bürgertum in den altbayerischen Städten unter dem zunehmenden Einfluß der Landesfürsten', in W. Rausch (ed.), *Die Städte Mitteleuropas im 17. und 18. Jahrhundert*, Linz, pp. 237–266.

Troeltsch, W. (1897) *Die Calwer Zeughandelskompagnie und ihre Arbeiter. Studien zur Gewerbe- und Sozialgeschichte Altwürttembergs*, Jena.

Tyszka, C. (1907) *Handwerk und Handwerker in Bayern im 18. Jahrhundert. Eine wirtschaftsgeschichtliche Studie über die bayerische Gewerbeverfassung im 18. Jahrhundert*, München.

Walter, R. (1990) *Die Kommerzialisierung von Landwirtschaft und Gewerbe in Württemberg (1750–1850)*, St. Katharinen.

11 Urban artisans and their countryside customers: different interactions between town and hinterland in Antwerp, Brussels and Ghent (18th century)

Harald DECEULAER, University of Brussels – VUB, Fund for Scientific Research (FWO-V)

I. Introduction

Recently, the interrelationships between urban and agrarian economies were mentioned as 'one of the key historical problems' of the early modern period. Attention was called for the role of cities as 'incubators of commercial facilities, linking subordinate market towns in extended commercial networks' (De Vries, 1999). This raises questions how the growing Western European rural demand (due to agricultural growth, rising prices and proto-industrial development) interacted with towns and urban trades, or with a developing rural service sector. De Vries has stated that the increase in agricultural income and the expansion of the volume of marketed farm output after 1750 gave impulses to small regional market cities (the 'new urbanisation' or 'urbanisation from below' of the eighteenth century) (De Vries, 1984). The effects of the growth of the countryside on the service sectors of larger cities, especially those offering relatively simple goods for countryside consumers, are less clear. In this paper, I will study the influence of rural demand on the occupational structures in the three largest towns of the Southern Netherlands in the eighteenth century: Antwerp, Brussels and Ghent. It is well known that the countryside of the Southern Netherlands experienced strong demographic and agricultural growth in the eighteenth century (see e.g. Billen, 1987; Dejongh, 1999). The analysis will deal with trades offering simple goods for local and regional markets.

Traditionally, general models have been constructed for the relationship between city and countryside, based on the services provided for the city's hinterland (Christaller's central-place theory). According to this theory, a connection exists between the rank-size of the town and the level of development of the service sector for the surrounding countryside. This connection is seen to be hierarchical, with the largest town as the largest 'central place', the second largest town the second central place, and so on. Of course, differences between towns have been taken into account, e.g. based on political roles (capitals) or economic functions (trade or industry) (Hohenberg and Lees, 1985). A differentiation between cities on the basis of their relations with the countryside is rarer.

I will not present a general model to describe the relations between 'the town' and 'the countryside'. Instead, a comparative approach of the three largest cities of the Southern Netherlands stresses the multitude of possible relations between town and countryside. I will argue that the different rural demographic and economic structures of the hinterlands profoundly influenced the size, composition and historical evolution of some urban occupations in Antwerp, Brussels, and Ghent in the eighteenth century. In this respect, attention will be given to the impact of proto-industrialisation in the hinterland of Ghent, of commercial agriculture in the Brussels area, and of poorer soils in the Antwerp hinterland. The specific positions of these three towns in the urban network will also be taken into account.

First, I present the demographic, geographic, and economic situation of the three cities and their hinterlands, along with their historical evolution in the eighteenth century. Second, a hypothesis about the interaction between these elements and the urban occupational structure will be related to a quantitative comparison of thirteen trades in the three cities. It must be stressed that this paper will not address the urban export trades. Third, the hypothesis will be tested through a focus on the garment trades. Although the garment trades are often portrayed as a sector operating on the local market, I will argue that the size and the composition of the urban clothing sector were influenced by relationships with the countryside. In fact, the differences in employment structure in specific market-segments of the clothing sector of the three towns were partly determined by the specific relationships with their hinterlands. The number and activities of the second-hand dealers are considered in some detail. In Ghent, they were extremely numerous and offered new, ready to wear clothes for the inhabitants of the countryside (and poorer city-dwellers). In Brussels, the second-hand dealers were also important, albeit at a lower level. In Antwerp, they became a marginal group in the clothing trades in the eighteenth century, and they shifted their activities to the trade in other (new or second-hand) goods. Data on the number of second-hand dealers in other towns of the Southern Netherlands suggest that this group could function as an indicator for the relationship between town and countryside. In this respect, I will make some tentative international comparisons with England, France, and the Dutch Republic.

II. Space and time: the Southern Netherlands in the eighteenth century

The Southern Netherlands were part of the region with the highest population density in Europe. From the late Middle Ages, this region has also been strongly urbanized. Its largest cities, however, were not giants of the size of Paris, London, Vienna or Berlin. The population of Brussels fluctuated between 50,000 and 70,000 inhabitants, Antwerp ranked second with 50,000 to 60,000, and Ghent was the third largest town in the Austrian Netherlands, with about 40,000 to 50,000 inhabitants. The differences were more important in the surrounding countryside of the three towns. Population density in the 'arondissement' of Antwerp grew from 43.6 inhabitants per square km in 1755 to 60.7 in 1784. The region around Brussel was more densely populated and grew stronger: from 88.3 inhabitants per square km in 1755 to 104.7 in 1784 (calculations on the basis of Klep, 1981). We do not have comparable information for the same years for the area around Ghent, but in 1796 a population of 158 persons per square km inhabited the whole region of eastern Flanders. In the region around Ghent this varied between 148 and 194 inhabitants per square km (Jaspers and Stevens, 1985).

Densities around Brussels and Ghent were not only high in comparison with other regions in the Southern Netherlands, but also with other regions in Europe. The average population density of all French *intendances* at the end of the Old Regime was 48.2

Figure 11.1 Map of the Southern Netherlands

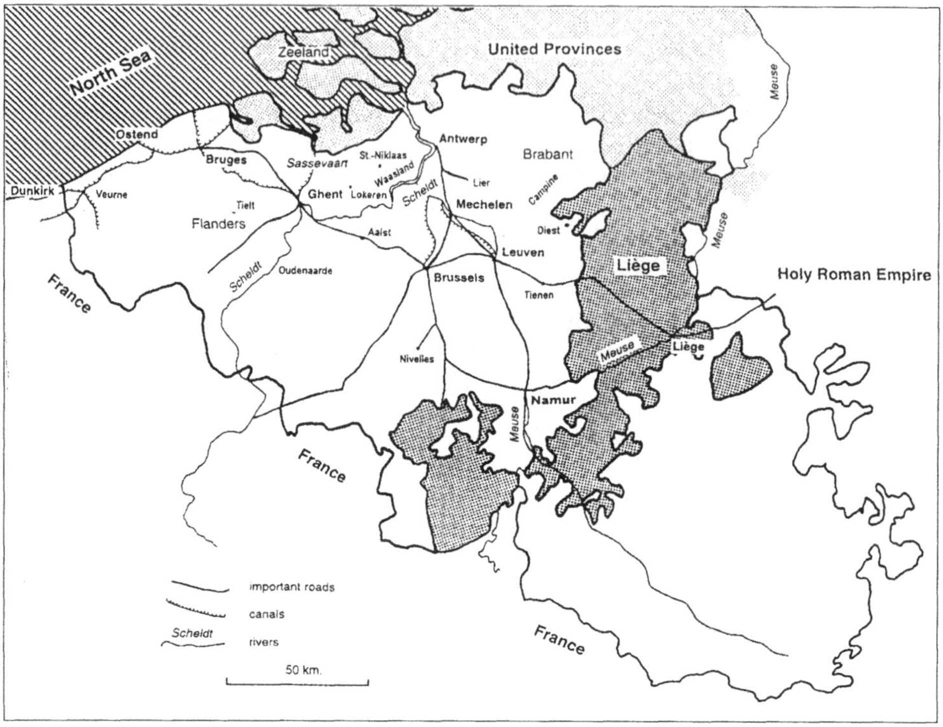

inhabitants per square km, with the region of Lille and Artois, Lyon and Paris reaching the highest figures of 81–87 (Dupâquier, 1988). For Northern France, even higher figures are sometimes mentioned. In most of southern England in 1801, population densities fluctuated from 48 to 57 inhabitants per square km, with the wider region around London reaching 100 to 150. Only in Lancashire and the area around a few towns (Birmingham, Bristol, Nottingham, London) were population densities of 150 to 300 inhabitants per square km registered (Barraclough, 1988).

The economic relations between Antwerp, Brussels, and Ghent and their hinterlands also varied strongly. From the late fifteenth century onwards, Antwerp was the 'gateway' of the Southern Netherlands. Its port remained the most important during the early modern period and even in the nineteenth and twentieth centuries. The relations between Antwerp and its hinterland, however, were less developed. Although the river Scheldt was a source of much wealth, it also created a natural barrier for the reach of Antwerp's hinterland. The fertile rural region on the western part of the river (the '*Waasland*') had fewer contacts with Antwerp, and in the eighteenth century turned increasingly to the small town of Sint-Niklaas (Blondé, 1999; Stabel, 1995). The polder villages north of Antwerp were sparsely populated. The countryside to the south of Antwerp was more populous and prosperous, but the competing role of other nearby towns (e.g. Lier, Mechelen) was quickly felt. From the river Ruppel onwards, the influence of Brussels became particularly strong. The main hinterland of Antwerp therefore consisted of the region to the east of the town: the Campine area. This was a region where navigable rivers were scarce, which made transport expensive (Van Uytven, 1992). The soils were poor and sandy, with a lot of forests and moorland. Agricultural production costs were high and profits low (Hannes and Vander Pijpen, 1973; Dejongh, 1991). As a lot of small farmers were burdened with debts, the rural population of the Campine was not likely to invest, to commercialize agriculture, or to purchase urban commodities. Agriculture in the region of Antwerp did not experience feverish growth in the eighteenth century. Brussels was the centre of an increasingly prosperous area of commercial agriculture. Many navigable rivers made transport easy in this region, and the construction of roads in the eighteenth century intensified the relations between town and countryside (Van Uytven, 1992; Blondé, 1999). The increasing commercialization and specialization of agriculture may very well have led to a rise in the rural market demand for goods and services (compare De Vries, 1975). Regional markets were of paramount importance for Brussels' industry, and the town was also a major regional service-centre (De Peuter, 1999). Brussels was the capital of the Southern Netherlands, and also formed the main fashion centre of the Netherlands. Costume historians have found, for example, that the clothing trade in Brussels clearly influenced the clothing worn in the nearby towns of Vilvoorde, Diest, Tienen and Leuven (Vanoppen, 1994).

The area surrounding Ghent was one of the most populous regions of northwestern Europe. Agriculture in the region of eastern Flanders became the most profitable in the eighteenth-century Southern Netherlands (Dejongh, 1999). Furthermore, this region was the main center of a very important proto-industrial linen industry, which developed strongly in the seventeenth and eighteenth centuries. The countryside weavers were institutionally obliged to sell their woven pieces at the weekly Friday market in Ghent, where a small number of merchants controlled the trade (Bastin, 1967). There, the weavers were paid in cash. At the same market, a lot of new and second-hand clothes, shoes, shirts and other commodities were sold. Quite a lot of weavers bought urban products at this market. Certainly in the first half of the eighteenth century, many contemporaries complained about the squandering on 'populuxe'-expenditures by the Flemish proto-industrial weavers (Vandenbroeke, 1984; 1996). It is, indeed, highly probable that most of these 'luxury' expenditures of the rural proto-industrial region were spent in Ghent. There were not many alternatives. Unlike Antwerp or Brussels, the city of Ghent existed in an 'urban void'. The closest smaller towns around Ghent were only about 25 km away from its city walls (Prevenier, Sosson and Boone, 1992).

III. The 'Countryside as external market – hypothesis'

It will be clear from this short overview that although the population size of the three towns was not fundamentally different, the demographic and economic structures of the countryside surrounding the towns differed quite strongly. Did this have any effect on the urban occupational structures? To check this, I compared the number of artisans in thirteen occupations in the three towns in a census ordered by the central government in 1738. In order to prevent possible distortions caused by differences in workshop size, a distinction is made between the total number of people employed (masters, journeymen and apprentices) on one hand, and the number of masters on the other. Not all data are exactly comparable, due to lacunae, or differences in institutional structures. We divided the thirteen occupations into two major groups: a first group in which the artisans of Ghent clearly dominated numerically, and a second in which this was not the case.

Table 11.1 Employment in thirteen occupations in Antwerp, Brussels and Ghent in 1738

	Antwerp		Brussels		Ghent	
Occupation	Total	N.Mr.	Tot.	N.Mr.	Tot.	N.Mr.
Shoemakers	450	149	492	118	528	133
Hatters	32	15	38	14	65	19
Second-Hand dealers	40?	40?	214	214	286	246
Hosiers	33	24	17	17	86	20
Mercers	?	?	518	292	839	364
Grocers	?	?	?	?	776	306
Butchers	85	55	130	110	354	136
Buttonmakers	116	61	?	140	96	43
Glovers	12	7	38	12	34	9
Wigmakers	100	50	195	75	?	?
Embroiderers	4	4	29	18	?	?
Tailors	839	350	956	294		226
Bakers	281	152	344	172	278	156

Note: N.Mr. = Number of Masters
Source: Smekens, s.d.; SAG, Serie 156, 3, 8; Van Honacker, 1994.

The table clearly shows that the classical rank-size hierarchy does not correspond to a numerical development of these occupations. Brussels was the largest town, but ranked second in the number of artisans involved. Antwerp was the second largest town of the Southern Netherlands, but its trades offering simple goods (shoemakers, hatters, second-hand dealers) were comparatively weakly developed. Of the three cities, Ghent was the smallest in population, but it had the strongest developed service sector. Historians have argued that unusual concentrations in certain trades point to the existence of external markets (Hohenberg and Lees, 1985; Cocula, 1987). Most of the Ghent trades in this table were not active on international markets, therefore we must probably turn to the countryside to find this external market.

Before we investigate that hypothesis, alternative explanations should briefly be considered and institutional elements should be investigated. The low figures for Antwerp cannot be explained by higher entrance-barriers, as in most trades, these were higher in Brussels. Could the higher numbers in Ghent be explained by lower entrance-barriers? Historians of early modern Ghent know very well that after the revolt of 1539–1540, Charles V changed the political and institutional structure of the town dramatically by imposing the *Concessio Carolina*. After 1540, obtaining the mastership in a guild in Ghent became much cheaper, at least on paper. Theoretically, this could influence the number of artisans in the town. This explanation, however, should be refuted. The deviations in the number of shoemakers, hatters or hosiers for example, were not caused by the number of masters, but by larger numbers of journeymen and apprentices. Furthermore, although the *Concessio Carolina* applied to all the guilds in Ghent, the number of tailors, bakers, glovers, wigmakers or embroiderers was not higher, but lower than in Antwerp or Brussels. However important the *Concessio Carolina* was on a political or institutional level, the economic consequences of this new local 'constitution' probably remained limited. Still, institutional differences probably do explain the higher number of butchers in Ghent. In Antwerp and Brussels (as in most towns of the Southern Netherlands) this trade was hereditary and closed to outsiders, in Ghent this was not the case.

The higher number of apprentices can explain the higher number of total artisans in Ghent in certain occupations. Indeed, among the Ghent shoemakers, tailors and hosiers the number of apprentices is remarkable compared to Antwerp or Brussels.

Table 11.2 Number of apprentices (N.A.) in Antwerp, Brussels and Ghent

Occupation	Antwerp N.A.	Brussels N.A.	Ghent N.A.
Shoemakers	59	57	193
Hatters	8	7	9
Second-handdealers	–	–	–
Hosiers	1	0	47
Mercers	?	50	238
Grocers	?	?	350
Butchers	9	0	84
Buttonmakers	22	?	25
Glovers	1	0	10
Wigmakers	20	25	?
Embroiderers	–	?	?
Tailors	102	75	133
Bakers	26	28	25

Source: Smekens, s.d.; SAG, Serie 156, 3, 8; Van Honacker, 1994.

This discrepancy must probably be related to the 'urban void' in Eastern Flanders, where Ghent offered one of the only available possibilities to learn a trade in an urban setting. The town was probably a centre of education for the surrounding countryside. This element, however, is not satisfactory to explain the differences for all seven occupations with deviations in numbers. Firstly, the total numbers of Ghent second-hand dealers and hatters was not really influenced by a higher number of apprentices. Secondly, the fact that Ghent shoemakers and hosiers could employ more apprentices is probably not simply determined by the demand for education, but also by the supply of apprenticeships by the masters involved. Therefore, the higher numbers for Ghent remain to be explained.

The 'countryside as external market-hypothesis' is probably a valid one, if we take a closer look at the nature of the products the deviant occupations offered. It is remarkable that most trades with an exceptionally high number of Ghent artisans offered rather simple and affordable consumer goods: shoes, second-hand clothing, hats, stockings, ribbons, etc. Most of these goods were sold at (or near) the markets where peasants and rural weavers came to sell their products. It seems probable that rural inhabitants bought some of these simple urban goods. The number of artisans offering expensive luxury products such as wigs, embroidery, clothes on order or gloves (products which were less likely to be purchased by rural inhabitants) were clearly not higher in Ghent. Tailors and bakers probably only worked for the local market as well, as their numbers were not exceptionally different from the ones in Antwerp or Brussels.

IV. Testing the hypothesis: the second-hand dealers in Antwerp, Ghent and Brussels

In order to test the hypothesis, and to try to grasp the social realities behind abstract figures, detailed archival research has been undertaken on a group with one of the most important numerical differences for the three cities: the second-hand dealers.

There is ample qualitative evidence that the Ghent second-hand dealers, indeed, sold clothing to rural customers. Already in 1536, the Ghent secondhand-dealers claimed to sell a lot to countryside customers (SAG, Serie 191, 6 (3), 1536). The accounts of a rich Ghent second-hand dealer between 1641 and 1691 showed that two thirds to three quarters of his customers were from the countryside (SAG, *Familiefonds handboeken*, 433). Four early eighteenth-century probate inventories of second-hand dealers registered sales to customers in the villages surrounding Ghent. In 1753 the city government accused second-hand dealers of hiring beggars to conduct countryside-dwellers to their shops or stalls. Thirty years later, the second-hand dealers were forbidden to run after the villagers when they entered the town, or to question the quality of the goods of their competitors (Deceulaer, 1998).

A quantitative analysis of the evolution of the number of Ghent second-hand dealers supports the importance of countryside customers, especially the ones active in the proto-industrial linen trade. In 1674, when the linen market shrank 164 second-hand dealers paid their yearly contribution to the guild. In 1719, in the early eighteenth-century boom of the linen market, no less then 323 were counted (SAG, Serie 199–17, 1674, 199–16, 1719). It is often argued that semi-proletarianised proto-industrial households had other expenditure-patterns than the agricultural rural population, for example that they spent more on clothing (e.g. De Vries, 1994). In more than one European proto-industrial region, there were complaints about the 'squandering' and the luxury consumption of the cottagers (Kriedte, 1983). Certainly in the first half of the eighteenth century, the number of Ghent second-hand dealers grew impressively.

In Antwerp, the number of second-hand dealers declined strongly during the course of the early modern period. In 1571, 170 second-hand dealers were active in the town, and in 1584 as many as 245. In the sixteenth and seventeenth centuries, Antwerp second-hand dealers sold ready-made clothing at moderate prices to rural customers and poorer city-dwellers. Often, they subcontracted with poorer tailors. This was probably related to the high number of inhabitants before 1585, to the prosperity of the countryside in most periods before 1650, and especially to the central place of the town in the Netherlands in the sixteenth and early seventeenth centuries. (Deceulaer, forthcoming). We do not have much information on the number and activities of the Antwerp second-hand dealers in the second half of the seventeenth century, but it is clear that sometime in the period between 1650 and 1750, a decline in their position took place. According to their dean in 1743, only twenty-six masters were still active (SAA, *PK*, 834, 3 august 1743). This count may be slightly low because in the population census of 1755 forty-two second-hand dealers were counted (Verbeemen, 1957). Another important difference between the second-hand dealers in Antwerp and Ghent was the evolution in the range of their activities. In Ghent they sold old and new ready-made clothing, in Antwerp they were forbidden to do so from 1742 onwards (Deceulaer, 1998). The Antwerp second-hand dealers increasingly concentrated on the sales of all kinds of other second hand goods, as they held a monopoly on public sales. This strategy of 'rent-seeking' can probably be partly related to a loss of rural markets for Antwerp industry and commerce. The first limited complaints about rural competition were heard during the twelve-year truce (1609–1621), but these cries multiplied in the second half of the seventeenth century. A royal ordinance from 1685 tried to extinguish certain artisan activities in the Antwerp suburbs, but this attempt failed. Other edicts vainly attempted to prohibit direct sales by skippers from the United Provinces in the villages on the waterways in 1684, 1698, 1724 and 1742 (Thijs, 1985; Dickshen, 1995). Therefore, it comes as no surprise that almost all Antwerp guilds complained about the growth of countryside shops in 1738 (Smekens, s.d.). The loss of market functions of Antwerp became painfully clear when the two fairs of the town were limited to a duration of only two weeks in 1732 and 1760. From 1770 onwards, the fairs were nothing more than a local kermis; only a faint memory from the all-important fairs of the early sixteenth century.

This process went hand in hand with a strong growth in the number of rural shops and artisans in the Brabantine countryside. Research on the occupational structures of twenty-seven villages between Antwerp and Brussels shows that the number of shopkeepers more than doubled between 1702 and 1755, and even quadrupled between 1702 and 1796. The number of countryside tailors quintupled between 1702 and 1755, and increased eight times between 1702 and 1796 (Leenders, 1983). This process was more important in the countryside near Antwerp than near Brussels, as villages were larger in the north of Brabant, which made the 'threshold demand' higher, and the presence of countryside-shops and artisans more probable (Van Uytven, 1972).

There is less precise information on the evolution of artisans or shopkeepers in the countryside near Ghent and Brussels, but indications about the second-hand dealers suggest a similar, though less extreme trend. In Ghent, the number of second-hand dealers decreased slowly from the 1730's onwards. The social evolution of this group also suggests a loss of wealth. At least, the number of masters supported by the guild more than doubled between 1674 and 1773.

Table 11.3 Number of supported masters on the total number of second-hand dealers in Ghent in 1673/74, 1738 and 1773

Year	Supported masters	Total masters	%
1673/74	23	164	14.0
1738	49	264	18.5
1773	86	228	37.7

A similar social evolution is suggested by the yearly contribution paid by second-hand dealers to cover the debts of their guild. They were taxed according to their means. A distinction was made between three categories (a rich, middle, and poorer group), and a very poor group which was exempted from the tax. The graph shows the evolution in percentages of these groups between 1705 and 1773.

Figure 11.2 Social categories among the Ghent second-hand dealers (1705–1773)

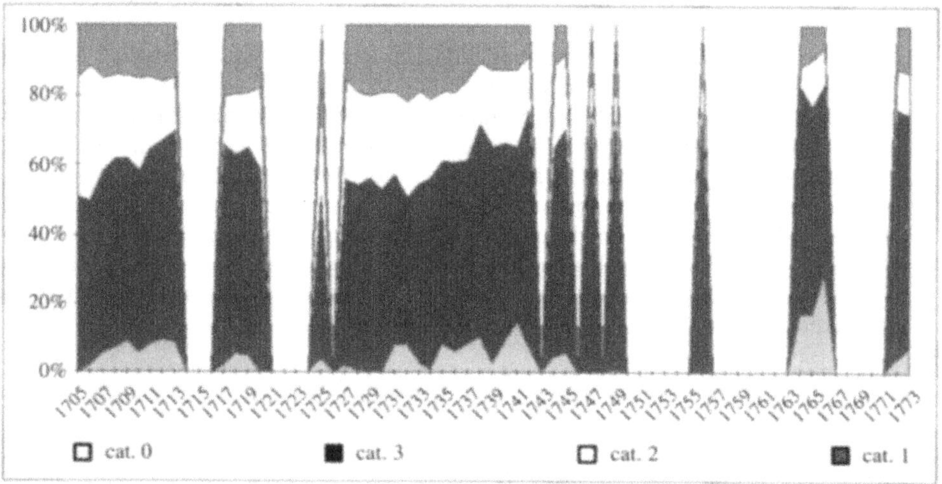

The figure seems to point to a gradual impoverishment from the 1730s onwards. In the three first decades of the eighteenth century, about 60% belonged to the two lowest groups, but this share increased to 80% in the 1760s and 1770s. The share of the middle group and the most prosperous likewise declined. Until the 1730s, about one in three second-hand dealers were counted among the middle group, but in the 1760s and 1770s this decreased to one in ten. In the early eighteenth century, some 15% paid the maximum contribution, only 5 to 10% did the same in the second half of the eighteenth century. We don't know which volume of business, or which levels in wealth corresponded to the categories in the corporate tax.

The evolution in the number of second-hand dealers, in the number of supported masters by the guild, and in the tax paid to the guild all seem to suggest a weakening of this group in Ghent. How can we explain this? A few explanations are possible. First, the living standards of the proto-industrial population seem to have declined in the second half of the eighteenth century (Vandenbroeke, 1996). The extreme rise in lease holds, the decline of the linen price after 1785, the rising age of marriage, the evolution in the number of rural people supported by poor relief, the growth of illiteracy, and the decline in body height in eastern Flanders all point in that direction. Detailed research on the '*land van Nevele*' in eastern Flanders has shown, however, that although the social positions of weavers and wage-labourers in the countryside weakened, farmers actually profited from the rise in agricultural prices (Schelstraete et al., 1986). A growth in countryside shops and artisans could also be seen in Flanders. This may also be related to a shift in the linen trade from larger cities as Ghent and Oudenaarde to new, smaller markets. This also harmed the crafts and shops of the older market centers (Dhondt, 1995).

A somewhat different evolution can be seen among the second-hand dealers in Brussels. The number of second-hand dealers rose slowly from 130 in 1709 to 168 in 1752, and 211 in 1796. The last figure, however, is probably not comparable to the earlier data, as no distinction was made between masters and hired help in the 1796 census. If we count the masters and journeymen second-hand dealers together in the 1738 census, we reach a figure of 214. Therefore, the 'rise' in number suggested by the 1796 census is more probably a stabilization. Overall, there is a strong impression of a positive and steadier development in Brussels, contrary to the sharp fluctuations and a certain tendency to decline in Ghent. We could speculate that the proto-industrial area surrounding Ghent was probably more sensitive to changes in business cycles on export markets than the area of commercial agriculture around Brussels. This region was much more strongly oriented on the domestic market, and probably profited from the agricultural upswing of the eighteenth century.

A detailed comparison with the evolution of other occupational groups would be interesting, but exceeds the scope of this paper. Comparing the censuses of 1738 and 1796 is possible for Antwerp and Brussels (the quality of the 1796 census for Ghent is too poor). A quick look suggests that the evolution of the shoemakers mirrors to some extent the one of the second-hand dealers. In Antwerp the number of shoemakers shifted from 450 in 1738 to 386 in 1796, or from 7.5 to 7.6 per 1000 inhabitants. The number of cobblers decreased from 194 to 108 (from 3.2 to 2.1) (Smekens s.d.; De Belder, 1973). In Brussels, the number of shoemakers and cobblers (counted together) increased from 777 in 1738 to 1243 in 1796, or from 11.6 to 18.7 per 1000 inhabitants (masters, journeymen, and apprentices in both trades were counted together). This does not seem to indicate a loss of markets (Van Honacker, 1994; Cosemans, 1966).

V. The second-hand dealers as an indicator for the relationship between town and countryside?

In other towns in the Southern Netherlands as well, second-hand dealers were oriented to customers living in the countryside. In 1725, the magistrate of Veurne wrote about 'les fripiers... qui vendent des habits et hardes pour les gens de la campaigne et le petit peuple' (ARA, *RvS*, 2020, 15 june 1725). For several towns, the number of second-hand dealers seems to be an indication for the intensity of the relations of the town with its hinterland. In Bruges in 1748 only eight, and in 1784 twenty-seven second-hand dealers were counted (0.2 and 0.8 per 1000 inhabitants). This low number is not really surprising. The population density in the countryside surrounding the town was rather low, particularly in the polders to the north of the town. In the town of Mechelen, the number of second-hand dealers decreased from 40 in 1740 to 30 in 1770 (2 and 1.4 per 1000 inhabitants). They complained that selling second hand clothing was not enough to survive, and just as their colleagues in Antwerp, they had to be dependent on their monopoly on public sales. At the same time a lot of lamentations were heard in Mechelen about the growth of shops in the countryside, which limited the outlets of local artisans and shopkeepers (ARA, *GR OR*, 1158 B, 23 September 1768, 9 November 1770, 10 August 1771). In the small industrial town of Lier, near the poor Campine area, only seven second-hand dealers were counted in 1796 (0.7 per 1000 inhabitants).

In smaller Flemish towns, in the census of 1796, second-hand dealers were only registered in Aalst (13), Tielt (7), Geraardsbergen (6), Lokeren (4), Oudenaarde (3) and Veurne (1). All these towns (with the exception of Veurne) were situated in densely populated proto-industrial areas (191.4 inhabitants per square km around Aalst, 207 around Geraardbergen, 180 around Oudenaarde, 171 near Tielt, 144 around Lokeren and 61 in the vicinity of Veurne). For these smaller centres, however, the number of second-hand dealers is often hard to specify, as tailors and second-hand dealers often combined the two occupations (ARA, *RvS*, 2020, 11 July 1716, 21 October 1716, 23 November 1723, 15 June 1725). Anyway, the number of tailors was also particularly high in Geraardsbergen and Oudenaarde (Jaspers and Stevens, 1985; Gyssels and Verstraeten, 1986). A remarkably high number of second-hand dealers were registered in Louvain. Their number rose from 60 in 1760 to 113 in 1794 (3.6 to 5.6 per 1000 inhabitants), although population density in the area around Louvain only rose from 41.7 to 67.4 inhabitants per square km (calculation based on Klep, 1981). The exceptional boom of Louvain's second-hand dealers can probably be related to agricultural growth in the Walloon-Brabantine area, and to the central place of Louvain in the grain trade. Louvain's grain market grew strongly after the construction of the brick road to Namur in the 1750s. The revenues of a tax on the grain trade levied at Louvain's city walls doubled between 1760 and 1788. This intensification of the contacts between town and countryside also explains a few typical deviations for Louvain. For example, it was the only town in which 'tailors for peasants' are registered in the censuses (Blondé, 1999). Also, in 1758, the second-hand dealers from Louvain obtained official permission to sell new, ready made garments, which was forbidden in Antwerp (Meulemans, 1958). The rise in purchasing power in the countryside due to agricultural growth in the Walloon-Brabantine area may also explain the rise in second-hand dealers in Nivelles (from 1 in 1755 to 9 in 1796, or 0.1 and 1.4 per 1000 inhabitants). It may also explain the large-scale activities of peddler networks in southern Brabant and northern Hainaut (Deceulaer, 1998).

VI. International comparison: France, England and the Dutch Republic

In other countries, second-hand dealers also seem to have sold their wares in the countryside. The author of a French *mémoire* from 1763 argued about the rural consumption of clothing: 'la plus grande partie de nos paysans achètent chez les fripiers à prix modique et dont ils se contentent' (cited in Pellegrin, 1986: 286). Peasants who visited the 'Halles' in Paris to sell their grain, flour or butter, were awaited by second-hand dealers, who tried to sell them old and new clothing. In early eighteenth-century Lille, some 1000 second-hand dealers were said to be active (Braudel, 1979). Earlier, we saw that the Lille and Artois region had the highest population density in France. Furthermore, Lille was the centre of a proto-industrial region. From the 1680s and 1690s, rural industry in the region grew strongly, and from 1696 it was customary for rural weavers to sell their pieces in Lille (Craeybeckx, 1976; Bossegna, 1988).

For England, preliminary figures by Beverly Lemire show that second-hand dealers were far more widespread in the agricultural and commercial south than in the industrial north (figures per county in Lemire, 1991).

Figure 11.3 High, average and low or unknown concentration of second-hand dealers in 18th century England

Source: based on Lemire, 1991.

Although population density in Lancashire and Yorkshire more than doubled the figures from the south, the clothing trades were less developed in the north of England. In this region, the share of less market-oriented small farmers and leaseholders was more important than in the South. Furthermore, the export industries of the industrial north were based on low wages which limited the growth of a service sector and a consumer goods industry (Hudson, 1992).

The Dutch Republic forms an interesting exception. The Dutch second-hand dealers have been portrayed as small peddlers without an urban base (du Mortier, 1991). In only four towns, second-hand dealers were organized in guilds from the late middle ages to the late eighteenth century (Bergen op Zoom, Dordrecht, Middelburg, Utrecht). In 's Gravenhage, a second-hand dealers guild was founded (probably) in the early seventeenth century, and in Haarlem and 's-Hertogenbosch in the eighteenth century (data from the database of the IISG-Amsterdam). More research is needed on the Dutch second-hand dealers to analyze their exceptional position (but see Panhuysen, 2000). Looking at the evidence from the angle of the interaction between town and countryside, however, a hypothesis can be built. The four mentioned towns were important centers of regional trade, and nodal points for town-countryside contacts. The fact that second-hand dealers were less organized, (and probably less numerous or prosperous) in other Dutch cities than in the Southern Netherlands, possibly points to a different interaction between town and countryside. Extensive research has stressed the strongly developed professional differentiation of the highly commercialized Dutch countryside in the eighteenth century. At least for simple goods as clothing or shoes, it was to a large extent self-supporting in the eighteenth century (probably already from the seventeenth century) (De Vries and Van der Woude, 1997). This may partially explain the lower numbers of Dutch second-hand dealers or other urban artisans offering simple goods, or may even be an element explaining the weaker position of certain urban 'artisan entrepreneurs' in the Dutch Republic (as found by Lis and Soly, 1997). Obviously, other elements should also be taken into account in this discussion (economic policy, position of merchants, institutional factors, etc.).

VII. Conclusion

The size and composition of urban trades making or selling such simple goods as second-hand clothing, or shoes was clearly influenced by the nature of the relations between town and countryside. The purchasing power of the surrounding countryside (determined by population density, agrarian structures, rents, proto-industrialization, etc.) and the extent to which this was spent in the towns (influenced by urban markets, size of villages, peddling-networks) had an important influence on the development of some urban trades.

Not one but several models of town-countryside interaction can be sketched. For the three towns, there were also major differences in historical evolution. A growth in countryside shops and rural artisans probably took place everywhere in Western Europe, but this does not preclude differences in the timing and the nature of its effects for urban trades. In Antwerp, a loss of rural markets for urban artisans was probably already felt from the second half of the seventeenth century onwards. The strong growth of a proto-industrialized countryside around Ghent enlarged the market for urban artisans in the first half of the eighteenth century, but this market was eroded in the second half of the eighteenth century, with living standards declining and the shift of the linen market to smaller centers. For Brussels, Louvain, and Nivelles, the town-countryside relations remained stable or intensified due to the commercialisation of agriculture and the improvement of roads.

The number and social positions of artisans offering simple goods were affected by these evolutions. The second-hand dealers can probably function as an indicator for the relations between town and countryside. The decline (Ghent), stabilization (Brussels) or rise (Louvain, Nivelles) in their numbers or social positions was influenced by the evolution of their access to regional, rural markets.

The effects of the 'new urbanisation' or 'urbanisation from below' on larger cities were therefore not unequivocal. There was no *general* deterioration of large town – countryside relations. The consequences on the urban occupational structure of large towns were strongly differentiated. In this respect, a distinction must be made between the rank-size of a town on the one hand and its function as a central place for the surrounding countryside on the other. The fate of the three cities shows that there is no linear connection between these two.

These conclusions may have certain implications, which are open for debate and further research. First, the differentiated access to rural markets clearly influenced the opportunities for urban artisan entrepreneurs. A possible deterioration in the social positions of urban artisans offering simple goods (e.g. the Ghent second-hand dealers) needs not necessarily be explained by an extension of the putting-out system controlled by merchants or large masters. The loss of rural markets to competitors in the countryside was probably another (more important?) factor (compare McIntosh, 1997). The growth of a rural service sector could have serious implications for urban trades.

Second, the strength of certain urban industrial entrepreneurs (second-hand-dealers, hatters, shoemakers, etc.) in different countries may be partially influenced by specific town-country relations, although we must repeat that this paper has not dealt with the export industries. The different evolution in town-country relations between the Northern and Southern Netherlands in the eighteenth century, for example, may possibly have influenced the different historical trajectories of the urban industries of both countries.

Bibliography

Manuscript sources[1]

Algemeen Rijksarchief (ARA), Brussels, *Geheime Raad (GR) Oostenrijkse Periode (OR)*, 1158.

Algemeen Rijksarchief (ARA), Brussels, *Raad van State (RvS)*, 2020.

Stadsarchief Antwerpen (SAA), Antwerp, *Privelegekamer (PK)*, 834.

Stadsarchief Gent (SAG), Ghent, *Familiefonds handboeken*, 433.

Stadsarchief Gent (SAG), Ghent, Series 191, 199.

Printed and secondary sources

Barraclough, G. (ed.) (1988) *The Times Atlas of World History*, London.

Bastin, J. (1967) 'De Gentse lijnwaadmarkt en linnenhandel in de XVIIde eeuw', *Handelingen van de Maatschappij voor Geschiedenis en Oudheidkunde te Gent*, new series, 21, pp. 131–162.

Belder, J. de (1974) *Elementen van sociale identificatie van de Antwerpse bevolking op het einde van de 18de eeuw. Een kwantitatieve studie*, Ghent. Unpublished doctorate thesis University of Ghent.

Billen, C. (1987) 'Een ingebeelde landbouwrevolutie?', in H. Hasquin (ed.), *Oostenrijks België, 1713–1794. De Zuidelijke Nederlanden onder de Oostenrijkse Habsburgers*, Brussels, pp. 95–120.

Blondé, B. (1999) *Een economie met verschillende snelheden. Ongelijkheden in de opbouw en de ontwikkeling van het Brabants stedelijk netwerk (ca 1750 –ca 1790)*, Brussels.

Bossegna, G. (1988) 'Protecting Merchants: Guilds and Commercial Capitalism in Eighteenth-Century France', *French Historical Studies*, 15, pp. 693–703.

Braudel, F. (1979) *Civilisation matérielle, Economie et Capitalisme XVe–XVIIIe siècle, II, Les jeux de l'échange*, Paris.

Cocula, A.M. (1987) 'Un critère qualitatif et quantitatif au XVIIIe siècle: les métiers urbains', in J.P. Poussou (ed.), *Les petites villes du Moyen Age à nos jours*, Paris, pp.161–164.

Cosemans, A. (1966) *Bijdrage tot de demografische en sociale geschiedenis van de stad Brussel, 1796–1846*, Brussels.

Craeybeckx, J. (1962) 'Les industries d'exportation dans les villes flamandes au XVIIe siècle particulièrement à Gand et à Bruges', in *Studi in onore di Amintore Fanfani*, vol. 4, Milan, pp. 413–468.

Database 'Gilden', Internationaal Instituut voor Sociale Geschiedenis (IISG), Amsterdam.

Deceulaer, H. (1998a) 'Guildsmen, Entrepreneurs and Market-Segments. The case of the Garment Trades in Antwerp and Ghent (Sixteenth to Eighteenth Centuries)', *International Review of Social History*, 43, pp. 1–29.

[1] Abbreviations: ARA = Algemeen Rijksarchief; GR = Geheime Raad; OR = Oostenrijkse Periode; PK = Privilegekamer; SAA = Stadsarchief Antwerpen; SAG = Stadsarchief Gent.

Deceulaer, H. (1998b) *Pluriforme patronen en een verschillende snit. Sociaal-economische, institutionele en culturele transformaties in de kledingsector in Antwerpen, Brussel en Gent, ca. 1585–ca. 1800*, Brussels. Unpublished thesis University of Brussels (VUB).

Deceulaer, H. (forthcoming) 'Entrepreneurs in the Guilds: Ready To Wear Clothing and Subcontracting in late 16th and early 17th century Antwerp', *Textile History*.

Dejongh, G. (1991) *Goederen en beheer van de abdij van Tongerlo in de achttiende eeuw*, Louvain. Unpublished M.A. thesis University of Louvain (KUL).

Dejongh, G. (1999) 'New estimates of land productivity in Belgium', *The Agricultural History Review*, 47, pp. 7–28.

Dhondt L. (1995) 'Plattelandslijnwaad en stadskatoen tegen en even na 1800. De organisatie van een oude en van een nieuwe industrie. Een memorie uit 1808 en haar relevantie', *Handelingen van de Geschied- en Oudheidkundige Kring van Oudenaarde*, 32, pp. 89–149.

Dickschen, S. (1995) 'De Antwerpse brouwersnatie en de dorpsbrouwers in de 17de en 18de eeuw', *Bijdragen tot de Geschiedenis*, 78, pp. 199–213.

Dupâquier, J. (1988) 'La peuplade', in J. Dupâquier [et al.] (eds), *Histoire de la population française, 2. De la Renaissance à 1789*, Paris, pp. 68–80.

Gyssels, C. and Straeten, L. van der (1986) *Bevolking, arbeid en tewerkstelling in West-Vlaanderen (1796–1815)*, Ghent.

Hannes, J. and Vanderpijpen W. (1973) 'Teeltplan, productie en productiekosten. De landbouw in enkele gemeenten van de provincies Antwerpen en Oost-Vlaanderen', *Belgisch Tijdschrift voor Nieuwste Geschiedenis*, 4, pp. 67–108.

Hohenberg, P. and Lees L.H. (1985) *The Making of Urban Europe, 1000–1950*, Cambridge (Mass.)/London.

Honacker, K. van (1994) 'De politieke cultuur van de Brusselse ambachten. Conservatisme, corporatisme of opportunisme?', in C. Lis and H. Soly (eds), *Werken volgens de regels. Ambachten in Brabant en Vlaanderen, 1500–1800*, Brussels, pp. 179–228.

Hudson, P. (1992) *The Industrial Revolution*, London.

Jaspers, L. and Stevens C. (1985) *Arbeid en tewerkstelling in Oost-Vlaanderen op het einde van het Ancien Régime*, Ghent.

Klep, P.M.M. (1981) *Bevolking en arbeid in transformatie. Een onderzoek naar de ontwikkelingen in Brabant, 1700–1900*, Nijmegen.

Kriedte, P. (1983) *Peasants, Landlords and Merchant Capitalists. Europe and the World Economy, 1500–1800*, London.

Leenders, G. (1983) 'De beroepsstructuur op het platteland tussen Antwerpen en Brussel (1702–1846)', in J. Craeybeckx and F. Daelemans (eds), *Bijdragen tot de Geschiedenis van Vlaanderen en Brabant. Sociaal en Economisch*, Brussels, pp. 167–228.

Lemire, B. (1991) 'Peddling fashion: Salesmen, Pawnbrokers, Tailors, Thieves and the Second-hand Clothes Trade in England, c. 1700–1800', *Textile History*, 22, pp. 67–82.

Lis, C. and Soly, H. (1997) 'Different Paths of Development. Capitalism in the Northern and Southern Netherlands during the Late Middle Ages and the Early Modern Period', *Review*, 20, pp. 211–242.

Meulemans, A. (1957) 'Leuvense ambachten, III, De Oudkleerkopers', *Eigen schoon en de Brabander*, 40, pp. 60–68, 134–142, 185–194, 301–314, 365–375.

McIntosh, T. (1997) *Urban Decline in Early Modern Germany. Schwäbisch Hall and its Region, 1650–1750*, Chapel Hill/London.

Mortier B.M. du (1991) 'Tweedehandskleding in de zeventiende eeuw', *Textielhistorische Bijdragen*, 31, pp. 39–59.

Panhuysen, B. (2000), *Maatwerk. Kleermakers, naaisters, oudkleerkopers en de gilden (1500–1800)*, Amsterdam.

Pellegrin, N. (1986) 'Chemises et chiffons. Le vieux et le neuf en Poitou et Limousin, XVIIIe–XIXe siècles', *Ethnologie Française*, 16, pp. 283–294.

Peuter, R. de (1999), *Brussel in de achttiende eeuw. Sociaal-economische structuren en ontwikkelingen in een regionale hoofdstad*, Brussels.

Prevenier, W., Sosson, J.P., Boone M. [et al.] (1992) 'Le réseau urbain en Flandre (XIIIe–XIXe siècle): composantes et dynamiques', in *Het stedelijk netwerk in België in historisch perspectief (1350–1850). Een statistische en dynamische benadering. Handelingen*, Brussels, pp.157–200.

Schelstraete, C., Kintaert, H. and De Ruyck, H. (1984), *Het einde van de onveranderlijkheid. Arbeid, bezit en woonomstandigheden in het land van Nevele tijdens de 17de en 18de eeuw*, Nevele.

Smekens, F. (s.d.) 'Schets van aard en betekenis der Antwerpsche nijverheid onder het Oostenrijks bewind', *Verzamelde Geschriften Frans Smekens*, s.l., pp. 49–67.

Stabel, P. (1995) 'De-urbanisation and Urban Decline in Flanders from 1500 to 1800: The Desintegration of an Urban System?', in D. McCabe (ed.), *Eurocit. European Urbanisation, Social Structure and Problems between the Eighteenth and Twentieth Century*, Leicester, pp. 87–108.

Thijs, A.K.L. (1986) 'The River Scheldt, closed for two centuries, 1585–1790', in F. Suykens [et al.] (eds), *Antwerp. A Port for all seasons*, Antwerp, pp. 169–273.

Uytven, R. van (1972) 'Peiling naar de beroepsstructuur op het Brabantse platteland omstreeks 1755', *Bijdragen tot de Geschiedenis*, 55, pp.172–203.

Uytven, R. van (1992) 'Brabantse en Antwerpse centrale plaatsen (14de–19de eeuw)', in *Het stedelijk netwerk in België in historisch perspectief (1350–1850). Een statistische en dynamische benadering. 15de Internationaal Colloquium, 4–6 september 1990. Handelingen*, Brussels, pp. 29–79.

Vandenbroeke, C. (1984) *Sociale geschiedenis van het Vlaamse volk*, Louvain.

Vandenbroeke, C. (1996), 'Proto-industry in Flanders: a critical review', in S.C. Ogilvie and M. Cerman (eds), *European Proto-industrialisation*, Cambridge, pp. 102–117.

Vannopen, H. (ed.) (1994) *Streekdrachten in onze gewesten. Antwerpen–Brabant–Limburg–Oost-Vlaanderen–West-Vlaanderen*, Ghent.

Vries, J. de (1975) 'Peasant Demand Patterns and Economic Development, 1550–1750', in W.N. Parker and E.L. Jones (eds), *European Peasants and their Markets. Essays in Agrarian Economic History*, Princeton, pp. 205–266.

Vries J. de (1984) *European Urbanisation, 1500–1800*, London.

Vries J. de (1994) 'The Industrial Revolution and the Industrious Revolution', *Journal of Economic History*, 54, pp. 249–270.

Vries, J. de (1999) 'Great Expectations. Early Modern History and the Social Sciences', *Review*, 22, pp. 121–149.

Vries J. de and Woude, A. van der (1997) *The First Modern Economy: Success, Failure and Perseverance of the Dutch Economy*, Cambridge.

12 The city and the forest: a privileged relationship? Some remarks on the case of the Soignes Forest, 16th–18th centuries

Sylvie LEFÈBVRE, University of Brussels – ULB

I. Introduction

A study of forestry-related issues in the Soignes Forest has allowed us to highlight the privileged relationships linking it to the city of Brussels. This paper does not seek to offer a systematic or statistical overview of the labour market conditioned by this relationship; the larger study, conducted in an altogether different perspective, does not contain that kind of data.[1] I would rather share with the readers some remarks on the work performed in the forest and the trade resulting from it; and thus draw the readers' attention to a number of issues ignored by the economic history of our regions. With this view in mind, I shall cast a light on hitherto unknown aspects of this type of activity, and notably on the exchanges in the Soignes Forest between the 16th and the 18th century. It will be observed that the large forest, characterised by its homogeneous crop of beech trees on the one hand and by its proximity to the capital on the other, offered considerable possibilities for labour and trade.

II. The city's needs in wood

The Soignes Forest, sprawling at the outskirts of Brussels, has always stood in total interaction with the city. Even today, it is still one of the favourite leisure spots for many Brussels citizens, who take pride in its beech groves and enjoy the beautiful forest walks. But under the Ancien Régime, the city and the forest were linked by stronger ties, as the life of all citizens, regardless of status or wealth, was affected by the forest. Brussels was a great consumer of wood, whether for heating, building, industry or the smaller trades. To cater for this demand the wood market offered a great variety of wood products: timber, splintwood and fuelwood in all forms and shapes: faggots, charcoal, timber of different species 'kricken' and 'spoelen'.[2]

At the time, wood was an inherent part of each individual's life. The citizens required wood for heating and cooking, to fuel their ovens and boilers, but also to manufacture their tools or luxury items. In the mid-18th century, Brussels (intra muros) counted a

[1] These remarks are part of a study of forestry management and operation in the Soignes Forest from the 16th to the 18th century.

[2] Each species was chosen for its energetic qualities. Thus, for example, the Brussels bakers preferred to work with alderwood charcoal (AGR, *CF*, 1633). The term designates small, cheap charcoal widely available on the Brussels market. The terms *spoelen*, *squettes* or *esclats* designate cull, scraps and other stumpwood.

Figure 12.1 Map of Brussels and the Forest of Soignes

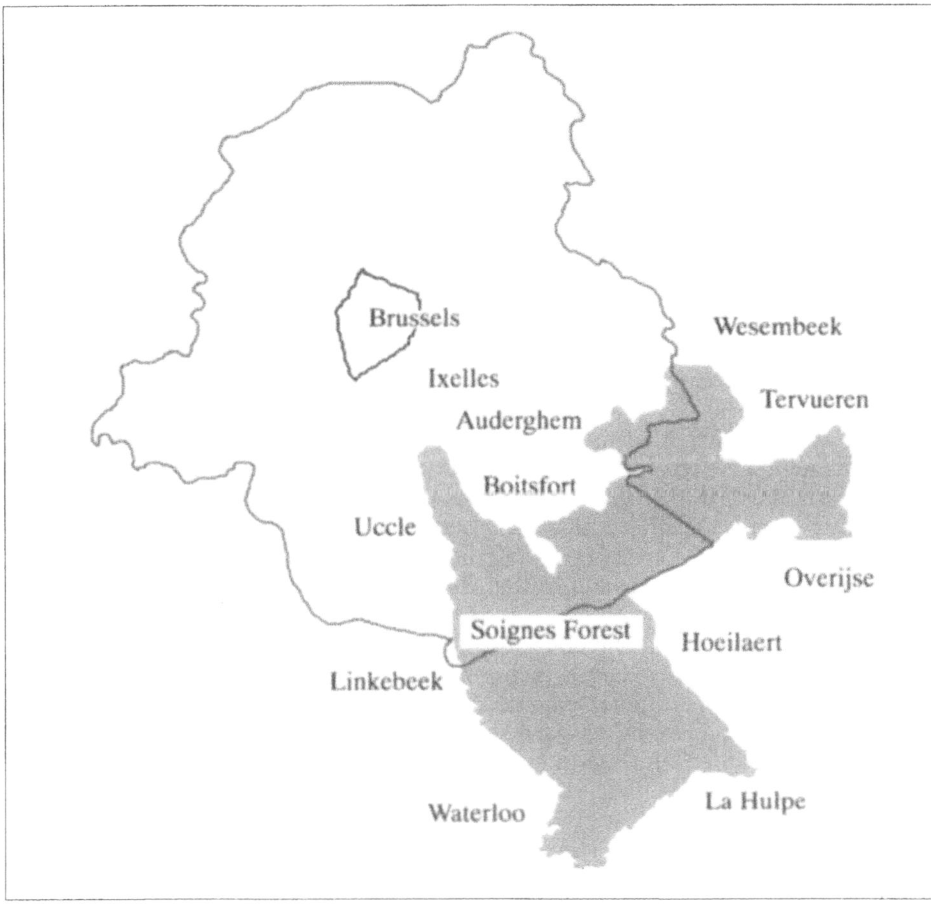

little less than 58,000 inhabitants, to which one may add some 15,000 more to include the population of contiguous villages which were eventually to be absorbed into the larger Brussels area (Hasquin, 1977: 17–18). Although the population figure may seem low in comparison to that of other European capitals,[3] Brussels was the city with the largest population in the Austrian Netherlands. Thanks to its privileged situation, the Soignes Forest was quite naturally poised to be an ideal source of wood for the city.

For fuel, the city used wood, especially charcoal, which was lighter to carry, burnt better and yielded better heat. But charcoal-burning destroyed the forest, as the manufacturing of 1 kg of charcoal required about 10 kg of wood. As early as the 17th century, coal was already used as more than a secondary source of fuel (Hasquin, 1970: 514–519), but its

[3] London, for example, counted 900,000 inhabitants at the time, and Paris 550,800 (Hasquin, 1977: 26).

general use was still slowed down by various obstacles. Thus, prohibitive customs rights jeopardised the import of coal for the use of lime-burners and brick-bakers (AGR, *AF*, 349, fol. 255–257; AGR, *CC*, reg. 510, fol. 101 vi–107), who would gladly have fuelled their kilns with coal. On the other hand, the corporative structure of some trades also hampered its introduction (Goblet d'Alviella, 1927: I, 441). Thus, the use of coal in industries like glassmaking or metallurgy did not yield the expected results. In the 16th and 17th centuries, the master glassmakers of Brussels and its suburbs who manufactured window-panes, bottles or fine crystalware refused to use coal, arguing that its flames damaged the glass (Chambon, 1955: 105; Engen, 1989: 151–163). Consequently, when the local authorities took steps to encourage the use of coal in small industries with a view to preserving the forest, they were faced with unexpected reactions. The order of December 5, 1623 (*Placcaeten van Brabant*: v.II, 146), which prohibited the use of wood by brewers and brick-kiln owners triggered a violent protest by brewers, who felt that coal gave their beer 'a bad taste and smell'. Certain kilns, ovens and forges ceased their activity for several years rather than to use coal (AGR, *AF*, 351/2, fol. 70).

Thus, wood was to remain the fuel most widely used by the inhabitants, the court and numerous religious communities established in town and outside, sometimes even in the middle of the forest.[4] To this use of firewood for everyday purposes the consumption of wood by small industries and trades in town and on its outskirts must be added: bakers and brewers, metalworkers (blacksmiths, smelters and casters, coppersmiths and boilermakers), brick-bakers and lime-burners.[5]

Wood was also a cheap and convenient construction material, widely used for the building and maintenance of houses, public buildings and fortifications (frames, shingles, floorboards, beams, stairs, poles, wharves, platforms, fences and boarding). The Soignes Forest provided wood for bridge- and shipbuilding, for the maintenance of roads and streets (ruts were filled with logs) and to lay the wooden foundations for cobbled streets (Rochette, 1972: 338, 341). To this list must be added the wood used in the manufacturing of furniture for dwellings and shops (ordinary furniture, but also stalls, benches and butchers' blocks) and luxury items like Spanish gilt-leather chairs or the famous coaches built by Jean Simons for the European courts and aristocracy. Between 1770 and 1790, Simons is reported to have exported 600 glass-paned coaches (Stengers, 1979: 120–121).

It is difficult to try and assess the capital's total consumption for the period studied; not only because of the wide variety of uses made of wood, but also because historians do not have any precise data at their disposal. Several studies have been made of the different Brussels corporations, but these do not account for their consumption either of raw materials or of fuel. Moreover, many craftsmen and small industries moved out of the city walls during the 18th century; some for economic reasons (lower land prices), some to meet demands of public salubrity, and some to escape from the grip of the cor-

[4] Notably, the Cambre Abbey, the Capucine Convent of Tervueren and the priories of Val-Duchesse, Groenendael, Rouge-Cloître, Sept-Fontaines and Ter Cluysen (*La Forêt*, 1987: 159–256).

[5] The full list of trades dependent on wood for their fuel inside and outside town cannot be given here, but can be found in Vernier, 1965: 328–329 and 415; Stengers, 1979: 120–122; Van Honacker, 1994: 183–185.

porations (Vernier, 1965: 433). As a consequence, these do not appear on the official lists and make objective assessment even more difficult. Approaching the issue from the other side, and studying the annual sales of plots of woodland does not yield any more satisfying results. Sales records are vague and incomplete (AGR, *FB*, 99–112), and the plots that are recorded fail to mention the species of wood growing on it, and thus jeopardise any systematic study of the destination to which the wood from the Soignes Forest was affected.

At the present stage of my investigation, I have therefore limited my ambitions to highlighting the importance of wood, a material all too often ignored in the accounts of our local historians.

III. The forest as a source of human activity

As pointed out, the Soignes Forest provided the craftsmen of the city and the adjacent villages both with raw material and with fuel to pursue their production: whether coach-builders, glass-makers, bakers, tanners, woodworkers, turners, chair-makers or even broom-makers, their needs for wood were multifarious. They obtained their wood from merchants, or applied to the local authorities for permits to go to the forest themselves to cut the trees required by their art, as is shown by the many applications filed with the authorities.[6]

The forest also offered employment to a multitude of people. These vocational activities can conveniently be classified into two major categories:

- on the one hand, officers, foresters, wardens and estate workers, that is, the whole forestry staff which performed daily rounds for the supervision and maintenance of the forest;
- on the other hand, workers involved in the various wood-trades, i.e. the loggers, lumberjacks, sawyers, cleavers, charcoal-burners, skidders, haulers and local wood merchants, all making a living out of the annual fellages organised by the local authorities.

III.1. Activities related to forest supervision and maintenance

Ever since the Middle Ages, the sheer size of the national forest estate has required the setting up of an important legal and administrative machinery. The officers in charge of forestry development and hunting held a privileged position in the institutional hierarchy of the Brabant Duchy, as the Soignes Forest represented a considerable source of revenue to the successive sovereigns.[7] Every year, fellages were organised for commercial purposes on those parcels whose revolution had come full circle. In addition to these 'ordinary' fellings, extraordinary fellages were carried out according to the needs of the authorities, of the army, or large building projects.[8]

---

[6] For instance, in the second half of the 16th c., cf. AGR, *CACC*, 2632.

[7] 'The revenues from woods and forests have been entered in the first column of receipts because these revenues constitute the most numerous and precious class of sources of income'. *Description des finances belgiques,* 1781, AGR, *CAPB*, 902, fol. 84–87.

[8] Such as, for instance, the reconstruction of the city centre after the bombing by the Maréchal de Villeroi in August 1695, or the construction of the new Tervueren Castle in 1749, both of which required important supplies of timber.

The organisation of these fellages, the supervision of the forest, the repression of forestry crimes and misdemeanours kept several officers active; among these, the master gamekeeper, the master venerer, the forestmaster or *wautmaître* and his lieutenant, the keeper of the marking-hammer, the measurer, the record-keeper, etc. All these officers and other members of the forest administration and jurisdiction were wealthy and educated men,[9] born in the city's aristocracy. Their respective activities have already been studied and described in great depth (Goblet d'Alviella, 1927: II, 21–33; Smolar-Meynart, 1991) and need not retain our attention. The activities of the subordinate staff members, however, are less well known and may conveniently be dealt with here.

The forest administration employed forest rangers and workmen, who worked within the forest area on a daily basis to fulfil supervision and maintenance tasks.

III.2. The forest rangers

The forest rangers acted as wardens supervising the forest estate. Their activity was varied, and involved responsibilities like recording offences, fining delinquents, assisting in measurements and fellings, marking trees for cutting, etc. These foresters, men of humble condition, usually were foresters from father to son; the names of the same families recur from the 16th until the late 18th century, across the reigns of successive rulers and notwithstanding different forms of government. An epitome of this continuity is the Vanderlinden family, which gave birth to two forestmasters in the 16th century,[10] and whose name is still to be found on the lists of foresters two centuries later. By the same token, under the French occupation, the lists of the forestry staff employed by the Republic display the same names as those of the early 18th century (AGR, *PD*, 496). Apart from those evicted from their charges because of old age, foresters would keep fulfilling their function for long stretches of time, some of them for as much as fifty years of service (Goblet d'Alviella, 1927: II, 159; Pierron, s.d.: II, 58).

These men would be hired for their skill as well as for their knowledge of the forest, as the authorities sought to employ people familiar with forest life, but also men in good physical condition to face the efforts and hardships of forest labour. When Cornelius Van Haelen was appointed in 1716, the nomination read: 'He is an able-bodied man, of sufficient health and strength to resist fatigue, and born in the forest, where he has long been a wood merchant, and thus familiar with its places and inhabitants, and acquainted with such offences as are or may be committed therein' (AGR, *AF*, 523–524).

With time, these rangers increasingly settled at the edge of the forest, in villages contiguous to their sphere of activity. From Emperor Charles V onwards, they were obliged, for the sake of efficiency, to spread their dwellings over the villages of La Hulpe, Hoeilaert, Tervueren, Duysburg, Waterloo, Linkebeek, Uccle, Boendael, Auderghem, Boitsfort, Ixelles and Brussels (Smolar-Meynaert, 1991: 118 ff). They were assigned well-defined sectors close to their homes, where proximity to the forest gave them more convenient

[9] They were held to be trained in forestry legislation.

[10] Philippe Vander Linden became forestmaster on March 20, 1569 and was succeeded by his son Ferdinand a year later, on July 29, 1570 (Pierron, s.d.: II, 29).

and faster access to the scene of an offence; but their number was not sufficient to cover all of the wooded area, and this left ample room for all kinds of offences. From 1548 onwards, there were 14 wardens in all, only two of whom rode horses. The figure was to vary very little. In the late 18th century, there were 19 foresters on foot, i.e. one per sector, assisted by 4 extras and 6 mounted wardens (Goblet d'Alviella, 1927: II, 159); a number altogether insufficient in view of the increasing insecurity and banditry. By virtue of its proximity to the city, the Soignes Forest was an area particularly exposed to all kinds of criminality. Every day, the forest would be entered by residents causing damage not only by acts of vandalism, theft or arson, but also by careless thoroughfare or under the cover of other users' rights.[11]

Only under the French government did an administrative report of the Dyle Department envisage a possible increase in the number of wardens in the Soignes Forest (AGR, *PD*, 469). On the 7th Floréal of the year VIII, the Inspector of Forest Administration called for the nomination of 78 rangers on foot, divided into 12 six-man brigades, and 6 mounted rangers. Each mounted ranger was put in charge of an area of 3000 ha of woodland with the assistance of 2 brigades of rangers on foot. This means that each brigade must supervise 1500 ha, which amounts to a 250-ha surface to be invigilated by each single ranger. It is easy to see how under those conditions, it was a daunting task to enforce law and order in the forest while at the same time fulfilling other, increasingly numerous, tasks related to the stocking and regeneration of the forest. The wardens, responsible for too large an area of jurisdiction, were obliged to cover long distances on foot, often hampered by bad weather and poor road conditions; as a consequence, they often arrived too late at the scene of an offence.

Although the forest wardens spent most of their time in the forest, they nevertheless maintained frequent contacts with the city, where they would often practise an extra trade. As they had difficulty subsisting on their meagre earnings, they frequently held another job despite the prohibition to do so stipulated in their statutes and regulations. In the city, they would be active as barbers or wood-merchants,[12] but also as crofters or keepers of woodside inns (Pierron, s.d.: II, 66–70). These side-activities not infrequently caused them to neglect their responsibilities. Some of them would condone offences against payment, others would engage in theft themselves. The Forestry Archives, kept at the General Archives of the Kingdom, abound in court cases implicating forest wardens.

Of course, not all rangers went to such extremes; but most of them did engage in more than one lucrative activity, and not infrequently, it can be observed that the extra workload exhausted the men and made them less efficient in their daytime tasks. Thus a sergeant, William Ficquart, apologised to his forestmaster that he no longer had 'the force and energy he used to have' and that he could no longer do 'tiresome work' because he was forced to spend too much time 'tilling the earth and ploughing the fields' in order to ensure his family's subsistence (AGR, *AF*, 369).

---

[11] Notably pasture and grazing rights, which caused little damage, but which allowed unscrupulous people to gain access to the forest (Lefebvre, 1997: 41). On the diversity of users' rights, see Smolar-Meynaert, 1991.

[12] These merchants would buy small batches with a view to selling them at a profit.

Some of the rangers were actually bold enough to accumulate more than two activities. Sander Pierron (s.d.: II, 58) relates the case of an individual who, in addition to his job as a forester, was or had been a wood-merchant, a contractor for forest road repairs and revenue service buildings, a church warden at Waterloo, a farmer at the Vivier d'Oie Gate and, last but not least, keeper of an inn along Waterloo road! Being an innkeeper was a popular extra job with many foresters, even if these ale-houses were frequently the scene of fights between foresters and peasants. And it was not rare for these innkeepers to attract their 'colleagues', wardens and other forest hands for 'a drink or two with their friends', thus keeping them away from their actual responsibilities. The authorities censured this practice on the grounds of an ordnance of July 10, 1628, which prohibited certain classes of officers 'to keep an inn or sell liquor', but failed to mention forest rangers. On other occasions, the Brabant Council condoned the practice, considering that the rangers' income was insufficient to provide for a living without some kind of parallel activity. Rangers could conveniently circumvent the ordnance by keeping the inn under their wife's name (Pierron, s.d.: II, 54–55), but until the late 18th century, and even later, court sentences condemning the practice were frequent[13] and sometimes harsh, as when a forest ranger was enjoined to forsake his inn at the Vert Chasseur within 24 hours, on pain of being dismissed from his charge as a forester.[14]

III.3. The forest workmen

The maintenance of the forest required a considerable workforce. The Soignes Forest had at its disposal no more than 8 sworn-in workers, lumberjacks assigned to forestry tasks like felling trees, cutting wood or binding faggots. They were also entitled to arrest delinquents. While their number increased during the 18th century, their charge was totally cancelled as an effect of the reforms later in the century. As the lumbermen were underpaid and demotivated, they were frequently found guilty of negligence and other abuses, and the forest authorities deemed preferable to pay piecework rates[15] for separate jobs to ordinary workmen who could be fired if they were suspected of incompetence or dishonesty.

It is not until 1760 or so that the government developed an awareness to the fact that the forest as a resource called for careful *management* rather than inconsiderate *consumption*.[16] The forest estate was badly damaged, and measures had to be taken to ensure its conservation and regeneration if the future supply of wood was to be guaranteed. For the first time ever, the forest authorities initiated a reforestation programme supported

[13] The General Archives of the Kingdom contain the minutes of trials of foresters arrested for selling ale or keeping ale-houses (AGR, *OFB*, 891, 928).

[14] The chairman of the Chamber of Revenue (la Chambre des comptes) specified on September 1783 that 'Wardens and other men at the service of His Majesty in the Soignes Forest are formally prohibited [to hold outside jobs] by virtue of a specific clause inserted in their contracts or commissions. This is all the easier to understand as it is in the unquestionable interest of the conservation of His Majesty's woods that his foresters should engage in no other vocational activity which might commit them to attitudes and behaviors susceptible to offend their fellow citizens' (AGR, *OFB*, 928/1, nr. 9737).

[15] i.e. on the basis of the number of faggots bound or ropes wound.

[16] The terms [in the French original] are borrowed from M. Faure (1991: 81).

by a marked increase in means. The budget tripled between 1760 and 1786, and 36,000 florins were henceforth allotted to the revegetation of the Soignes Forest. The programme entailed a great many structural changes as well. Within the new perspective of rational management, the forest administration supplied its staff with detailed guidelines on how to implement the planting programme. Nothing was left to chance: the programme took into account the soil type and the orientation of each plot to be replanted, and sought to work with competent staff. In order to exert better control over the operations, in 1774 the forest was divided into three sectors, each assigned to one of the three main forest officers, i.e. the Brussels estate tax collector, the forestmaster and his lieutenant.[17]

This reforestation programme was to give rise to a certain amount of specialisation in forestry, as its various stages called for new procedures like field nurseries or cutting and layering techniques. These new techniques allowed a further diversification of the forestry tasks and, consequently, the enlistment of more subordinate staff assigned to plantation tasks; and notably, an increase in the female workforce, hired for seed-gathering or for hoeing and weeding between the saplings. In order to obtain satisfactory results, the transportation and planting of seedlings must be performed carefully. On the whole, all the stages in the process called for increased skill and precision, and the performance of those tasks demanded a competent staff with increasingly specific assignments. As a consequence, the idea of worker training emerged (Lefebvre, 1992–1993: 67–69), and the forestmaster's lieutenant of l'Escaille even offered to instruct in person the workers charged with pruning the trees (AGR, *ACC*, 2410, anno 1779).

The reforms, then, entailed more stringent demands on the enlistment of workers. The status of sworn-in worker was abolished, and strict regulations were drawn up with regard to the amount and quality of work to be performed. Each worker was assigned a specific task, described at his enlistment, and remunerated on the basis of the number of days or half-days actually spent at work.[18] In order to allow close supervision, the staff employed for precision tasks (like dealing with the seedlings and pruning) was limited to 45 members.

This staff was recruited by the forest rangers,[19] who were to submit their lists for approval to the officer on whom they depended. They were seasonal workers, frequently whole families – men, women and children from neighbouring villages[20] – who left their fields in the winter to seek employment in the forest. The men would take on the heavy logging jobs (felling, sawing, and pruning) while the women, children and even the

[17] This division into three sectors was guided by a motive: it sought to abolish the hierarchical relationship between the three officers and thus to increase their efficiency. But the operation did not run as smoothly as anticipated, cf. Lefèbvre, 1997: 42–52.
[18] Cf. the instructions in 41 points drawn up by the l'Escaille forestmaster in 1779 for the use of foresters charged with planting tasks. They specify the working hours, the number of hands to be hired, the skills demanded and a precise description of the task to be performed (AGR, *CF*, 1783, reproduced in Lefèbvre, 1992–1993: 168–174).
[19] From 1784 onwards, rangers must be able to read and write (Goblet d'Alviella, 1927: II, 159).
[20] In his account of socio-vocational structures in 9 villages of the Brussels suburbs, H. Hasquin (1977: 24) notes that the forest villages of Auderghem and Boitsfort feature the highest number of forestry day-workers.

elderly would bind faggots and clean up the sites after completion of the actual logging work. They would carry out these jobs for a few months only, and leave the forest in late March. As soon as the sap started rising, the wood had to be evacuated and the forest floor cleaned up to avoid trampling the regrowth. And of course, the arrival of spring also heralded in a new season of agricultural activity at home.

Thus, the forestry jobs provided an extra source of income for the inhabitants of woodside villages, and this revenue seems to have responded to a real need, as is shown by the following episode. In the year X, a report of the Dyle Department deplores a noticeable increase in forestry offences (mainly thefts and damage to the crops). The author of the report explains the phenomenon by a decision, taken two years earlier, to cease all planting and pruning activity in the Soignes Forest. The measure deprived a number of underprivileged families of small woodside villages of their additional revenue, while they had previously 'been accustomed to live on a salary habitually earned by their forest employment'. Each year, from 800 to 1000 workers were hired by the foresters for about five months during the winter to participate in regeneration and pruning. Thus occupied, they had neither the will nor the time to commit offences. By offering work and a modest salary to the rural populations 'for as long as can be remembered', the forest administration protected its estate from a series of aggressions (AGR, *PD*, 813).

IV. Activities linked to the wood trade

The wood merchants would buy their merchandise in batches at sales organised by the authorities at the Broodhuys in the Town Hall Square and sell the trees in the form of timber or charcoal on the Brussels markets to the inhabitants or craftsmen, according to the demand. Thus, the bakers would consume 'practically all of the produce of periodical cutting coppice of the Heeghde'[21] because they favoured charcoal made of alderwood, which abounded in this hunting reserve.[22] In principle, these batches could be purchased by anyone, but the merchants constituted a kind of closed corporation. Little can be inferred from the sales records (AGR, *FB*, 99–112). The clerks seemed to be so familiar with the merchants that their records bear only their initials or nicknames; but the same names keep appearing throughout. The data are vague, and only occasionally indicate the merchants' place of residence, i.e. Brussels or villages adjacent to the forest.[23]

While the wood-merchants did not actually constitute a full-fledged corporation, they nevertheless seem to have been linked by strong ties, and to have formed a faction which could if necessary co-ordinate their efforts to lobby for a common cause. The

[21] The coppice forest closest to Brussels, situated at Uccle (AGR, *CF*, 1633).

[22] The bakers appreciated this wood 'for its lively fire, practically without any smoke, and for the excellent charcoal it yields'. This type of wood was favored in the Heeghde area, where wildlife was important, because it offered the advantage of being resistant to damage by large game (Lefèbvre, 1997: 43, 46).

[23] Cf. the records of extraordinary sales in 1784. Here, most buyers come from Brussels, Ixelles, Etterbeek, Stockel, Tervueren, Auderghem, Overijse, Duysburgh or Wesembeek, but never from villages outside the present-day suburban Brussels area (AGR, *FB*, 103).

wood trade was extremely sensitive to the overall economic climate, as demand fluctuated not only with the growth and decrease in population, but also with factors like public works[24] or military conflicts. Faced with the inescapable realities of the economy, the wood-merchants sought to take advantage of their position to regulate sales. Of course it was difficult for a merchant to increase the volume of wood offered on the market, but on the other hand, it was in his power to diminish or postpone sales. Thus, for example, in 1625, the authorities proposed to carry out extraordinary fellings to counter a rise in wood prices due to a growth in population and a degradation of the forest crops caused by the military conflicts at the turn of the century. In taking this measure, they hoped to keep speculation in check by increasing the supply on the market. The merchants, on their side, feared that the measure might have effects adverse to their interests, since dumping more wood on the market might make their supplies harder to sell. As a consequence, they compounded their forces to oppose the decision.[25] Nor was this an isolated reaction: a few years later, in 1645, the merchants deplored the excessive fellings performed by the authorities with a view to increasing the estate's revenue, and threatened to boycot ordinary sales if they received no formal guarantee that no cuttings would be scheduled between ordinary regulated fellings (AGR, *AF*, 371/2). In either case, the authorities complied with their demands.

The wood trade provided employment for a host of workers. Felling, sawing, cutting, cleaving and banking wood required a considerable workforce. A. Corvol (1987: 109) estimated that it took a good worker over 7 hours to produce a 'stere' of wood (m^3). But forestry work involved a variety of skills. On the felling sites, the loggers and lumberjacks would be followed by sawyers and cleavers, and subsequently by the charcoal-burners. Skidders and haulers from the contiguous villages would be called in to collect the merchandise and take it into the city. And finally, the clearing and cleaning of the site would provide jobs for unqualified workers. It is likely that the merchants resorted to the same seasonal workers as those recruited by the forest authorities for the reforestation campaigns.

Unfortunately, this work market is hardly accounted for by historiography, as the data on the woodmerchants' trade are scarce. It can be studied only indirectly, by resorting to very diverse archival data collections like the records of the forest administration, judicial records or the archives of the various Brussels trades who depended on wood for their activity. Yet the work market offered by the forest is far from negligible. It allowed woodside residents to find additional revenues. The craftsmen and manufacturers from the city who bought their wood on the market or who would go to the forest to choose and collect their raw materials themselves would also depend on this workforce. Thus, the glassmakers, blacksmiths, carpenters, bakers, brewers, cabinetmakers, brick makers and coach builders would employ more people in the forest to provide fuel or raw material than personnel in their own workshops. Thus, besides the three or four workers generally employed in the glass manufacture in Brussels, it also provided work for a host of loggers and haulers to fuel its glass-oven (Engen, 1989: 88–89). It is, however, difficult to give

[24] For example, the construction of public buildings, repairs on fortifications, or reconstruction projects like that of central Brussels in 1695.

[25] This phenomenon, which is at present being investigated within the framework of a study on Soignes Forestry from the 16th to the 18th century, will be dealt with in a forthcoming publication.

precise figures, as the work prior to the providing of raw material covered a great variety of aspects, ranging from the measurement to the transportation of wood or charcoal, and might include cutting, sawing and site clearing. We do have access to studies allowing us to assess the number of craftsmen within the city,[26] but these provide little useful information about their respective wood consumption. Moreover, the numerous craftsmen living outside the city walls are hardly known at all. Only a thorough study of the accounts held by these various industries could shed a new light on these markets.

But a few case examples may, nevertheless, help us gain a more detailed view of the importance of forestry on the work market. In the mid-18th century, the Brussels suburbs were largely rural in character. H. Hasquin (1977: 22–23) shows that in 1755, half of the heads of families in that area were engaged in an activity closely linked to agriculture and forestry. Certain villages actually drew most of their revenue from the forest like, say, Boitsfort, where a number of inhabitants lived from the manufacture and sale of besoms made of birch twigs gathered in the forest (Vernier, 1965: 329). Grazing, acorn- and seed-gathering also constituted job opportunities for a number of villagers. Keeping cattle was vital to these village people, as it played a central role in their food supplies (milk and meat), and moreover allowed them to gather manure for their fields, produce wool, and even sell or lease their animals to haulers for their for carriages.

The large building projects also required an important work-force on the forestry sites. Thus, in 1599, repair works on the short Ixelles-Vleurgat road entailed the felling of no less than 2665 oak trees. Other, particularly large orders, required the enlistment of an additional workforce. After the bombing of 1695, the Magistrate of the city allowed foreign master carpenters to come and work in town with an unlimited number of workmen (Culot, 1992: 131). And in 1671, the government forced workers from woodside villages to work in the Heeghde to bundle a million faggots to fuel the lime- and brick-kilns catering for the construction of fortifications (Pierron, s.d.: II, 137).

In addition to this 'professional' use of the forest, there existed an 'occasional' use as well. Because of its closeness to villages and religious communities, the Soignes Forest was entered by a number of people, sometimes totally deprived and penniless, who would gather wood clandestinely or under pretence of users' rights, for their own use or to be peddled in the streets. In August 1626, the revenue service deemed that six to seven thousand indigent made a living out of their permit allowing them to gather deadwood for fuel (AGR, *CC*, 179). This peddling, though prohibited by the regulations, allowed some of them to make a modest living. Again, parallel-market sales like these are hard to quantify. The only clue to their existence is constituted by records when a cheater was caught and a statement booked. Part of the subordinate forestry staff, gathered in a brigade of sergeants on foot, was assigned the task of ensuring at the city gates that no illegally gathered wood be carried into town (Goblet d'Alviella, 1927: II, 31; Smolar-Meynaert, 1991: 122). Any wood thus seized would be put up for auction by order of the forestry administration at the Grass Market, where the citizens of Brussels, whether burghers or craftsmen, would generally purchase their wood (Pierron, s.d.: II, 124).

[26] Cf., notably, the studies by G. des Marez (1904) and K. Van Honacker (1994).

These illegal sales tended to concentrate in the winter season, but also at the beginning of spring, when the seasonal workers would desert the lumbering sites and leave them to the underprivileged at the margins of society, who had no other means of subsistence. To these, the forest offered not only enough to heat themselves, but also the means to make a living, however modest. These people would live from wood-gathering, fruit-picking and poaching, for their own use or for hawking in town, as is recorded in a document of 1634 which deplores that many young children 'are taking up the habit of gathering wood to sell it to brewers, bakers, innkeepers and others'.

But the poor were not the only ones to peddle illegal wood. The forestry staff themselves engaged in the practice and would clandestinely sell wood or charcoal in town.[27] Those 'offences' would be committed during the delivery of wood to the court and to the wealthy, or even at the marking of trees.[28] Any opportunity was tempting; all the more so since foresters' salaries were far from attractive.

V. The city, the forest and the countryside: a privileged relationship?

Thanks to its situation on the outskirts of the city, the Soignes Forest enjoyed, and still enjoys, strong links with the city of Brussels, as if fate had bound them together. The forest provided wood and charcoal for the city, but also provided employment to its population, giving rise to a considerable work market as well as a considerable variety in social status, ranging from forestry officers to an ensemble of small workers, on whom Brussels craftsmen depended for the raw material and the fuel required by their trade. A thorough study of this interaction would allow one to view economic and social realities in a new light.

The need to compensate for an employment deficit attracted the rural population to the forest, too. The Soignes Forest provided a considerable number of them with an indispensable occasional revenue. Work was of a varied nature and offered the advantage of being carried out in a period during which rural activity was less intense. The peasants easily accustomed themselves to the harsh conditions of forest life. Of course forest work was very different from their usual agricultural tasks, but the inhabitants of woodside villages had long been used to this kind of work and were familiar with the forest. Thus, the forest, the city and the countryside were dependent on each other and fulfilled each other's needs.

On the other hand, the forest has always been perceived as a 'frontier', a separate, mysterious universe, the refuge of hermits and vagrants. People would migrate to the forest to seek employment in the winter, and return to their country villages in the

[27] One practice was the illegal sale of wood received as part of their salary; another fiddling with the weight of bags of charcoal by including stones or other waste.

[28] The lieutenant-forestmaster of l'Escaille managed in 1785 to bring to light an important case of fraud, discovering that the marking-hammer used to identify oak-trees had been counterfeited. Thus a large number of trees had been cut and sold without the knowledge of the forest administration. This fraud had been going on for eleven years and had entailed considerable losses of revenue for the estate (Lefebvre, 1997: 41).

spring. The forest demanded particular knowledge and skills. This fact is reflected in the recruitment of forestry staff, characterised not only by a high degree of continuity across several centuries, but also by increasing specialisation and training, a fact which heralded the advent of the 19th century.

Bibliography

Manuscript sources[29]

Archives générales du Royaume (AGR), Brussels, *Avis en finances* (AF), 349, 351/2, 369, 371, 523–524.

Archives générales du Royaume (AGR), Brussels, *Acquits des chambres des comptes* (ACC), 2410.

Archives générales du Royaume (AGR), Brussels, *Chambre des comptes* (CC), 179, 510.

Archives générales du Royaume (AGR), Brussels, *Chancellerie autrichienne des Pays-Bas* (CAPB), 902.

Archives générales du Royaume (AGR), Brussels, *Conseil des finances* (CF), 1633, 1783.

Archives générales du Royaume (AGR), Brussels, *Correspondance administrative des Chambres des comptes* (CACC), 2632.

Archives générales du Royaume (AGR), Brussels, *Foresterie de Brabant* (FB), 99–112.

Archives générales du Royaume (AGR), Brussels, *Office fiscal du Brabant* (OFB), 891, 928, 9737.

Archives générales du Royaume (AGR), Brussels, *Préfecture de la Dyle* (PD), 469, 813.

Printed and secondary sources

Biget, J.-C., Boissière, J. and Hervé, J.C. (1991) *Le bois et la ville*, Paris.

Chambon, R. (1955) *L'histoire de la verrerie en Belgique du IIe siècle à nos jours*, Brussels.

Corvol, A. (1987) *L'Homme aux bois. Histoire des relations de l'homme et de la forêt XVIIe–XXe siècles*, Paris.

Cosyn, P. (1978) 'Soignes à travers les âges', *Soignes, Ancien droit de chasse*, 59/4, pp. 14–29.

Culot, M., Hennaut, E., Demanet, M. and Mierop, C. (1992) *Le bombardement de Bruxelles par Louis XIV et la reconstruction qui s'en suivit 1695–1700*, Brussels.

[29] Abbreviations: ACC = Acquits des chambres des comptes; AGR = Archives générales du Royaume (AGR); CACC = Correspondance administrative des Chambres des comptes; CAPB = Chancellerie autrichienne des Pays-Bas; CC = Chambre des comptes; CF = Conseil des finances; FB = Foresterie de Brabant; OFB = Office fiscal du Brabant; PD = Préfecture de la Dyle.

des Marez, G. (1904) *L'organisation du travail à Bruxelles au XVe siècle*, Brussels (Mémoires couronnés de l'Académie Royale de Belgique; v. 65).

Engen, L. (ed.) (1989) Le *verre en Belgique des origines à nos jours*, Brussels.

Faure, M. (1991) 'La forêt et l'incendie: quelques leçons du passé', in *La Forêt*, Actes du 113e congrès national des Sociétés Savantes-Strasbourg 1988, Paris, pp. 77–88.

La forêt de Soignes. Art et histoire des origines au XVIIIème siècle (1987), Catalogue de l'exposition à Auderghem-Trois Fontaines, Europalia Autriche, Brussels.

Goblet D'Alviella (1927–1930) *Histoire des Bois et forêts de Belgique*, 4 vols, Paris/ Brussels.

Hasquin, H. (1970) 'Charbon des Pays-Bas espagnols et sidérurgie du Hainaut français aux confins des XVIIe et XVIIIe siècles', in *La Vie wallonne*, 44, pp. 514–519.

Hasquin, H. (1977) 'La population de l'agglomération bruxelloise au XVIIIème siècle', in *Etudes sur le XVIIIè siècle*, Groupe d'étude du XVIIIe siècle de l'Université Libre de Bruxelles, IV, pp. 13–26.

Honacker, K. van (1994) 'De politieke cultuur van de Brusselse ambachten in de achttiende eeuw: conservatisme, corporatisme of opportunisme?', in C. Lis and H. Soly (eds), *Werken volgen de regels. Ambachten in Brabant en Vlaanderen 1500–1800*, Brussels, pp. 179–228.

Lefebvre, S. (1992–1993) *Un aspect de la politique forestière du gouvernement autrichien: les pépinières en Brabant, Hainaut et Namurois*, Brussels. Unpublished licentiate thesis University of Brussels (ULB).

Lefebvre, S. (1997) 'Les pépinières dans les Pays-Bas autrichiens: le cas de Soignes', in *Etudes sur le XVIIIème siècle*, Groupe d'étude du XVIIIe siècle de l'Université Libre de Bruxelles, Brussels, 25, pp. 39–77.

Pierron, S. (s.d.) *Histoire illustrée de la forêt de Soignes*, 3 vols, Brussels.

Rochette, D. (1972) 'L'emploi du bois pour la réparation des routes', *Le Folklore Brabançon*, 196, pp. 337–347.

Smolar-Meynart, A. (1987) 'Les droits d'usage de Soignes des origines au XVIIIe siècle', in *La forêt de Soignes, massacre ou survie?*, Europalia Autriche, Brussels, pp. 83–94.

Smolar-Meynart, A. (1991) *La justice ducale du Plat Pays, des forêts et chasses en Brabant (XIIe–XVIe siècle)*, Annales de la Société Royale d'Archéologie de Bruxelles, t. 60.

Stengers, J. (ed.) (1979) *Bruxelles, croissance d'une capitale*, Antwerp.

Verhaegen, A. (1953) 'Note sur le travail et les salaires au XVIIIe siècle', *Bulletin de l'Institut de Recherches économiques et sociales*, 19/1, pp. 71–87.

Vernier, L. (1965) *Un millénaire d'histoire de Bruxelles. Depuis les origines jusqu'en 1830*, Brussels.

PART IV

MODERN PERIOD

Introduction to part IV

Eric VANHAUTE, Ghent University

The four contributions on the late 18th – early 20th centuries show the impact of the accelerated interaction between and integration of rural and urban labour markets. The female and child labourers in the Madrid region (Nieto Sánchez and López Barahona), the butchers on the Brussels' meat market (Libert), the maids in the service of the urban bourgeoisie (Piette), or the day labourers in Flemish agriculture (De Moor), the social position of all of them was considerably altered by the ongoing opening of the urban/rural labour markets.

Nieto Sánchez and López Barahona show how Madrid merchant capital was able to develop proto-factories and extensive putting-out networks in nearby rural areas. This generated a high demand for unregulated labour, mainly women and children. This new (rural) labour market was created by (urban) state and guild mediation and expanded within older, rural social institutions.

Libert describes the effects produced by the abolition of the crafts monopoly enjoyed up to then by the Brussels meat trade at the end of the 18th century. The local family networks lost their hold on the trade as a growing number of non-local butcher families moved in. The latter came from the 'traditional' areas surrounding the capital, linked to the economic and tax power of Brussels.

Piette reports on how the new Brussels urban bourgeoisie generated a new demand for labour, i.e. from young maids. These too mainly came from the rural belt around Brussels, thus reinforcing the interaction between both labour markets, which used to be quite separated.

De Moor investigates how paid labour vanished from early 20th Century Flemish agriculture. This phenomenon is closely related to a more in-depth national labour regulation as well as a greater mobility of labour.

The four contributions make it clear that the greater interaction between urban and rural labour markets does not automatically imply the creation of a national, unified labour market. Indeed, the survival of earlier economic and political influence, as evidenced by Madrid and Brussels, is striking. The information channels seemed to operate along traditional lines for some considerable time. Right into the 20th century local and regional differences remained important, as illustrated by the widely different manners in which Flemish day labourers responded to the same external signals. The greater interaction was not a one-way affair, as many maids returned to their village after a few years. Moreover their journey to town often included several intermediary stops. In no way does the record show the existence of a linear urban attraction.

In the 19th Century the labour markets, up to then considerably determined by local and regional factors, opened up even more, both in the city (trades and crafts) and in the country (the rural subsistence economy). This process produced differentiated effects, which need to be investigated by means of further research.

a) The differences in time play an important part. The late 18th and 19th centuries were characterised by a far-reaching deregulation of labour markets, cancelling old arrangements and setting new rules to ensure maximum flexibility and openness of the labour market. This deregulation undermined the closed production systems, like urban crafts or the household economy, while paving the way for fresh inflows of labour migrants. Notwithstanding this process local and regional networks survived for a long time. In the 20th century an active government embarked on a fast regulation of the labour market (cf. De Moor's 'social wage'). Only at this stage was the national labour market able to break through finally, thus consigning the reign of regional determinants to history.

b) The more integrated labour market produced different effects in urban and rural settings. Here, the decisive factor was the ability of more or less independent family businesses to survive.

c) The various social groups reacted differently to these shifts, as did men, women and children. The new urban middle classes used the new opportunities offered (hiring maids, buying lace, consuming meat), whereas peasant families continued to depend on an income combination for a considerable time, which partially protected them from market mechanisms. More open and unregulated labour often created new labour possibilities for women and children, but also made them more dependent of low and uncertain wages.

Further research into the integration versus the survival of regional labour markets needs to be sensitive to the interaction between these three fields of tension. As stated by Jan De Vries in a recent contribution, this will not be a smooth process all the way: 'The interaction of the urban and rural economies remains, in many ways, the site of the most difficult conceptual issues in economic history. They are certainly the most ideologically contested issues' (De Vries, 1999: 132).

Bibliography

Vries, J. de (1999) 'Great expectations. Early modern history and the social sciences', *Review: a journal of the Fernand Braudel Center for the Study of Economies, Historical Systems and Civilizations*, 22, 2, pp. 121–150.

13 Women's work and proto-industrialisation: Madrid and New Castile (1750–1850)

José A. Nieto Sánchez and Victoria López Barahona, Universidad Autónoma de Madrid

I. Introduction

The stage of proto-industrial capitalism, which revived interest in the eighteenth century, was vital both to the process of capital accumulation and to the restructuring of labour markets along crosscutting geographical and social lines. Among the latter, gender divisions of labour markets have been calling scholars' attention, as they reveal special methodological significance for the ongoing discussion concerning the phase of transitional expansion before full industrialisation. Increasing evidence is being brought forward which show how women and children's labour were singled out to actively contribute to the diversification of the labour markets, urban and rural, in early modern and modern Europe (Lis and Soly, 1982; Gullickson, 1986; Berg, 1987).

In the following discussion we shall examine two major aspects of the relations between Madrid and the surrounding rural areas of New Castile in the period from 1750 to 1850: the process of proto-industrialisation and the creation of a gender-oriented labour market. These are subjects that remain unexplored in Spanish historiography.[1] More specifically we shall focus on the relations between Madrid's merchant capital and female, rural labour markets through case studies of the *escuelas de hilazas* (spinning schools) and of the evolution of the lacemaking industry in Campo de Calatrava (Ciudad Real). Before exploring this, however, let us digress briefly to comment on the way in which historians have often conceived of Madrid as playing a passive or 'parasitical' role in relation to her surrounding rural areas. An overemphasis on the flow of basic supplies that were, indeed, directed to the capital through administrative coercion has overshadowed the circulation of resources that went the other way – from Madrid to the countryside – as part of a process of continuous exchange of commodities, people, and information. If we wish to achieve a full understanding of the nature of town and country relations in the case study of early modern Madrid, this 'active' role of the capital should be taken into consideration too. This paper intends to be a small contribution to it.

Recent research has shown how the interplay of private and state-sponsored initiatives fostered the expansion of both putting-out networks that operated over varying distances from Madrid, and semi-centralized proto-factories. It is not our concern here to assess

---

[1] A few relevant works have been produced about different aspects of women's labour (Iradiel, 1986; *El trabajo*, 1992; Sarasúa, 1994 and 1995; López Cordón, 1996), but within the context of proto-industrial developments only the region of Catalonia has been approached thus far (Narotzky, 1988; Carbonell, 1989; Vicente, 1994).

the extent to which these capital ventures succeeded or failed.[2] As has been assumed (Nieto, 1999), the Castilian path to proto-industry evinces some traits which make it differ from the classic proto-industrial model, namely the predominance of *kaufsystem* relations, traditional patterns of labour organisation, and poor technological innovation. Yet the Spanish eighteenth century provided an opportunity for industrial growth because of rising demand and the policy of encouragement to industry followed by the Bourbon monarchy. It is also the case that this opportunity was not taken advantage of equally by different Spanish regions.

The character of eighteenth-century Castilian proto-industrialization, however, conformed to the proto-industrial paradigm insofar as it was predominantly a rural industry whose product was mostly 'exported' to other parts of the Iberian peninsula and to oversea territories, there was an integration between agricultural activity and industrial work within the producers' households, some developments in the organisation of production became apparent, and the commercial (though not the production) side of the trade was partly dominated by merchant capitalists, occasioning some possibility for accumulation of capital. The latter benefitted from a pre-existing sexual division of labour that rendered a cheaper and more disciplined labour force, that of women and children. Definitions of the kind of work seen as appropriate for women, in which contemporary social reformists like Campomanes[3] took so much interest to make clear and distinct, must be contemplated as deriving, at least in part, from ideological mechanisms of social control governing the allocation of women's 'time' so as to make it adaptable to the demands of the new industries.

The ideas presented in the following brief account might also contribute to more general comparisons of women's work patterns across several phases of economic and social organisation in European countries.

II. Madrid's merchant capital and rural labour markets

The seventeenth-century crisis in Spain followed the collapse of Castile's celebrated urban textile industry, and led to stagnation in both craft industries and demographic rates. One solution was to transfer most stages of the production process to rural areas where heavily levied peasants were forced into market-oriented handicraft industry in the home. But the whole point of the relocation of the textile industry from town to countryside was the search for cheap labour. Madrid's merchants found an infinitely expandable labour pool in the large numbers of 'idle' women and girls who, according to Campomanes,

[2] On the 'failure' of Spanish industrialization interesting literature has been produced (Nadal, 1975). On the 'success' of Spain as a peripherical country some investigation has recently been carried out too (Ringrose, 1996).
[3] Pedro Rodríguez de Campomanes was Attorney General of the Council of Castile from 1762 to 1783 and held other relevant offices. In 1774 and 1775 he published two of his most important works: *Discurso sobre el fomento de la industria popular* (of which 30,000 copies were issued), and *Discurso sobre la educación popular de los artesanos y su fomento.* Some cites from the former will be reproduced hereby from the Spanish edition of G. Anes in our own translation into English.

were 'fit for work' in the textile industry (*industria popular*). In this way, he argued, women in turn should benefit from a means 'to help themselves contribute to their families' unkeep (...) seeing to housework duties as well'.

In Castile a large part of rural production took place in unspecialised households that were rather oriented to self-sufficiency. The small independent textile producer – or small clothier – was predominant in a country where both increasing competition from foreign manufactures and the export of raw materials had notably contributed to check domestic industrial growth. Though it has been assumed by some historians that Madrid's merchants were not at all interested in industrial investment (Cruz, 1996), they nonetheless took a leading role in facilitating the shift of textile production to the countryside. Some of these merchants, who had formerly invested in the urban textile trades, would foster the structuring of both putting-out relations and proto-factories in rural contexts, a process which, while not entailing a revolution of the productive forces, did to a certain extent attain control over some aspects of the organization of production, and contributed to the creation of an increasingly wage-dependent labour market (Nieto, 1997). The following represent a sample of this significant group.

Between 1765 and 1778 overseas commerce saw a process of liberalisation that enabled shareholding-based merchant companies to be added to the 'traditional' and still vigorous merchant guilds. Thus, the *Compañía de lonjistas* (grocers' company) was founded in Madrid in 1764 by members whose identity remains thus far unknown. We know, however, that twenty years later this company was composed of fifteen merchants of Basque origins. They were engaged in the overseas commerce of cocoa, sugar, cinnamon, and dye-stuffs, the returns of which were swelled through investments in Toledo's silk industry. A network thus operated whereby spices where brought from America, silk-stockings and other items of different qualities were supplied by Toledo's silk industry, and Madrid served as the central storehouse and hub of mercantile traffic. The company moreover undertook the management of an old textile factory in Valdemoro (25 km from Madrid), whose output – including cloth, silk, worsted, cotton, and linen – was delivered to various storehouses in Madrid, Medina de Rioseco, La Coruña, Aranjuez, Toledo, Sevilla, and Cádiz (Larruga, 1787, vol. I: 295–301; Corella, 1992; AHPM, prot. 19,970, f.237).

The textile industry was both urban and rural. In towns it was usually based on a network of rural outworkers organized by middle-men *fabricantes*.[4] The *Gremio de mercaderes de ropería de nuevo* (ready-made clothing merchants' guild), who seem to have been prosperous master tailors, embarked upon large scale commercial enterprises employing as many as 4,000 people of both sexes just in Madrid city. Their influence extended over an area 170 km around the city, which included, within Toledo's province, the locality of Ajofrín, where 1,100 spinners worked for the local weavers in 1748 on orders from these merchants, and those of Novés and Sonseca, with 600 and 450 spinners respectively (Larruga, 1787: I, 342; 1790: IX, 30 and 136; García Ruiperez, 1988: 360).

[4] *Fabricante* is the contemporary Spanish term for manufacturer.

During the early years of the nineteenth century other merchants from Madrid profited from putting-out the embroidering of *mantillas* to rural women workers in nearby villages (Villaverde, Parla, Getafe, and Fuenlabrada). Moreover, in 1804 a master embroiderer and large-scale *fabricante*, Francisco García, had forty women working in his central workshop in Madrid as well as 124 more throughout the city. But he also established a business branch in the village of Getafe where another group of forty women were allocated to seven different workshops under the supervision of a 'mistress'. These women also spun yarn for the coarse-textile factories of Getafe and nearby Fuenlabrada. It was not infrequent for women to diversify their industrial labour and thus set a competition for their labour among employers (AGS, *Consejo Supremo de Hacienda, Junta de Comercio y Moneda*, file 315, exp. 38; Regás, 1825: 73–74; Madoz, 1848).

The hold of these capitalists, however, was challenged by the largest and most powerful merchant corporation in Madrid – and indeed in the nation as a whole –, the *Confederación de los Cinco Gremios Mayores de Madrid* (Confederation of the Five Major Guilds), to whom the Crown was so conspicuously indebted (Capella and Matilla, 1957). This is partly the reason for their having been granted the management of the royal cloth factories of Guadalajara and Brihuega for a ten-year period (1757–1767), including the branches of San Carlos (in Guadalajara's city) and San Fernando (a town in Madrid's province). The *Cinco Gremios* were also granted the royal silk factory of Talavera de la Reina (in Toledo's province), and the royal cloth factory of Cuenca. These large enterprises involved an organisation of production whereby weaving and the subsequent stages of the process were centralised on the factory's premises. Former stages such as spinning, carding, etc., were performed by means of a network of disperse, smaller units of production, contemporarily known as *escuelas de hilazas*. In order to secure sufficient and regular supplies of yarn, increasing the labour contingent of women and children was deemed essential, as well as introducing spinning lathes for higher productivity. This meant the creation *ex novo* of a large network of lathe-spinners over which to hold a monopoly, thus bypassing the control of local *fabricantes* to whom the existing networks of women spinners were attached, usually by community bonds.

III. An enlightened organisation of women and children's labour: *Las escuelas de hilazas*

The reliance on low-paid labour entailed higher proportions of female and child labour, which was already undervalued because of cultural assumptions about the complementary nature of dependant's incomes. Both urban and rural children and women were thus to be given the opportunity to hire their work out in special training establishments, the *escuelas de hilazas* (spinning schools). Campomanes never ceased to emphasise the indispensability of these establishments for children's apprenticeships as a crucial pre-requisite to extending disperse handicraft production. Earlier labour-recruiting experiences, such as that of using the labour of imprisoned women, had met with failure.

There were mainly three types of *escuelas de hilazas* as far as the ownership of their premises was concerned. Most of them belonged to the royal factories themselves and were managed by a salaried master craftsman. A second group were those set up by charitable boards or by civic institutions like the *Sociedades Económicas*, whose directing boards also appointed salaried masters or 'mistresses' for training and supervising purposes. Individual owners, usually independent *fabricantes* who also undertook the managerial tasks or delegated them to their wives, composed a third type of *escuelas*. These last two often acted as subcontractors for the royal factories or other merchant companies.

The royal factory of Guadalajara organised a large network of *escuelas de hilazas* (up to 190) in 157 villages and towns across New Castile, where as many as 18,500 spinners, mostly women and children, spun yarn for the factory in the later part of the eighteenth century. As new factory branches were established, more *escuelas* grew at further distances, including the provinces of Cuenca, Toledo, Ciudad Real and Albacete (Table 13.1). The branches of San Carlos and San Fernando were even forced to put out spinning work to independent household producers.

Table 13.1 Spatial distribution of spinning schools (escuelas de hilazas) belonging to the Royal Factory in Guadalajara, 1783–1787

Premises	Guadalajara		Cuenca		Toledo		Madrid		Others		Totals	
	N	%	N	%	N	%	N	%	N	%	N	%
Guadalajara	27	45.8	10	17.0	11	18.6	11	18.6	–	–	59	100
Brihuega	45	81.9	9	16.3	–	–	–	–	1	1.8	55	100
S.Fernando	17	36.8	14	31.9	5	11.3	1	2.2	7	16.0	44	100
S.Carlos	1	2.5	17	41.4	17	41.4	–	–	6	14.7	41	100
Totals	90	45.3	50	25.1	33	16.6	12	6	14	7	199	100

Source: Our own elaboration from González, 1980: 481–489.

The running of the *escuelas*, however, was frequently far from smooth. Work conditions must have been extremely hard as peasants were usually relunctant to send their children out to do low-paid intensive work in an industry that was socially considered 'an indecent and vile occupation'. This was a justification that underlies a general perception of the *escuelas* as actual sweatshops for children and women. In consequence, managers had to face dramatic difficulties in labour recruitment. For example, in 1783 the person in charge of the *escuela* located in Aranjuez (Madrid) was unable to gather a sufficient number of children even though a special board – constituted by the town's mayor, a council officer, and the parish priest – was created for the purpose. In 1786 twelve *escuelas* had to be closed down as no labour could be hired. And not even the poor harvests of the following year seemed to have encouraged people from Torrejón de Ardoz (Madrid) to increase their families' income by seeking employment out in the local *escuela*. Meanwhile, the director of Guadalajara's factory complained about the dearth of yarn, and in 1788 attempts to set up new *escuelas* in Ciudad Real met with failure too. A year later in Ocaña (Toledo) the *escuela*'s workers, whose numbers had formerly escalated to 300, quit alleging low wages (González, 1980: 473–475). Though not all *escuelas* were equally affected by labour shortages, the ways authorities had contrived to obtain and retain workers is worthy of notice. For example, in Alameda de la Sagra (Toledo) the *Real Junta de Comercio* offered rewards to those willing to work at the local *escuela*. This strategy seemed to have worked out in this case for in sixteen months one hundred spinning lathes were kept busy at the premises.

Within the *escuela* the work process was organised by an internal hierarchy of age. While the master – or mistress – apprenticed the children from ten to fourteen years old, single young women above sixteen were committed to lathe-spinning, and widows – plus 'needy married women' – performed the carding procedures. The prizes endowed by the *Junta de Comercio* gave women incentives to compete against each other so that productivity would be stimulated (ADT, Descripciones del Cardenal Lorenzana). State and guild mediation was thus essential for proto-factories to be able to recruit a cheap and plentiful labour force for the early stages of the production process. This is how, in 1800, Cuenca's cloth royal factory attracted 1,109 women and girls working in different rural *escuelas*, including lathe and hand spinners, warpers, combers and others (Troitiño, 1984: 40; AHN, Estado, file 3,182, box 2, exp. 150).

The *escuelas de hilazas* represented the limit of decentralisation that a centralised enlightened proto-factory could allow. This system was to choke, however, the full decentralisation proposed by Campomanes, who had conceived of the *escuelas* just as a means for women and children to acquire the basic skills of a trade (lathe spinning) that was meant to be performed thereafter in independent households. As Campomanes' argument goes, state-sponsoring of 'industria popular' should not be aimed at the expansion of putting-out relations but rather to the consolidation of what was the actual predominant kind of relation between capital and labour, that of *kaufsystem*, in which the producer remains independent (Díez, 1990). He was convinced that merchant capital's penetration into the production process and organisation would be likely to bring about the impoverishment of rural producers, and in turn stagnation in population rates. Couched in his own terms, 'these (the merchants) would turn rural producers into day-labourers at their beck and call'. For this reason, he argued, merchants would be useful only 'to facilitate outlets and often provide some credit to the manufacturers'. In this vein he suggested that 'the cloth royal factories (...) should take steps to progress if weaving frameworks were allocated in independent manufacturers who own their industry' and rely on household and community members to undertake the preliminary tasks.

These pronouncements notwithstanding, royal factory managers tried to tie women and children workers to roofed-in intensive production under the close supervision of a foreman at the premises of the *escuelas*. This pattern of behaviour and organisation among the largest merchant capitalists was likely to have served as example by other textile *fabricantes*. In 1798, the Hermanos March, from Catalonia, started a factory of cloth, silk, and linen in Morata de Tajuña (Madrid) that included a local *escuela* – where twenty-two women were 'apprenticed' –, another one in Vallecas (Madrid) and even a third one further down in La Mancha. In the same way, the factory of Valdemoro, run by the *Compañía de lonjistas*, was supplied with yarn by *escuelas* scattered over twenty villages (Corella, 1992; 1997).

Conflicts over the control of spinners were frequent among merchants. They could only meet their immediate needs for women and children's labour by hiring them – which meant hiring the local middle-men to whom they were attached – away from other companies. In 1778 the aforementioned *Compañía de lonjistas* had thus managed to gain control over four *escuelas* that had formerly been subcontractors for Guadalajara's royal factory, even though this caused the seizure of the *escuelas*' materials and the exile of the masters in charge. Likewise, the expansion of Valdemoro's factory in the early years of the nineteenth century was accomplished by subcontracting the carding and spinning procedures with the weavers' network at Ajofrín, whose prosperous textile industry had already declined (González, 1980; Paz, 1990).

IV. The lace-making industry of Campo de Calatrava

It has been argued that for merchant capital and rural out-workers relations to become clearly entrepreneurial capitalist relations, three interconnected developments usually had to take place: producers are deprived of alternative sources of livelihood and thus become completely dependent on the wage; they lose possession of the means of production, often by falling into debt with the merchant; and they become forcibly attached to a single employer (Middleton, 1985). Two of these processes, at least, seemed to have occurred in the later part of the eighteenth century when Madrid's merchant capital ventured into the lace-making industry of Campo de Calatrava (Ciudad Real). Although lace-making, which was almost exclusively a female trade, did not require investment in machinery – performed as it was just by means of a bobbing pad –, the women lace-makers in Campo de Calatrava seemed to have found themselves and their families on the margins of subsistence, and so relied heavily on the earnings of all members of the household, especially women and girls. Moreover, they became attached to Madrid's merchants as these gained the monopoly of raw materials and hence the hiring of labour.

In the throes of the eighteenth century the real estate in this region was still concentrated in the hands of the Order of Calatrava, who held the manorial jurisdiction over the vast majority of villages and towns. The landless peasants were thus cut-off from farming activities save for seasonal day-labouring at the harvest as well as olive and grape collection. Local sales in nearby fairs of surpluses derived from seemingly highly productive orchards were, for peasant families, a means of raising money for dues or the purchase of commodities not obtainable otherwise. In one of Campo de Calatrava's largest towns, Almagro, the mercantile community was comprised of 130 individuals, 34 of whom were lace traders, and 24 kept shops and dealt with textiles including lace and blond lace. All of them retailed yarn and lace patterns to be pinned to bobbing pads, and purchased the finished product from the women producers, which was then distributed to peddlers in Castile and Andalusia (Sarasúa, 1995; Almagro, 1994).

Although the property register carried out in the mid-eighteenth century does not enable us to accurately assess the number of women from Calatrava engaged in lace-making – only 300 were registered –, their mere presence suggests a handicraft of likely Flemish background dating back at least to the mid-seventeenth century.[5] In 1766 a married couple from Madrid, Manuel Fernández (a mining businessman) and Rita Lambert

[5] Cervantes depicted Sanchica Panza, Sancho's daughter, as an industrious lacemaker who earned 8 maravedíes by this activity, 'savings that she keeps in a box to help her trousseau'.

Table 13.2 Lace-makers working for Torres factory in Almagro, 1846

Localities	Total population	Total of women	Female workers	A	B
Dep. de Almagro					
Almagro	10,273	5,311	2,262	22.01	42.59
Granátula	2,484	1,288	623	25.08	48.36
Pozuelo	1,713	834	566	33.04	67.86
Aldea del Rey	2,386	1,217	192	8.04	15.77
Bolaños	2,852	1,379	184	6.45	13.34
Valenzuela	1,169	587	314	26.86	53.49
Carrión	3,120	1,532	184	5.89	12.01
Pardillo	–	–	52	–	–
Torralva	3,977	2,008	901	22.65	44.87
Caldaza	4,504	2,293	126	2.79	5.49
Daimiel	12,503	6,381	99	0.79	1.55
Puertollano					
Puertollano	2,856	1,438	614	21.49	42.69
Argamasilla de Calatrava	2,190	1,069	164	7.48	15.34
Almodóvar del Campo	5,875	2,732	41	0.69	1.50
Vallamayor	1,353	705	114	8.42	16.17
Mestanza	2,093	1,002	50	2.38	4.99
Hinojosa-Cabezasrubias	2,076	995	234	11.27	23.51
Villar	219	99	18	8.21	18.18
Dep. del Corral					
Corral de Calatrava	1,737	872	255	14.68	29.24
Cañada	505	238	81	16.03	34.03
Caracuel	314	161	42	13.37	26.08
Ballesteros	1,037	547	191	18.41	34.91
Moral y Retamal	4,359	2,112	731	16.76	34.61
Totals	69,625	34,800	8,038	11.54	23.09

A = workers percentage on total population
B = workers percentage on female population

Source: Our own elaboration according to Madoz, 1847 and *Censo de población de 1857*.

a highly skilled lace-maker) were granted permission to teach new lace-making techniques to the women in Almagro. Rita Lambert's school soon saw dramatic growth. In 1767 there were about 140 women and girl apprentices which increased to over 400 in two years time. By the end of the century lace-makers in Almagro amounted to 2,000 – from six-year-old little girls to aged women –, a number that escalated to 3,730 in the district as a whole (Larruga, 1792: XVII, 294–296).

It was not, however, until the arrival in 1785 of the privileged, Madrid-based *Compañía de Mercaderes de la Puerta del Sol* that Rita Lambert's enterprise declined. But these merchants were to reap substantial gains from her work, since they found a readily available army of skilled lace-makers, and were, in addition, granted the right to import 1,500 pounds of tax-free yarn from Haarlem for a four-year period. They soon monopolised the supply of raw materials (yarn and silk) and offered it to the women out-workers on regular terms (Larruga, 1792: XVII, 297–304). The latter thus became completely dependent on Madrid's merchants and were even forced to make do with payments in kind (usually linen).

Catalonian merchant capital, represented by Félix Torres' factory, took over from Madrid's merchants the control of the lace-making industry of Campo de Calatrava in the second half of the nineteenth century. In this case roofed-in production displaced domestic work. In 1850 Pascual Madoz's *Diccionario Geográfico* registered 23 villages and towns where a large number of women were employed in Torres' factory. This gave employment to 8,000 people at that time in the whole region of Campo de Calatrava. Besides Torres' there were a number of other factories, like the one belonging to Ildefonso Aparicio, and a set of small shops. One out of three women in the region was employed in lace-making, which in some villages represented half the female population. The semi-centralised organisation of lace-making industry combined an urban central plant with disperse rural units of production that resembled the *escuelas de hilazas* promoted by the royal factories. In Torre's premises as many as 806 little girls from four to five years of age were committed to making plain lace, whereas 677 girls up to nine years old were in charge of the finer work. The adult women and their 'mistresses' – who seem to have been assistants to a foreman – topped off the labour hierarchy within the factory.

Although occasional unemployment could play havoc with family budgets, women lace-makers were usually less than enthusiastic about a sweating activity often carried out by candlelight and hence sight-consuming even to the point of blindness – as contemporary doctors certified –. Again, it was not infrequent for employers to face serious difficulties in recruiting women for intensive production, since payments were usually three to four-fold beneath the actual value of their production. The women from Argamasilla de Calatrava got a daily payment of 4 *maravedíes*, which does not stand a comparison with that of 2 *reales* obtained by the 'lucky' women ribbon-makers in the village of Mascaraque (Toledo). It is not surprising that large *fabricantes* like Félix Torres fell back on rewarding productivity by endowing clothing and different sorts of dowries to the women producers (Madoz, 1847).

V. Conclusions

The interplay of state-sponsored enterprises and the private initiative of Madrid's merchant organisations stimulated a process of proto-industrialisation in New Castile that was partly a response to the strong urbanisation of the sixteenth-century Spanish textile industry. Madrid's merchant capital was thus able to develop proto-factories and extensive putting-out networks in nearby rural areas to supply markets in Madrid and other regions. However, Madrid's merchants did not always get direct control over production but made use of pre-existing labour structures so that rural localities kept control of production processes. Several types of organisation could be combined in one industry in one region. This organisational diversity responded to the increasing demand of the eighteenth and nineteenth centuries and rested on a large, cheap, adaptable, and unregulated rural labour force where women and children constituted a majority.

Labour markets were deeply embedded in social institutions other than the market itself. Among them charitable institutions together with more labour-linked social organisations such as guilds may be found. The latter played a crucial intermediary role in textile putting-out networks. In early stages of textile production the bulk of the labour market was comprised of domestic out-workers, mostly women and children, controlled by local merchants and/or *fabricantes*. There was co-operation between rural and urban based corporations and companies in that urban masters sometimes organised rural work, especially spinning, which had never been organised in a guild and always undertaken by out-workers whether urban or rural. All these elements enabled the development of a dynamic rural industry capable of producing not just staples but also more fashionable items demanded by a new and growing market.

It has been pointed out by some scholars that out-work, home-work and handicraft work, much of it involving women, survived into this century. It certainly did in Spain where, today, a large part of the 'submerged' and unaccounted economy – (amounting to roughly a thirty per cent of the gross national product) is based upon these activities. In the current phase of world-wide capitalist relations of production, which seemingly puts an end to the 'industrial age', the still cheaper female labour force from developing – and some so called developed – countries keeps on feeding 'post-fordist' multinational enterprises. The upsurge of a new gender-oriented 'reserve army', which usually impinges on children to varying degrees, is evident everywhere. As Maxime Berg pointed out, parallelisms between proto-industrial and current processes may become very revealing.

Bibliography

Manuscript sources[6]

Archivo Diocesano de Toledo (ADT), *Descripciones del Cardenal Lorenzana.*

Archivo General de Simancas (AGS), *Consejo Supremo de Hacienda, Junta de Comercio y Moneda*, file 315, exp. 38.

Archivo Histórico Nacional (AHN), Madrid, *Estado*, file 3182, box 2, exp. 150.

Archivo Histórico de Protocolos de Madrid (AHPM), prot. 19970, f. 237.

Printed and secondary sources

Almagro, 1751. Según las Respuestas del Catastro de la Ensenada ([1994]) Madrid.

Berg, M. (1987) *La era de las manufacturas, 1700–1820. Una nueva historia de la Revolución industrial británica*, Barcelona.

[6] Abbreviations: ADT = Archivo Diocesano de Toledo; AGS = Archivo General de Simancas; AHN = Archivo Histórico Nacional; AHPM = Archivo Histórico de Protocolos de Madrid.

Capella, M. and Matilla, A. (1957) *Los Cinco Gremios Mayores. Estudio crítico-histórico*, Madrid.

Carbonell, M. (1989) 'Hecho y representación sobre la desvalorización del trabajo de las mujeres (siglos XVI–XVIII)', in *Actas de las III Jornadas de investigación interdisciplinar: Mujeres y hombres en la formación del pensamiento occidental*, vol. 2, Madrid, pp. 157–171.

Censo de población de 1857. Instituto Nacional de Estadística.

Corella, P. (1992) *Reales manufacturas de Valdemoro: tejedores franceses y flamencos*, Madrid.

Corella, P. (1997) 'Coyuntura económica e Ilustración. La fábrica de tejidos e hilados de Morata de Tajuña (Madrid) a fines del siglo XVIII', in *Jornadas sobre el Real Sitio de San Fernando de Henares y la Industria en el siglo XVIII*, Madrid, pp. 243–257.

Cruz, J. (1996) *Gentlemen, bourgeois and revolutionaries. Political change and cultural persistence among the Spanish dominant groups, 1750–1850*, Cambridge.

Díez, F. (1990) *Viles y mecánicos. Trabajo y sociedad en la Valencia preindustrial*, Valencia.

García Ruipérez, M. (1988) 'La industria textil en Castilla-la Mancha durante el siglo XVIII', *I Congreso de Historia de Castilla-La Mancha. Tomo VIII*, Talavera, pp. 351–397.

González Enciso, A. (1980) *Estado e industria en el siglo XVIII: la fábrica de Guadalajara*, Madrid.

Gullickson, G.L. (1986) *Spinners and weavers of Auffay. Rural industry and the sexual division of labor in a French village, 1750–1850*, Cambridge.

Iradiel, P. (1986) 'Familia y función económica de la mujer en actividades no agrarias', *La condición de la mujer en la Edad Media*, Madrid, pp. 223–260.

Larruga, E. (1787, 1790, 1792) *Memorias políticas y económicas sobre los frutos, comercio, fabricas y minas de España*, Madrid.

Lis, C. and Soly, H. (1982) *Pobreza y capitalismo en la Europa preindustrial (1350–1850)*, Madrid.

López Cordón, M.V. (1996) 'La rueca y el huso, o el trabajo como metáfora', in A. Vaca (ed.), *El trabajo en la Historia*, Salamanca, pp. 175–198.

Madoz, P. (1847) *Diccionario geográfico de España*, Madrid.

Madoz, P. (1848) *Madrid: Audiencia, Provincia, Intendencia, Vicaría, Partido y Villa*. Madrid.

Middleton, Ch. (1985) 'Women's labour and the transition to pre-industrial capitalism', in L. Charles and L. Duffin (eds), *Women and Work in Pre-industrial England*, London, pp. 181–207.

Nadal, J. (1975) *El fracaso de la Revolución industrial en España, 1814–1913*, Barcelona.

Narotzky, S. (1988) *Trabajar en familia. Mujeres, hogares y talleres*, Valencia.

Narotzky, S. (1997) *New Directions in Economic Anthropology*, London/Chicago.

Nieto Sánchez, J.A. (1997) 'Industria rural y clases sociales bajo el impacto de la Corte: la provincia de Madrid durante el siglo XVIII', in *Jornadas sobre el Real Sitio de San Fernando de Henares y la Industria en el siglo XVIII*, Madrid, pp. 259–275.

Nieto Sánchez, J.A. (1999) *La protoindustrialización en Castilla, 1350–1850*, Universidad Autónoma de Madrid. PhD dissertation.

Paz, D. de, Rodríguez, J.M., and Cruz, L. de la (1990) *Historia de la Villa de Ajofrín*, Madrid.

Regás, A. (1825) *Estadística de la provincia de Madrid*, Madrid.

Ringrose, D. (1996) *Spain, Europe and the "Spanish Miracle", 1700–1900*, Cambridge.

Rodríguez de Campomanes P. (1991) *Discurso sobre el fomento de la industria popular (1774). Discurso sobre la educación popular de los artesanos y su fomento (1775)*, Oviedo. Edition of G. Anes.

Sarasúa, C. (1995) 'La industria del encaje en el Campo de Calatrava', *Arenal, Revista de historia de las mujeres*, 2, pp. 151–174.

Sarasúa, C. (1994) *Criados, nodrizas y amos. El servicio doméstico en la formación del mercado de trabajo madrileño, 1758–1868*, Madrid.

El trabajo de las mujeres. Pasado y presente (1992) Málaga.

Troitiño, M.A. (1984) *Cuenca: Evolución y crisis de una vieja ciudad castellana*. Madrid.

Vicente, M. (1994) 'Mujeres artesanas en la Barcelona moderna', *Las mujeres en el Antiguo Régimen. Imagen y realidad (s. XVI–XVIII)*, Barcelona, pp. 57–90.

14 The butcher's trade in Brussels during the French period (1797–1812): between corporatist traditions and deregulation

Marc LIBERT, University of Brussels – ULB

I. Introduction

In 1845, Alexandre Henne and Alphonse Wauters published *Histoire de la ville de Bruxelles,* a history of Brussels which even today still constitutes one of the indispensable reference tools for anyone with an interest in the history of this city. In the second volume, the butchers' trade under the Ancien Régime is presented in the following terms: 'after lengthy disputes with the local administration, the butchers managed to prohibit access to their trade to anyone who was not of their blood; a circumstance which has allowed it to subsist within the same family circles up to the present day' (Henne and Wauters, 1845). This suggests that in the early decades of the Belgian State, nepotist and endogamic practices resulted in a majority of the capital's butchers being of local stock; and this in turn could be taken to mean that the laws which abolished the trade corporations and their regulations exerted little or no impact on the evolution of membership of the butchers' trade.

On a first-sight basis, this reluctance to change may seem plausible. The butchers' trade was, admittedly, one of the most powerful in town, and one may without difficulty imagine that its long-established members resorted to various devices, including intimidation, to keep outsiders from gaining access to the trade.

We feel it would be of interest to study the butchers' trade during the French period in order to assess the efficiency of the Brussels butchers' resistance to change during the first few years following the enforcement of d'Allarde and Le Chapelier's Laws, and, by implication, to measure the impact of these laws upon a trade characterised by its closedness to outsiders.

Our study is based on the census carried out in Brussels in 1812.[1] We have also carried out a significant albeit incomplete perusal of the census data of the year IV of the Republic (i.e. 1797) to study the situation in the fifth sector of the city, which housed no less than 62% of the Brussels butchers.[2]

---

[1] We must here record our debt to M. Antoine Massin, who processed the full set of census data kept at the Brussels City Archives, Register 79–97, and granted us the advantage of access to his research data relative to the butchers.

[2] AGR, *ACDD*, n. 3528 (Cosemans, 1966). Brussels had at the time been divided into eight administrative sectors by the French authorities. Sector Five covered the eastern part of the city contiguous to the Large Butchers' Hall (Rue Marché aux Herbes).

Figure 14.1 Map of Brussels

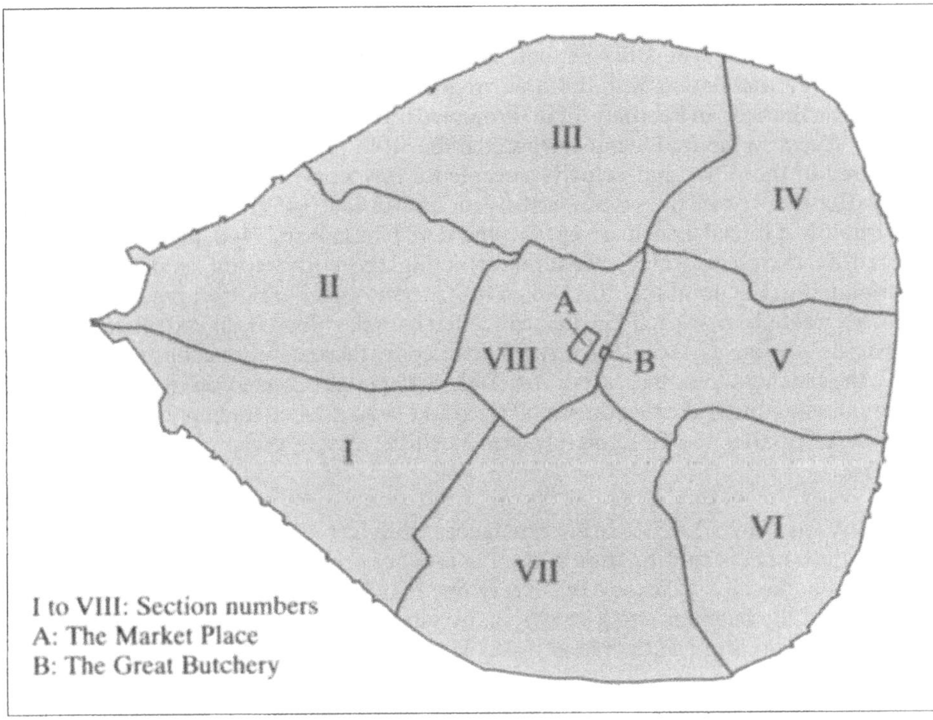

Source:
Ph.J. Maillart, *Plan itinéraire de la ville de Bruxelles*, an VII (1799), in Danckaert, 1989.

II. The Brussels butcher's trade

In Brussels, the trades started displaying internal organisation in the late 13th century, but only in the late 14th century were nineteen among them granted statutes by the Magistrate (Magistrat). The corporations kept growing in number as time advanced, and by the 18th century, the city counted as many as 49 corporations, which yet did not represent the bulk of the city's economic activity. It has been estimated that in 1615 the trades gathered about 38% of the total active population in Brussels, and that by 1738 this ratio had fallen to a mere 25%.

Initially, the butchers formed a single corporation together with the fishmongers, but this was to split into separate corporations. On July 31, 1446, the butchers were granted by Philip the Good, Duke of Burgundy, the privilege of heredity, which restricted access to the corporation, and hence to the status of master, to the sons of master butchers only. The Magistrate attempted to oppose this privilege, but in vain: the Duke confirmed his ruling on January 17, 1458.

In 1451, Philip the Good had granted the city the right to hold a weekly free market. As a consequence, market butchers were free to sell meat in town once a week, on Friday. They were, however, obliged to bring in the live cattle and have them slaughtered by a sworn skinner. The Brussels butchers attempted to obtain the monopoly on the meat trade on that day as well, but their request was rejected by the Brabant Council (Conseil de Brabant) in February 1458. Prompted by this victory, the Magistrate reinstated general access to the trade, and confiscated the 1446 privilege.[3] The butchers initially submitted to the order and actually accepted a few non-Brussels candidates in their midst. But their obedience was short-lived, and in late 1459, a candidate whom the Magistrate had forced them to accept was murdered. In January 1460, the local authorities reacted by taking coercive measures affecting the corporation, and the situation deteriorated to the point that the Duke was forced to deal with it in person. In March 1467, he granted a new privilege that cancelled both the blood right and the terms of the Magistrate's ruling of 1460. The city failed to apply these new decisions and in August 1467, the butchers took the case to the Duke's Council (Conseil du duc), at the same time reminding the Duke that the blood right had been granted them previously. In May 1470 Duke Charles the Bold merely sentenced the city to compliance with the 1467 privilege.

Finally, on March 2, 1519, in circumstances which remain obscure, Charles the Fifth granted the butchers confirmation of their hereditary privilege, which was subsequently integrated in the city's Customary: 'Every one may be admitted to the trades, with the exception of the butchers' trade to which, by virtue of a special privilege, no one shall be admitted who is not of the blood' (Des Marez, 1903).

The city of Brussels was governed by three discrete Councils: the Magistrate, the Large Council (Large Conseil) and the Nine Nations (les Neuf nations). The Magistrate was in charge of the everyday management of the city and enacted the urban legislation. It was composed of the amman or the lieutenant-amman (a ducal officer), of ten patricians chosen among the seven lineages, and nine representatives of the corporations.

The Large Council was composed of former members of the Magistrate and the Eight members of the Guild.[4] In the 18th century, it was to be composed of twelve men of lineage and twelve members of the corporations. The Council met only upon request of the Magistrate or the Duke.

In 1421, the corporations were associated to the city's political powers through a council named the Nine Nations. The trades were gathered in nine bodies placed under the patronage of the city's most venerated saints. Thus, the butchers became members of the Nation of Our Lady (nation de Notre-Dame) together with the salted-fish merchants, the green-

---

[3] The Magistrate considered that the privilege granted to the butchers in 1446 was tacitly cancelled by virtue of the dismissal of their claims concerning the free market.

[4] The Guild, founded in the second half of the 13th century, was charged with the supervision of the city's cloth industry (regulations, wages, operation of the cloth market hall, judicial functions, ...). It was composed of two deans and eight members, originally all belonging to the lineages; but after 1421, non-lineage members were accepted as well.

grocers and the goldsmiths. Like the Large Council, the Nine Nations played a consultative role in cases which were explicitly referred to them by the Magistrate.

The butchers' trade was represented by several members in each of these three bodies, and could thus make its voice heard at all levels of decision-making.

From 1673 until 1786, the entire meat trade fell under the control of the butchers' corporation, which levied on behalf of the township the rights due on butchered meat. The butchers' political involvement was thus compounded by a considerable financial interest.

The sale of food products was carried out in specific locations in town equipped for the purpose (markets and halls). Thus, from the 13th century onwards, meat was sold in the Large Butchers' Hall[5] in the centre of town, at a stone's throw from the Town Hall Square. The ground floor[6] featured benches and stalls belonging to individual butchers, which were handed down from one generation to another (Des Marez, 1903; Van Honacker, 1994; Bruneel, 1998).

III. The abolition of the butchers' corporation

The laws of the French Republic brought an end to the system of corporations, but similar attempts had already been made in the Austrian Netherlands, with various degrees of success.

The late 1760s were marked by a steep rise in food prices in the Netherlands. In 1770, the Antwerp and Brussels butchers raised the meat prices. In order to avoid complaints from the government, the butchers in the capital had even decided to sell meat at the usual price to wealthy customers, and to put a higher price tag only on those portions sold to common people. As the Brussels Magistrate failed to take any measures to put an end to these wild increases, the Privy Council (Conseil privé) charged the Brabant Council to force the city authorities into taking action. When they did, the price of meat returned to its original level, but the butchers started selling meat that included bones and other waste to increase the weight of the portions they sold. In order to obviate these practices, the Magistrate unilaterally fixed the price of meat at 3.5 sols a pound. The butchers, however, refused to sell their meat at less than 4 sols a pound, arguing that the cattle were too expensive. In response, the Brabant Council proposed a series of measures aiming to curtail the power of the butchers over the meat market. These measures were approved by the Privy Council and by the Governor General (gouverneur général), Charles Alexander of Lorraine, but the Magistrate showed little readiness to enforce the regulations. During the decade that followed, the Brabant Council sought, upon order of the Privy Council, to reform the free market held on Fridays in order to relax the butchers' stronghold on the Brussels meat trade; but their attempts were to remain unsuccessful (Bruneel, 1998).

---

5 The hall came to be known as 'large' after other meat halls had been built to house the butchers' trade. Thus, an additional 'small' butchers' hall was built in the Rue de Bavière in 1702 when the 'large' hall became too exiguous.

6 The upper floors housed the corporation's assembly halls.

While the attempts to curtail the privileges of the Brussels butchers' corporation took the form of a series of subtle compromises which were to prove totally inefficient, the local and central authorities booked more convincing results in Bruges. Here also, the attempt to impose a fixed meat price was soon to prove impracticable. On April 2, 1772, the Bruges Magistrate enforced an imperial ruling allowing all citizens to sell meat two days a week, while the other four days were reserved for the butchers. The butchers immediately took legal action to counter this attack on their privileges, but unsuccessfully so.[7] In 1790–1794, the Bruges corporation of butchers counted 40 members belonging to three families, but there were also 18 non-free butchers owning stalls, as well as 133 pork butchers (Van Den Berghe, 1970).

In France, the corporations associated the masters, the journeymen and the apprentices of the same trade. In parallel to these, the workmen had developed their own trade-guilds (*compagnonnages*), more or less secret organisations which allowed them to support each other and to defend themselves against their masters' demands. From the beginning of the Revolution on, the corporations were considered as privileges, and their abolition was soon envisaged. Yet, the issue was not broached by the National Constituent Assembly until 1791, as part of a discussion of the law on licences. On February 16 of that year, a deputy by the name of d'Allarde submitted a bill ruling the abolition of guilds and masterships (*jurandes* and *maitrises*). The bill was voted on March 2nd and promulgated on the 17th.[8] The ruling satisfied both masters and workers: the former viewed it as a liberation from the compelling regulations of the corporations, while the latter interpreted it as a recognition of their workers' associations, and thus as an acknowledgement of their right to defend their own interests.

The demands of the Paris carpenters, felt to be excessive, were eventually to lead the Constituent Assembly to take position against the workers' associations. A deputy by the name of Le Chapelier defended on June 14, 1791 a bill ruling the abolition of workers' associations, which he equated to corporations. The law, voted on the same day,[9] prohibited citizens from the same class or trade to group themselves in organised associations (Godechot, 1951).

Our provinces, occupied by the Republic as a result of the Fleurus battle of June 26, 1794, were split up into nine departments and annexed by France over a year later, on October 1st, 1795. D'Allarde and Le Chapelier's laws were not enforced in our regions before November 10, 1795.

---

[7] The corporation displayed great activity during the Brabant Revolution, and almost regained its former privileges, but the annexation by France brought the attempt to a final standstill.

[8] 'Décret posant suppression de tous les droits d'aides, de toutes les maitrises et jurandes, et établissement de patentes'. *Pasinomie,* Brussels, 1834, 1st series, vol. 2, pp. 230–234.

[9] The text was promulgated on June 17, 1791. 'Décret relatif aux assemblées d'ouvriers et artisans de même état et profession', *Pasinomie,* Brussels, 1834, 1st series, v. 3, p. 22.

IV. Immigration among Brussels butchers

Between the mid-18th and the mid-19th century, the number of butchers in Brussels kept growing: in 1755, there were 60. There were 109 in 1797, 118 in 1812, and 160 in 1842. This growth, however, was not proportional to that of the population as a whole; nor did it display the same growth rate. The proportion of butchers was of 1 per thousand inhabitants in 1755, of 1.7 per thousand in 1797, of 1.6 per thousand in 1812 and of 1.4 per thousand in 1842.

Table 14.1. Number of butchers and population of Brussels between 1755 and 1842 (per thousand)

	1755	1797	1812	1842
Number of butchers	60	109	118	160[1]
City population	58,000	66,000	75,000	113,000
Per thousand	1	1.7	1.6	1.4

Note:
[1] This figure represents the number of licensed merchants in the meat, fowl and fish trades in 1847.

Sources: Cosemans, 1966; Jaumain, 1996; Verbeemen, 1962–1963.

The steep rise at the end of the Century of Enlightenment corresponds to an important growth of the city's population. The slight decrease in the subsequent fifty years tends to confirm a relative decrease in the consumption of meat in the cities.

Thus, in Brussels, the annual per capita consumption of meat has been evaluated at 61 kilos between 1806 and 1825, at 47 kilos between 1826 and 1840, and at 42 kilos between 1841 and 1860. In Ghent, the decrease was more perceivable in the 18th century, since the per capita consumption was 43 kilos between 1701 and 1750, and only 30 kilos between 1751 and 1790. In the first half of the following century, the Ghent situation displays a steep increase between 1806 and 1825 (47 kilos) and a sharp fall between 1826 and 1860 (40 kilos). In Antwerp, the first fifteen years of the 19th century lead up to a peak per capita consumption of 56 kilos in 1816, but from 1817 onwards the average drops below 45 kilos and never moves above the 40-kilo barrier between 1830 and 1859 (Vandenbroeke, 1983; Lis and Soly, 1977).

The cities of Eastern and Western Flanders display a similar profile, characterised by a slight decrease in the proportion of butchers between 1796 and 1815 (Gyssels and Van der Straeten, 1986). We may then infer that in rural Brabant, the number of butchers decreased considerably, just as was the case in the rural areas of the two other provinces at the same period.

Table 14.2. Origins of the Brussels butchers in 1797 and 1812

	1797	%	1812	%
Brussels-born	56	82	74	63
Non-Brussels-born	12	18	44	37
Total	68	100	118	100

In 1797, Brussels counted 18% of butchers of non-Brussels origin, but by 1812 this proportion had risen to 37%. It thus appears clearly that a mere two years after the enforcement of the d'Allarde and Le Chapelier laws, the butchers' trade was already open to non-Brussels-born butchers. And apparently this openness met with little reluctance, since fifteen years later, the trade in hands of genuine Brussels natives represented a little less than two-thirds of the total.

But these hasty inferences deserve more careful qualification. It must be noted that in 1797, all the butchers were of Brussels stock, and that the outsiders are found only among the young butchers' assistants. This situation is an accurate reflection of the reality of the trade under the Ancien Régime: whereas the position of master-butcher was the exclusive prerogative of certain families, this exclusiveness did not apply to the butchers' assistants.

Nor was this maximum protection of access to the trade restricted to the butchers or, for that matter, to the city of Brussels. In general terms, in all the butchers' corporations of the Austrian Netherlands and the Principality of Liège, the trade was maintained at the hands of a few families by facilitating their sons' access to the corporation and by the practice of endogamy. In Huy and Namur, the butchers' trade was at the hand of veritable dynasties, and in Tongres, it was shared between five or six families (Bruneel, 1998; Discry, 1953; Matthieu, 1998). The situation was slightly different in Malines, where only a third of the butchers' marriages were endogamic – but all of them between spouses of local stock. The Malines fishmongers also recruited natives only, while the corporations of apothecaries and surgeons of the city counted only 40% of natives among their members (Van Werveke, 1948; Verbeemen, 1954). The persistence of endogamy and the exclusive recruitment of the Brussels butchers at the time shows that this trade had not yet undergone the evolution that may be observed elsewhere.

In 1812, more than a third of the butchers were from outside Brussels. This proportion of immigrants is not very important, and admittedly less spectacular than that found among the slaughterers and pork-butchers, where the ratio of outsiders reached, respectively, 66 and 80%, but it nevertheless reflects a significant shift. A count which makes allowance for the difference between master butchers and butchers' assistants evinces that both trades had now become accessible to non-natives of Brussels in identical proportions (i.e. about 36%).

Table 14.3. Origins of the Brussels butchers and butchers' assistants in 1812

	butchers	%	butchers' assistants	%
Brussels-born	60	63	14	64
Non-Brussels-born	36	37	8	36
Total	96	100	22	100

It is important to note that the trade of butcher (previously 'master-butcher') opened up both rapidly and consistently, since outsiders represented one third of the trade in 1812, whereas they were still totally absent from it fifteen years earlier. The French laws had, then, fostered a radical transformation in the butchers' trade, which at the end of the French period showed features unheard of under the Ancien Régime. But it is equally important to note that in 1803, the food trades in sectors 1 and 3 of the city[10] displayed a respective ratio of 30 and 50% of Brussels natives (Bruyninckx and De Metsenaere, 1981). From this comparison, the butchers emerge as having one of the most conservative trades in the local food business.

Among the thirty-two places of provenance recorded in the data, it has been possible to identify twenty-six villages, all in Brabant, which yielded thirty-three individuals, and five towns which were the origin of ten butchers. Only one locality could not be identified. These figures clearly illustrate the variety in the immigrants' geographical, as well as the high ratio of rural labour in the workforce.

Six among the ten butchers of urban origin came from Ninove, while the other cities (Alost, Binche, Ghent and Liège) were represented by only one individual each. This high ratio of Ninove-born migrants can be explained by the fact that throughout the 18th century, the butchers from this town had already been selling meat on the Brussels markets (Vangassen, 1959). The opening up of the Brussels trade now made it accessible to individuals who had previously been accepted as merchants only, but who were familiar with the handsome profits that could be made on the meat market in the former capital of the Austrian Netherlands, and who had long been trying to reap the benefits it could yield.

The overwhelming number of immigrants originating from the province may be explained by the attraction that the city has always exerted on the countryside. Some butchers may also have been incited by the slumping meat consumption in the rural areas to seek a better fate in the city, where demand was likely to be both stronger and more stable.

By 1797, all butchers' assistants in sector 5 of the city who were not Brussels-born came from rural Brabant; and so did all the non-Brussels immigrants in the butchers' trade in 1812. This common background was less clearly marked among the immigrants into the Brussels trades as a whole since in 1803, workers of Brabant origin represented 59 and 81% of the incoming rural workforce in sectors 1 and 3.

[10] Sector 1 was situated at the south of the city, and sector 3 covered the northwestern part (cfr. Figure 14.1.).

Under the Ancien Régime, Brussels wielded economic and fiscal control over the outskirts within a radius of 22 km around the city (Bruneel, 1994). In 1812, two thirds of the non-Brussels butchers came from within this zone, a fact that underscores the permanent influence of this area on the Brussels economy on the one hand, and on the other, the limited appeal that Brussels exerted on rural areas beyond this circle. One explanation for this phenomenon resides in the high urban density of the former duchy of Brabant, where each city commanded a zone of influence to which other cities had only limited access. This suggests that even in 1812, the narrow confines of traditional economy had not yet been broken through.

By and large, the immigrants were spread across the various sectors of town in the same proportion as the local natives[11]. On the other hand, it may be observed that the spread of butchers over the city as a whole had undergone a slight evolution, since the quarters contiguous to the Large Butchers' Hall near the Town Hall Square remained the most populous areas, but no longer hosted as high a concentration of butchers as in 1797. It cannot be determined, however, whether this centrifugal movement was triggered by the natives or by the immigrants.

Table 14.4. Number of immigrants in the butchers' trade per year, according to the 1812 census

	< 1786	1786–1790	1791–1795	1796–1800	1801–1805	1806–1810	1811 1812	date unknown
Number of Immigrants	4	4	6	16	7	3	1	3

The post-1795 period witnessed the highest rate of immigration. Out of 44 immigrants recorded by the 1812 census, 14 arrived before 1795 and 27 after that date. The year of arrival of the last three is not known.

In other terms, the years immediately subsequent to the enforcement of d'Allarde's and Le Chapelier's laws are characterised by a spectacular increase in the number of immigrants, since no less than 16 individuals (i.e. 36% of the immigration over 25 years) settled in town between 1796 and 1800. Closer observation of the period between 1791 and 1795 evinces that three of the six new arrivals moved in 1792, i.e. during the first French occupation, and that there were no new arrivals during the Austrian restoration, in 1793 and 1794. It seems, then, that the renewal heralded by the French revolutionaries transcended the date marking the enforcement of a new legislation, and contributed significantly to the liberalisation of the trade.

The sudden drop in attraction just after the peak of 1796–1800 could be explained by a relative decrease in meat consumption in the urban centres, a phenomenon already referred to above.

[11] Sector 5 still featured the highest population rate in 1812, and about 45% of the butchers, both Brussels-born and non-native, were to be found in this area.

Table 14.5 Age of immigrants at their arrival in Brussels

Age	< 10	10–14	15–19	20–24	25–29	30–34	> 35	Unknown
Number	2	4	8	12	9	4	2	3

The figure recording the immigrants' age of arrival shows that butchers immigrating in early youth, i.e. with their parents, were rare. A vast majority of butchers moving into Brussels (about seven out of ten) arrived in town between 15 and 29 years of age. The same pattern can be recognised in male domestic servants moving into Brussels in 1797. English studies have shown that 60% of youngsters left home between the age of 15 and 19 (Daelemans and Van Honacker, 1988). This age range is wider than in the two Brussels examples, where young adults tended to leave home between 20 and 29 years only.

V. Family relationships between Brussels butchers

Observing the family relationships between Brussels butchers, we have recorded 81 patronyms in the butchers' trade in 1812. Among these, 67 belonged to isolated individuals, while 14 belonged to families, which represented 51 persons in all. The vast majority of family links were paternal or fraternal filiation. Only two cases of linkage by marriage were observed.

Between 1753 and 1794, seventeen families shared between them the 47 charges of dean granted by the butchers' trade (Wauters, 1888). In 1812, only eight of these families were still present, and six of these were represented by only one individual. This forces us to conclude that these once powerful families had lost considerable ground.

In 1812, then, the family profile in the Brussels butchers' trade had undergone considerable change with regard to their situation fifteen years earlier. But it must be pointed out that the four families which had achieved the status of dean of the trade in the late 18th century and which were still present in 1812 counted 33 members at that time, i.e. a little below 28% of the total trade; and it is just between two of these families that the two cases of endogamy mentioned above were found. The marked tendency towards the liberalisation of access to the trade still met with opposition of a significant minority which kept living according to the ancient customs.

VI. Conclusion

Summing up, it appears that Henne and Wauters' claims which constituted the original incentive to our research need to be revised. However, while it is inaccurate to claim that access to the butchers' trade was still governed by rules which prevailed under the Ancien Régime, and while the enforcement of the revolutionary legislation did not meet with any strong opposition, it would be equally inaccurate to suggest that the trade became totally open to outsiders. For towards the end of the French occupation, there remained a significant nucleus of butchers' families little given to change. These families were the ones which had wielded authority over the trade under the Ancien Régime.

In 1812, the butchers' trade was no longer closed to non-Brussels natives, but the rate of immigrants in the trade was generally lower than that observed in the other Brussels trades as a whole in 1803. Practically all rural immigrants came from Brabant, and more specifically from an area which traditionally fell within the ambit of Brussels' economic and fiscal influence; while other trades welcomed immigrants with more remote geographical origins. Moreover, the only town providing several butchers to the former capital of the Southern Netherlands had already been linked to Brussels by narrow meat-trade relationships for over a century.

It is interesting to note that the public authorities initiated all the changes, regardless of their eventual impact. The Austrian attempt to curtail the privileges of the corporations had collided with the powerful butchers' trade in Brussels, but operated a real change in Bruges. It took more than laws to deal with the stubborn opposition of the Brussels butchers, who moreover enjoyed solid political support: it required in addition a radical change in the political and institutional build-up of the country before the structure of the trade could eventually be modified.

Bibliography

Manuscript sources[12]

Archives de la Ville de Bruxelles, Brussels, Register 79-97.

Archives générales du Royaume (AGR), Brussels, *Administration Centrale du Département de la Dyle* (ACDD), 3528.

Printed and secondary sources

Berghe, Y. van den (1970) 'La lutte contre le corporatisme à la fin du 18e siècle. Un exemple: l'opposition, demeurée vaine, des bouchers brugeois', *Bulletin du Crédit Communal de Belgique*, 92, pp. 88–92.

Bruneel, Cl. (1994) 'Les migrations entre villes et campagnes. L'exemple des Pays-Bas méridionaux', in *Le migrazioni in Europa secc. XIII–XVIII. Atti della "Venticinquesima Settimana di Studi*, Prato, pp. 501–532.

Bruneel, Cl. (1998) 'Sus au monopole des bouchers bruxellois: le franc marché du vendredi (1771–1787)', in *"Proeve 't al, 't is prysselyck" Verbruik in Europese steden (13de–18de eeuw). Liber amicorum Raymond van Uytven*, Antwerp, pp. 115–125. (Bijdragen tot de geschiedenis; 81).

Bruyninckx, R. and Metsenaere, M. de (1981) 'De rekrutering van de Brusselse bevolking op basis van de telling van het jaar XI', *Taal en sociale integratie*, Brussels, 4, pp. 183–197.

Cosemans, A. (1966) *Bijdrage tot de demografische en sociale geschiedenis van de stad Brussel, 1796–1846*, Liège.

[12] Abbreviations: AGR = Archives générales du Royaume; ACDD = Administration Centrale du Département de la Dyle.

Daelemans, F. and Honacker, K. van (1988) 'Het Brussels dienstpersoneel in 1796', in *Arbeid in veelvoud. Een huldboek voor Jan Craeybeckx en Etienne Scholliers*, Brussels, pp. 161–169.

Danckaert, L. (1989) *Bruxelles. Cinq siècles de cartographie*, Tielt-Knokke, 1989.

Des Marez, G. (1903) *L'organisation du travail à Bruxelles au XVe siècle*, Brussels.

Discry, F. (1953) *Histoire de l'ancienne corporation des bouchers de Huy*, Huy.

Godechot, J. (1951) *Les institutions de la France sous la révolution et l'empire*, Paris.

Gyssels, C. and Straeten, L. van der (1986), *Bevolking, arbeid en tewerkstelling in West-Vlaanderen*, Ghent.

Henne, A. and Wauters, A. (1845) *Histoire de la ville de Bruxelles*, 3 vols, Brussels.

Honacker, K. van (1994) 'De politieke cultuur van de Brusselse ambachten in de achttiende eeuw: conservatisme, corporatisme of opportunisme ?', in C. Lis and H. Soly (eds), *Werken volgens de regels. Ambachten in Brabant en Vlaanderen 1500–1800*, Brussels, pp. 179–228.

Jaumain, S. (1996) 'Les bouchers bruxellois avant 1914', *Les cahiers de la Fonderie*, 20, pp. 6–11.

Lis, C. and Soly, H. (1977) 'Food Consumption in Antwerp between 1807 and 1859: A Contribution to the Standard of Living Debate', *Economic History Review*, 30, pp. 460–486.

Mathieu, G. (1998) 'La corporation des bouchers de Namur au XVIIIe siècle: étude sociale d'un métier fermé', in J. Toussaint (ed.), *Corporations de métiers à Namur au XVIIIe siècle*, Namur, pp. 91–103.

Vandenbroeke, C. (1983) 'Kwantitatieve en kwalitatieve aspecten van het vleesverbruik in Vlaanderen', *Tijdschrift voor sociale geschiedenis*, 9, 31, pp. 221–257.

Vangassen, H. (1959) *Geschiedenis van Ninove*, vol. 2, s.l.

Verbeemen, J. (1954) 'Mechelen in 1796. Demographische en sociaal-economische studie', *Handelingen van de Koninklijke Kring voor Oudheidkunde, Letteren en Kunst van Mechelen*, 58, pp. 135–179.

Verbeemen, J. (1962–1963) 'Bruxelles en 1755. Sa situation démographique, sociale et économique', *Bijdragen tot de Geschiedenis*, 14, pp. 203–233; 15, pp. 65–133.

Wauters, A. (1888) *Liste chronologique des doyens des corps de métiers de Bruxelles de 1696 à 1795 dressée d'après des documents inédits*, Brussels.

Werveke, H. van (1948) 'De Gentse Vleeshouwers onder het Oud Regime', *Handelingen der Maatschappij voor Geschiedenis en Oudheidkunde te Gent*, 3, pp. 3–32.

15 Women going to the cities: migration and stereotypes. The example of servants in Brussels in the nineteenth century

Valérie PIETTE, University of Brussels – ULB

I. Introduction

In the present article, I propose to draw attention to an essential element of migration: the migration of women. When historians have drawn their attention to the study of population migrations, they have usually devoted their studies to male workers, probably because they have felt that men constituted the majority of the workforce necessary for the development and the economic growth of the host countries. Indeed, 'men who were uprooted, expropriated from their family patrimony and from their home industries, requisitionned by the army or the factories, hallucinated by the lights of the city, like seabirds that flock in the light of lighthouses when the sun goes down' (Vandervelde, 1899: 330).

Today the necessary exchanges and interactions between the country and the city are better understood as far as heavy industry, craftwork, seasonal work and trade are concerned. Migrations of women, apart from a few exceptions, have rarely aroused the same interest as migrations of men. Migrations of women nevertheless increased during the nineteenth and twentieth centuries: 'to such an extent that women (would) soon win in number in many cities', as Abel Chatelain notices for France (Chatelain, 1969: 26).

II. A 'feminisation' of big cities?

The attraction of cities on women is undeniable. At the end of the nineteenth century, the male/female ratio in Belgium is relatively narrow: 98 men per 100 women. However, there are a few exceptions to this rule and these exceptions are of importance because they apply to two large Belgian cities, Brussels and Ghent. In Ghent and its suburbs the ratio is 87 men to 100 women. In the capital city the phenomenon is even more noticeable, only 85 men to 100 women. In the case of Ghent this phenomenon can be easily explained because of the attraction of cotton and (to a larger extent) of linen manufacturies, which were traditionally great purveyors of female workforce. In Brussels, however, the importance of servanthood is the main cause of the discrepancy.

Domestic service increases the sex differences in certain areas of the city. In 1842, Quetelet places the emphasis on the fact that the seventh section of the capital city, the Park section, (the most well-off) was the most feminised area (122 women for 100 men) and had the greatest number of 'strangers' (by 'strangers' he means Belgians born outside Brussels). These two phenomena were closely interwoven and were directly related to the presence of maids in well-off households. Quetelet concludes, 'it is in the most well-off areas that the greatest number of female servants can be found' (Quetelet, 1843: 52).

Domestic service, a female job 'par excellence', plays an important part in the way cities were populated and in their subsequent feminisation. During the nineteenth century, both in Brussels and in other big cities, between 75% and 90% of domestic workers were servants. The countryside offered a wealth of workers, which was often considered inexhaustible by contemporaries. Because they had no specific training, numerous young rural girls used domestic work as a way to settle down in big cities. This urban and feminine phenomenon has already been the object of some studies.

Domestic service as an occupation was first studied in the United States, and more generally in English-speaking countries. In the 1970s, the first historical studies were released which remain major references to this day. Included among them are *The Domestic revolution. The Modernisation of Household in England and France 1820–1920* by Theresa Mc Bride (1976) and *Seven Days a Week: Women and domestic service in Industrializing America* by Katzman (1978). French historians rapidly followed the movement. At the end of the 1970s and the beginning of the 1980s pioneering books were released such as *La vie quotidienne des domestiques en France au XIXe siècle* by Pierre Guiral and Guy Thuillier (1978) and above all *La place des bonnes* by Anne Martin-Fugier (1979).[1] Since then, the study of domestic work has slowly become the centre of interest for European historians such as the Dutch Jannie Poelstra, the author of *Luiden van een andere beweging. Huishoudelijke arbeid in Nederland 1840–1920.*

In these various studies, the strange interaction between the country and the city regarding domesticity was underlined. In 1851 two thirds of British servants were the daughters of farm workers. In 1850 in France and more particularly in Versailles, three fifths of the servants came from the country. In Bordeaux, the proportion reached fifty percent whereas in Marseille, all the maids came from outside the city.

In Brussels during the 19th century, one female worker out of three happened to be a servant. Before 1850, domesticity was the second most important professional occupation for women in Brussels: in 1842, craft industry acounted for 48% of working women, domesticity 30% and the retail trade 10%. Work as a domestic can consequently be considered one of the prototypical female jobs. The origin of servants should certainly not be neglected in this phenomenon. Indeed, as underlined by Emile Vandervelde, large cities always count a 'floating population', which varies according to the individuals, who compose it 'and which can reach proportions that vary between 25 and 30% of their total population'. He refers among others to 'garrisson soldiers, servants, female factory workers who stay in the city for a certain time' (Vandervelde, 1903: 215).

---

[1] As far as France is concerned, we must quote: G. Fraisse, *Femme toutes mains. Essai sur le service domestique*, 1979; J.-P Gutton, *Domestiques et serviteurs dans la France d'Ancien Régime, 1981*; C. Petitfrère, *L'oeil du maître. Maîtres et serviteurs de l'époque classique au romantisme*, 1986.

III. Amplified speeches

As soon as domestic work is refered to, stereotypes and prejudices inevitably abound. The perception of servants is quite interesting and deserves a good deal of attention. Servants were seen as poor girls who came from the country, got lost in big corrupting cities and were exploited by the local (most of the time French-speaking) upper class. This prototypical representation of the servant reflects the ideas of the time and grows considerably by the end of the century.

Indeed, as soon as the domestic service crisis was felt and the recruiting of servants became more difficult, comments multiplied. These went together with the moral crisis that shook the Western societies of the time. The intensity of this crisis grew parallel to the successive discoveries of the trade in white slaves. Work as a servant was gradually considered a risky profession. These young rural women who came to town in search of a job seem to have been an easy prey. Because their liberty and (of course) their virginity needed to be saved, a real quarantine line was deployed around these young girls and a new moral cruisade began.

Domesticity (referring in this paper to domestic work) does not elude the concomitant and closely linked ideas suggested by the depopulation of the country and by the perception of the city as 'tentacular and corrupting'. The servant who migrated to the city was often regarded as a major cause of the depopulation of the country. She partly symbolised the rural exodus feared by moralists.

Criticism abounded inextricably mixing considerations about rural exodus and the dangers of big cities. Criticism took several forms. Firstly, the arrival of these country girls who rapidly discover urban luxury and vice was often denounced: 'their endlessly renewed legions enrich tawdry jewellery dealers and rubbish mongers' (Gange, 1901: 88). The taste for luxury they had acquired made the return to the village even more difficult. Their clothes were astonishing because they singularly contrasted with those of the local peasants. Servants returned to the country with city behaviours and manners. The hiring of women in cities both as servants and as factory workers was always subject to fear and suspicion. The village of Roclange[2] is cited as an example; 25 percent of girls would try to go and find a job in Brussels and Paris, 'some of them stay there, in the gutter; others leave alone but come back with a child. All of them bring the customs, the clothes and the manners of the Paris factory workers to this remote part of Limburg. Nothing is more curious to see than the loads of spruce young girls on the market square of Roclange-la-Belle whose dressing singularly contrasts with the garnments of the surrounding peasants.' (Vandervelde, 1899: 338).

But critics also laid the emphasis on the country girls' probable definitive departure from their birthplace: the servant starts a home and family, marries in the city and then decides to stay there. And what is even worse: the servants would not only be 'the most

[2] The village dealt with is undeniably Roclange-op-Jaer, a small commune of Limburg near Tongeren which counted a little more than 1000 inhabitants. In the 19th century, it specialized in the manufacture of straw hats.

active factor of the depopulation of the country', but they would lead peasants out of their villages and make them settle down in the city where they would join their country girl 'transformed into a lady'. In fact, domesticity definitely appears as an eminently risky profession for rural districts. If the servant came back to the village, she had often transformed and adopted the manners, the tastes and the traditions of city women; if she did not come back to the village, she contributed to the rural depopulation and the gradual desertion of the countryside.

IV. Walloon or Flemish?

These moral talkings and the numerous stereotypes are clearly influenced by the beginning of anthropology. For example Charles De Quéker, the City of Brussels' chief of division and the right-hand man of the mayor, Charles Buls. He published the results of a study concerning 6000 Brussels-based servants. Because he realized that 4/5th of them came from the country, he established a relationship between their origin and a specialisation of the profession. The Flemish country 'mainly provides maids of all work whereas Wallonia provides nannies and servants for the nicer areas' (*Bulletin du Travail*, 1893: 17). He went further in his argumentation and suggested qualities and failings according to origin. So 'are Flemish servants generally heavier, more stubborn but also hardier than the Walloon who is winsome, polite and often very pretty'. In Paris, Belgian and, above all, Flemish servants were much sought after at this time: 'for their cleanliness, their taste for housekeeping, their strength at work, their love of children and in certain cases, their catholicity' (Schirmacher, 1908: 73).

It should be noticed that stereotypes based on supposed qualities linked with the geographic and linguistic origin of servants were present. These stereotypes remind us of the distinctions made today between cleaning ladies of different nationalities. Generally accepted ideas also abound about the cleanliness of the Poles, the know-how of the Portuguese, the carelessness of the Africans, etc.

If it is undeniable that domesticity played a considerable role in the relationships between both rural and urban areas and that it is fairly easy to collect stereotypes and clichés, methodological problems, however, make it very difficult to undertake a thorough study of these migrations. Before addressing these migrations, some realities should be mentioned. One must first consider the period and the state of urbanisation. Belgium has always been a country of internal migrations. Because it is a small and densely populated country (200 inhabitants/square kilometre at the end of the nineteenth century), Belgium had an excellent communication network from an early date. Communication between the countryside and the cities was encouraged at the outset because it was believed that keeping the workforce in the countryside would avoid the formation of a dangerous industrial proletariat. In the beginning of the twentieth century more than one third of the active population commuted to the city for work (Pasleau, 1995: 173). But this separation between residence and workplace did not at all apply to servants. Indeed, live-in young women from the countryside were in high demand by landlords; women who were ready to work at any time of the day or night and who were consequently 'at their disposal'. This need was all the more pressing because servants had to be at work very early in the morning (to start the fires, prepare breakfast, etc.) and late at night (to prepare and serve meals, put out the fires, etc.).

Belgian workers have always moved across the entire territory. The socialist leader E. Vandervelde even evoked 'the inborn nomadic instinct of Belgians and of Flemish in particular' (Vandervelde, 1899: 333). These typically Belgian characteristics must be kept in mind when the geographic origin of workers is examined. In this case there is not always a clear relationship between the place of birth and the membership of a community (Flemish, Walloon, Brussels). Population movements are such that knowing the place of birth is obviously interesting but does not solve all the problems in a country of commuters.

V. Available sources: population registers

The population censuses are of little help except as far as the study of immigration of workers after 1910 is concerned. Internal professional migrations were neither analysed nor detailed. Population registers contain extremely valuable information. Every household is recorded, individuals are identified by their name, profession, date and place of birth, marital status and last residence, which proves to be an essential source of information for the social historian.

However, this *source reine* is the victim of its own richness. Indeed, the source includes a significant number of servants and only a database of the entire Brussels population could offer exhaustive answers. No one has yet undertaken this painstaking task! Working with selections of samples can often reveal numerous and unsuspected difficulties. It is almost impossible to establish a really significant sample of the urban community since important differences become apparent depending on the areas or even the streets taken into account.

Frank Daelemans and Karin Van Honacker's study of domestic work in Brussels under the French regime can be cited as an example. They focussed on the origin of domestic staff and analysed two sections of the city beginning with the 1803 census. The results vary from one section to the other. The Brabant and Hainaut provinces represented the most important suppliers of servants in the first section whereas the Hainaut province was practically non-existant in the second one (Daelemans and Van Honacker, 1988: 167). It is consequently impossible to extrapolate the results of the study of particular areas to the rest of the city without making methodological mistakes and distorting the historical reality.

Moreover, the social composition of an area influences and determines recruitment patterns: the servants who were recruited by the shopkeepers of the city center did not have the same profile and the same origin as those recruited by the large families of wealthy areas. These differences from street to street, from area to area and from section to section shed light on the networks and the paths that made it easier for workers to go and work in the city. Aristocrats who were important employers of servants would in most cases recruit their employees in the villages near their country estates.

Despite all these reservations, population registers remain a major source of information as far as the geographic origin of servants is concerned. Beside the date of birth, they provide information about the last residence, the dates of arrival in the city and of departure, and shed light on the duration of the job in the city. Unfortunately these data are not systematic and vary from register to register according to the degree of conscientiousness of the city employee and depend on the information given by both employers and employees.

If it is fairly easy to collect information about the arrival in the city and the departure of servants, it is often difficult to follow them within Brussels and the suburbs. As soon as they leave the city of Brussels itself, the probability of following them is slight because of the poor state of the population registers of the suburban towns.

VI. The servants who married in the city: a sample

In order to bypass some of the problems mentioned above, an exploratory test has been carried out in an often neglected source: wedding registers. These also offer interesting and relevant information for our research subject. The sample is naturally not completely accurate. The population taken into account is a very specific one; the servants in question had already made a choice. They chose to marry in Brussels, which for most of them meant that they wanted to leave their employment as servants, stay in the city and in some cases to settle down permanently in Brussels. Despite these drawbacks, these sources have many advantages. They even offer a double advantage since they make it possible to define the geographic origin of servants as well as to analyse their social mobility.

In the registers it is easy to find the names, professions and places of birth of the husband and wife but also the names and occupations of the parents and of the witnesses, so that is easier to have an insight into the couple's integration within the urban environment. However, the situation is not always so ideal. The parents' occupation is never mentioned when they are deceased and is rarely given for mothers. While the place of birth of the couple is referred to in most cases, a lot of exceptions remain. The absence of precision in the reference to homonymous communes located in various provinces does not always make it possible to identify them with a high level of certainty.

These few methodological comments having been made, we shall now carry out a systematic analysis of the wedding acts of the servants who got married in Brussels in 1847. At the outset it must be noticed that 168 marriages out of the 992 contracted in Brussels in 1847 concerned a servant. Nearly 1 out of 5 women who got married was in service. This discovery goes against all stereotypes about domesticity, which is often considered the profession of spinsters par excellence. It proves on the contrary that domesticity was only a transitory occupation for a majority of women.

However, this proportion of servants is a minimal one. Indeed, only unambiguous cases were taken into account: servant, cook, nanny, chamber maid. It is obvious that under the name dressmaker, governess, shopkeeper, etc. a certain number of servants will appear. These were not taken into account in order to avoid any misunderstanding.

VII. The importance of cooks

If servants represent the largest number of domestic workers the same does not apply to marriages. Sixty-six percent of married domestic workers were cooks. This high proportion of cooks could even substantiate the 'popular common sense' notion according to which working class men of the time would try to find a model wife among the cooks of wealthy families. This very pragmatic vision of marriage was taken over by several moralists of the end of the century. Because they advocated women's return to the home and tried to shape the ideal image of a housewife who is capable of keeping her husband (certainly if he was a working man) in his family, she proves the validity of this assertion. The working man had all that he could want and soon became a model husband as opposed to the less happy one who, because he made a wrong choice and married a bad housewife, spent his time in pubs to forget about his miserable condition.

Cooks and servants in general conveyed the image of the ideal wife 'because these former servants who are so good at keeping their husbands at home simply take advantage of the knowledge they acquired at their master's. They take care of their families and prepare good meals that owe everything to the seasoning. The well-fed and well-pampered husband looks forward to going back home and spending happy hours after having worked hard' (Parent, 1891: 4).

VIII. An ideal age?

Figure 15.1 Age of marriage of servants in Brussels in 1847

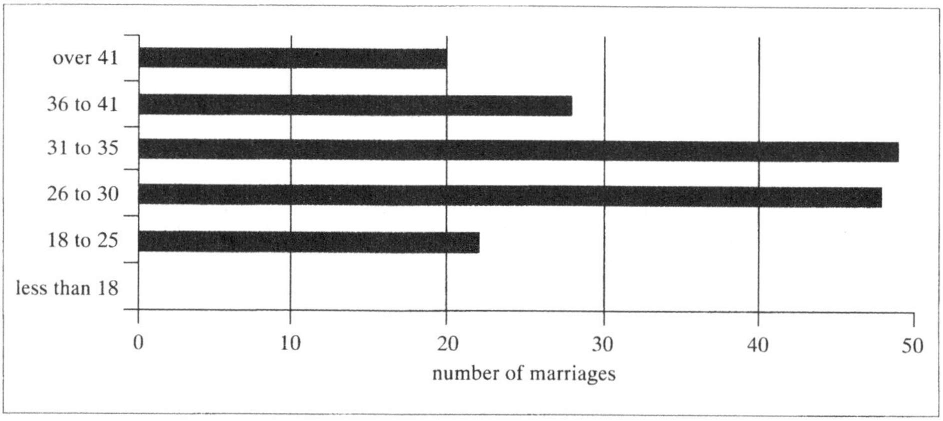

Domestic workers did not marry very young, which distinguishes them from working-class women. Their average age was comparable to that recorded in the country. This is naturally linked with the condition of servants, the contacts they established in the city and their objectives. The aim of domestic work was often to enable the servant to save a reasonable amount of money, which would facilitate her marriage and sometimes the establishment of a small business (a small retail shop in most cases). The existence of savings is confirmed by an analysis of the marriage contracts available in notarial records. When they married, servants often brought significant amounts of money. Furthermore, servants rarely married to legitimise a pregnancy. No trace of legitimatisation of children was found.

The servant/cook dichotomy is also present when it comes to the study of the age of marriage among domestic workers. While the age bracket 31–35 prevails in both cases (24 servants and 25 cooks), cooks generally and proportionally married later than servants (12 are older than 36 years old and 13 are older than 41 years old). This was the case of Marie-Therese Vercammen, born in Hasselt in 1806, who married François Vromant, a typograph from Kortrijk who was 10 years younger than she was (AVB, Registres de mariage, 1847, n° 359). Catherine Hauwaert, born in Tourneppe in 1804, similarly married Louis Janssens, a cobbler from Glabbeck 16 years younger than she was (AVB, Registres de mariage, 1847, n° 236).

IX. Geographic origin

Figure 15.2 Origin of married servants in Brussels in 1847

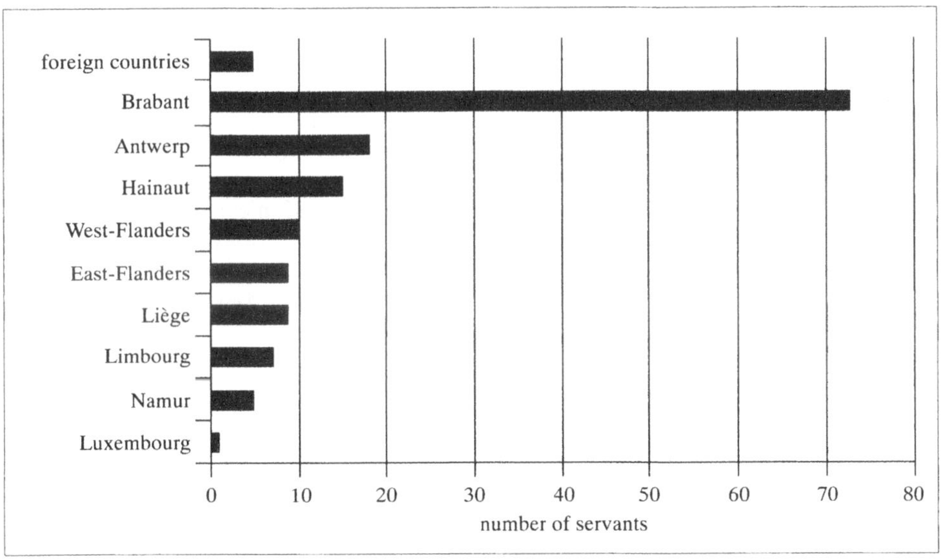

At first glance, the places of birth of domestic workers can be surprising. Indeed, surprisingly enough, they seem to be spread over the whole country, which contradicts numerous generally accepted ideas according to which there would be 'servant networks' in certain villages. The geographic origin of servants is really atomized. All provinces are represented, including the province of Namur (five cooks) and the province of Luxemburg (one cook). A few foreigners are also recorded such as Dutch, French but also Prussian servants who confirm the presence of the much sought after German speaking servants in the upper-class families of Brussels. Anne Beissel, born in Prussia in 1824 married Pierre Geeurincks, a gardener. Before her marriage, she was a nanny in the rue du Marais (AVB, Registres de mariage, 1847, n° 64). It was indeed very frequent for upper-class families to hire German speaking nannies or governesses in order to familiarize their children with the language of Goethe.

Nevertheless, the main recruitment took place in the 19 peripheral communes of Brussels. Servants who were born in Brussels were a rarity. These were in most cases girls who were abondonned by their parents in their early years.

Marie Deroever, born in Brussels of an unknown father in 1810, declared, when she married, that she hadn't had news of her mother for 35 years (AVB, Registres de mariage, 1847, n° 762). Young orphans and girls born of unknown parents were taken into custody by the authorities whose aim was, among other things, to make good servants of them.

Brussels held a real attraction for girls from the rural outskirts of the capital city (today's Flemish and Walloon Brabant provinces) (73 domestic workers out of 153 whose place of birth could be identified). The greatest number of domestic workers originated from the villages neighbouring Brussels. The provinces of Antwerp and of Hainaut were far behind Brabant (18 and 15 servants respectively).

Generally speaking, it can be noticed that the attraction is regional and does not take administrative or political borders into account. The analysis of domesticity in the cities of the north of France is very significant in this respect. The cities of the Department du Nord found their servants in their own hinterland, even if the latter belonged to another country, in this case to Belgium. More than 20% of the servants in the department were Belgians (5972 out of 26841) (Piette, 1998: 86). This situation can of course be seen in reverse. In Mons a lot of servants came from France. In 1842 the mayor of Mons informed to the administrator of public security that 'a fairly large number of girls from French border communes come every year to find domestic work in our city' (AGR, *Sûreté Publique*, Dossiers généraux, n°112).

X. Social origin

As can be noticed in Figure 15.3, Brussels domestic workers originated equally from the working class and the agricultural class. However, the statement that servants were usually farmers' daughters, needs to be qualified. The country did not only count small farmers but also craftmen, workers (carpenters, masons, brickmakers, etc.) and tradesmen. Furthermore, the term 'farmer' could refer to very different situations. It is even more surprising to find two servants whose fathers were schoolteachers. Marie for example, born in Moorsel, who married Pierre Neukermans, an apprentice baker, was the daughter of Pierre Cordon, a schoolteacher (AVB, Registres de mariage, 1847, n° 743). The sources unfortunately do not make it possible to provide more precision about her parents' standard of living. In any case, the sordid image of the poor young peasant who tries to find a job in the city has to be reconsidered.

Figure 15.3 Profession of the father of the servants, Brussels 1847

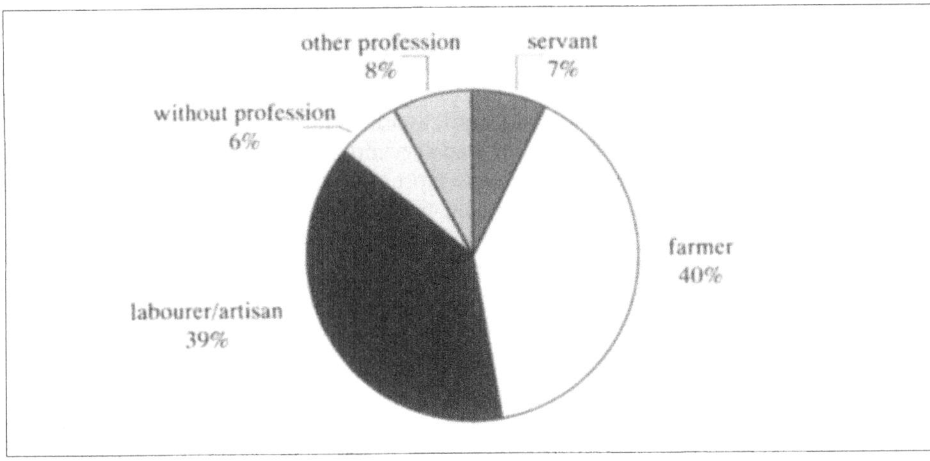

XI. The choice of the husband: a social rise?

A few husbands were not easy to classify in an appropriate heading. They are gathered under the term 'others'. The husbands recorded are a waterman, two carriage operators, a town sergeant, a security officer, the guard of the Galleries Saint-Hubert, a shoeshiner and four restaurant waiters.

Figure 15.4 Profession of the husbands of the servants in Brussels, 1847

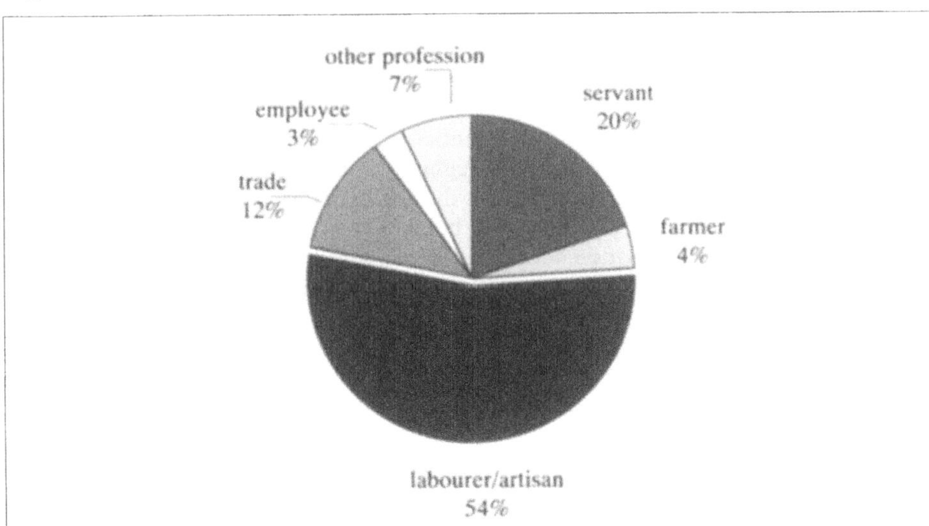

The difference in occupation of the servant's father and her husband is obvious. Farmers appear in very scarce number. This phenomenon is of course related to the irreparable reduction of the place of agriculture in Brussels and its outskirts. It also emphasizes the deliberate (or less deliberate) choice to settle down in the city and to change lifestyles for good.

Contrary to what may be believed, domestic workers rarely married each other. If the phenomenon existed, it most often concerned servants who worked in the same family. Workmen and craftsmen are obviously more represented. Clerks timidly appear even if they are less well represented. Tradesmen and shopkeepers form a significant group and thus sustain the commonly accepted idea according to which shopkeeping and consequently the access to a self-employed occupation would be the aim, the (almost) inaccessible dream of numerous servants. The presence of shopkeepers can also be explained by the lifestyle of servants and reveals the existence of meetings and exchanges during the outings to go to the market and do the family's shopping.

XII. Conclusion

In 1903 E. Vandervelde noticed that 'When workers desert the countryside or, at least the farm, to find jobs in urban or industrial centers, they of course do so with the hope of improving their situation and in particular to earn higher salaries' (Vandervelde, 1903: 183). We certainly agree with him but his statement needs to be qualified in some respects.

Women contributed to migration between the countryside and the city, and to some extent increased the rural exodus that was so feared by moralists and other conservative observers. Servants can for that reason not be excluded from the history of these workers who went to cities in search of a better standard of living. This better standard of living had different implactions: to leave in order to earn more also implied to leave a village, a family, a background. This 'movement, is a necessary (if not sufficient) condition to a change and sometimes to a liberation and indicates the willingnes to break with the past, which creates the possibilities of a future' (Perrot, 1991: 480).

The emphasis has been laid on the essential role of the placement of children and adolescents as servants during the Ancien Régime. A real circulation of children is attested in France, England and Germany from the 17th century onwards, which does not necessarily correspond to a material need but rather to a wish of sociabilisation and education. This system has often been assimilated with a kind of schooling and is the origin of the expression 'life cycle servant' as opposed to professional domestic workers (Burguière et al., 1986: 42 ff).

Most probably, the phenomenon has too often been neglected by contemporary historians. If the analysis of marriage acts does not make it possible to provide a satisfactory answer (even though they emphasize the transitory character of domesticity), other sources shed new light on the motivations of the girls who came to the city. A record book held by the Brussels police between 1813 and 1815 contains astonishing information. The aim of this record book was to watch the domestic workers living in Brussels and to facilitate contacts with potential masters. For that reason the police administration meticulously recorded the family name, first name, place and date of birth, addresses, age and other complementary data such as the motivations of the girls who were newly arrived in the city. A more detailed study of this record book is under way but a first and quick analysis confirms the schooling system of the Ancien Régime. Marie Group for example who tried to find a job as chambermaid says that she 'came to Brussels to learn the French language' (AVB, Sujets à gages, 1812–1816). Domesticity is certainly considered a period of household schooling, but also probably of social and linguistic schooling during which it was possible to save money. Many girls built up a dowry for a possible marriage or to settle down. Historians cannot ignore these motivations.

It is unfortunate that, despite the richness of the wedding acts, no information is given about the itinerary of servants. It may be believed that it was a straight line, the starting point of which was situated in the village of origin and the arrival in a Brussels family. However there may have been numerous stages between these two geographic points. Recent studies have highlighted the way in which these migrations took place. It was 'essential to know what their progress was and amongst other things to know their itineraries' (Poussou, 1995: 9). Because 'as marriages do not take place haphazardly, the vast majority of migrations are guided by itineraries' (Poussou, 1995: 18). The servants who came to Brussels to find their first employment were a rarity. Most of them had already worked in provincial upper-class families.

Rosalie Brande, 28 years old, looked for a job as a cook or as a servant in Brussels. She came from Havré in the province of Hainaut and had already worked for five years in Mons and 15 months for the mayor of Ath. The geographic progression seems logical. Because she was born in Hainaut, she first worked in the towns of the province before going to Brussels (AVB, Sujets à gages, 1812–1816). But this particular case is by no means representative. Désirée Provost, born in Mons (Hainaut) and aged 24 had already found a job in Aalst (two years) and in Ghent (nine months) before going to Brussels (A.V.B. Sujets à gages, 1812–1816).

The results of the present study naturally can not be systematically generalized. Further quantitative analyses should be carried out for other years. A first quick survey does not invalidate the results discussed in the present study. This brief study sheds light on the migration of country girls and their subsequent settling in the city, which represents a genuine mutation because, as underlined by Theresa Mc Bride 'servanthood was a cross-cultural experience of immense significance' (McBride, 1976: 119). The range of this unique contact between two traditionally opposed and compartimentalized cultures (urban and rural) and between two social classes (upper-class and rural working-class) remains practically unknown to this day. Exchanges certainly took place even though this process certainly did not take place mechanically. Indeed, as underlined by Edward Higgs 'it may be too simplistic, therefore, to view domestic service as a bridging occupation between the rural and the urban world. It may have been a physical but not a cultural bridge. Indeed the institution may have served to maintain rural deference in the urban milieu and thus to insulate part of the ex-rural population from the dominant ideology of the urban working classes' (Higgs, 1986: 143).

The servant's marriage or return to the village are both synonymous with the end of domestic service and undeniably accelerated both the integration process in a new job environment and cultural exchanges.

Bibliography

Manuscript sources[3]

Archives de la Ville de Bruxelles (AVB), Brussels, Registres de Mariage, 1847.

Archives de la Ville de Bruxelles (AVB), Brussels, Register called Sujets à gages, number IV, 1812–1816.

Archives générales du Royaume (AGR), Brussels, *Ministère de la Justice, Sûreté Publique*, Dossiers généraux, nr. 112

Printed and secondary sources

Burgière, A., Klapisch-Zuber, C., Segalen, M. and Zonabend, F. (1986) *Histoire de la famille*, vol. 2, *Le choc des modernités*, Paris.

'Rapport sur les opérations de la bourse du travail pendant l'exercice 1892–93' (1893), *Bulletin du travail.*

Chatelain, A. (1969) 'Migrations et domesticité féminine urbaine en France XVIIIe siècle–XXe siècle', *Revue d'histoire économique et sociale*, pp. 512–524.

Daelemans, F. and Honacker, K. van (1988) 'Het Brussels dienstpersoneel in 1796', in *Arbeid in veelvoud. Een huldeboek voor Jan Craeybeckx en Etienne Scholliers*, Brussels, pp. 161–171.

Gange, R. (1901) *Comme on vit à Bruxelles*, Louvain.

Higgs, E. (1986) 'Domestic Services and Household Production', in J. Argie (ed.), *Unequal Opportunities. Women's Employment in England 1800–1918*, Oxford, pp. 125–150.

McBride, Th. (1976) *The Domestic Revolution*, London.

Parent, M. (1891) 'Servantes et ouvrières', *La voix de l'ouvrier*, 31 may 1891, p. 4.

Pasleau, S. (1995) 'Les migrations de main d'oeuvre en Belgique' in Y. Landry, J.A. Dickinson, S. Pasleau and C. Desama (eds), *Les chemins de la migration en Belgique et au Québec XVIIe–XXe siècles*, Louvain-la-Neuve, pp. 173–194.

Perrot, M. (1991) 'Sortir', in G. Duby and M. Perrot (eds), *Histoires des femmes en Occident*, vol. IV, *Le XIX siècle*, Paris, pp. 467–494.

Piette, V. (1998) 'Les servantes belges à Paris', in A. Morelli (ed.), *Les émigrants belges. Réfugiés de guerre, émigés économiques, réfugiés politiques ayant quitté nos régions du XVIe siècle à nos jours*, Brussels, pp. 79–100.

[3] Abbreviations: AGR = Archives générales du Royaume; AVB = Archives de la Ville de Bruxelles.

Piette, V. (2000) *Domestiques et servantes. Des vies sous condition. Essai sur le travail domestique en Belgique au 19e siècle*, Brussels.

Poussou, J.-P. (1995) *Les chemins de la migration en Belgique et au Québec XVIIe–XXe siècles*, Louvain-la-Neuve, pp. 9–20.

Quételet, A. (1843) 'Sur le recensement de la population de Bruxelles en 1842', *Bulletin de la Commission centrale de statistique*, vol. 1, pp. 27–163.

Schirmacher, K. (1908) *La spécialisation du travail par nationalités à Paris*, Paris.

Vandervelde, E. (1899) 'Les villes tentaculaires', *Revue d'économie politique*, 13, pp. 329–351.

Vandervelde, E. (1903), *L'exode rural et le retour aux champs*, Paris.

16 The occupational and geographical mobility of farm labourers in Flanders from the end of the 19th to the middle of the 20th century[1]

Martina De Moor, Ghent University

I. Introduction

The Western European labour market in its present form is, among other features, characterised by a minor part of the population working in the agricultural sector. In Belgium it was around the third quarter of the nineteenth century that it became obvious that the agricultural sector could no longer claim to be the biggest employer. From then onwards the number of people employed in agriculture was less than half of the working population. By 1896 the sector only guaranteed work to a third of the total working population (as a full-time job). Only fifteen years later this had diminished to little more than one fifth. Between 1937 and 1961 this percentage would drop to 7.7%. Thereafter the employment in agriculture would stay under 5% (De Brabander, 1983).

This article focuses on a specific segment of the labour market in rural Flanders, namely the labour market where farm labourers and farmers met each other. This is important for two reasons. Firstly, the decline of people employed in agriculture from 1895 until the middle of the twentieth century was primarily caused by the decline of paid labour in agriculture. As will be shown in this article, this decline was the expression of a growing occupational and geographical mobility of farm labourers, which was a direct consequence of the growing interaction between countryside, town, and (especially) industrial centres.

Secondly, the reasons for the mobility, and thus the decline of farm labourers, can not simply be regarded as a consequence of the overall decline in the number of people employed in agriculture since the middle of the nineteenth century. For example, the fact that paid labour and family labour did not diminish at the same pace nor period, suggests that the causes of the decline of both groups somehow differed.

These two reasons for specific research have lead to the question: which factors played a causal role in the occupational and geographical mobility of farm labourers? Before actually presenting the research on the push- and pull-factors involved in this mobility, some characteristics of the area and period of research, the source material, and the social-economic group of farm labourers must be set out. It has to be stressed beforehand that this article aims primarily at explaining the mechanism that lies behind the mobility of farm labourers, without going into detail on specific data.

---

[1] With special thanks to Prof. E. Vanhaute (Ghent University) and Prof. E. Green (Royal Holloway College, University of London, Egham) for their usefull comments.

The provinces of East and West Flanders were selected as the area of research since the relative number of people actively employed in agriculture in these provinces stayed well above the national average for a long time. While in East and West Flanders this percentage between 1896 and 1947 diminished from 38.5% to 18%, the employment in agriculture in the whole of Belgium diminished from 31% to 13%.

The period of research, from the end of the nineteenth century until the middle of the twentieth century, was chosen, with an emphasis on the inter-war period, because of its importance as the transition period from traditional to modern agriculture. During this transition period new technologies were introduced and integrated into the system without changing it fundamentally. According to Blomme 'it was a slow, but steady mutation in which elements of both traditional and modern agriculture coexisted and complemented each other' (Blomme, 1993). One of the most important differences between the two forms of agriculture is the different role labour played in the production process. While in traditional agriculture, land and labour played the leading role as production inputs, capital was less important and was in most cases the result of the use of labour for land improvements. Modern agriculture, however, needed a far greater capital input in the production process by the input of labour-saving and land-saving capital goods (Blomme, 1993). During the transition period, the nature of labour and its relationship with the other factors of production changed fundamentally. The story of the wage labourers is one aspect of this changing nature.

As main source material, the Enquête sur le travail agricole of 1920 and the general agricultural censuses of the years 1895, 1910, 1929 and 1950 were used.[2] The Enquête sur le travail agricole is a unique historical document and formed a common thread through the research. It was set up by the Ministry of Agriculture as an enquiry on the moral, intellectual, and economic situation of the farm labourers in order to stop, among other things, flight from the countryside. The pre-war information available, for example the studies of Vliebergh and Ulens, were considered outdated.

The questionnaire used for the Enquête covered a wide range of subjects about the economic situation of farm labourers, their social situation, their education, their living and working conditions, and it also contained questions on the reasons the labourers had for leaving their jobs and/or the countryside. The results were, however interesting, never processed properly nor used as a policy instrument.

The Enquête and the censuses can be seen as complementary on several levels. On time-scale, the general agricultural censuses allowed us to highlight continuities and changes over a longer period, while the questionnaire only dealt with one single year, 1920. On the geographical level, most general censuses dealt with large administrative units of grouped villages (cantons), while the questionnaire was mostly filled in for just one village or a unit of a few villages.[3] Above all, the data in the censuses were primarily dealing

---

[2] *Enquête [...]*, 1920; *Agriculture*, 1900, 5 vols; *Agriculture*, 1920; *Recensement [...]*, 1920; *Agriculture*, 1937; *Recensement [...]*, 1937; *Algemene [...]*, 1954.

[3] Since not all the censuses could garantuee an analysis by village, the second lowest level, the canton, was chosen as geographical unit of analysis.

with rather general and mainly quantitative information on agriculture and agricultural labour, while the questionnaire contained very specific and mainly qualitative information. This information should, however, not be regarded as less interesting, on the contrary, the qualitative data could give indications for the explanation of the census-data.

II. Farm labour and the income pooling strategy

The socio-economic group of farm labourers is not a group that can be easily specified because of the position wage labour could have in the income structure of a rural family. According to Bouché a farm labourer always regarded his situation as 'un pis-aller': wage labour was only an interim solution since a wage labourer regarded himself/herself as 'un candidat à la terre' (Bouché, 1913). He/she generally preferred independent farming, preferably on his/her own patch of land. Wage labour in Flanders, and especially in some parts of our study area, whether full-time or part-time, whether on a continuous or discontinuous basis, was part of what can be called 'an income pooling strategy'. This specific income pooling strategy was linked to the overall predominance of extremely small farms in Flanders. In such areas income pooling was the key mechanism in the survival policy of the rural population. The rural population searched for a balance between independent farming, proto-industry, sweating industries, wage labouring at farms and factories, and possibly some other activities. This balance could vary over time: dependent on the economic situation of the family, one had to seek other income or not. The system of income pooling can, this way, explain temporary declines in the number of wage labourers. Over the long term we see, however, an overall decline, and this can no longer be explained by labourers temporarily choosing independent farming.

The decline fluctuated slightly but the downward trend could not be reversed. During the period 1895–1950 the number of wage labourers in agriculture in East and West Flanders had diminished by more than half (Table 16.1). In 1950 only 5% of the total agricultural labour input came from wage labourers. At that time their number was no more than one eighth of 1895. The number of family labourers however dropped less drastically. In 1950 they were still working with more than half of their 1895 number. During the period 1929–1950 the number of family labourers even rose in absolute terms.

Table 16.1 Absolute and relative number of family labourers and wage labourers in the agricultural sector in the provinces of East and West Flanders (as a whole)

Year	Family labourers	% of total	(1895=100)	Wage labourers	% of total	(1895=100)	Total
1895	339,466	81.94	100	74,822	18.06	100	414,288
1929	166,012	87.81	48	23,040	12.19	30	189,052
1950	176,580	94.39	52	9,903[1]	5.31	13	186,483

Note: [1] 88 foreign labourers
Sources: General agricultural censuses: *Agriculture*, 1900; *Agriculture*, 1937; *Algemene [...]*, 1954.

The fact that by the middle of the twentieth century family members provided nearly all labour input, this, linked to a decrease in the number of farms, indicates that the intensification of family labour was preferred instead of paying for the, by then increasingly expensive, wage labour. A strong correlation between the number of full-time wage labourers and the number of family labourers and the weakening of such a correlation later on, indicates that this intensification took place just before the middle of the twentieth century.

Regionally, some differences in the input of farm labourers during the period 1895–1950 can be pointed out. The western part of West Flanders and more specifically the area close to the French border (cantons Poperinge and Veurne) had the highest concentrations of wage labourers. By 1950 their number had declined the least in this area too. This can probably be explained by the specific nature of the farms in these regions: mainly large farms in permanent need of farm labourers throughout the year, with some peaks during the harvest periods. Some cantons in the north-east, close to the border of the province of Antwerp had an intensive paid labour input too, but it declined rather fast to a level in 1950 that was as low as in the rest of the area.

Figure 16.1 only concerns full-time labourers. As income pooling played an impor tant role in Flemish agriculture, part-time wage labour was a widespread phenomenon. The labour input of part-timers was, however, only counted in 1929, shows that in all cantons of both provinces at least a tenth of the total paid labour input came from part-timers. In most cantons however this was at least one third of the paid labour input. Without long-term figures it is difficult to estimate the importance of part-timers before and after 1929, but it can be supposed that beforehand they were numerous in areas where full-time labourers were numerous too, as a strong positive correlation between full-timers and part-timers for 1929 suggests.

A comparison of the figures with the figures of the active population in the provinces and the rest of the country, indicated that mobility must have caused an important outflow of labourers. Which places farm labourers went to, which jobs they choose and to what degree, can not easily be retrieved. Regarding geographical mobility, it must be noted that reliable migration statistics are rather rare and if available, they only rarely mention the occupation of the migrant. Concerning the farm labourers, the following can be said about their geographical mobility behaviour. On the level of international migration, farm labourers mainly chose short-distance, short-term intra-European migration, so the seasonal or circular migration to the North of France was of particular importance for farm labourers in East and West Flanders during the period of research and until the Second World War. In some villages in this area 1/5 to 1/3 of the population went harvesting in the North of France (Schepens, 1973). After the First World War, farm labourers no longer primarily worked at the French farms but were increasingly employed in the devastated French areas. Due to the shortage of French labour wages were high, this in addition to well-organised syndicates and an advantageous exchange rate. From the thirties onwards seasonal labour would steadily diminish due to more job opportunities and improved working conditions closer to home, and a more xenophobic attitude of the French regarding migrant labourers. Migration to other countries was less important but was nevertheless significant until the beginning of the twenties. 1920 was on all

Figure 16.1 Regional differences of paid labour input over time (1895, 1929 and 1950) in East and West Flanders

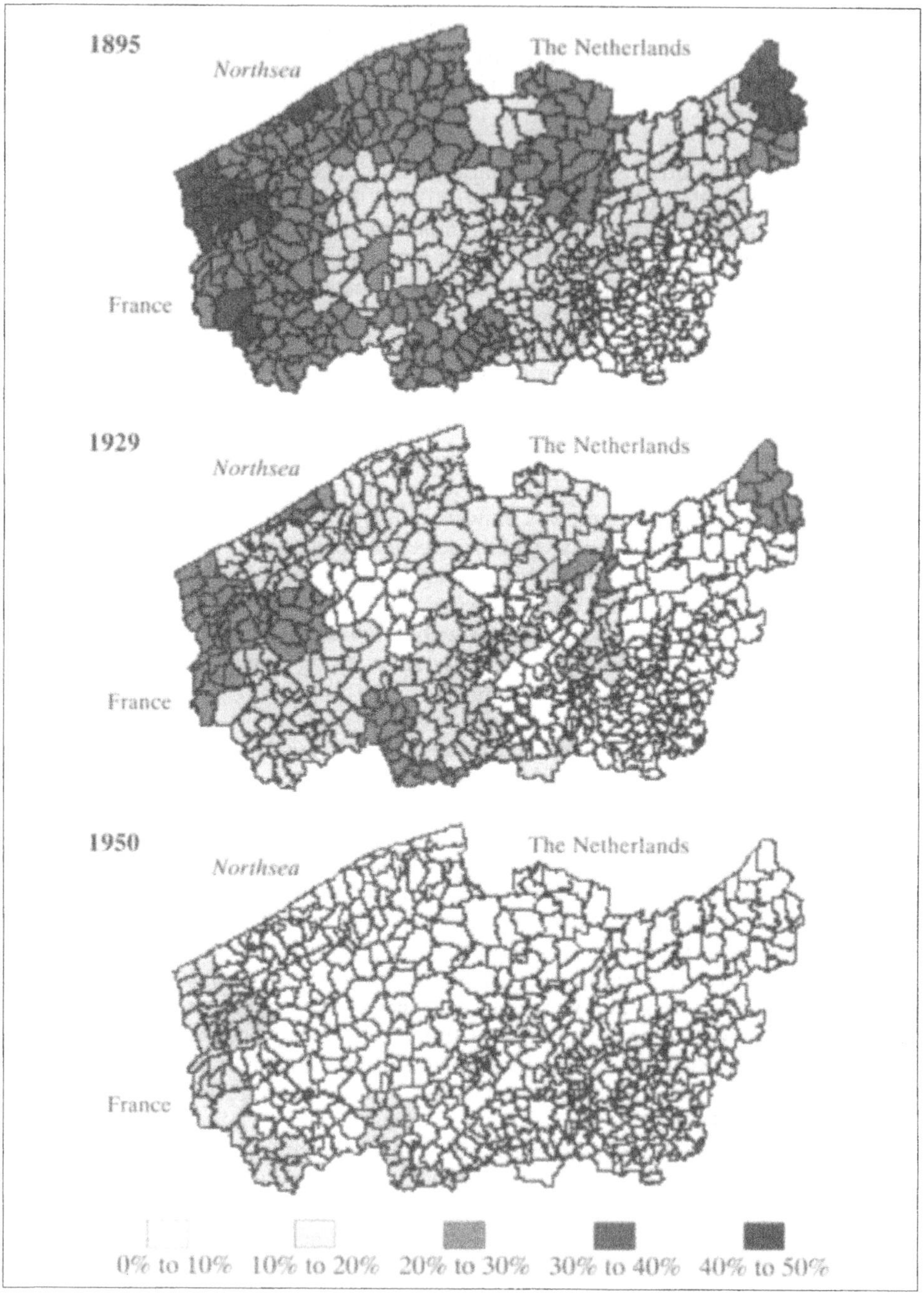

Figure 16.2 Part-time wage labour in percentages of the total paid labour input in East and West Flanders, 1929

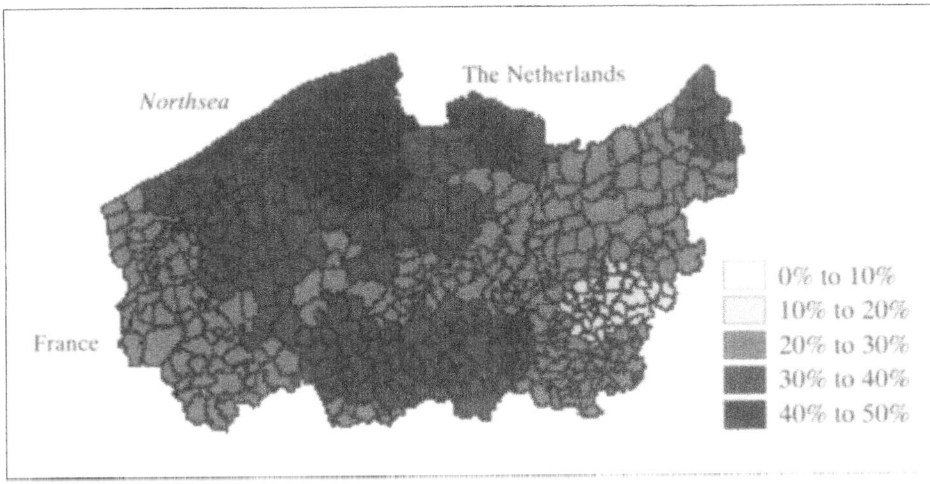

levels a peak year for migration. The French government gave special conditions for foreign farmers, willing to move to France and start a farm. This attracted a significant number of Flemish farmers, to the North of France but also to Normandy, Ile-de-France and the Champagne-area (Dupacquier, 1991). In 1920, the migration to 'le pays du dollar', the U.S.A., peaked as well. The Enquête held in 1920, concurs with the statistics: France was, in the whole area, a popular destination, the U.S.A. was mentioned in five communities. Thereafter permanent international migration declined, while seasonal migration would stay important until the 1950's.

Internal migration is even more difficult to trace than international migration. For farm labourers especially, (short-term) migration to the mines and industrial sites in the Walloons, and rural-urban migration were important (Poulain and Foulon, 1981). The move to the Walloons was mostly undertaken once a week and would be steadily replaced by daily commuting by train from the last quarter of the nineteenth century onwards (1871: introduction of season-tickets for labourers). More and more the Walloons would be replaced by the new economic centres of Antwerp and Brussels as a popular commuting destination. The answers on the Enquête showed that by 1920, migration to towns, and especially Brussels and Antwerp was far more important than the migration to the Walloons.

Since farm labourers were overall not used as skilled labourers, their job opportunities were mostly limited to jobs in industry, service sector (as servants) or public works (for example road construction). The Enquête data showed that industry was undoubtedly the most important destination in the whole area, followed by reconstruction works (for example the works at the ports of Gent and Zeebrugge) where high wages were paid. Working as a servant in the towns played an insignificant role as destination for farm labourers in 1920.

The study of the age structure of wage labourers showed that wage labourers left agriculture when still young. Once they reached age 18, it became more difficult for wage labourers than for family labourers to leave the sector. It was especially the young wage labourers who left agriculture; a decline in the number of farm labourers was, thus, mainly caused by the fact that retiring parents (formerly wage labourers) were not replaced as farm labourers by their children.

III. Examining the causal factors of farm labourers' mobility

What caused the mobility among farm labourers? Why did they choose to look for another job? Which factors influenced their perception and expectations of work in the countryside or which elements repulsed them so strongly that they wanted to leave it behind?

In neo-classical studies differences in employment opportunities and wage levels are regarded as the most important incentives for labourers to change jobs and/or places. Bublot (1957) and Blomme (1993) for example suggest that farm labourers chose other jobs because of a lack of employment possibilities within agriculture and higher wages elsewhere. What has not been researched, however, is the degree to which these factors were actually responsible for mobility and whether other factors (not suggested by neo-classical studies) played a role. Two questions will be dealt with hereafter: 1. Were the labourers really pushed out of agriculture because there was no demand for them? 2. Were wages elsewhere in fact so much higher that they left their jobs for them?

III.1. Employment and mechanisation as push-factors?

III.1.1. Employment

Firstly, employment should be examined as a causal factor. In the Enquête of 1920 many complaints of farmers about the lack of wage labourers can be found. This was not simply due to circumstances of war: before the war, and even later in the forties, the same complaints can be found in other sources. Just before the First World War Bouché wrote about 'l'antinomie agraire: trop peu de terre pour ceux qui voudraient la cultiver pour leur compte, trop peu d'ouvriers pour ceux qui cultivent pour leur compte et dont la famille est insuffisante comme main-d'oeuvre' (Bouché, 1913). To solve this problem more and more foreign labourers were employed in agriculture. The study of the evolution of two indicators, farm size and mechanisation, proved that these complaints were of a structural nature rather than isolated instances.

Differences in farm size can indicate roughly the need for extra hands on the farm. Though the relationship between the size of a farm and its production is dependent among other things on the soil and has been a point of discussion, one can roughly say that with a farm of about 1 to 2 hectares a family could provide for itself. A farm size between 2 and 5 ha would enable the family to produce a surplus for market. With a farm larger than 5 ha, however, the family would be able to sell a larger part of the production. For the period under research, a farm larger than 10 ha would need at least

1 full-time wage labourer. For smaller farms, hiring labour would on average not be necessary the whole year through.

For the whole of Belgium, we see from the aftermath of the crisis at the end of the nineteenth century until 1929 a growth of small (beneath 1 and 5 ha) farms, and the number of farms greater than 10 ha diminishing. Thereafter, until the 1950 census, farms smaller than 5 ha decreased by nearly 15%, but those between 5 and 30 ha doubled. The number of companies had diminished substantially too.

For East and West Flanders a similar pattern can be found. The average farm size grew substantially during half a century. While in 1895 the average was 1.3 ha, it rose to 1.8 in 1929 and to 6.4 ha in 1950. Taking into account that after 1929 the average size of the farms would grow continuously, subsistence agriculture, which was a of kind of agriculture farm labourers often combined with their work, became less important. Commercial agriculture was becoming more and more important. Blomme estimated the percentage of the non-commercial labour input (input for subsistence agriculture), in the total labour input in agriculture in 1929 at 12.7%. In 1950 only 9.1% of the total labour input was still dedicated to self-sufficiency.

III.1.2. Mechanisation

Mechanisation is another factor that can indicate the need for labourers. Until the middle of this century, mechanisation stayed a rather marginal phenomenon in agriculture. A lot of improvements in machinery gave the advantage to small to average sized companies. Machines for the larger companies which employed many labourers, would not become widespread until after the Second World War. Because of the labour intensive nature of the work, the evolution of threshing machines was examined for the first half of the century. While in 1895 1% of the farms had a threshing machine, this was about 5% in 1929 and in 1950 this had risen to 12% which represents quite a limited number of farms. Mechanisation should however not always be seen as a push-factor. The Enquête learned that in many cases the shortage of labourers was a reason for farmers to hire or buy the costly machines. Several locals who filled in the questionnaires of the Enquête noted that the influence of machines on emigration was negligible while the flight from the countryside influenced the use of machines significantly. According to Bouché 'les ouvriers agricoles ont induit la mécanisation et n'ont pas été induites par elle' (Bouché, 1913). At about the same time of the Enquête, Mr. Demain wrote in his work *Les migrations ouvrières à travers la Belgique* that the introduction of machines 'a supplée avantageusement en maintes circonstances à l'insuffisance de la main d'oeuvre' (Demain, 1919). During the second half of the twentieth century, the use of machines would rise significantly and, though mechanisation can not be regarded as a push-factor before 1950, would have a more significant influence on the mobility behaviour of farm labourers. Mechanisation would, like many other capital goods, increasingly replace expensive labourers.

When comparing the evolution of these indicators with the evolution of farm labour, two conclusions must be drawn. Firstly, a structural shortage in the supply of paid labour can not be denied for the period and place of this research. Though the First World

War must have had a considerable impact on the supply of wage labour, the structural nature of the shortage before and after the war can not be denied. Secondly, when linking both elements, the moment or period when Bouchés candidat-à-la-terre-theory comes into play is no longer valid. A certain moment or period during which many labourers no longer tried to combine farm labour and independent farming but started trying other options, can be pointed out by the following explanation.

The figures have shown us that, especially during the first half of the inter-war period (before 1929), the number of farms and especially small farms (<1ha) must have risen slightly while the number of (full-time) labourers declined. This suggests that wage labourers saw a chance to combine a small farm with possibly (but not necessarily) some extra part-time wage labour either in agriculture or in industry (no doubt under influence of the positive economic climate at that time). After 1929 (until 1950) however the number of small farms (including the farms up to 5 ha) declined. Beforehand such an evolution would most likely be accompanied by a rise in the number of people dependent on wage labour on a farm. This was however not the case after 1929. The declining number of farm labourers combined with a decline in the number of smallholdings explains the outflow to other sectors. It seems that other options than independent farming alternating with wage labour at other farms had become more attractive. In the meantime average farm size was growing. It is clear that farmers found a solution for the chronic shortage of hired labour in the intensification of family labour, the hiring of foreign labour, and the growing use of machines. During the 1930s and 1940s, the mechanism of income pooling that enabled a supply of cheap and especially flexible labour broke down because of various internal and external pressures and formed thus one of the causes of a profound re-organisation of labour-input in agriculture.

III.2. Higher wage levels as pull-factors

III.2.1. The importance of wage structure

The other classical explanation of mobility is the difference in wage levels between two employment opportunities. The real impact of wage differences must be evaluated with a study of the wages of the labourers and a comparison with other wages farm labourers might have received elsewhere. Besides the actual wages, attention must be given to differences in the wage structure. Various historical and sociological studies have pointed out that these might have played an important incentive for farm labourers to find other work.

Sources for research on wage levels in agriculture are rather rare, even in the twentieth century. The wage data found in the Enquête gave an indication of the local wages in the communities. Before their actual processing, the data were set in order by sex and function in order not to mix completely different kinds of wages. After data processing, it turned out that wages of farm labourers could vary significantly from place to place, from function to function, and between both sexes. On average a farm labourer in East and West Flanders in 1920 earned little more than 5 Belgian francs daily. The analysis by function showed that domestic labourers could be found at the bottom end of the wage scale, while task labourers could earn the most. Male domestics earned on average 4.4

francs a day while their colleagues who worked per task got on average 10.4 fr. Day labourers got about 6.4 fr. a day on average. The discrepancy between these wages can be explained easily. Task labourers were hired for a limited period, during the busiest time of the year, to work fast and efficiently. They mostly worked in groups and were thus able to negotiate a good wage; their negotiation position even improved because of the lack of wage labourers. Apart from these elements, task labourers could only partly be paid in kind, while for many wage labourers payment in kind formed an important part of their wages. The importance of payment in kind should not be underestimated. Especially those receiving the lowest wages were supplemented with payment in kind, but nevertheless those earning the highest wages received supplements too. For domestics we find high proportions of payment in kind by means of board and lodging; day labourers received a lot of food as payment. A census of 1937 teaches us that still more than 78% of the wage labourers in agriculture received payment in kind at that time.

In the Enquête, the locals were asked to estimate the value of the payment in kind. In many cases the goods received as payment in kind turned out to be as valuable as the wage received in money. Extra payment in kind could thus mean that the wage was doubled. Notwithstanding its value, it is likely that payment in kind became increasingly unattractive for the wage labourers compared to jobs where the remuneration was only paid in money. Besides, in the Enquête it was mentioned several times that farmers tried to tie their workers to them by putting a plot of land at their disposal for free: the labourers could use the land but were obliged to work for the farmer. In the areas where this was common practice (e.g. the area the French border with mainly large and average sized farms), most farmers could easily miss a plot of land thus assuring their supply of labour. This tie was, for some labourers, a reason not to work at a specific farm. Moreover, during the inter-war period several initiatives to encourage small-scale land owning made it easier for factory workers to use or buy a plot of land without being dependent on a farmer. It is thus not surprising that a labourer would not want or did not need to work any longer for certain farmers.

Comparing the wages of farm labourers with the wages for other jobs they might have changed to, is not a straightforward task. Firstly, no precise figures on the destinations of the farm labourers can be given. Secondly, the cost of living between town and countryside could differ significantly. The marginal return of a wage at an industrial site compared to the farm labourers' wage could be lower than expected because of the cost of living at towns and industrial sites. Thirdly, contrary to the wages in industry from 1919 onwards the farm labourers' wages were not linked to the retail price index.

A short comparison of the wages of a farm labourer in 1920 with the monetary wage of an unskilled factory labourer in Belgium shows that in several places the latter wages were even higher than the wages of task workers in agriculture.[4] Besides, it has to be stressed that during the aftermath of the First World War, for example in 1920, the wages at factories rose at a serious speed when indexed (and in a period of serious inflation). This fast rise probably created certain expectations among the farm labourers and attracted them.

[4] For the comparison, data of the *Enquête Davin* were used (Scholliers, 1979).

The wages over the border, in the North of France were even more impressive, though these could mostly only be earned during a certain period of the year. In the Enquête it was noted in Bottelaere, East Flanders that in some places French farmers offered 1350 fr. for three months of work, including board and lodging, while in that village men could earn only 100 to 125 fr. a month including board and lodging. It should not be a surprise then that farm labourers were prepared to emigrate for three months to France.

III.2.2. The social wage: an underestimated factor

Closely linked to the qualitative elements which might have functioned as incentives for labourers to leave agriculture, is what is described as 'the social wage' i.e. the social advantages which are linked to a certain job (McLean Petras, 1981). During the inter-war period a dichotomy grew between the agricultural sector and other sectors. A. Pfeiffer from Dendermonde warned in the Enquête that it was dangerous 'de vouloir empêcher d'un côté l'exode rural, alors que d'autre part les avantages les plus variés sont réservés aux professions non agricoles. Les pouvoirs publics sont assaillis de demandes en faveur de toutes les classes de la population, sauf pour l'agriculture, et la population se dirige naturellement vers les lieux et les professions favorisés'. It would indeed take a long time before farm labourers would be able to enjoy the same social advantages as their colleagues in the other sectors. Various reasons can be given for the delay in labour and social security legislation, and especially the implementation of the legislation. Firstly, the fact that the number of farm labourers in Belgium was relatively small compared to other social-economic groups made it difficult for them to draw attention to their specific problems. Labour unions of farm labourers were extremely weak, possibly due to their shrinking number, their isolation in the countryside, and a still paternalistic relationship between the farmer and his labourer. A sense of class awareness (as a class 'für sich') among farm labourers did not exist. The reason for the weakness of the unions and the lack of class awareness is no doubt the specific income pooling strategy which has been mentioned several times already. Farm labourers were used to receiving their income from several sources, and depending on the economic evolution of the industry contributing a certain part of their income (e.g. the evolution of the goods made in the sweating industries), they tried to keep their income in balance. Their actual living expenses were covered by several income sources. The need to organise themselves in a union was thus less obvious. Secondly, the fact that their number declined probably discouraged politicians from defending the rights of wage labourers. The Enquête sur le travail agricole was a rare initiative taken to improve the working and living conditions of farm labourers. The actual reason for the Enquête was certainly not of a purely humanitarian nature: the general single vote system had just been introduced and the elections were coming closer. Undoubtedly the Catholic Minister of Agriculture took the initiative for the Enquête hoping to keep the support of farm labourers and of farmers too. Improving the living and working conditions of farm labourers might keep them in the sector and thus stop the complaints of the farmers about the shortage of labourers. Further significant losses in the advantage of the Socialist party had to be avoided. A third and last element that explains more specifically the delay in implementation of the legislation concerning farm labourers is the discontinuous basis on which the labourers worked on farms. The legislation did not take into account that the farmers' need for wage labourers depended a great deal on unpredictable factors (e.g. climatic change).

This would discourage the actual implementation. Finally, it would take quite a few decades before farm labourers had become entitled to the most basic social security and labour legislation. By that time their number had become neglegible.

IV. Conclusion

Several conclusions can be drawn. Concerning the causal factors, it can be concluded that some premises made by historians in the past have proven to be right, others to be wrong. Employment probably was not a push-factor: there were plenty of job opportunities for wage labourers in agriculture in this period. Wages and specifically the wage structure and the lack of a 'social wage' in agriculture, however, might have played an important role. This is not surprising since wage labour was often regarded as a complementary income. The role this wage could play was no doubt dependent on the level of the wage and the opportunities of earning more (or a 'better' wage) elsewhere. Because of these opportunities and the characteristics of the transition the agricultural sector went through at that time, the link between land (small farms) and labour, such as that found before the second half of the inter-war period, disappeared. This means that the income pooling strategy lost a great deal of importance in the countryside. Other income structures were built. The new wage and income structures of the twentieth century whereby a full-time wage accompanied by a social security network obviously influenced the farm labourers in their choices. The old income pooling strategy was pushed off the market.

Exogenous factors, such as better employment and wages, but also the introduction of machinery and other capital goods, combined with endogenous changes in the income structure of the rural family (the breakdown of the income pooling strategy) caused the mobility and changes in labour-input in agriculture.

To replace paid labour, family labour had to be intensified and in some cases foreign labour had to be hired. By the middle of the twentieth century, farm labour had become what McLean Petras calls a bottom job: a job for which it was difficult to find locals because of the low wages, bad working conditions, and the low prestige level of the job. Just as *les petit'belges* went to France to get the bottom jobs done in the nineteenth century, we see some foreigners, on a certain level, take the farm labourers' vacancies in the middle of the twentieth century.[5] Machines would take over some work later on. The sector adjusted itself to changes in the supply of wage labour. Wage labour was no longer needed in the ways and in the amount it had been used before the post-war era.

[5] The censuses indicate that foreigners were taken into service as farm labourers. it has to be stressed, however, that this happened in a very limited number of farms. Mostly machines replaced the farm labourers.

Bibliography

Agriculture: Récensement général de 1895 (1900) 5 vols, Brussels.

Agriculture: Récensement général de 1910 (1920) Brussels.

Agriculture: Récensement général au 31 décembre 1929 (1937) Brussels.

Algemene landbouwtelling van 1950 (1954) Brussels.

Blomme, J. (1993) *The economic development of Belgian agriculture 1880–1980. A quantitative and qualitative analysis*, Louvain.

Bouché, B. (1913) *Les ouvriers agricole en Belgique*, Brussels.

Bublot, G. (1957) *La production agricole belge. Etude économique seculaire 1846–1955*, Louvain-Paris.

Brabander de, G.L. (1983) *Regionale structuur en werkgelegenheid*, Brussels.

Demain, H. (1919) *Les migrations ouvrières à travers la Belgique*, Louvain.

Dupaquier, J. (1991) 'La contribution des belges à la formation de la population française (1851–1940). Etude quantitative', in *Historiens et populations. Liber Amicorum Etienne Helin*, Louvain-la-Neuve, pp. 331–347.

Economische en sociale telling van 27 februari 1937. Enquête nopens het arbeidsstelsel en de loonen in de landbouw (s.d.) Brussels.

Enquête sur le travail agricole (1920) Brussels.

McLean Petras, E. (1981) 'The global Labor market in the Modern World-Economy', in M.M. Kritz, *Global trends in migration: theory and research on international population movements*, New York, pp. 44–63.

Poulain, M. (1984) *Urbanisation et migration en Belgique: une vue d'ensemble de 1800 à nos jours*, Louvain-la-Neuve.

Poulain, M. and Foulon M. (1981) 'L'immigration flamande en Wallonie. Evaluation à l'aide d'un indicateur antroponomique', R*evue d'histoire belge contemporaine*, 12, pp. 205–244.

Schepens, L. (1973) *Van vlaskutser tot Franschman. Bijdrage tot de geschiedenis van de West-Vlaamse plattelandsbevolking in de negentiende eeuw*, Bruges.

Scholliers, P. (1979) *Lonen in de Belgische nijverheid, 1913–1940: de Enquête Davin*, Brussels.

Lightning Source UK Ltd.
Milton Keynes UK
UKOW06f0407050915

258071UK00005B/78/P

9 782503 512815